Irving Penn

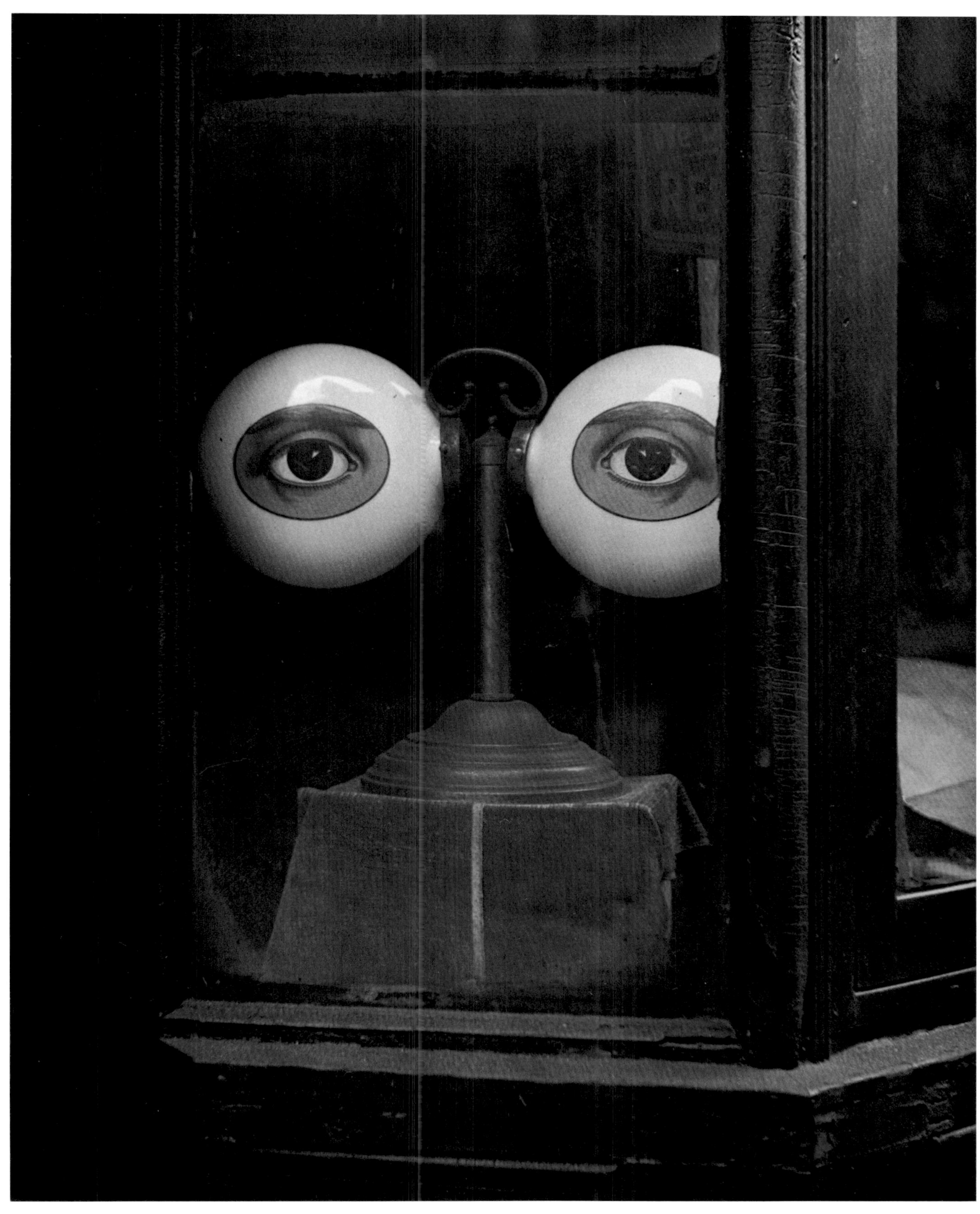

1. Optician's Window. New York, c. 1939

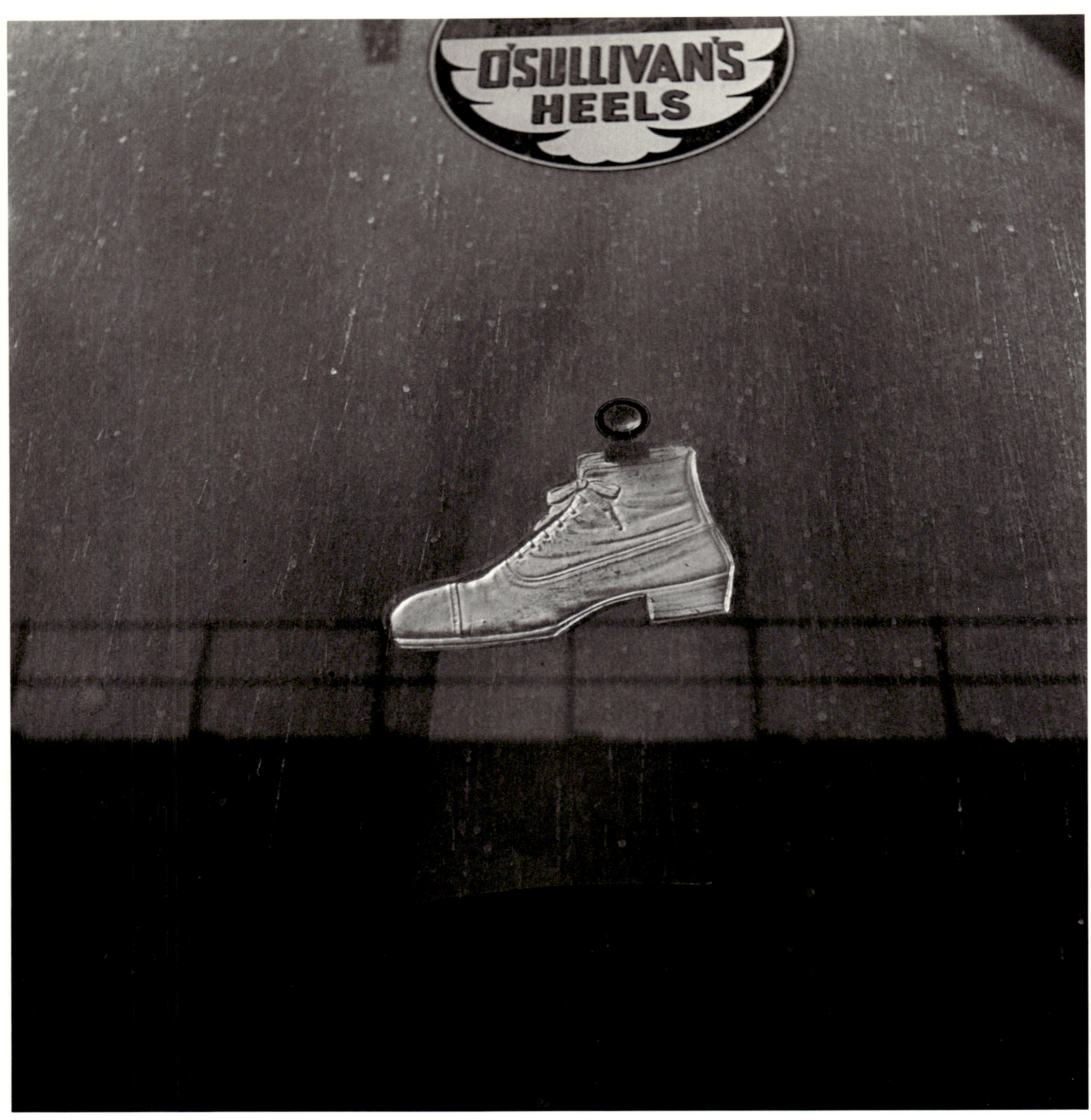

2. O'Sullivan's Heels. New York, c. 1939

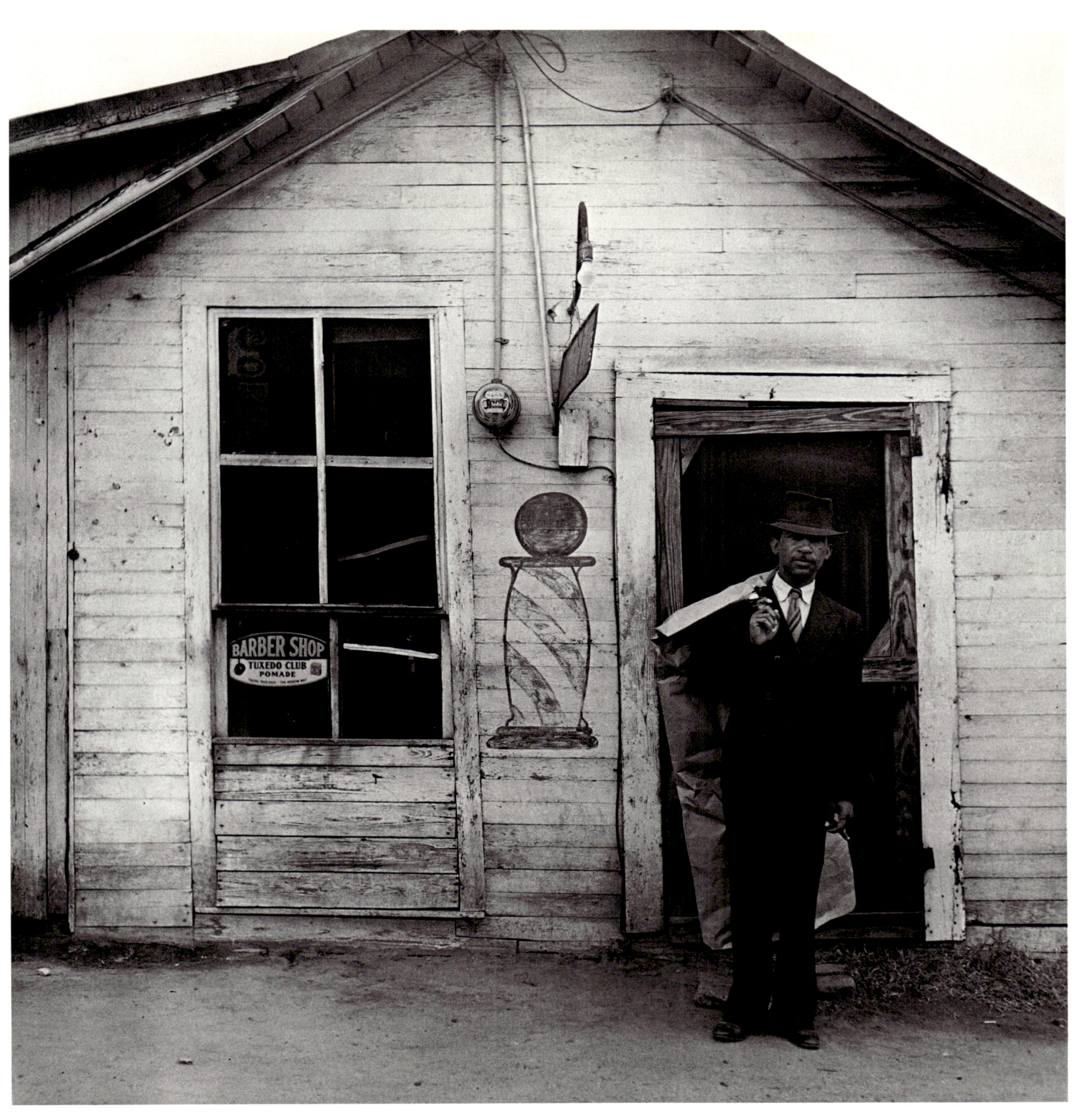

3. Man with Clothing Bag. American South, 1941

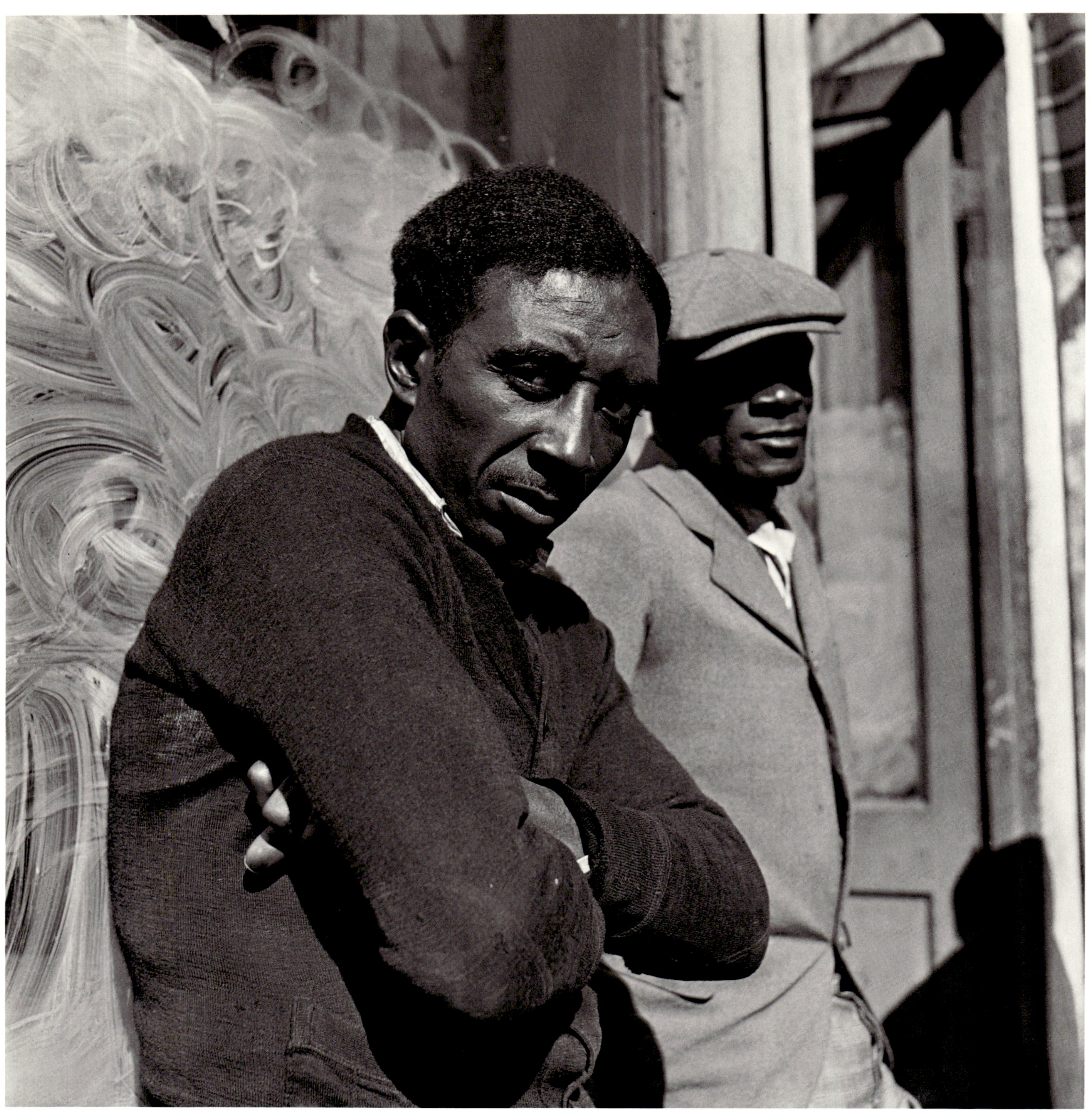

4. **Two Men.** American South, 1941

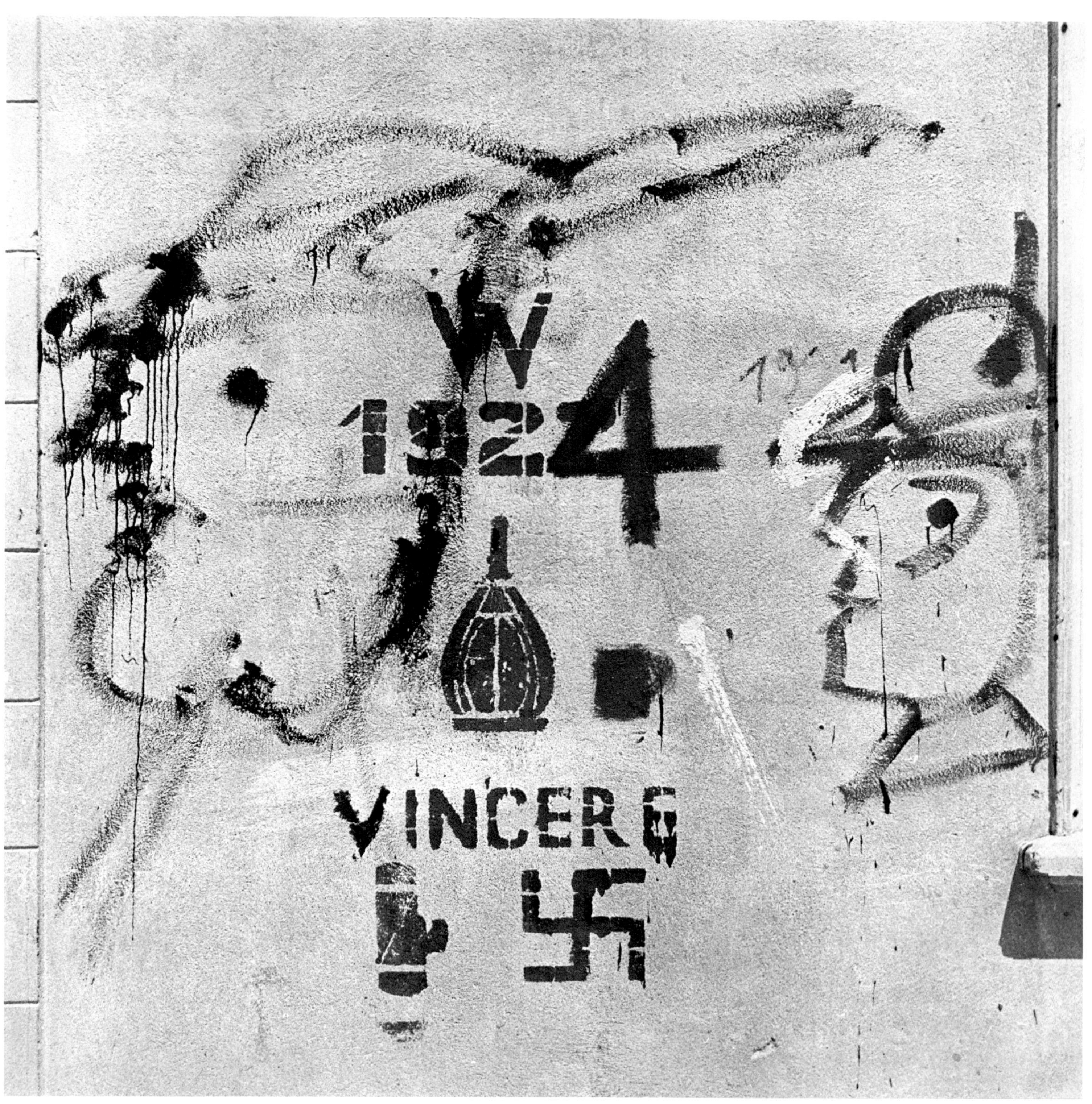

5. Italian War Wall. Northern Italy, 1944–45

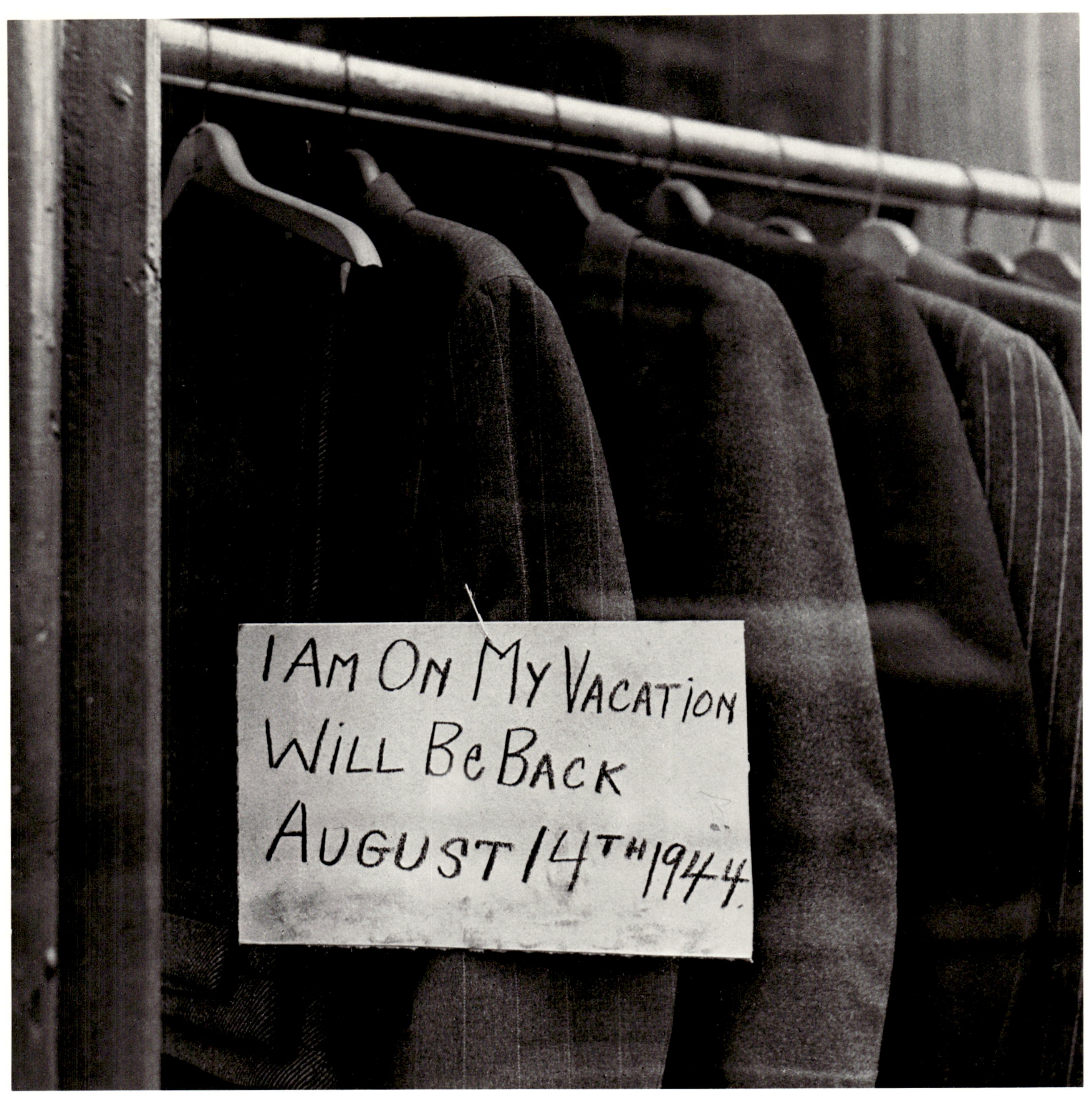

6. I Am On My Vacation. 1944

Irving Penn

John Szarkowski

The Museum of Modern Art, New York

This book and the exhibition it accompanies have been made possible by generous grants from the SCM Corporation and the National Endowment for the Arts. On behalf of the Museum and its audience I thank them.

Many people have contributed in many ways to the realization of this project. My efforts to understand better the circumstances in which much of Penn's work has been done have been greatly assisted by conversations with Alexander Liberman and the late Marvin Israel. Transcripts of several sessions of the Brodovitch Workshop, given to the Museum by Ben Fernandez, were also very rewarding.

In addition to those authors cited in the Introduction, the writings of Nancy Hall-Duncan and Owen Edwards on the subject of fashion photography were especially helpful.

For assistance with special research problems I am grateful to Diana Edkins, Robert Gilka, Kate Lloyd, William Orrick, and Peter Schub. Jo Ann Baker, of Mr. Penn's staff, has provided essential cataloging information.

I am grateful to Timothy Baum for permission to reproduce the Man Ray photograph shown in Figure 16, and to Chanel Inc., Chrysler Corporation, and General Foods Corporation for permission to reproduce photographs made for them. The Condé Nast Publications Inc. has granted permission to reproduce those pictures listed on page 216.

Of the many members of the Museum's staff that have made important contributions to this project, I will thank here only three. As editor of the text, Susan Weiley has rescued it from most of its infelicities, and has tolerated those to which I was most attached. Tim McDonough has been responsible for the planning and the supervision of the book's production. Catherine Evans has collaborated with sensitivity and precision in all aspects of the realization of the book and the exhibition.

Penn's prints characteristically make important use of the extreme ends of the photographic gray scale, and present a formidable challenge to half-tone reproduction. In this regard the advice and counsel of Richard Benson was of enormous help.

It is not hyperbole to say that this project could not have been done as it has been done without Pat McCabe, Mr. Penn's extraordinary assistant, whose knowledge of Penn's work and archives, and whose graciousness, have made even the most unreasonable requests seem reasonable.

I am of course most deeply indebted to Irving Penn. The privilege of studying his remarkable achievement has been enlarged by the pleasure of working with an artist of such generosity of spirit and so keen an intelligence.

JOHN SZARKOWSKI

Introduction

In 1934 Irving Penn enrolled in the Philadelphia Museum School of Industrial Art—since 1964 the Philadelphia College of Art—largely, he claims now, because of their forgiving admissions standards, and the liberality with which they awarded scholarships. At the age of eighteen he had no focused ambitions that he now remembers, and during his first year he contentedly and absent-mindedly drew from plaster casts and modeled clay figures. He recalls his fellow students as being more or less equally divided between purists, who hoped to emulate Franklin C. Watkins,[1]* the faculty's best-known painter and a man who had won many honors, including the coveted Carnegie Prize, and pragmatists, who leaned toward the example of Henry Pitz, a highly successful illustrator and follower of Newell Wyeth.[2] Penn does not

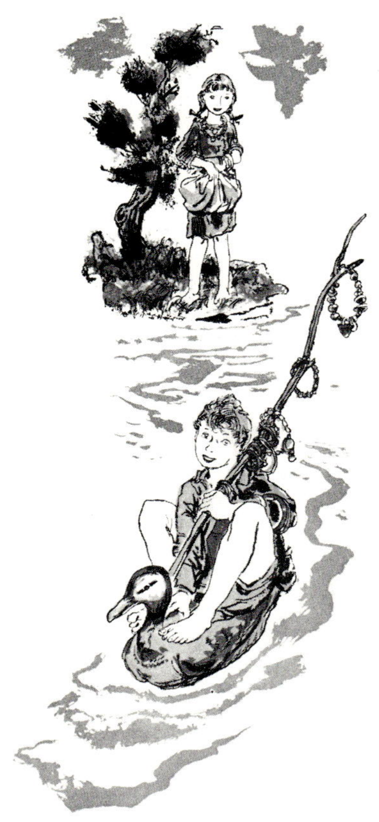

2. Henry C. Pitz. Watercolor illustration for *Hansel and Gretel*. The Limited Editions Club, New York, 1952

think he was influenced by either man, although he did admire Watkins because he looked and carried himself like an artist, and paid students no more attention than they demanded.

In his second year Penn met Alexey Brodovitch, who taught at the school every other Saturday. Brodovitch was the son of petty Russian gentry, a former cavalry officer who had fought for the Imperial Army before and

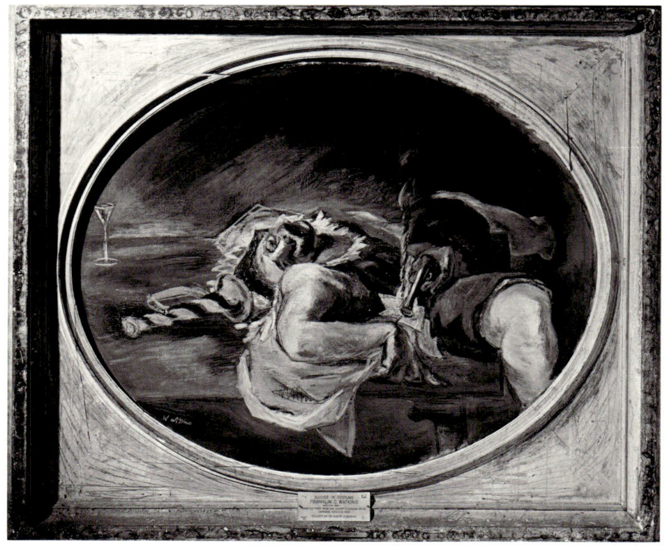

1. Franklin C. Watkins. *Suicide in Costume.* 1931. Oil on canvas. Philadelphia Museum of Art, given by a group of donors

*The footnote numbers in the essay refer to text illustrations.

after October 1917, an émigré to and then from Paris, and a graphic designer of great influence.[3]

Those who have known privilege, once relieved by revolutions of the traditional obligations that accompany the ownership of land and its peasants, sometimes enjoy for a generation or two the best of two worlds: their sense of natural authority remains intact, while tedious responsibilities have been lifted from their shoulders. Brodovitch's stature might be best measured not in terms of work done at his own drawing table, but by the great influence that his restless curiosity and quiet artistic arrogance had upon the impressionable. Few were more impressionable than the teenaged Penn, who after a few sessions in Brodovitch's Saturday class decided that it was his ambition to learn to make art so fine that it would be worthy of inclusion in the most elegant magazines of the time, including *Harper's Bazaar*, which Brodovitch served as Art Director.

During the summers of 1937 and 1938 Penn worked for Brodovitch at *Harper's Bazaar*. Although he was not paid, it would be imprecise to say that Penn was Brodovitch's serf, for serfs were given shelter and a garden plot, whereas Penn (an American, and therefore not a serf) required no such coddling. In the event, Brodovitch was right. Penn presumably leaned on his family, survived, and enjoyed that higher happiness known only to acolytes, for whom the most trivial task, done in the small hours of the morning, represents a special privilege.

Among the perquisites of Penn's position during these summers with Brodovitch was that of opening the mail and having the first look at drawings by Cocteau, Tchelitchew, Dali, and other olympian role models.

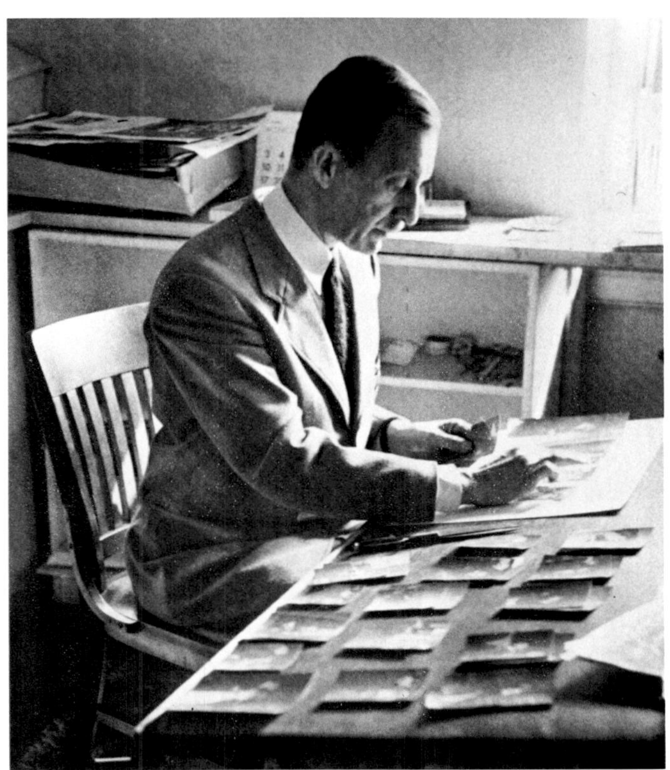

3. Maurice Tabard. Alexey Brodovitch at his desk at *Harper's Bazaar*. c. 1950

One day in 1937 a drawing by Rufino Tamayo arrived, intended to accompany a text by Edwin Lanham. Brodovitch suggested that Penn try his own hand at the problem, in his free time, and would he please have his solution on Brodovitch's desk in the morning. Penn, assuming that the assignment was a continuation of his academic apprenticeship, delivered his drawing on schedule and thought no more of the matter until it appeared in the *Bazaar* with the Lanham text. Carmel Snow was said to adore it, and Penn was deeply depressed. The

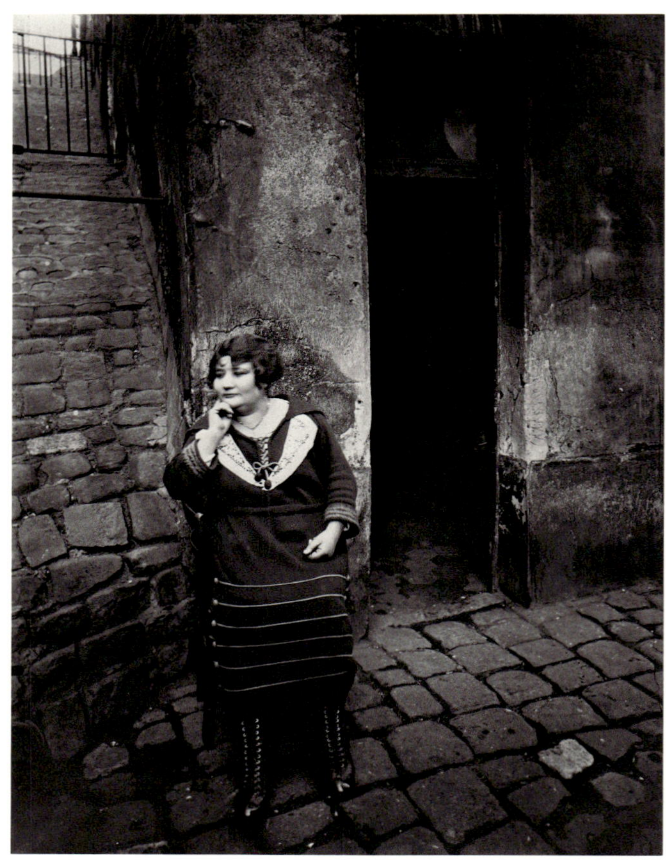

4. Eugène Atget. *Prostitute.* 1921. The Museum of Modern Art, New York, Abbott-Levy Collection, partial gift of Shirley C. Burden

goal that he had hoped to achieve after years of study and devoted effort had come to him as a casual accident.

After graduating from the Museum School in 1938 Penn moved to New York and began a career as a freelance commercial artist, working chiefly but not exclusively for Brodovitch, who in addition to being Art Director for *Harper's Bazaar,* had a variety of other irons in the fire. In 1940 Penn went to Saks Fifth Avenue with Brodovitch, who had been retained to redesign that store's advertising strategy. Brodovitch's role was largely conceptual and critical. "I think we should have drawings by Bemelmans. I would like to see Bemelmans's drawings on these pages. Penn, would you speak to Bemelmans?" When the layout had been completed in keeping with Brodovitch's general directive, he would say yes or no, or move an element, or sometimes change the size of a typeface, without agonizing, or even much apparent thought.

After one year Brodovitch left Saks and recommended to Adam Gimbel that Penn be his successor. Gimbel agreed; Penn took the job and remained one year. Having never been a Russian cavalry officer, he found the job difficult and the buyers—to whom it was self-evident that ten dresses on the page were ten times as good as one—impossible. Disillusioned, he resigned without strenuous protest and went to Mexico, where he recalls painting for a year from morning until night.

This cannot be entirely accurate, for he also made photographs in Mexico. He had in fact made them earlier, and although he now tends to dismiss (or defend) these early pictures as the photographs of a non-photographer, a disinterested observer might think they exhibit much of the personal character that identifies the best of his later professional work. The most obvious models for these early pictures are photographs by Eugène Atget and Walker Evans. Brodovitch had shown his students Atget in reproduction; Penn remembers pictures of second-hand clothes shops, with hanging clothes blurred by the wind, and the portrait of the prostitute seated by her doorway, with her tall laced

18

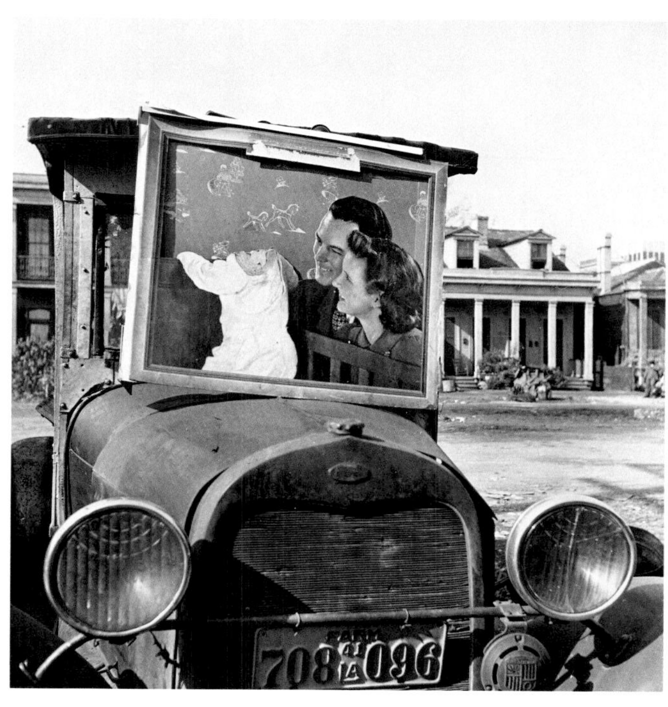

5. Irving Penn. *American South.* 1941

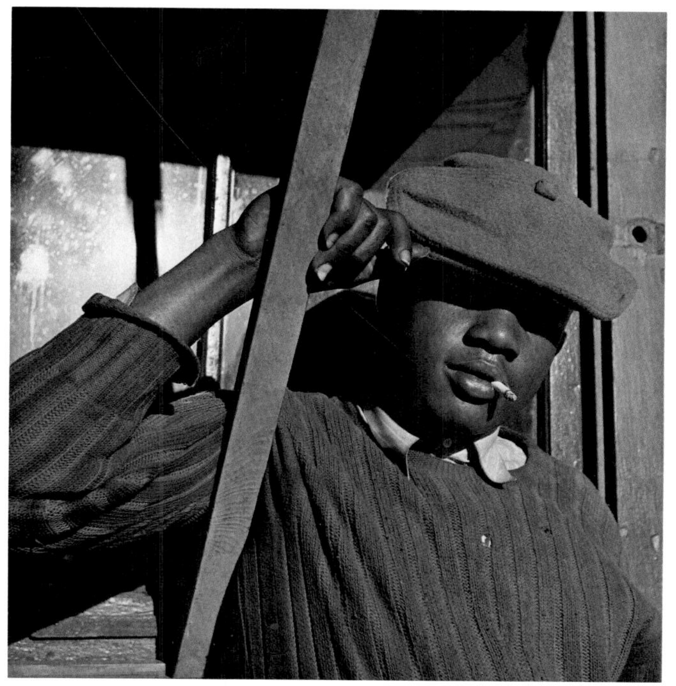

6. Irving Penn. *Young Man with Cigarette.* New Orleans, 1941

boots and the cobblestones of the sidewalk racing upward.[4] Penn was not a regular visitor to The Museum of Modern Art, but thinks he saw the Walker Evans show there in 1938, and his familiarity with Evans's work dates from this period.[5]

The subject matter of Penn's earliest photographs closely echoes that of Atget or Evans: shop windows, handmade signs, barbershops, and informal portraits of people on the street. But it also seems clear that there is a personal sensibility in these pictures, whether or not it was visible to the young photographer. A street portrait like *Young Man with Cigarette*[6] possesses a lan-

guorous elegance of line and pose, a pleasure in satiny textures, a stylishness that does not relate to Evans. The raw materials of *Optician's Window* (pl. 1) are as humble as those of Atget's working-class shops, but in Penn's picture they seem dear enough for Tiffany's.

Penn had bought his first Rolleiflex with money earned by doing drawings of shoes, at five dollars each, for *Harper's Bazaar;* by the time of his year in Mexico he also had a 4 x 5 stand camera, and he used both often and well. Nevertheless, it had not occurred to him that photography might become central to his artistic ambitions.

19

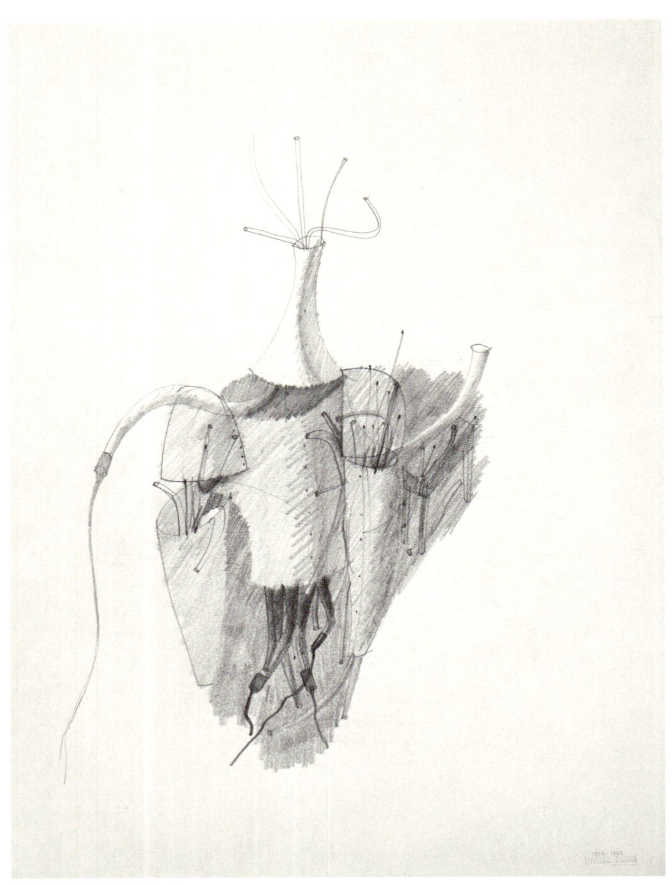

7. Irving Penn. Untitled. 1939–42. Pencil drawing

Penn's principal models were de Chirico and Matta.[7]

Before leaving for Mexico Penn had met Alexander Liberman, another artist from Russia by way of Paris. He had even wondered in passing whether Liberman, who had been Art Director for Lucien Vogel at *Vu*, might want his job at Saks, but quickly decided that the new man deserved, and would find, more interesting adversaries than the buyers Penn was fleeing. When Penn

After a year in Mexico Penn returned to New York, dissatisfied with his painting. It is said that Penn, a man who respects quality, disliked his paintings but loved the beautiful linen canvases they were painted on; thus he did not burn his failures, but scraped them and washed them clean, so that he could continue to admire them as cloths for small tables. Some undated drawings survive from the approximate period; they suggest that

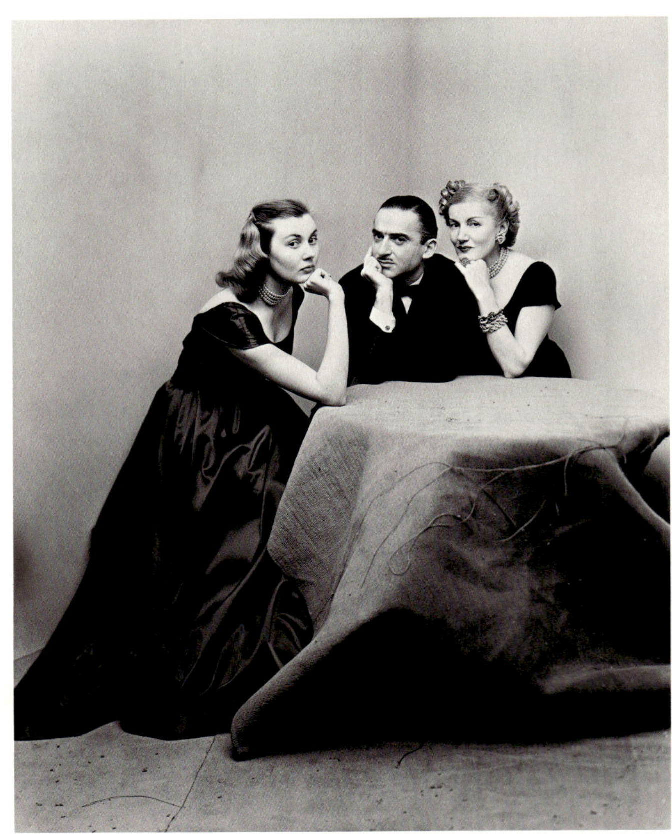

8. Irving Penn. *Francine du Plessix and Mr. and Mrs. Alexander Liberman.* 1948

returned to New York, Liberman was at *Vogue*, where he became Art Director in 1943, succeeding M. F. Agha, who had served this role for all Condé Nast publications since 1929.[8] Liberman quickly hired Penn as his assistant, and established the beginnings of a creative collaboration of remarkable durability and fecundity. (So close has their working relationship been that it is often impossible to disentangle their individual contributions to shared creative problems.)

Vogue was then one of the irrational glories of the great days of the magazines. From the outside it seemed to possess the self-certainty of an ancient, lavishly endowed institution. During its best years it was not in fact financially secure; its poise was an attribute of style and steady nerves, not wealth.

The duties of Penn's new job were undefined, and after having familiarized himself in general terms with the personal and architectural landscape of the *Vogue* offices and studios, Penn asked Liberman what he was supposed to be doing. After a little thought Liberman replied that Penn might think about covers. After thinking about covers, Penn brought his sketches to the magazine's distinguished photographers—Horst, Blumenfeld, Beaton, Lynes, Rawlings—who were often polite but invariably too busy to play games with the young assistant. When Penn finally reported to Liberman that the idea wasn't working, it was suggested that in that case he might like to make the photographs himself, and was assigned a studio assistant to explain the peculiarities of an 8 x 10 studio camera and how to calculate exposures. Penn became a photographer and proceeded to work at his new calling every day. The first color photograph of his new career was the cover of *Vogue's*

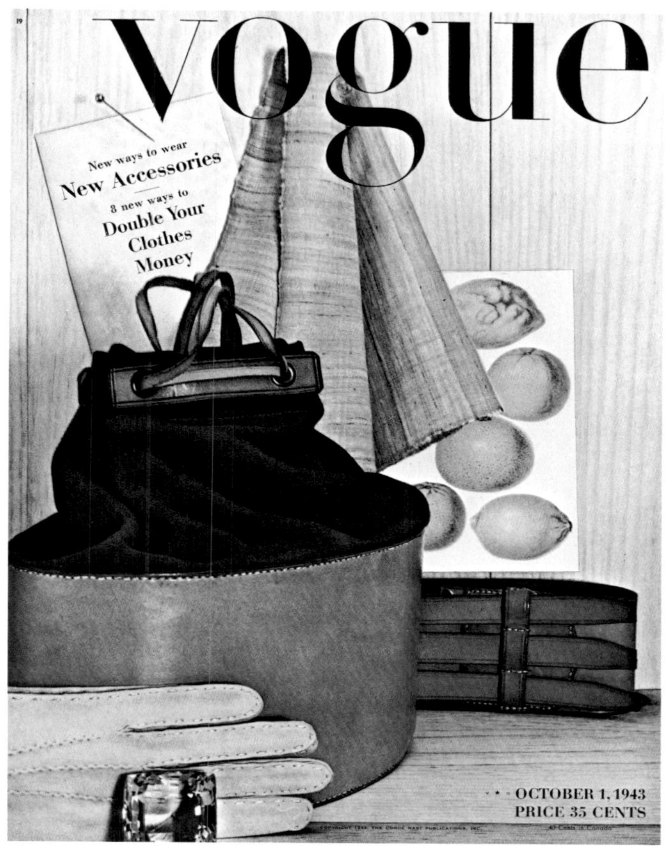

9. Irving Penn. *Vogue* still-life cover. 1943

October 1, 1943 issue, and it was the first still-life cover in the magazine's history.[9]

In 1944 Penn took leave from *Vogue* to join the volunteer American Field Service, which he served as an ambulance driver and photographer, primarily in Italy and briefly in India, until the war's end. In these years he again enjoyed the freedom of photographing as an amateur. During his free hours he photographed his

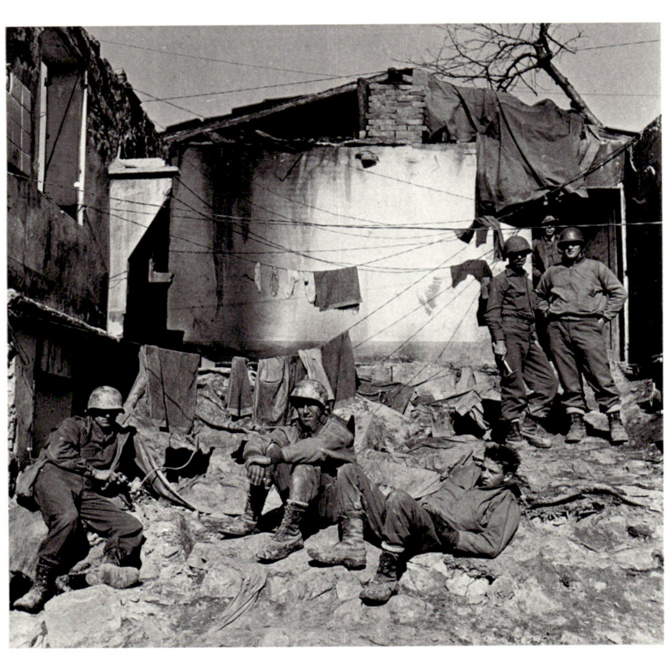

10. Irving Penn. *American Mortar Crew, San Clementi Front.* Apennines, 1944

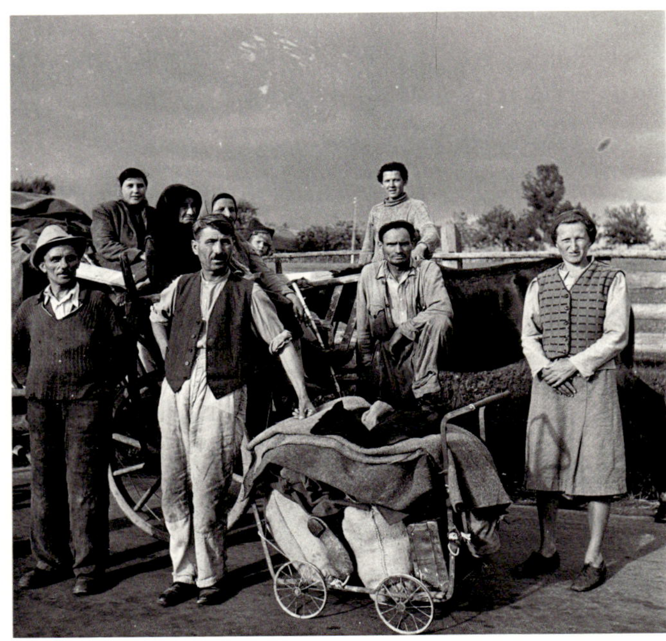

11. Irving Penn. *Austrian Family.* 1945

friends and allies and those aspects of the larger war that presented themselves to him. Among the most interesting of these casual records are three group portraits[10, 11, 12] that may be seen as sketches for a species of picture that Penn would later revise and perfect in the studio (see *Twelve Most Photographed Models*, pl. 28, and *Ballet Theater*, pl. 15). Like the later, fully formed versions of this idea, the three wartime documents remind us of tableaux vivants, in which the specificity of natural fact stands in tension with the abstract perfection of grand design. The somnolent grace of the combat soldiers in figure 10, and the lazy, elastic asymmetry of

their patterning across the sheet, creates an image that is disconcertingly stylish and foreign to our sense of the proper look of war. The photograph of the Georgian cossacks (fig. 12) recalls a romantic, anachronistic notion of warfare, one related to the dashing officer that Penn had photographed on the wall of the Mexican pulquería three years earlier.[13] The aura of glamour in the photograph resides perhaps less in the soldiers' Rudolph Friml costumes than in the athletic elegance of their comportment. They would have made superb fashion models, for as long as their patience lasted.

After the war Penn returned immediately to *Vogue,*

22

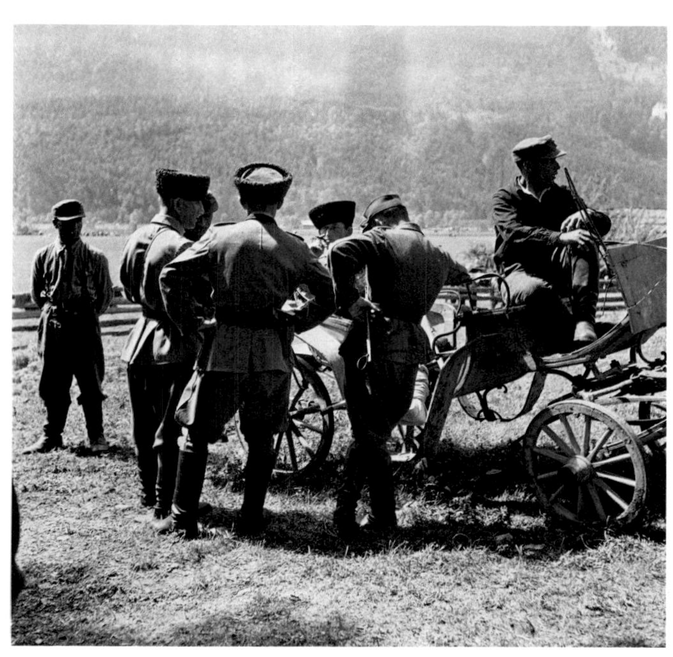

12. Irving Penn. *Russian Soldiers.* Austria, 1945

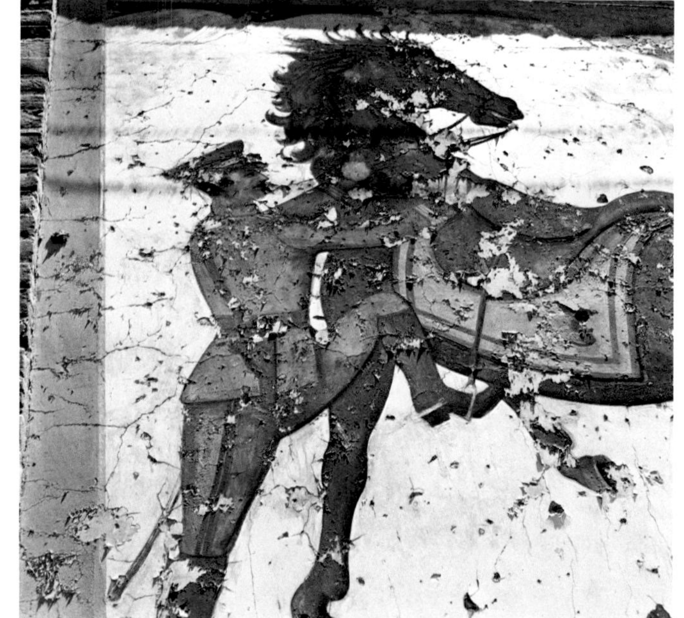

13. Irving Penn. *Pulqueria Decoration.* Mexico, 1942

where he photographed continually, making fashion pictures, still lifes, portraits, and clever, atmospheric confections that touched more or less directly on the world of theater. During 1947, the second year after his return, the essential Penn—what now might be called the historic Penn—emerged. The calm spareness of vision and manner in his pictures was breathtaking. Seen against the background of the various trilling, ornamental styles that had seemed intrinsic to the very substance of fashion magazines, they seemed to represent a new beginning.

It was perhaps in portraiture and in still life rather than in fashion that Penn first found full confidence in his own intuitions. Several of his earliest memorable portraits, including *George Jean Nathan and H. L. Mencken* (pl.7) and *John Marin* (pl. 14), were made in 1947, as was his riotous, joyful *Still Life with Watermelon* (pl. 63), one of the triumphs of color photography. Beginning the next year Penn made many portraits in Europe, whose older painters and writers had been largely hidden from American audiences during the war years, and whose younger ones were generally known only to specialists. The portraits of artists, especially, were an adventure for the youthful Penn because he knew and admired their work. His 1948 photograph *Joan Miró and his Daughter Dolores* (pl. 11) is in part a homage to the painting made ten years earlier by Balthus.[14]

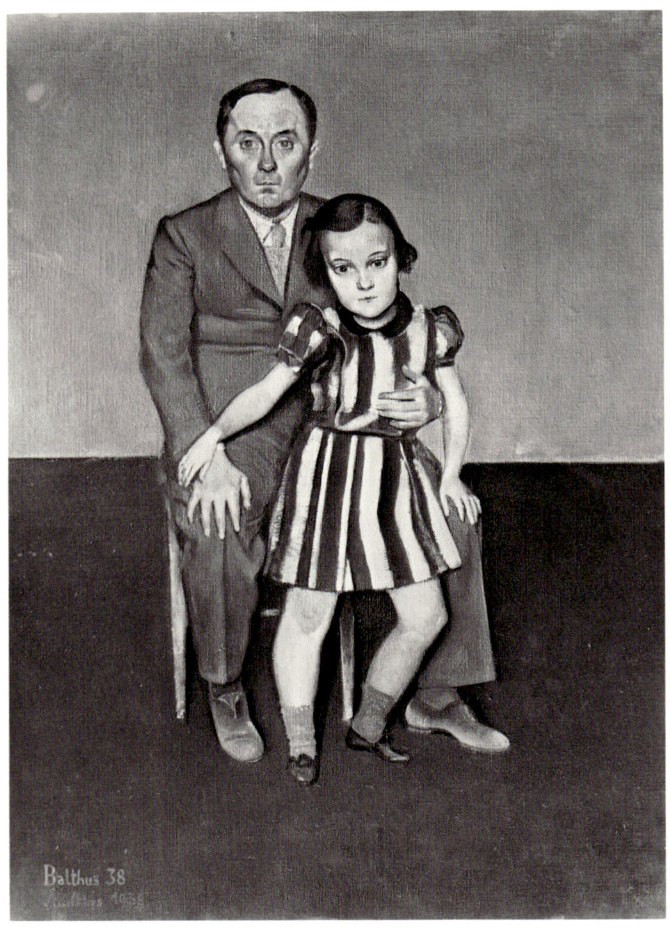

14. Balthus (Baltusz Klossowski de Rola). *Joan Miró and his Daughter Dolores.* 1937–38. Oil on canvas. The Museum of Modern Art, New York, Abby Aldrich Rockefeller Fund

It is not likely that a free-lance photographer would have gained access to so impressive a list of subjects; the support and influence of an important magazine was essential. At times the largess of *Vogue's* support was almost overwhelming. When the car bearing the photographer, photographic equipment, an editor, and assistants pulled up before the entrance to the subject's fourth-floor, cold-water walk-up, it did not improve the chances of a successful sitting. Penn learned to find a plausible excuse to be dropped off around the corner so as to present himself to the sitter as unencumbered and as quietly as possible. It was (and is) his idea that the portraitist must seem a servant to the sitter (even if sometimes a stern and demanding one), one whose function it is to attend and encourage the sitter's self-revelation. Whether the portraitist should actually be what he seems is a more complex question.

Recalling his early years at *Vogue,* Penn remembers himself, probably disingenuously and surely hyperbolically, as a street savage surrounded by sophisticates. This neat equation is perhaps suspect at both ends. In the photographs of the youthful Penn he seems to resemble not so much a street savage as a schoolmate of Keats.[15] As for the sophistication of the others at *Vogue,* it is surely true that some of them were people of broad culture and experience, and that most of the rest had learned to play that role. It is also surely true that the aspect of sophistication was in those years the magazine's most precious asset, and one that would not be sold cheaply.

In 1949 Liberman told Penn to buy a dinner jacket

and go to Paris to see the new collections—not to work, but to familiarize himself with the world in which he was working: how it talked, walked, ate, and drank, and how it conducted business. Penn enjoyed the visit very much.

In 1950 Penn photographed the Paris collections and produced a series of photographs that remain almost equally memorable (pls. 45-47, 54, 58), and that revised the terms on which future fashion photographs would, for a while, be considered. The best of the earlier work—by de Meyer, Steichen, Beaton, Hoynigen-Huene, and others—now seems close to theater, with the dress and its model playing a role. But Penn's 1950 pictures provide no references to plot or circumstance, no suggestions of old châteaux, or perfect picnics, or delicious flirtations in Edwardian drawing rooms, or footlights, or *avant* Freudian dream worlds. They are not stories, but simply pictures. Within the boundaries of a classically simple photographic vocabulary, they effect a translation, into pictorial terms, of the idea and the spirit of another artist's work—the couturier's work.

Penn claims, with a modest and disarming smile, that the simplicity of his approach to fashion was inspired by ignorance. He did not know which sideboard or candelabra or period wallpaper to use with which dress, and therefore discovered by necessity the beauties of the seamless-paper background. Without questioning Penn's candor, it can be pointed out that the traditional solution to this problem, if it was a problem, was to greet anachorism as a creative ally, and to photograph the ball-gowned models with a horse in what appears to be

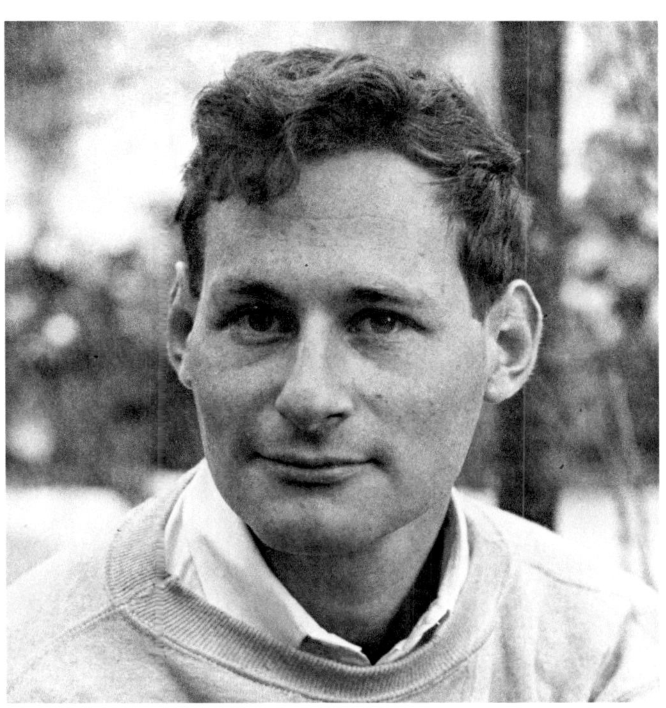

15. Photographer unknown. *Irving Penn.* c. 1938

an immaculate abattoir, as Steichen had; or to seat the subject in a surrealistic wheelbarrow, as Man Ray had.[16] Beaton wrote later that the fashion photographers of the thirties had indulged themselves in a "recklessness of style....Badly carved cupids from junk shops on Third Avenue would be wrapped in Argentine cloth or cellophane. Driftwood was supposed to bring an air of neo-romanticism to a matter-of-fact subject. Christmas paper chains were garlanded around the model's shoulders, and wooden doves, enormous paper flowers

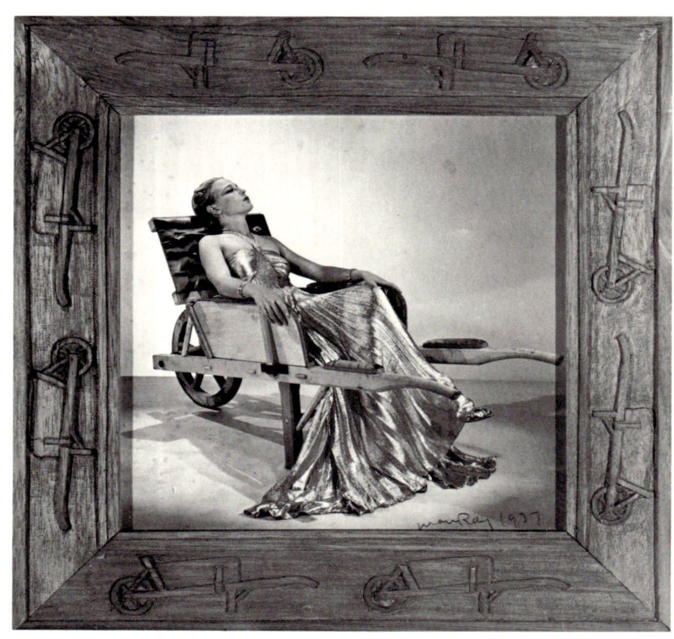

16. Man Ray. Untitled. 1937. Courtesy Timothy Baum, New York.
©Man Ray Estate, ADAGP, Paris

from Mexico, Chinese lanterns, doilies or cutlet frills, fly whisks, sporrans, egg beaters, or stars of all shapes found their way into our hysterical and highly ridiculous pictures."*

The economy and concentration of Penn's fashion pictures echoed his work in portraiture. In contrast to the prevalent magazine style of the years around 1950, his portraits are free of reference to the sitter's work or habitual environment. Writers are not photographed at their work tables, or even walking on the beach, thinking,

*Cecil Beaton, *The Glass of Fashion* (Garden City, N.Y.: Doubleday & Co., 1954), pp. 228-29.

but in a photographer's studio, or in an improvised space made to appear as anonymous, as value free, as a photographer's studio. In many of Penn's early portraits the presence of the studio is insistent; we are allowed to see the electrical cables, or the edges of the backdrop, and feel the impersonal, conventional north light (real or contrived) falling on these subjects as it had on a thousand others before them. There is a suggestion of shabbiness about this studio. The floor bears the scars of earlier sittings, and the somber gray carpet, artfully spread over coffee tables and soft-drink cases, is raveled at the edges. The studio presents itself as the functional workroom of an honest craftsman who is clearly unaware of the requirements of high elegance. After all those badly carved cupids and all that driftwood this would have been a perfect strategy, even for a photographer of modest talent who, after the novelty of simplicity had worn thin, could have adopted or adapted a new idea, and then another, etc.

Penn has never changed his first idea of portraiture; he has merely simplified what at first seemed almost irreducibly simple, so that by the late fifties even the anonymous studio disappeared, and there remained no environment at all, only a wordless conversation between the photographer and the sitter. If both principals are alert, and willing to accept the risk of humiliating failure, and if they are lucky, the collaboration may produce a picture that seems to touch the subject's soul.

Such high success may be hoped for, but the odds of achieving it are statistically not good. Not even Holbein or Velázquez always achieved it. It is, however, not the product of arbitrary chance. Among photographers, Nadar had no apparent skills or esoteric knowledge that

26

were unavailable to the other distinguished French portrait photographers of his day, but he succeeded more often in giving us a person who would, if not mute, tell us something marvelous. Or to start with the sitter, one might consider why there are so many moving portraits of Abraham Lincoln and so few, or none, of his contemporary Napoleon III, who apparently spent much of his career as Emperor being photographed. Perhaps it is because Lincoln had so deep a curiosity about other men that he did more than half the work, and brought even ordinary photographers to a state of alert participation and confidence that made them, for a time, equal collaborators.

One of Penn's recent sitters, the anthropologist Lionel Tiger, has written with unusual candor and perception of the demands required of the person portrayed, and of the possible rewards. As his sitting proceeded, and he entered into the spirit of the peculiar event,

> The act became a duet...I was a performer—not even of my own self, but in the context of something new to me, which demanded a highly complex effort. I had both some grasp of distance from myself, and yet a full sense of immersion in that person who was Penn's subject....I recall the sense of giving more than I had, of being more than I was, of telling more than my story...a symmetry of intent between myself and Penn seemed to have become created. *

An extraordinary portrait is by definition rare. The successful professional will, however, produce with regu-

*Lionel Tiger, "Encounters," *Camera Arts* (September-October 1981), pp. 43-44.

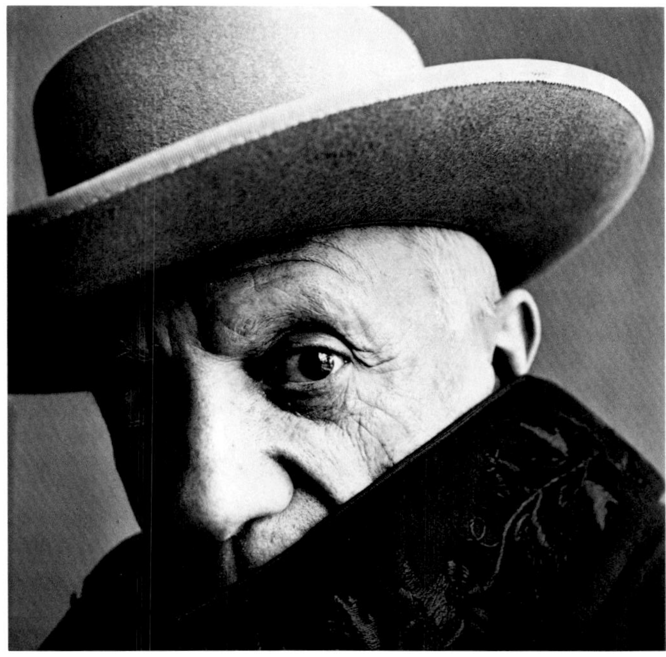

17. Irving Penn. *Picasso.* La Californie, Cannes, 1957. The Museum of Modern Art, New York, gift of the photographer

larity a picture that looks good, that has some variety of quality or style, and that will satisfy or delight the client and perhaps even the sitter, who in the world of high fees are almost never the same person. Penn's famous portrait of Picasso,[17] with the great cyclopean eye, the bullfighter's cape, the ethnic hat, the dramatic lighting, etc., seems to this viewer a marvelous triumph of skill, an admirable act of legerdemain, but something less than a true portrait, if one takes as a standard the picture of S. J. Perelman, for example (pl. 139). This is the record of a collaborative disclosure, or discovery, of a self.

The first ten or fifteen years after the war was perhaps the most satisfying time for Penn in terms of his public work. In 1950, at a symposium at The Museum of Modern Art, he stated a creed that every professional photographer would prefer to believe, and that many then did believe. He said,

The modern photographer, having, as most creative people, the urge to communicate widely, is inevitably drawn to the medium which offers him the fullest opportunity for that communication. He thus works for publication. He is, in fact, a journalist.... For the modern photographer the end product of his efforts is the printed page, not the photographic print. The technical limitations of his medium are the limitations not of the sensitive photographic materials, but of the reproductive process by which the printed page is made. The modern photographer works within their technical limitations. He even uses them to his advantage. He is not surprised and saddened by the published result. He has to a great extent pre-envisioned it.*

Fourteen years later, among colleagues and prospective colleagues at a session of the Brodovitch Workshop, Penn stated a different view:

The printed page seems to have come to something of a dead end for all of us. It is the main thing we've headed for, for so many years. Now the printed page degenerates in quality.... The next step, as I see it, is the area of manipulation, of control, breakdown, and

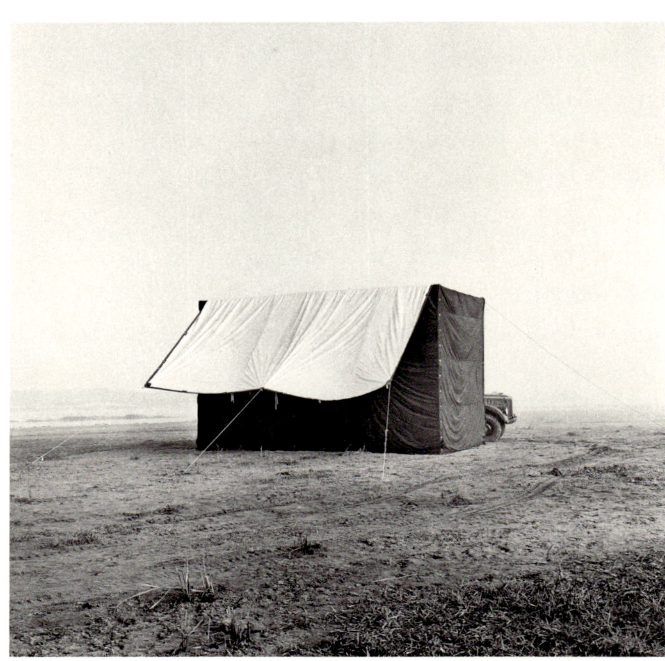

18. Per Boije. *Portable Studio.* Nepal, 1967

the reconstruction of the image in the making of a print. A beautiful print is a thing in itself, not just a halfway house on the way to the page. Because this way it's heartbreak as far as I'm concerned. And I've learned the discipline of not looking at the magazines when they come out, because they hurt so much.*

Penn's change of heart was not merely, or even primarily, a personal issue. The years between 1950 and 1964 were, approximately, the years during which photographers lost their faith in the opportunity that the magazines had seemed to promise. *Life* still sold seven million copies every week, and most of the others seemed fat and rich, and paid their photographers better than ever; but the sense of high adventure that had sustained the photographers earlier—the belief that an exceptional photographer, by virtue of the justice and accuity of his own vision, might with the magazines as his instrument revise the world—was failing. The content and style of magazines that depended on photography were decided by progressively larger committees of art directors, editors, advertising experts, market analysts, and accountants, and the photographers' effective authority declined proportionately.

It is true that the principal photographer of *Vogue* was allowed great freedom and given lavish support. If Penn wished to photograph the people of a place so obscure that it could be located only with the help of an excellent atlas, Alexander Liberman would make it possible, and a team would be galvanized to make sure that the project would not fail for lack of enough good camels or translators. And Liberman would not burden the photographer with long lists of requirements, shooting scripts, tentative numbers of pages to be filled, or similar claptrap. He would say, "Good luck, friend. Bring us back a treasure for Christmas."

Nevertheless, morale can erode under the best of officers, for reasons perhaps beyond their control. The nature of fashion magazines and the nature of fashion were changing. The question of which changed first is beyond the competence of this writer, but it does seem clear that until approximately the time of the Eisenhower administration fashion had been understood to stand for superior artifice, for the high craft of produc-

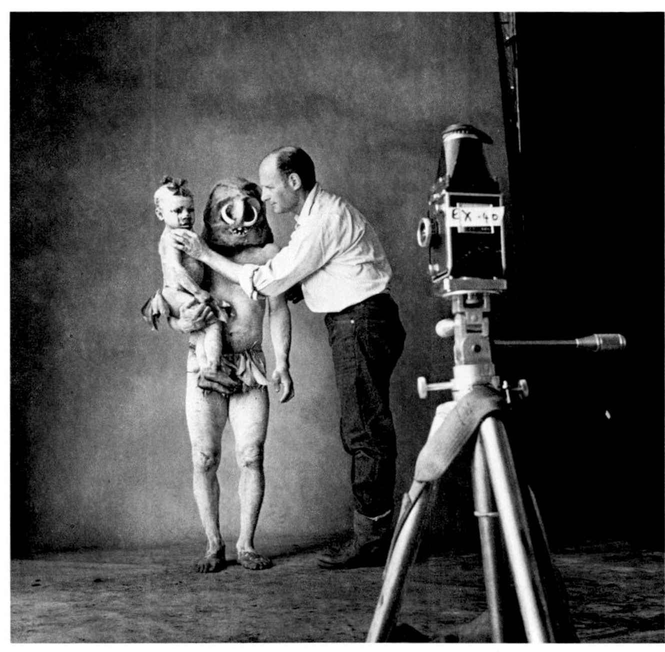

19. Lisa Fonssagrives-Penn. *Penn with Asaro Mud Man and Child.* New Guinea, 1970. ©1974 Lisa Fonssagrives-Penn

ing the illusion of beauty and mystery, for an exceptional and precious variety of art object that privileged women might wear—might *inhabit*—as a badge of their station, wealth, and taste. During the fifties the word changed its meaning, and fashion came to stand for lifestyle, a matter that was concerned less with art or craft than with popular psychology. As the clothes in the magazines became progressively ordinary, the model who wore them came to represent a progressively larger demographic sample; she became more active, and finally frenetic; less discriminating in her choice of amusements and friends; and progressively younger—finally too young to drive her own car. Without judging from a philosophical point of view the relative merits of the two ideas, one might guess that Penn found a woman in a Balenciaga suit more richly conducive material for his own art than a teenager in designer denim.

As haute couture declined and finally died, Penn found a substitute in the even more passionate and costly pursuit of style that had survived in corners of the world not yet completely absorbed by the West. First in Peru, then in West Africa, Nepal, Morocco, and New Guinea, Penn photographed people who had not

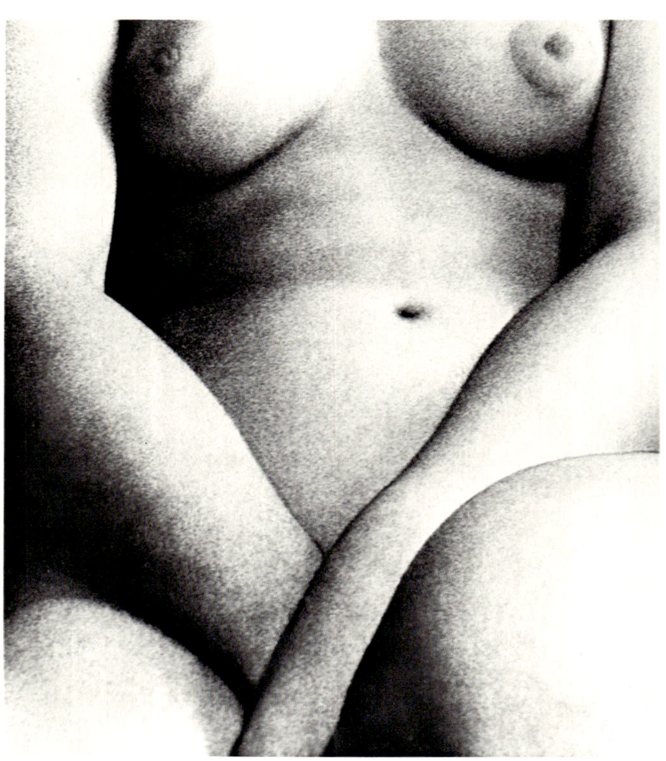

20. Bill Brandt. From the series Perspective of Nudes. 1953. The Museum of Modern Art, New York, purchase

yet learned to be embarrassed by the art of adornment. Penn's brief introduction to *Worlds in a Small Room*, a collection of these pictures, suggests that he thinks of them as portraits, and on occasion they are. But they are consistently photographs that describe the larger, impersonal issues of style, ornament, beauty, and role.

Most photographers, even though not anthropologists or ethnologists, would prefer to photograph exotic people in the undirected flow of their normal lives, in the environment that they have formed and that has formed them. Penn, characteristically, declined the potential riches and the untidiness of the large world and has instead taken his insular and abstracted studio, his hopefully neutral ground, along with him.[18] The audacity of the attempt is not in itself quite an adequate defense against the inevitable charge that he is removing his subjects from the real world, and the problems that it represents to them. The charge seems unanswerable. Penn shows us nothing of the circumstances of the New Guinea tribesmen, and nothing of their world beyond their sense of style. This fundamentally aesthetic issue Penn confronts with seriousness, skill, precise attention, and admiration, but it would be ingenuous to suggest that his art will be of greater use to them than Fragonard's was to Marie Antoinette.

Penn's relationship to his elegant subjects in Peru, Dahomey, Nepal, and so forth, may from the photographer's point of view have represented a less radical departure than we would suppose. When he worked with ordinary high-fashion models, it was presumably not necessary to reach a shared intellectual understanding of the problem. Such communication as was necessary may have been more like that sufficient for dancing:

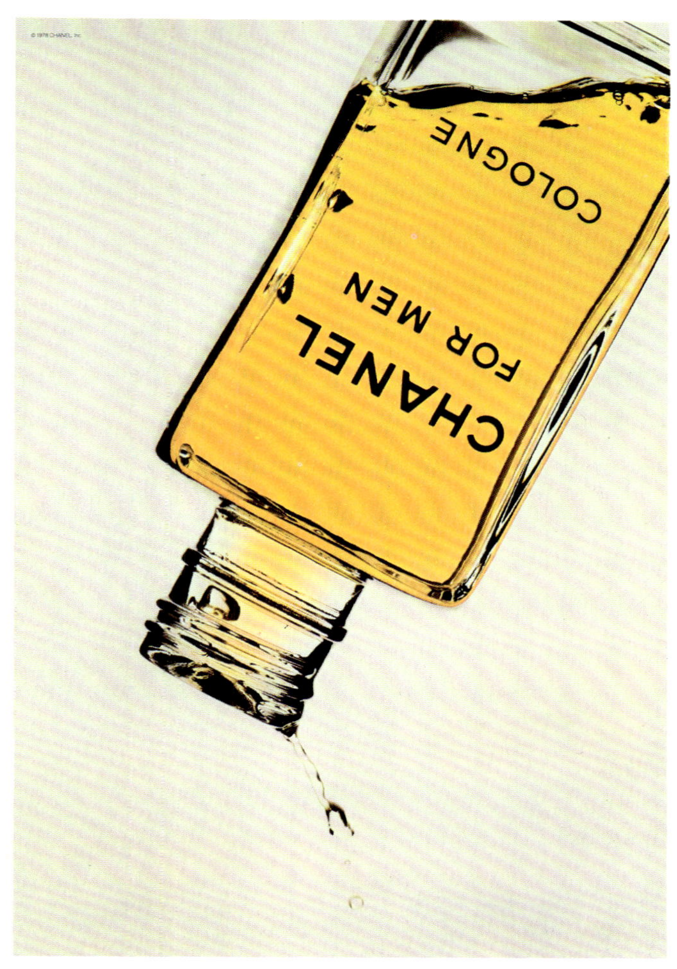

21. Irving Penn. Chanel for Men. 1978. © 1978 Chanel, Inc.

dresses created between the end of the Edwardian decade and the beginning of World War II. The dresses were included in an exhibition that Diana Vreeland had directed for The Metropolitan Museum of Art. In Penn's photographs the dresses are modeled by plastic mannequins whose patience and perfect stillness help the photographer describe his subject—which is not the evanescent beauty and charm of specific women, but the art of couture. The quiet perfection of the photographs seems an elegy to the past they memorialize.

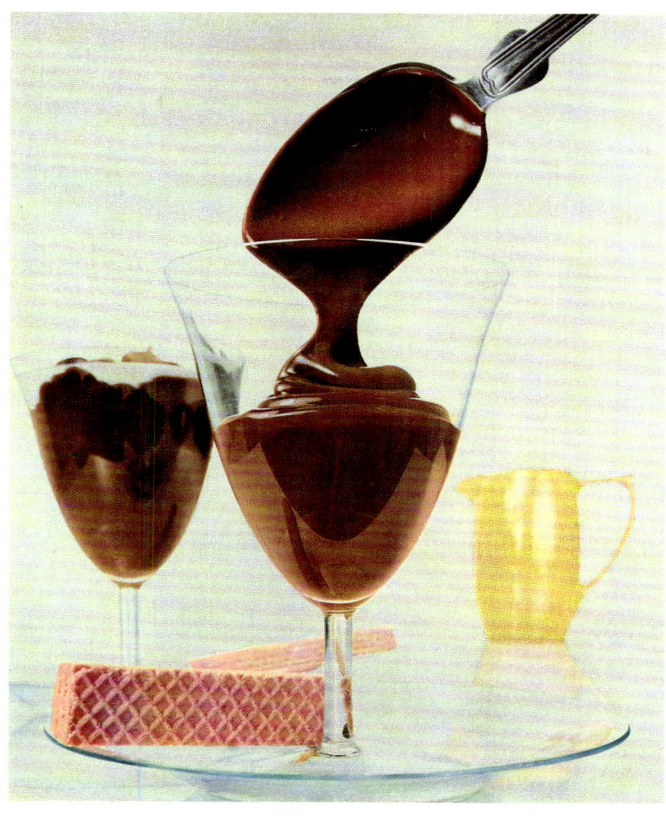

22. Irving Penn. Jell-O® Pudding. c. 1953

subtle guidance by the hand, body language, and a variety of appreciative murmurs may have been enough.[19]

Almost thirty years after his first Paris collection, Penn returned to high fashion to produce a book of perfectly conceived and exquisitely realized photographs, *Inventive Paris Clothes*, which describes forty-eight

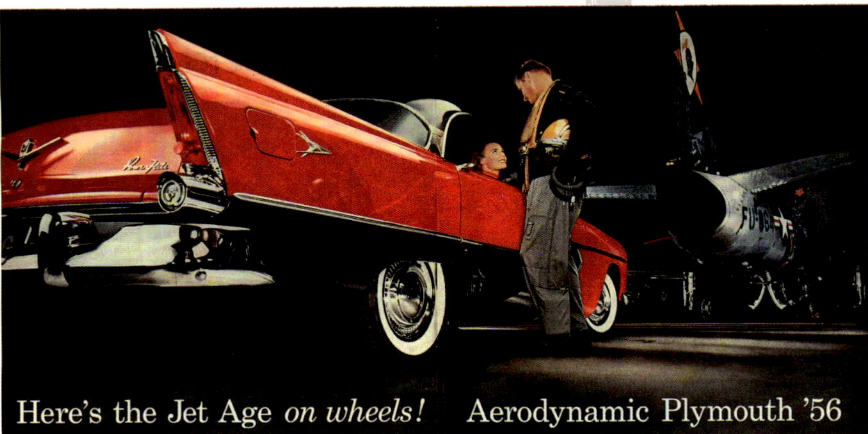

23. Irving Penn. 1956 Plymouth Belvedere. 1955

Each fashion model is of course unique; nevertheless the range of their uniqueness describes a fairly narrow segment within the total spectrum of human aspect. Although unique they do tend toward a slim, smooth, youthful minimalism, which might in time come to seem an arbitrary limitation. In 1949 Penn began a series of nudes for which he soon turned to the traditional model of art schools, a grown woman whose body has tangible weight, and volumes complexly modulated by ropes and pouches of abundant flesh.

There are no other nudes like these in the history of photography. They do, however, invite comparison with the magnificent nudes of Bill Brandt, which were begun at about the same time.[20] One might say of both series that their abstraction is directed not toward the end of formal perfection, as it is in Edward Weston's nudes of twenty years earlier, but toward the expression of an erotic idea. In Brandt's pictures the idea is more nearly transmuted into memory, almost assimilated into the calm euphoria of pure seeing. The most radical of Penn's nudes, though no less thoroughly resolved, retain a trace of primitive, animistic vitality, and recall demons. With very few exceptions, these pictures were withheld from publication and public exhibition until they were shown at the Marlborough Gallery in New York in 1980.

The nudes also represent Penn's first intensive and extended effort to revise and expand the technical vocabulary of modern photography. The prints were grossly overexposed, then bleached and redeveloped. In this way tone could be subtracted (the print made lighter) not in proportion to the values of the negative, but equally from all areas of the gray scale. (The result—in which the darkest values are affected only slightly, and the middle and high values are raised almost to white—is perhaps similar to that which in theory would be produced by an unprintably dense negative.)

It is interesting that Penn was apparently at work on the nude series when he made the public remarks, quoted earlier, to the effect that the printed page was sufficient problem for him. This will surprise those who think that artists should be free of contradiction, and that they should both understand their changing motives and ambivalent values, day by day, and be able and willing to explain them simply and clearly.

During all these years, between the public editorial projects and the private experiments and the portraits of the famous or the glamorous, Penn did the work that successful commercial photographers do: he made photographs for advertisements of perfume, packaged pudding mixes, cosmetics, automobiles, shoes, ready-made shirts, and many other salable commodities.[21, 22, 23] Many of these pictures are perfect, within the narrow boundaries that are assigned them, and some have provided genuine aesthetic pleasure; but it must be admit-

24. Irving Penn. *Vogue* beauty page (Kathy Wallace). 1957

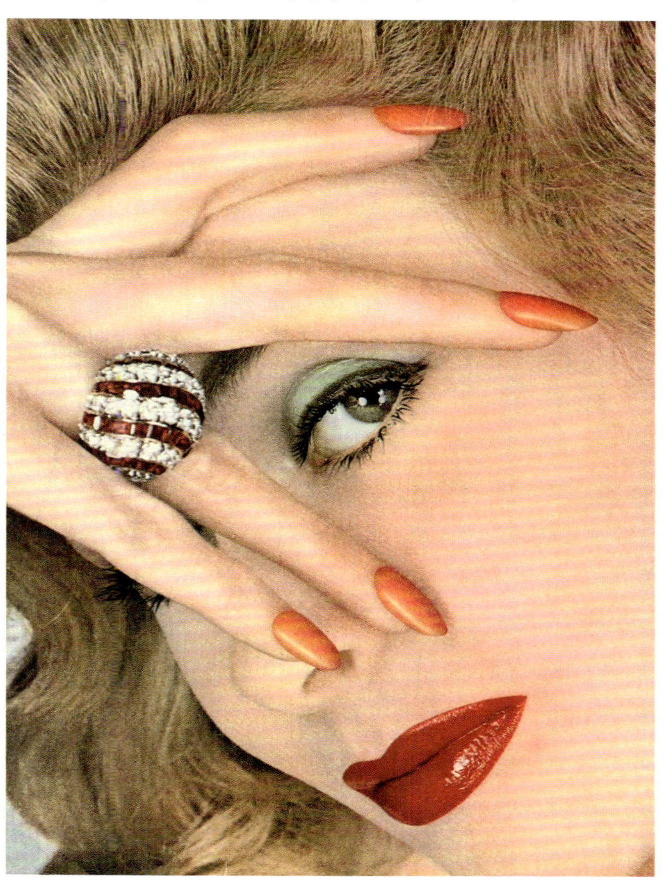

ted that they are for the most part less interesting than the earlier pictures from which they are derived. The earlier pictures were most often done for the magazines' editorial pages, for which a degree of free play and experiment was encouraged, and occasional failure expected. Advertising, in contrast, is a rigidly conceptual art. The poetry, such as it is, is in the idea. The execution, whether skillful and elegant or amateurish and lumpen, is only documentation.

Penn has also continued to make editorial fashion photographs, pictures that report the news of the world of fashion. As a random guess, it seems possible that he may have published five thousand such pictures. Whatever the number, an objective observer (meaning a person in another line of work) might think that the really essential fashion news could have been reported more economically. It is surely true that news of all varieties could be reported more concisely, if a way could be found to make concision profitable. It is probably true that the effort to make any variety of news perpetually fresh results in comic excess, or vulgarity.

Some might think that a serious interest in fashion is in itself vulgar, but to despise fashion and love art requires an athlete's balance. Even the issue of vulgarity is not as simple as it might seem. Kennedy Fraser has pointed out that in the world of fashion the word vulgarity has two almost polar meanings.* Among those who value the conservative virtue of taste, vulgarity means shrill and flashy overreach; for those like Baudelaire, on the other hand, or Beau Brummell, for whom style

*Kennedy Fraser, "Style," *The Fashionable Mind* (New York: Alfred A. Knopf, 1981), p. 77.

is a matter of high artistic aspiration, vulgarity means the cautious conventionality of the herd. In the commerce of fashion both varieties of failure lie precariously close to success. They may even be rewarded as success. It is in fact possible for a fashion photograph—like other works of art—to be vulgar in both senses simultaneously, and achieve gaudy conventionality.[24]

In Penn's fashion work what seems remarkable is the frequency of his success in converting predictable disasters into artistic victories. Consider the chances of artistic success in making a close-up color photograph of a

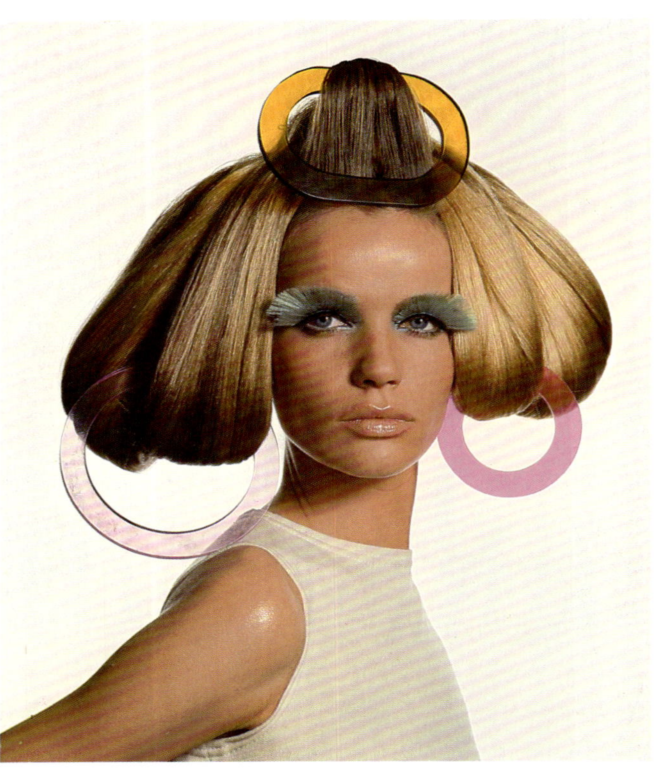

25. Irving Penn. *Vogue* fashion photograph (Veruschka). 1966

woman's wide-open mouth while the woman applies lipstick (pl. 100), or of another woman in the act of inserting a contact lens (pl. 101). We may despair at the thought of the sequence thus unleashed, and still admire these triumphs—these heroic last-minute rescues of artistic virtue.

More frequently, Penn's professional work elevates itself and its role by virtue of its great refinement of craft. The grace, wit, and inventiveness of his pattern-making, the lively and surprising elegance of his line, and his sensitivity to the character, the idiosyncratic humors, of light make Penn's pictures, even the slighter ones, a pleasure for our eyes.

Penn has mourned the disappearance of the skylight, and the incomparable "sweetness and constancy" of the light that fell from it. Nevertheless, his understanding of the functional qualities of that light have allowed him to simulate it closely enough (for example, in *Still Life with Food,* pl. 73) to deceive at least this viewer. He is equally alert to the potentials of qualities of light that he loves less, like the glittering, paper-thin light of electronic flash, which can shrink-wrap its subject in a plane of light as bright and brittle as zircons.[25] But it is not sufficient to understand the qualities of the various kinds of light, and how to produce them; it is necessary that the design and character of the picture as a whole be homogeneous with the meaning of the light that reveals it. In this intuitive awareness of light as an organic part of his subject, Penn is perhaps unmatched in the long and honorable tradition of studio photography.

For this viewer, Penn has been less successful when he has worked out-of-doors. To say that he has preferred to work in the studio, which he has, is merely to restate

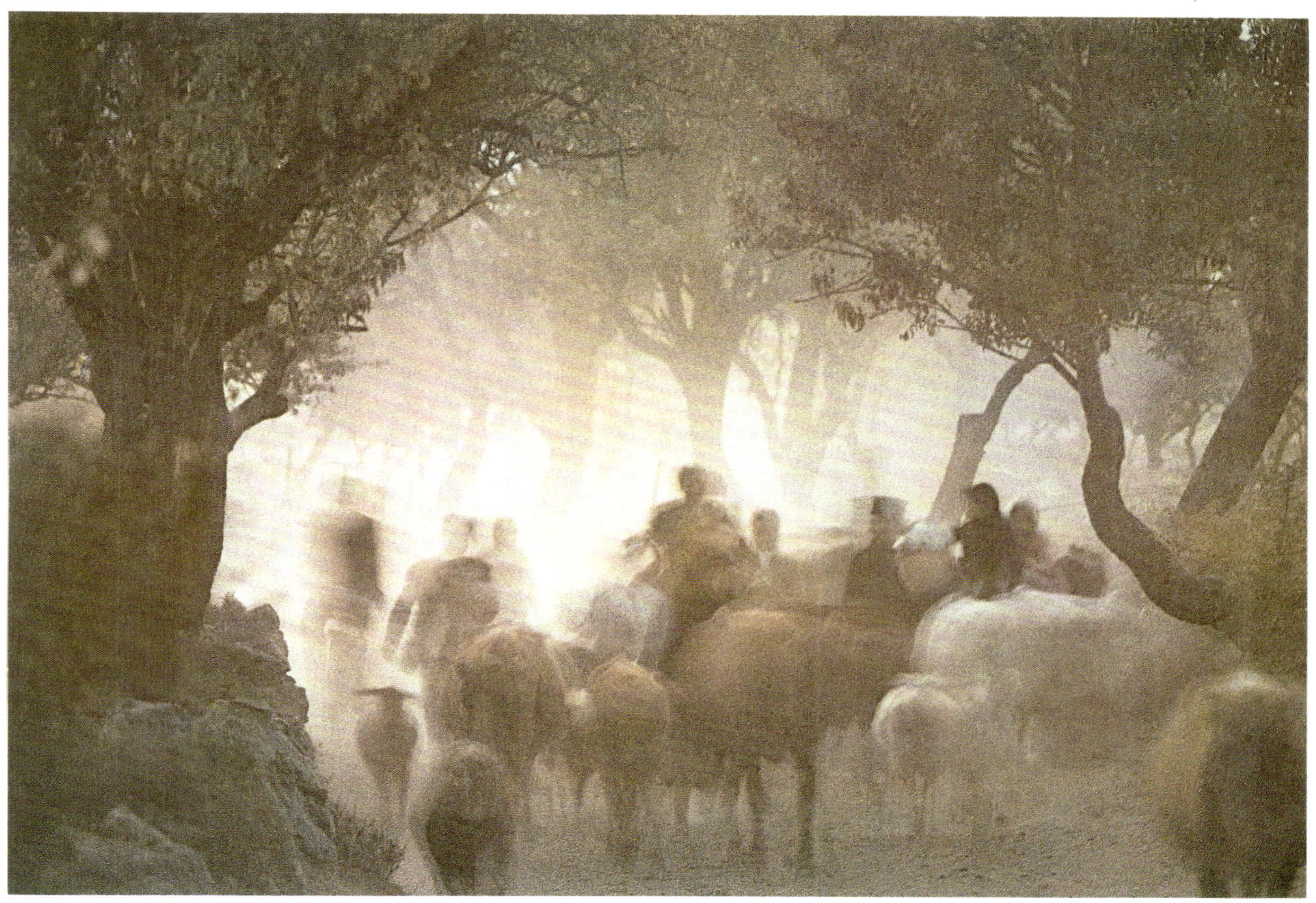

26. Irving Penn. *Cretan Landscape.* 1964. Three-color pigment print on porcelainized steel

the implied question. It would seem that Penn, a model of poise and patience in his studio, has been overcome by ambition when he has worked outside, as though one could by talent, will, and bravura compel quick compliance from the landscape. In Penn's work from the studio we see with perfect limpid clarity his subject. In his work from out-of-doors we see, perhaps too clearly, his artfulness.[26,27]

In 1950 *Portfolio* magazine asked Penn to identify some of the sources that had helped define his own sense of photography's potentials. In his answer he cited the dramatic foreshortening of space in Ucello, the

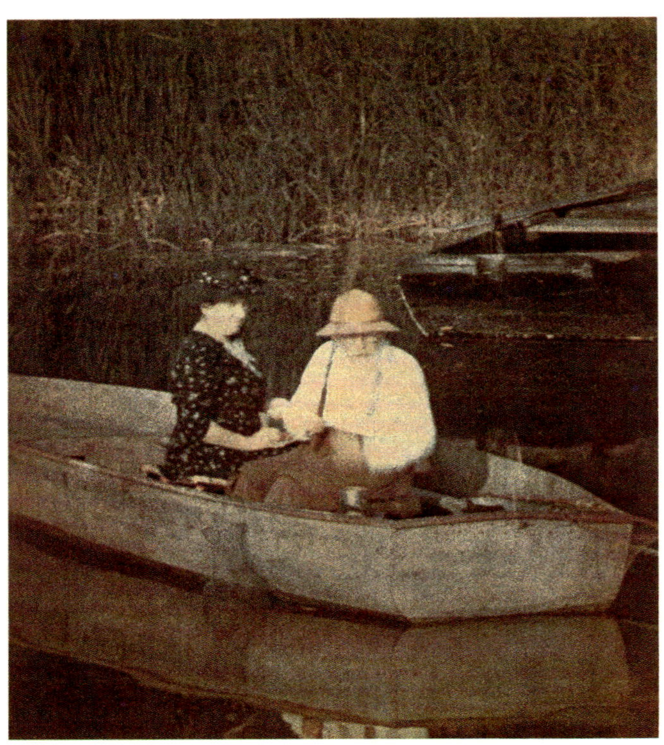

27. Irving Penn. *Old Couple on the Seine.* 1953. Seven-color pigment print on porcelainized steel

psychological force of dislocation in de Chirico, the direct simplicity of Mathew Brady's portraits, and the stylish elegance of Goya's. As a metaphor for the photographer's studio he cited the baseball diamond—a circumscribed field within which limited options allow infinite variety. Most surprisingly, he called attention to an amateur snapshot published by the *National Geographic* in 1932 that had remained in his memory. It showed the image of a solar eclipse, projected many times on the wall of a house by the pinhole lenses created by the tiny interstices between the leaves of a tree.[28] Penn did not suggest that the picture could be called a work of art by any useful definition of that term. It is, however, a minor photographic miracle, the kind of extravagantly seductive accident that occurs by chance once in every billion photographs but that can be mistaken for something close to an epiphany, a revelation of principle. It is not that; it is only a suggestion, like a fragment of conversation overheard on the street. The suggestion made by the eclipse photograph might best be pursued inside the studio, within the tradition of still life. The idea it proposes is a risky one, suggesting that nature can be made to perform like trained lions. It is perhaps too ambitious an idea to be pursued out-of-doors, where the best artistic successes have been won not by magicians but by supplicants.

In Penn's portraits from the late forties, the frayed threads of the carpet remind us that the general elegance of effect is invented, is a matter of stagecraft; but they remind us also of the omnipresence of decay, imperfection, corruption, of dustballs under the beds even of princesses. The raveled carpet or its equivalent is a recurring motif in Penn's work. The elegant still life is compromised by the stain of spilled coffee in the demitasse saucer, or by a rank ash tray. The fairy-tale kitchen of 1950, with prosciutto and provolone hanging as prescribed from the wall, has a mouse at the baseboard. The burlap sack of grain has a beetle on it.

One of Penn's most famous pictures, *Summer Sleep* (pl. 99), originated as a suggestion from Alexander Liberman, accompanied by a rough sketch.[29] The draw-

ing indicated a fan of the sort that revolved slowly over
Sidney Greenstreet in rumpled linens as he sat in the
Hong Kong bar; beneath the fan a woman, presumably
beautiful, reclines; the circles at the lower left represent
a still life; the cross-hatching stands for a mosquito net,
a variant of the familiar veil that had served so many

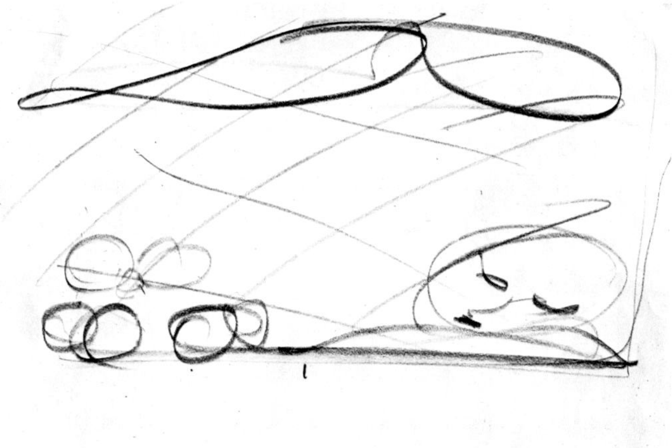

29. Alexander Liberman. Untitled. 1949. Pencil drawing. ©1949
Alexander Liberman

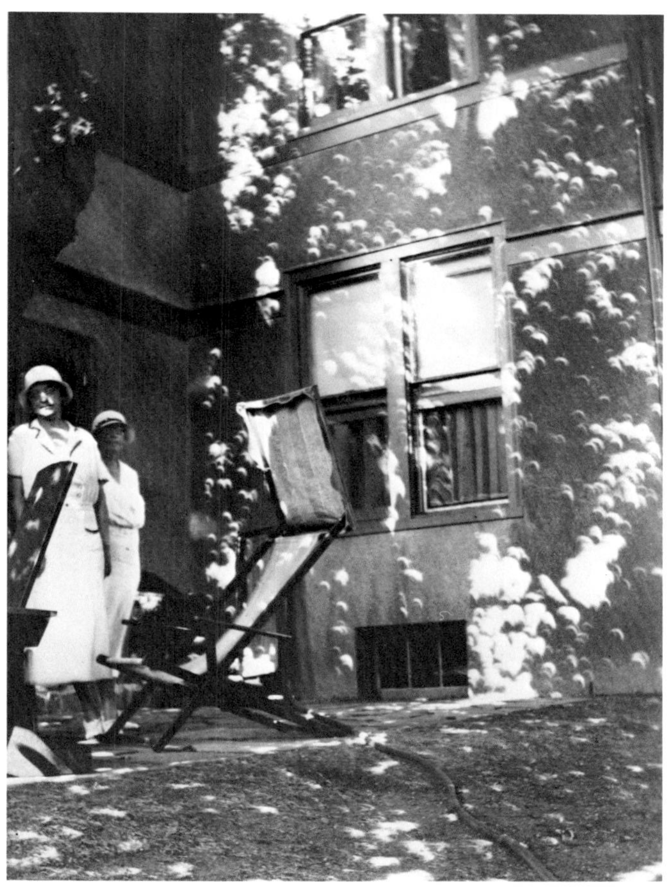

28. Photographer unknown. *Splotches of Light from a "Crescent Sun."*
1932. ©National Geographic Society, courtesy Mrs. George
Harrington

fashion photographers so well, providing in one stroke
ancient mystery, old-fashioned flattery, and modern
flatness.

In broad conceptual terms, Penn's answer is respon-
sive to Liberman's question; the sketch was not intended as a diagram. Perhaps Penn's most characteristic
addition to the subject matter of the picture was the
flies, which were acquired in mid-winter from the horse
armory and brought, deep-frozen, to Penn's studio, where
their feet were carefully glued to the mosquito net. In
the photograph the flies and the net are sharply focused,
the woman indistinct and romantically remote.

The lipstick on the dead cigarette butt, the beetles,
flies, stains, mice, raveled carpets, and moldering walls [30]
that recur with such frequency in Penn's work might be
explained as a quiet dissent from the general model of
perfect elegance that prevailed at *Vogue* during Penn's
early years there. Alternatively, one could find in Penn's

first photographs, made long before his first encounter with high fashion, evidence of a taste for the special beauties of decay and imperfection, as in *Tattooin*[31] and its sequel, *Ta tooin*,[32] made on a subsequent visit to the same motif.

A decade ago the detritus that had long figured in Penn's work as a *sotto voce* aside, an almost audible cavil whispered behind the hand, became a central subject. The change was announced in the early seventies by the

30. Irving Penn. *The Empty Plate.* 1947

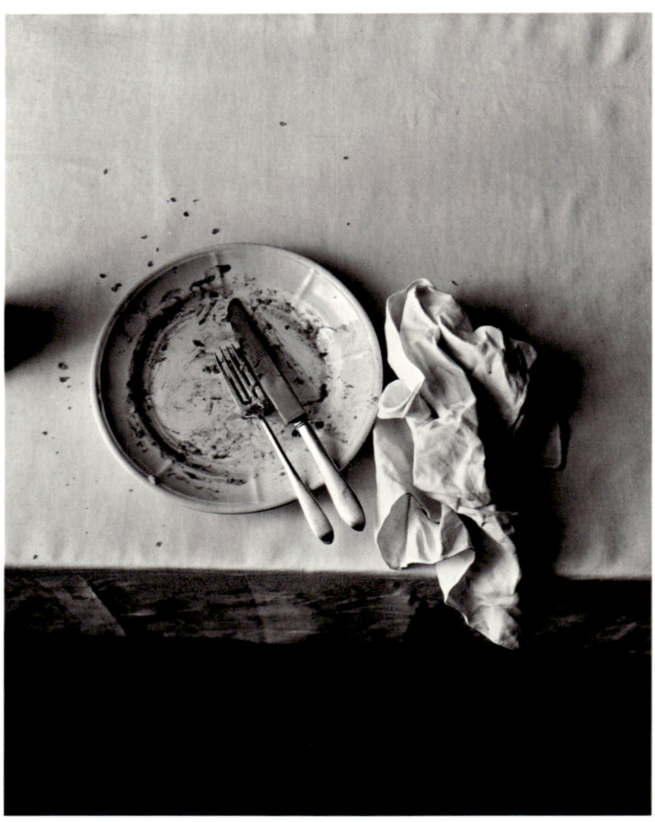

Cigarette series; Street Material followed in the middle of the decade, and Recent Still Lifes at the beginning of the eighties.

The Cigarette pictures were printed in platinum and palladium metals. By the early seventies, after long, meticulous, and expensive experiment, Penn had perfected his command of this demanding alternative to the prevalent silver print. Because of its costliness and complexity, and because of its irrelevance to work intended for magazine reproduction, the process had been widely neglected for half a century. (The late Laura Gilpin had continued to print in platinum throughout her life; George Tice, Richard Benson, and others made the process their own at approximately the same time as Penn.) The platinum-palladium process is prized for the richness and delicacy of its tonal scale, and thus for its ability to make the nicest of photographic distinctions. In this respect Penn's prints surpass in subtlety, clarity, and power even those of Frederick Evans and Clarence White, the turn-of-the-century photographers who are the most conspicuous historical masters of the technique. It is perhaps not too much to say that in Penn's prints the descriptive resources of the photographic gray scale have never been more fully exploited.

Penn's first work in platinum consisted of prints from negatives that had been made in anticipation that they would be printed in the conventional gelatin-silver process. The Cigarette series represented Penn's first major effort to make pictures that were conceived in terms of platinum. The objects described in these pictures are nominally inconsequential. We may if we wish think of them as metaphors—as shards of ancient sculpture, or architectural fragments, or the discarded

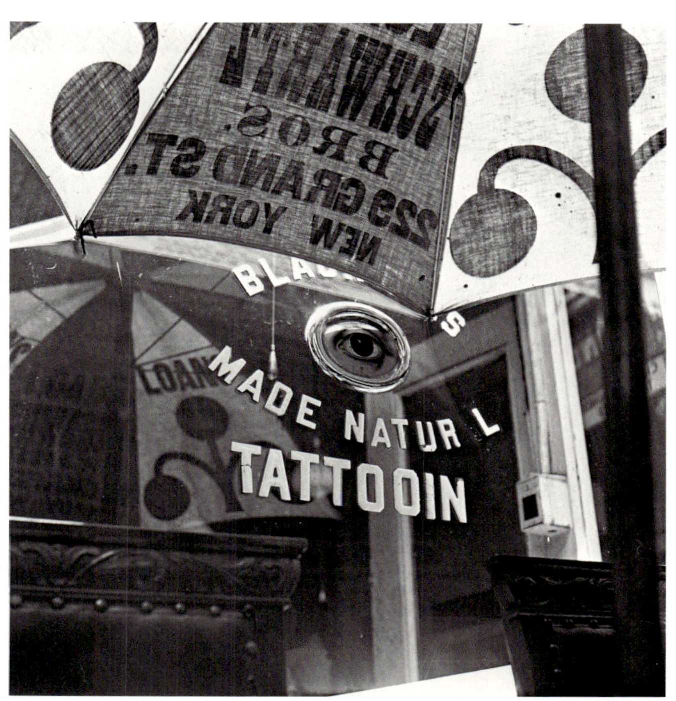

31. Irving Penn. *Tattooin.* New York, c. 1939

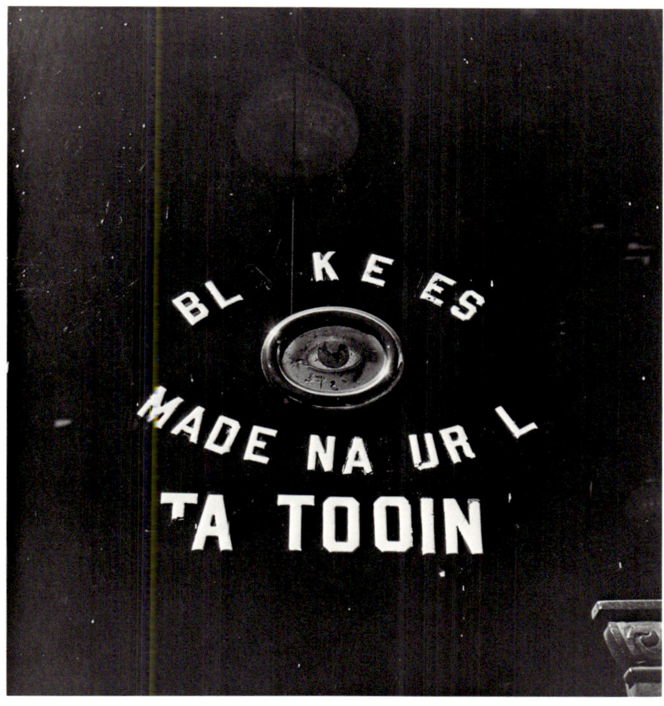

32. Irving Penn. *Ta tooin.* New York, c. 1939

costumes of kings and jugglers—but it is important that we remember also their inconsequence, for otherwise their new nobility and eloquence, their classical rectitude, would not so deeply touch our hearts.

The space of the Cigarette pictures, although very shallow, is sculpturally complete; the pictures of the subsequent Street Material series (pls. 125-128) are, in contrast, graphic in conception and uncompromisingly flat, as though Penn had selected this trash in the wake of a street roller. The change in conception allowed the photographer to make these prints with a marginally less refractory printing method, or perhaps the change in method proposed a new view of the raw material. In

comparison to the Cigarettes, these pictures are less classical in spirit, and more expressively indulgent.

The Recent Still Life series (pls. 149-156) might be seen as an effort to synthesize the beauties of the still lifes he had made years earlier for *Vogue* with the less ingratiating beauties of the pictures of discarded cigarette ends and other gutter debris. Although the negatives for the new still lifes were made within a period of a few months, the pictures themselves were begun in Penn's mind earlier, in scores of casual sketches made at odd hours during the routine waiting that sometimes fills much of a commercial photographer's day (waiting for the make-up man, the coiffeur, the stylist to complete their preliminary arrangements; waiting for the color tests; waiting for consensus).[33] Unlike the drawings of his youth, these are sketches for sketches, minimal indications that suggest the possible parts and plan of a picture. Sometimes the drawings indicate objects that have been possessed and observed for years, and sometimes things to be sought out in junk shops and hardware stores, or in the deepest recesses of the attic.

One might ask why a photographer would be tempted or driven to make these stern and uncompromising pictures rather than advance along the line that he had claimed earlier, in *Still Life with Watermelon*, or *Still Life with Food*, or *After-dinner Games*. It is perhaps because it is difficult to imagine improving on these earlier pictures. They are within their own frame of reference perfect pictures, or as close to perfect as they are likely ever to get. If the photographer who made them wishes to pursue further the idea of still life he

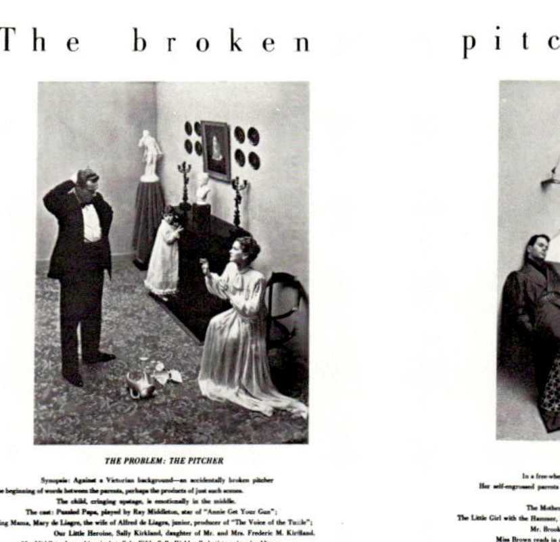
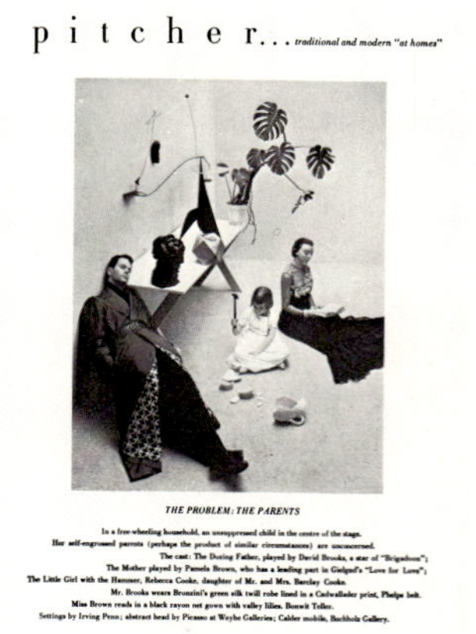

34. Irving Penn. *The Broken Pitcher.* 1947. From *Vogue* (June 15, 1947), pp. 56–57

must change the question, not the answer. In his recent arrangements of old bones and plumbing fittings and machined steel fragments and broken pottery Penn has discarded all references to the conventional pleasures of the good life and to the comforts of deception. *Still Life with Food* is perhaps finally too demanding a fiction. No sideboard ever supported so improbable a confluence of profane delights, described in so immaculate a light, proposing so perfect a harmony of spirit and flesh and good taste. *Collapse* (pl. 155) proposes a similar but simpler and more realistic ideal, one that asks from us only a competence of the spirit.

In 1947 Penn conceived and executed a two-page spread for *Vogue* that bore the title "The Broken Pitcher."[34, 35] The two pictures are professionally made and conventionally stylish, but would be of little interest to us now

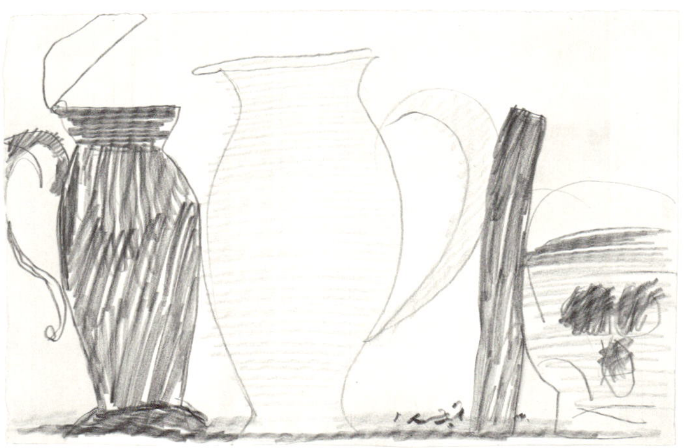

33. Irving Penn. Untitled. 1978. Pencil drawing

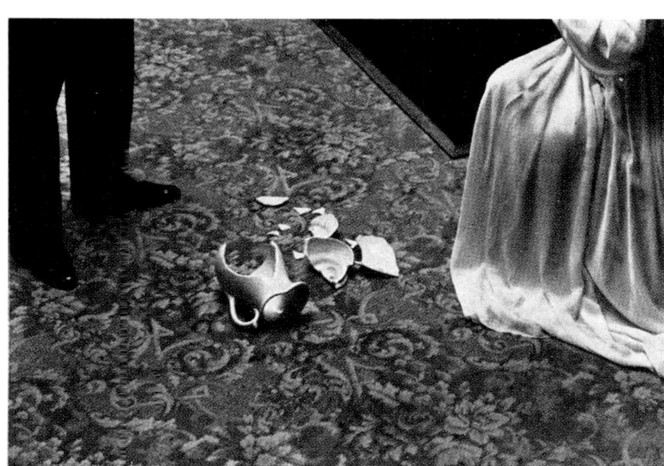

35. Irving Penn. *The Broken Pitcher* (detail)

except for the broken pitcher on the floor, which sticks in our minds like a line of half-remembered verse. There is no reason to believe that this pitcher relates to those in the recent still lifes (e.g., pl. 149), other than our knowledge of the tenacity with which artists retain the trace memories of their earlier pictures.

Irving Penn has made his best-known and many of his best pictures in a professional world that has for the most part secretly held a determinist view of its own work. It has believed that the content of that work is the product of market forces, cultural gestalt, communication technology, and second-class postage rates, and that the artists, writers, and editors who are listed as the magazines' creators are in fact only their stylists. This secret perception is probably no more true for the makers of magazines than it is for politicians or architects or bankers, and it is least true for those of largest talent, stamina, discipline, and will, among whom Penn is conspicuous. His self-discipline and self-containment are legendary; at sixty-seven his powers seem undiminished and his privacy intact, and we can expect that his work will continue to surprise and challenge us. Until now it has demonstrated for photography in our time what must be relearned by most arts in most times: that the apparently inconsequential can be redeemed by artistic seriousness; that a plain vocabulary is the most demanding; that high craft is the just desert not only of monuments and ceremonial vessels, but of the ordinary baggage of our lives.

Penn's private, stubborn, artistic intuitions have revised our sense of the world's content. His essential work is Spartan in its rigor, in its devotion to the sober elegance of clarity, in the high demands that it makes of us regarding poise, grace, costume, style, and the definition of our selves. We have failed to meet those demands— naturally—but we will not forget them.

Plates

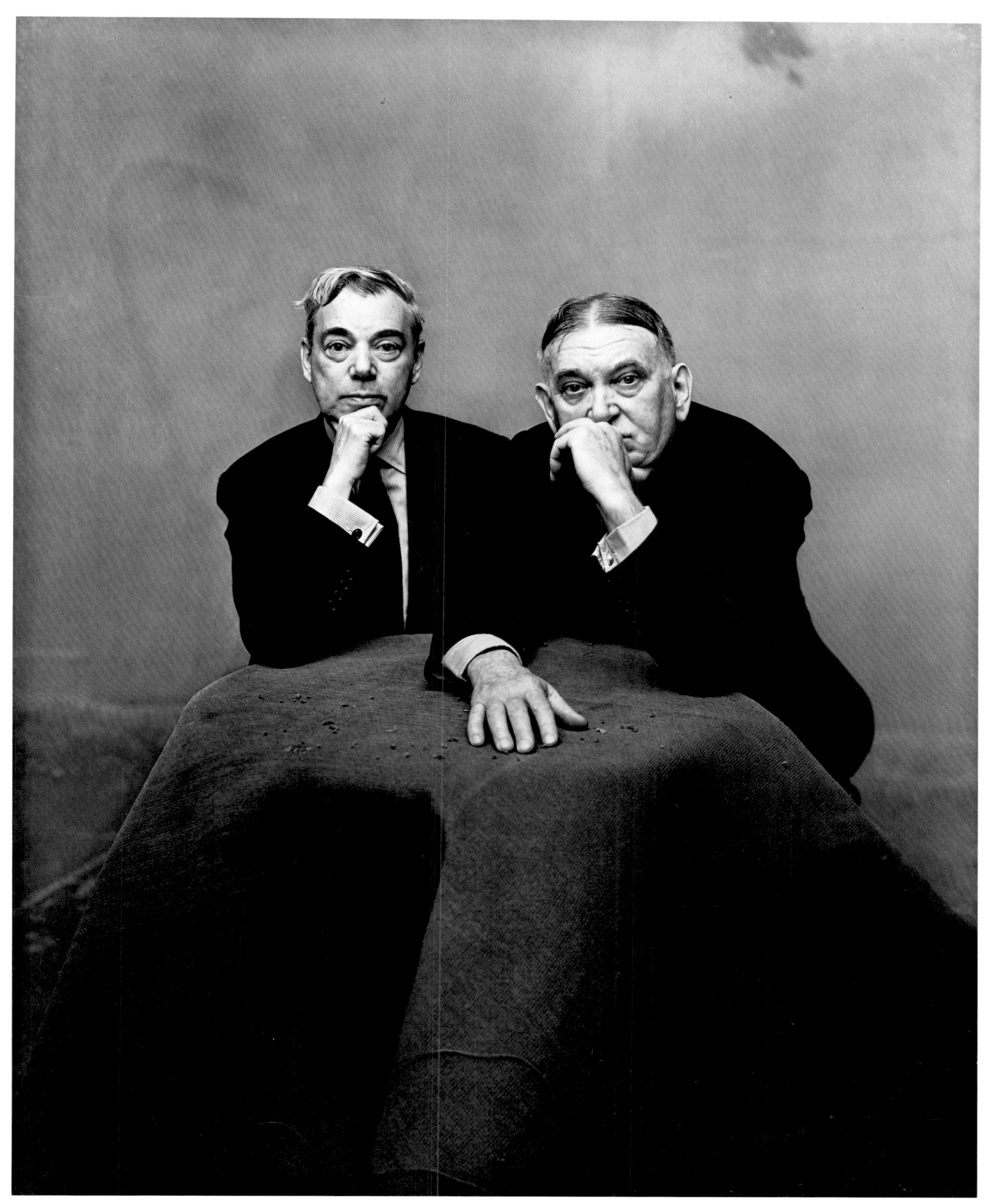

7. George Jean Nathan and H. L. Mencken. New York, 1947

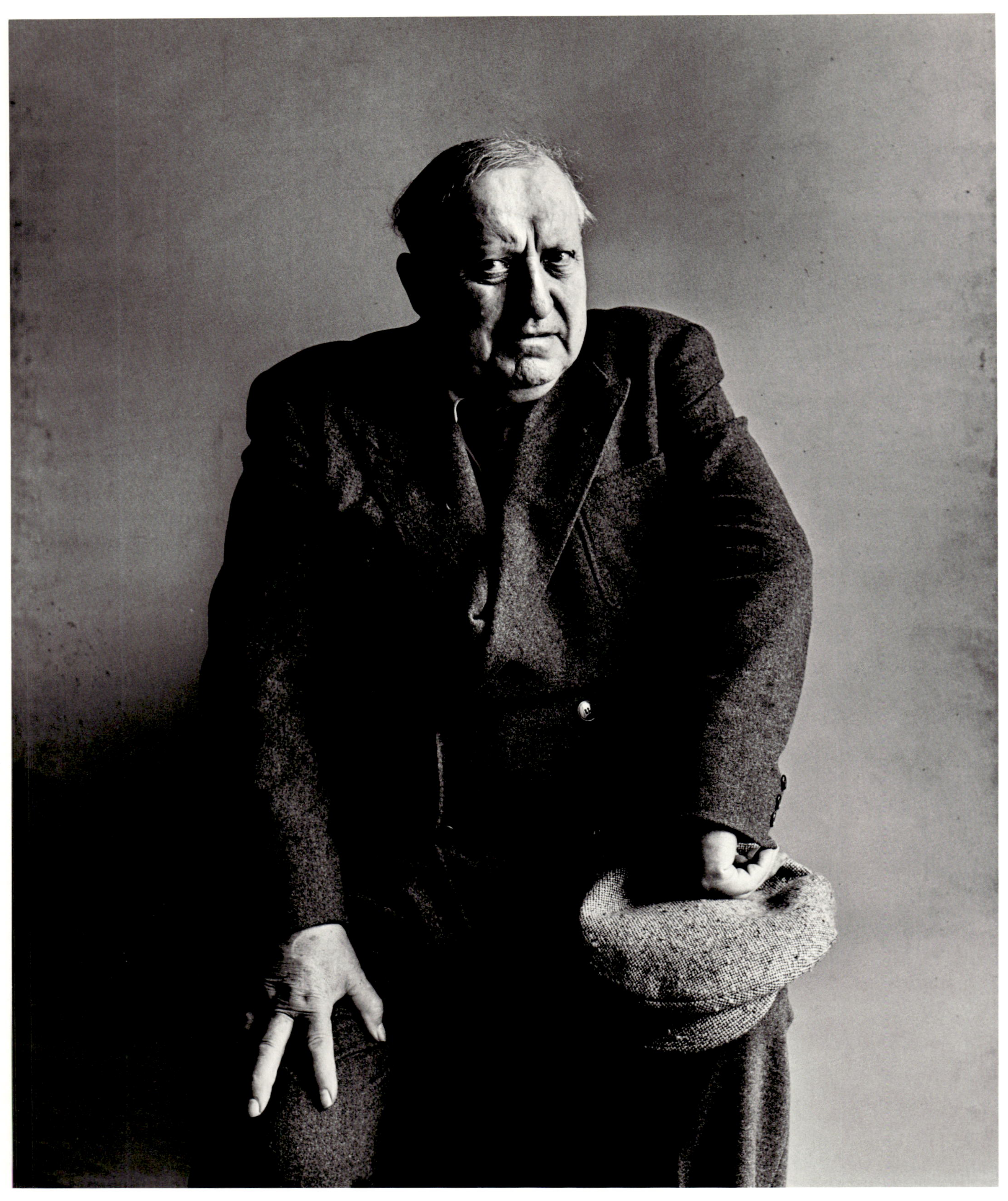

8. André Derain. St. Germain, France, 1948

9. Truman Capote. New York, 1948

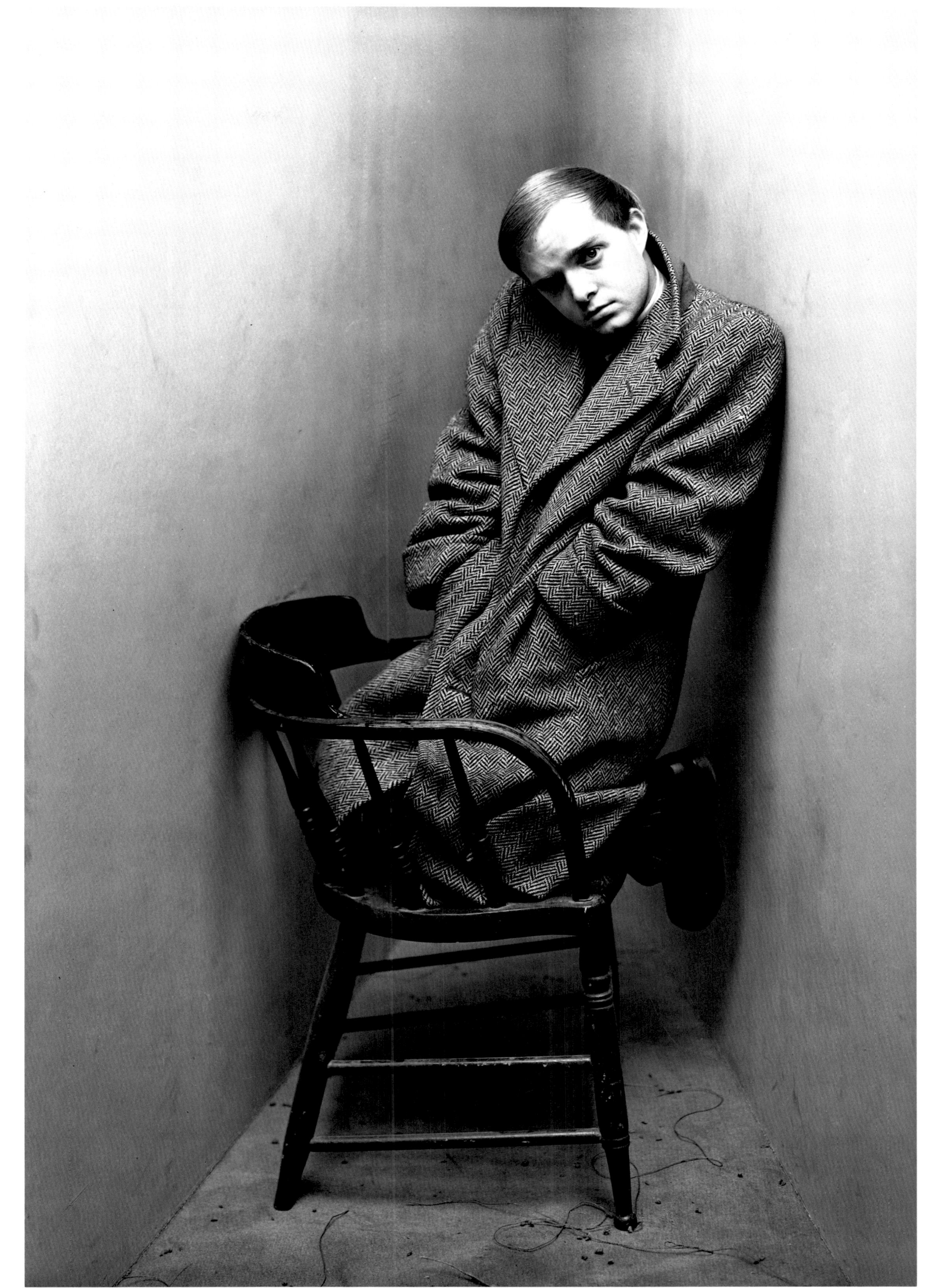

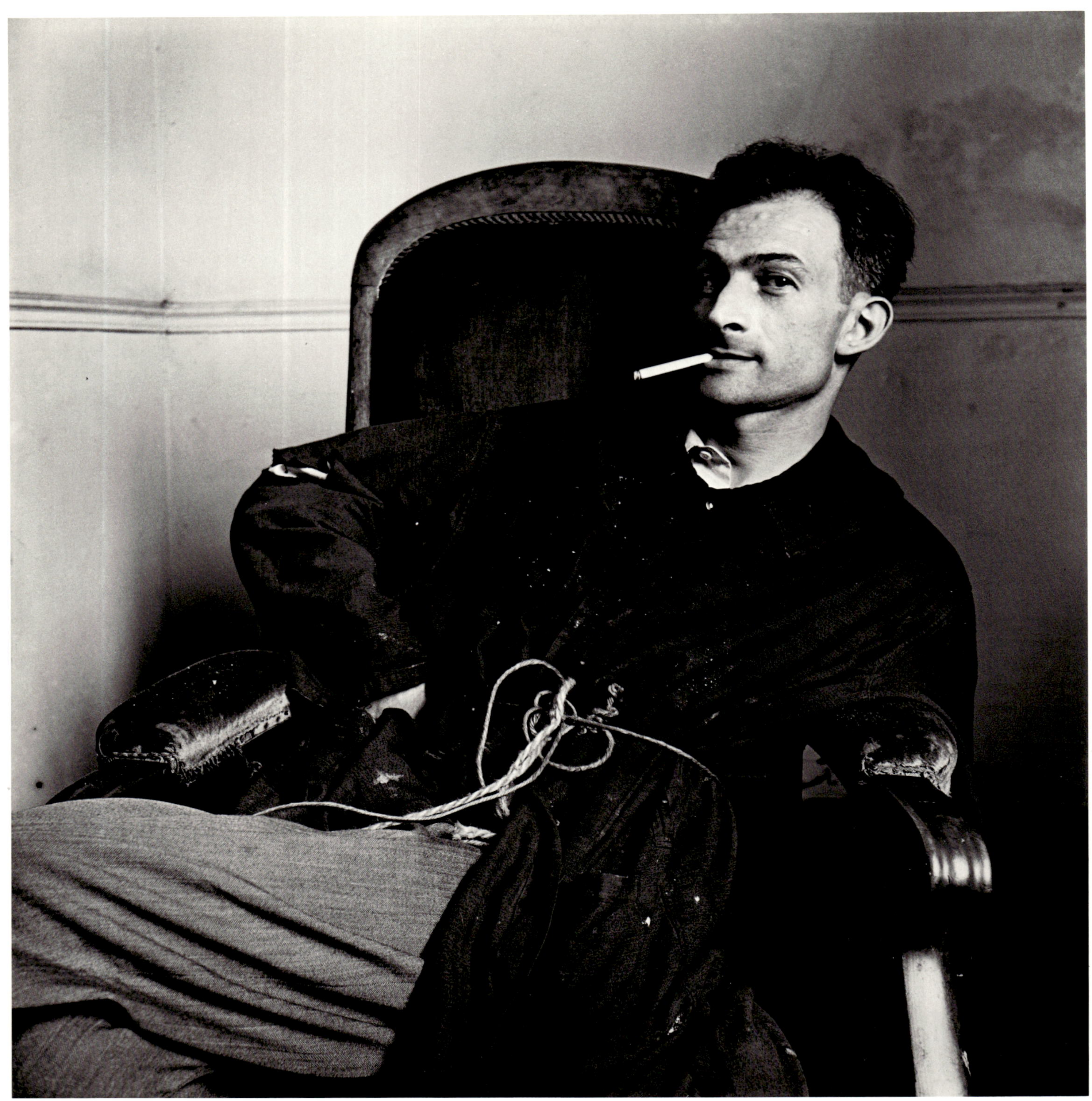

10. **Balthus** (Baltusz Klossowski de Rola). Paris, 1948

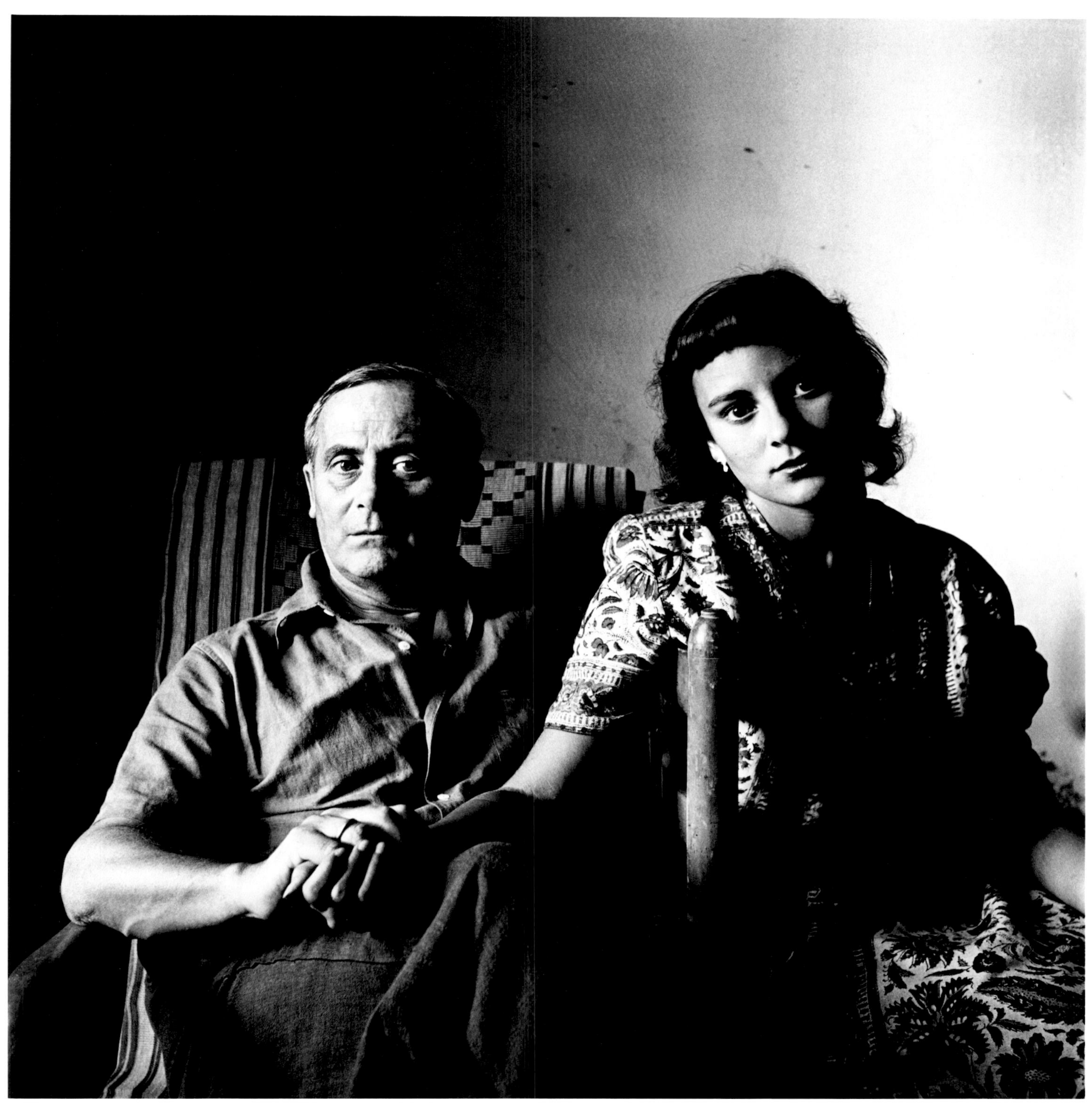

11. Joan Miró and Daughter Dolores. Tarragona, Spain, 1948

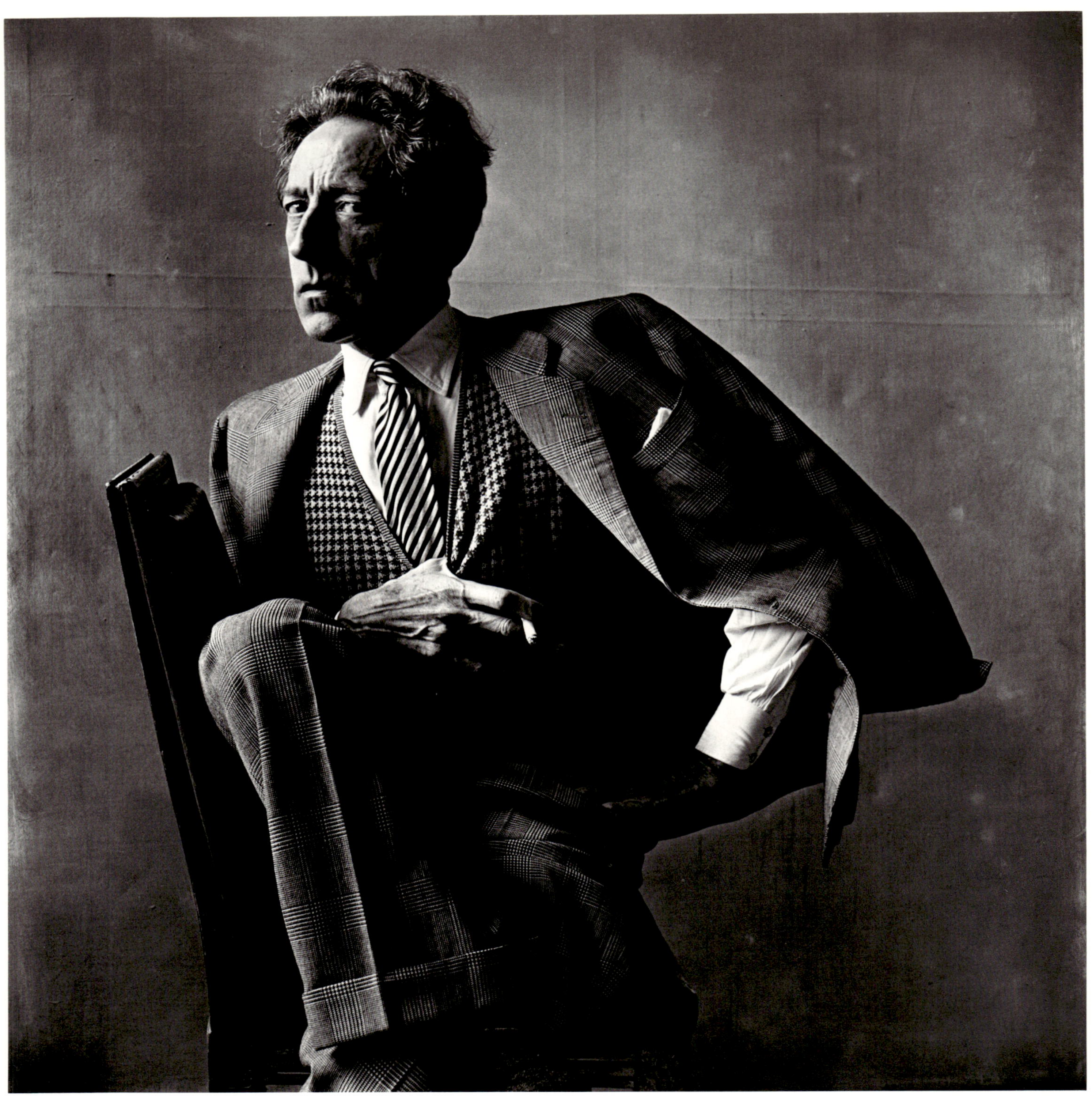

12. Jean Cocteau. Paris, 1948

13. Marcel Duchamp. New York, 1948

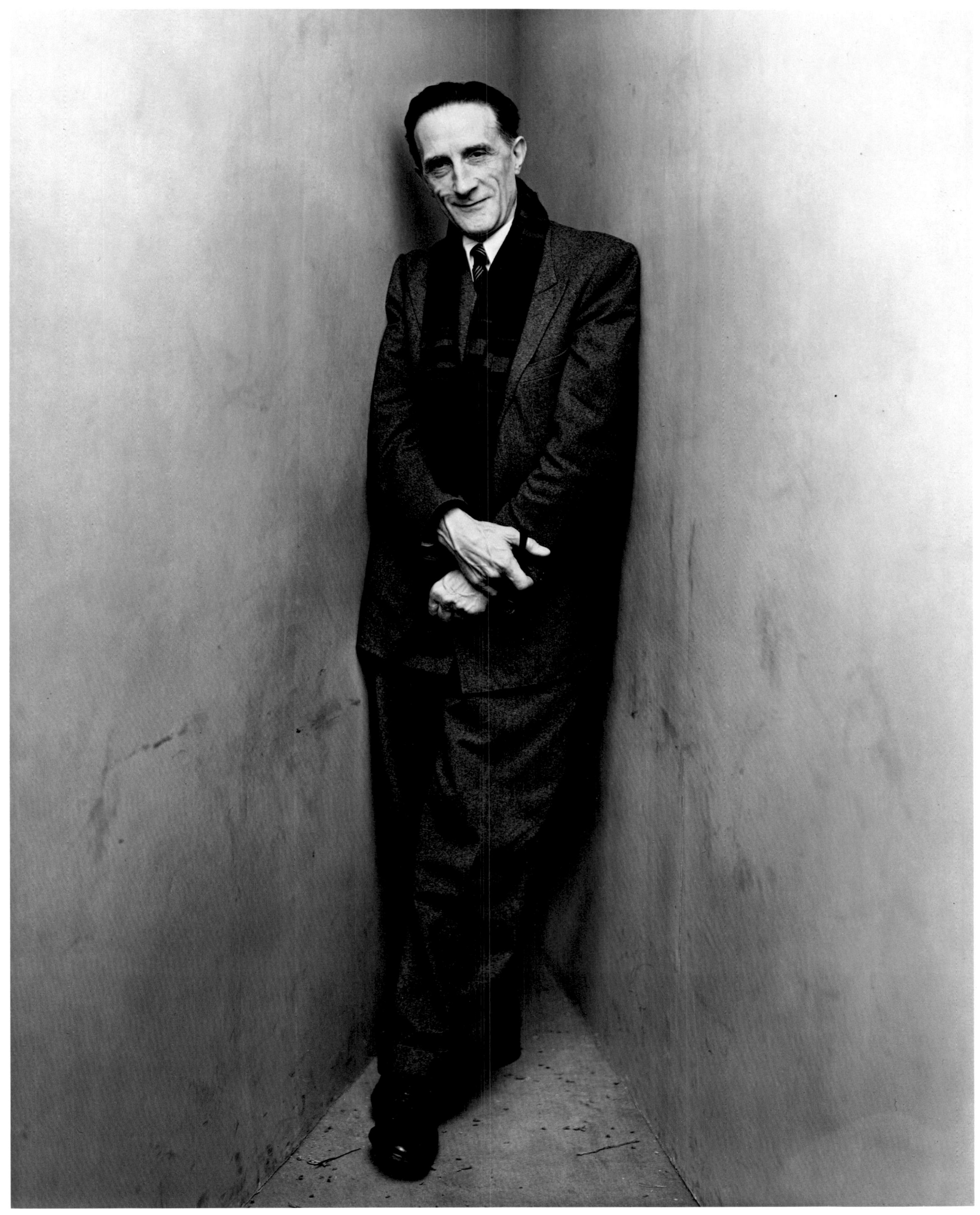

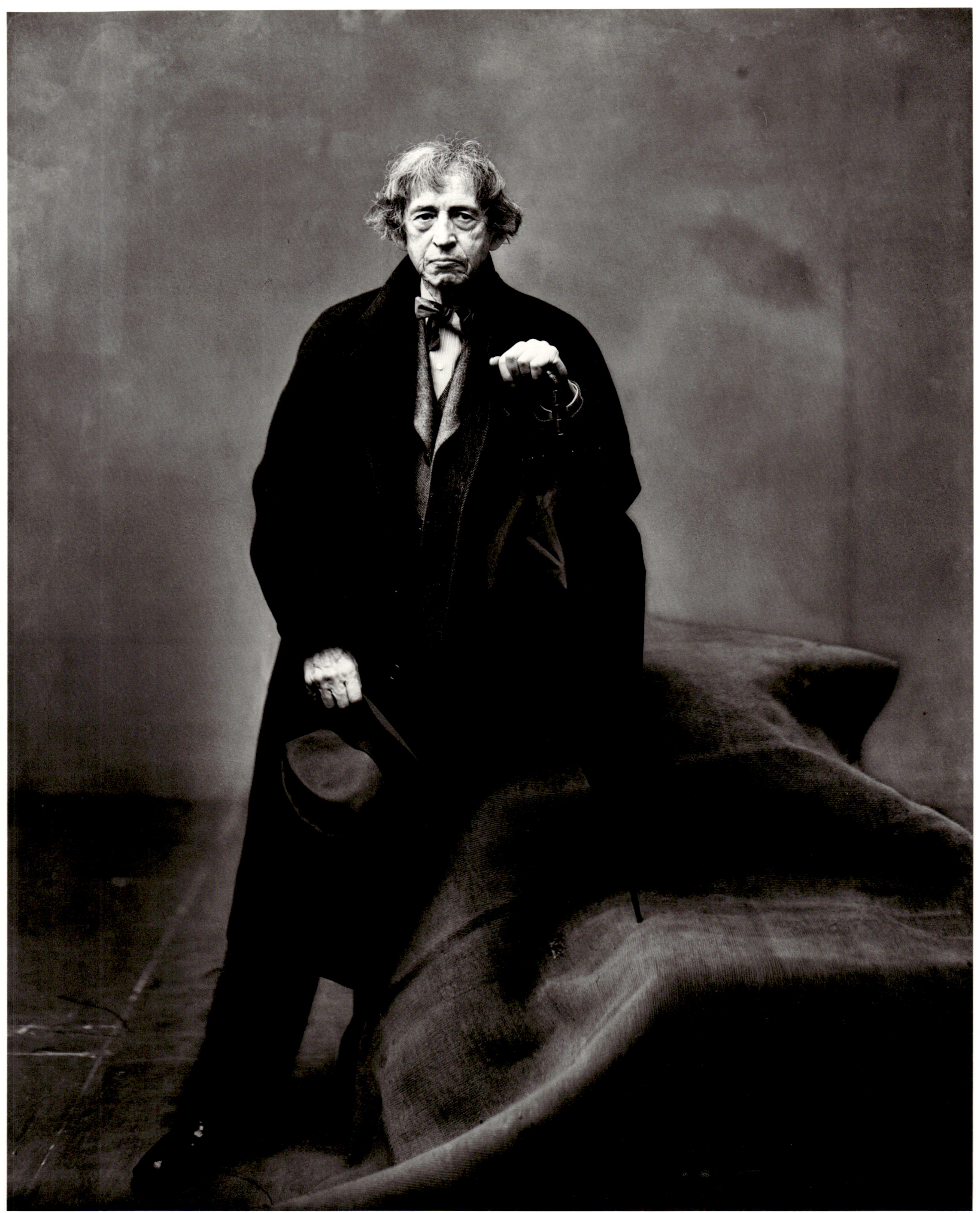

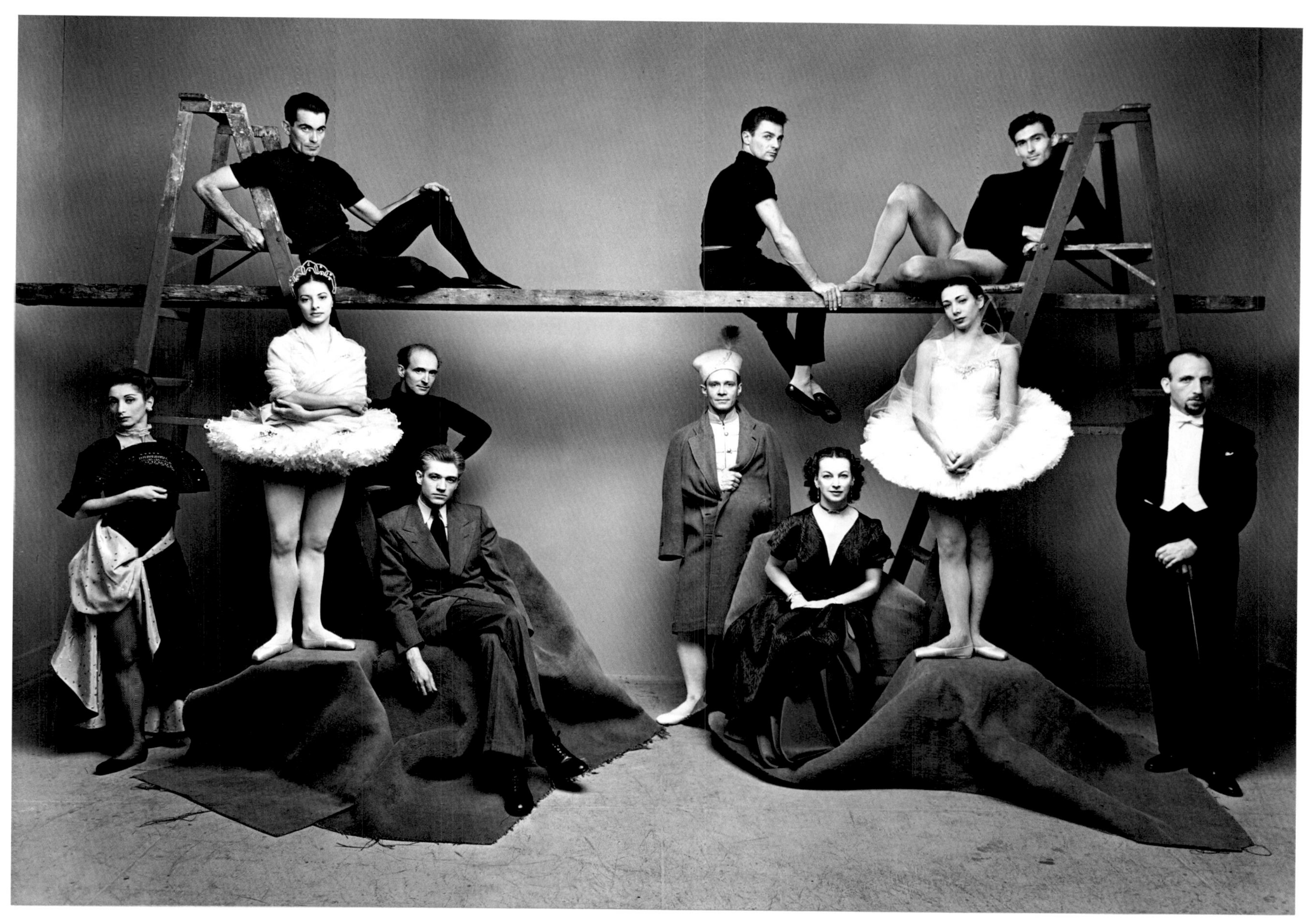

14. John Marin. New York, 1947

15. Ballet Theater. New York, 1947

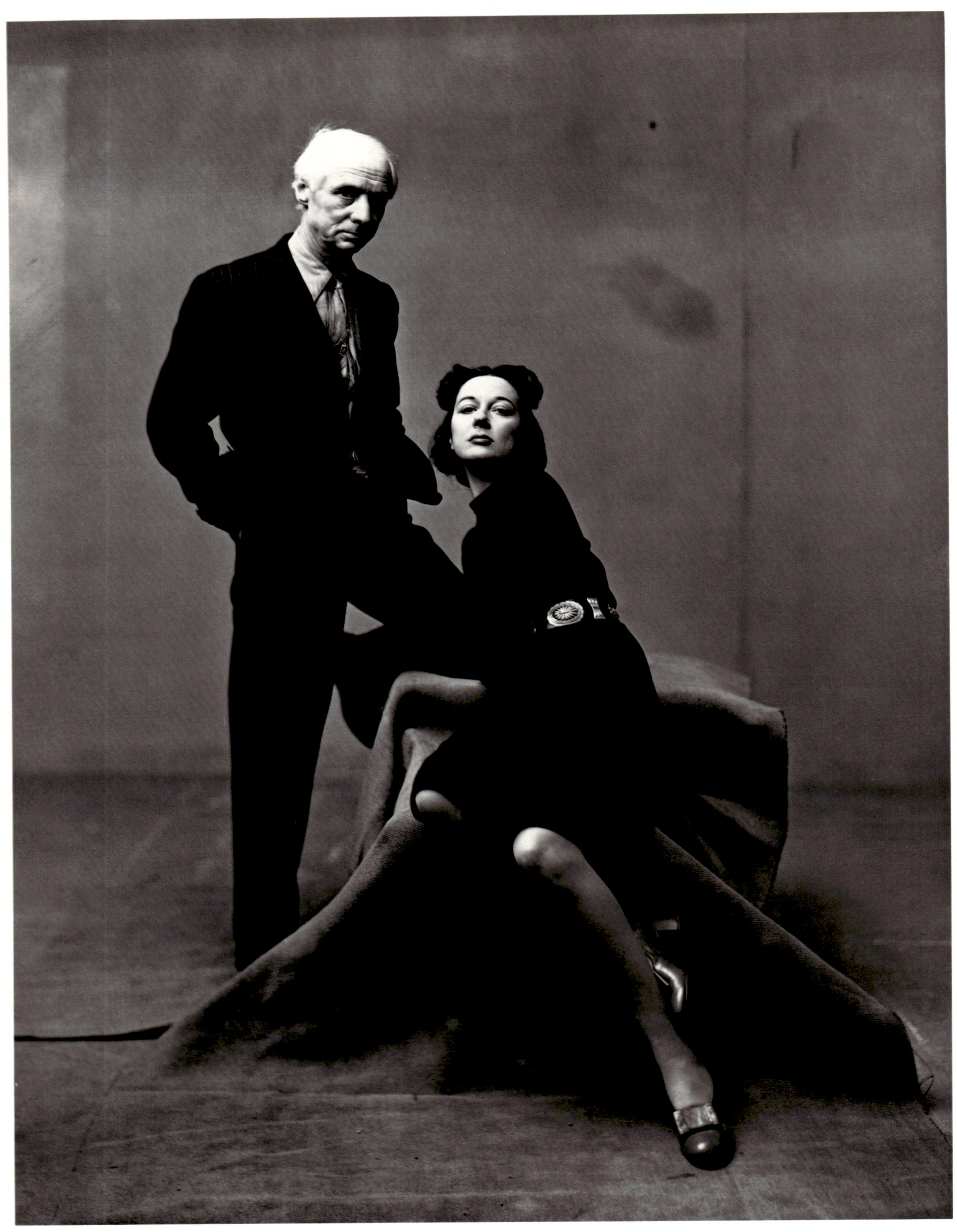

16. **Max Ernst and Dorothea Tanning.** New York, 1947

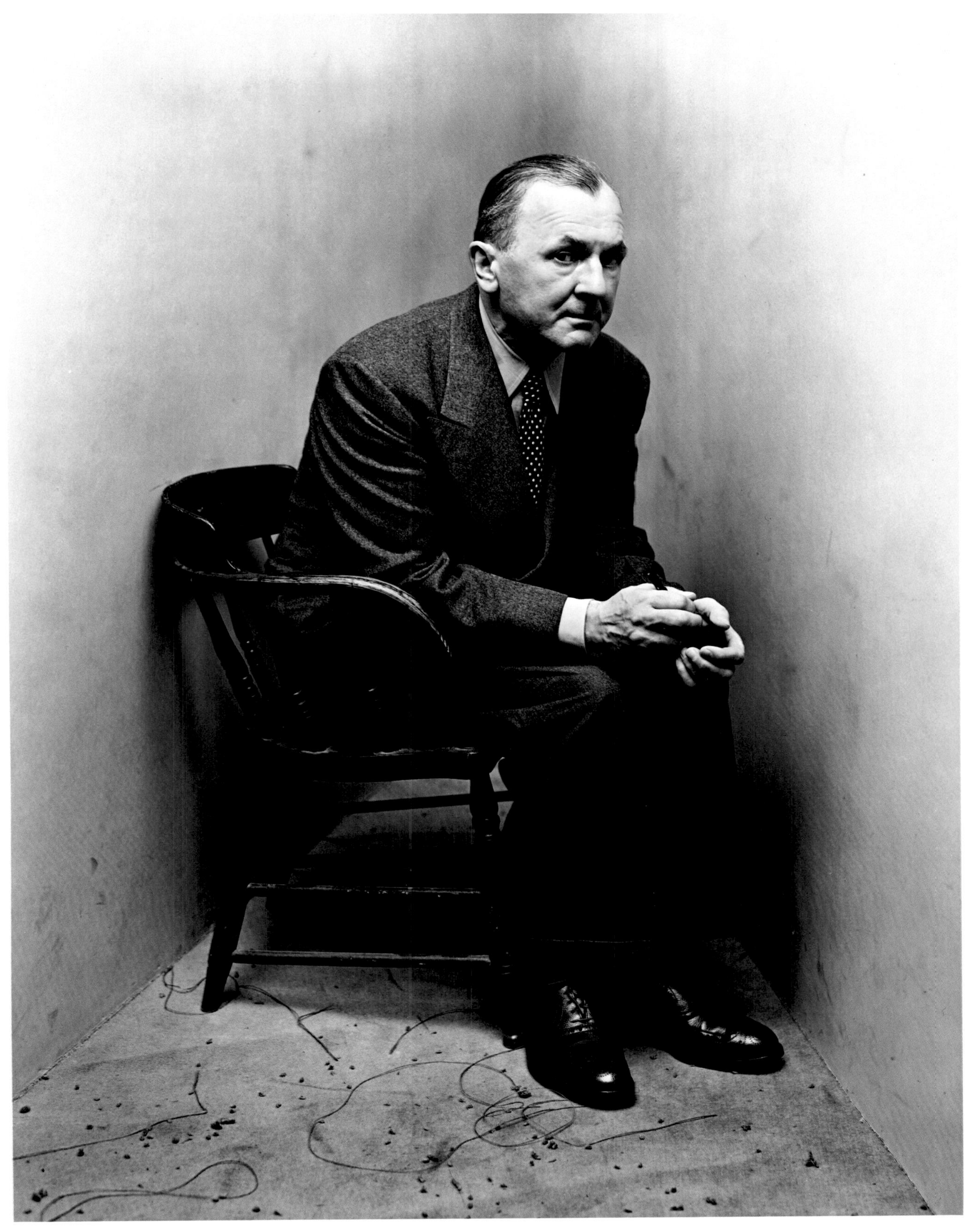

17. George Grosz. New York, 1948

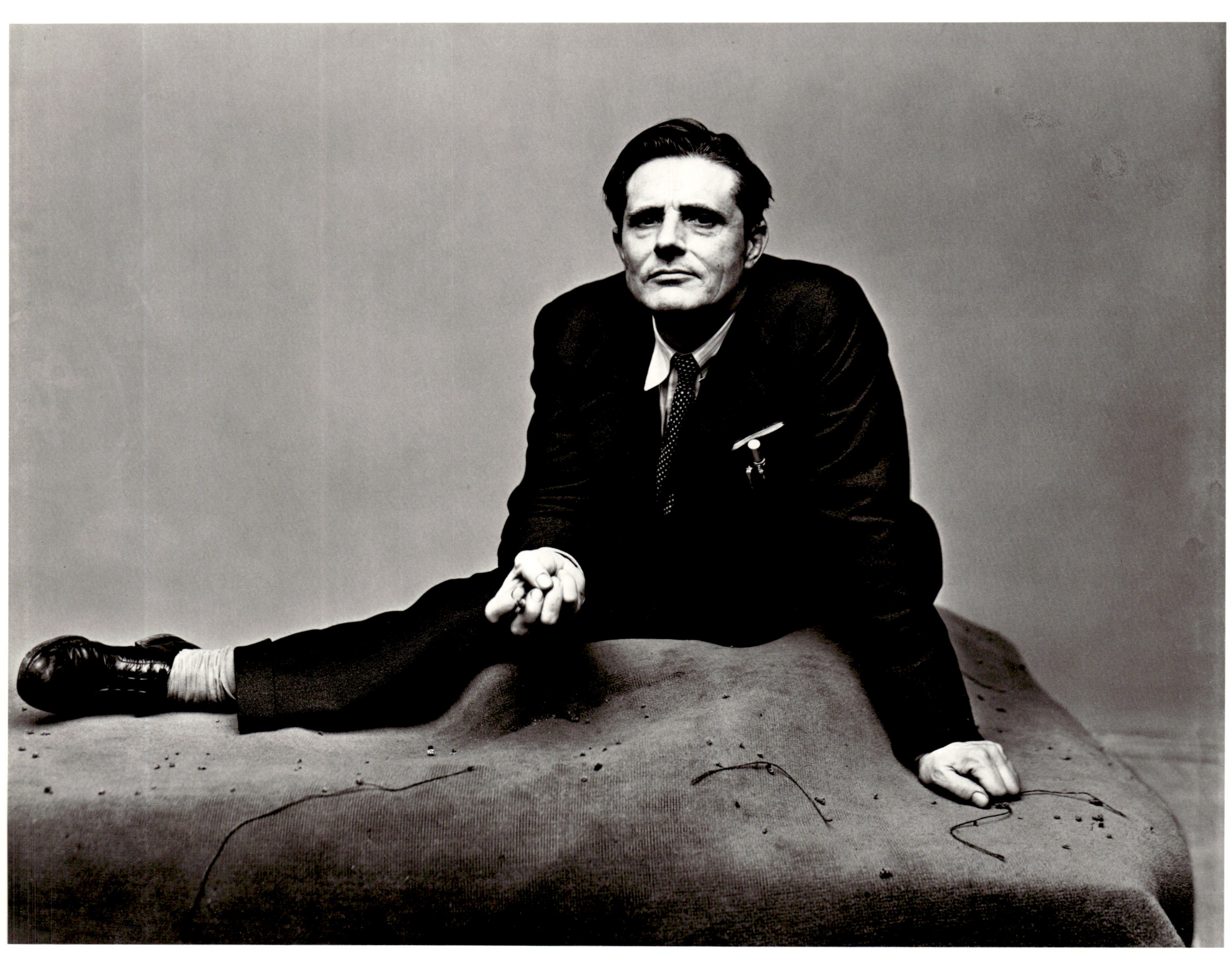

18. Stanley W. Hayter. New York, 1947

19. Ballet Society (left to right: Corrado Cagli, Vittorio Rieti, Tanaquil LeClerq,
    and George Balanchine). New York, 1948. Platinum-palladium print, 1980

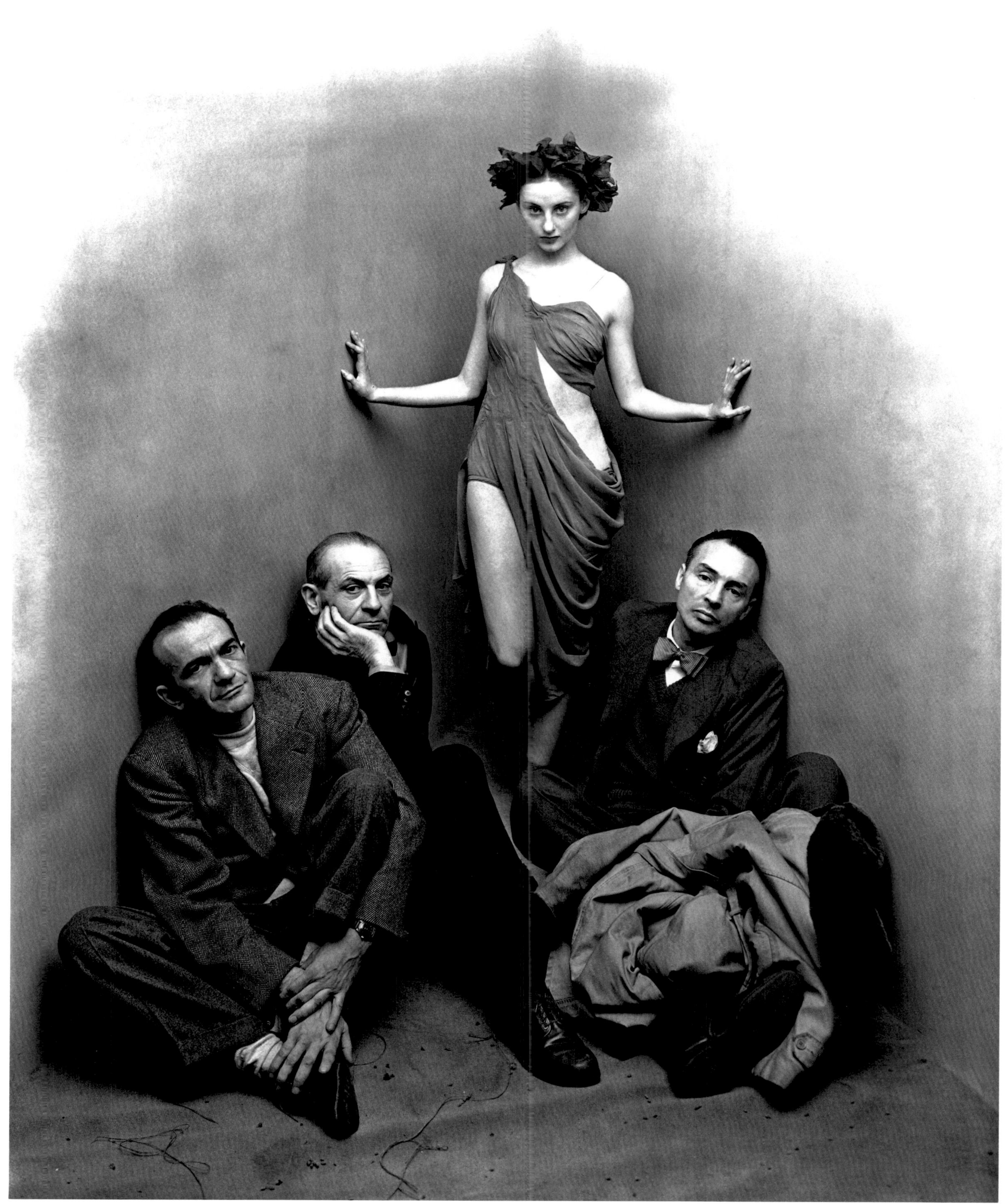

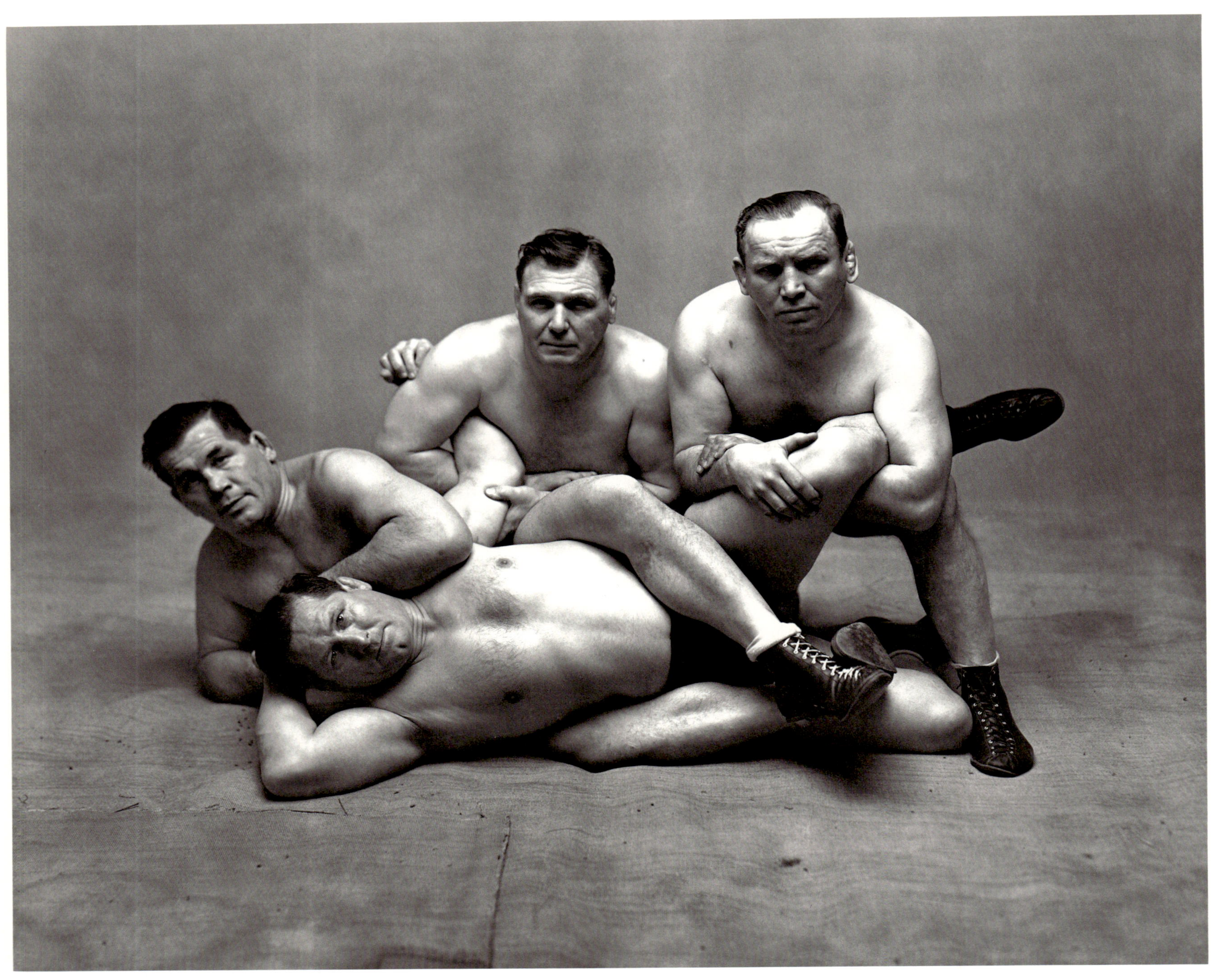

20. Four Dusek Brothers. New York, 1948

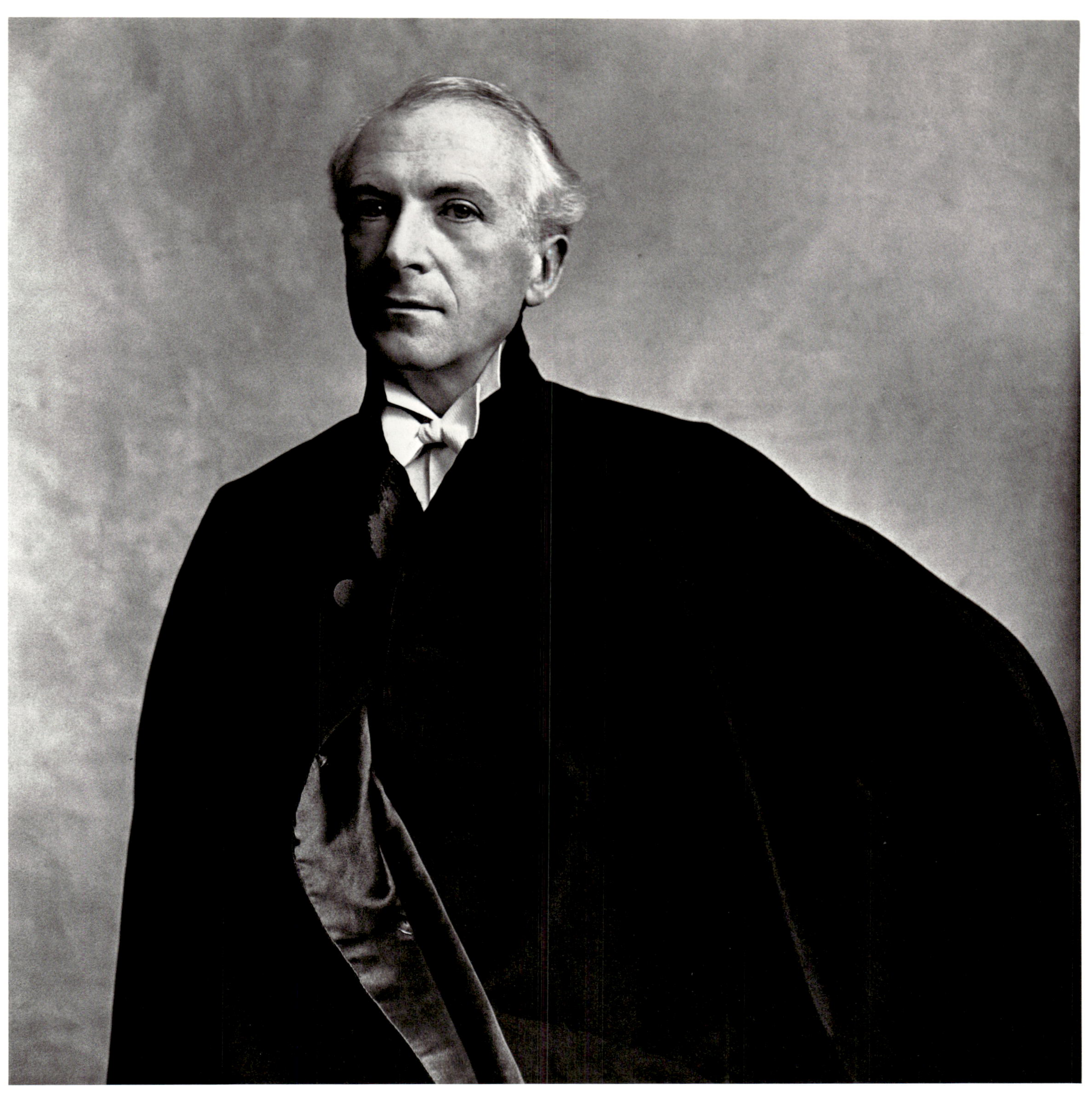

21. Cecil Beaton. London, 1950. Platinum-palladium print, 1977

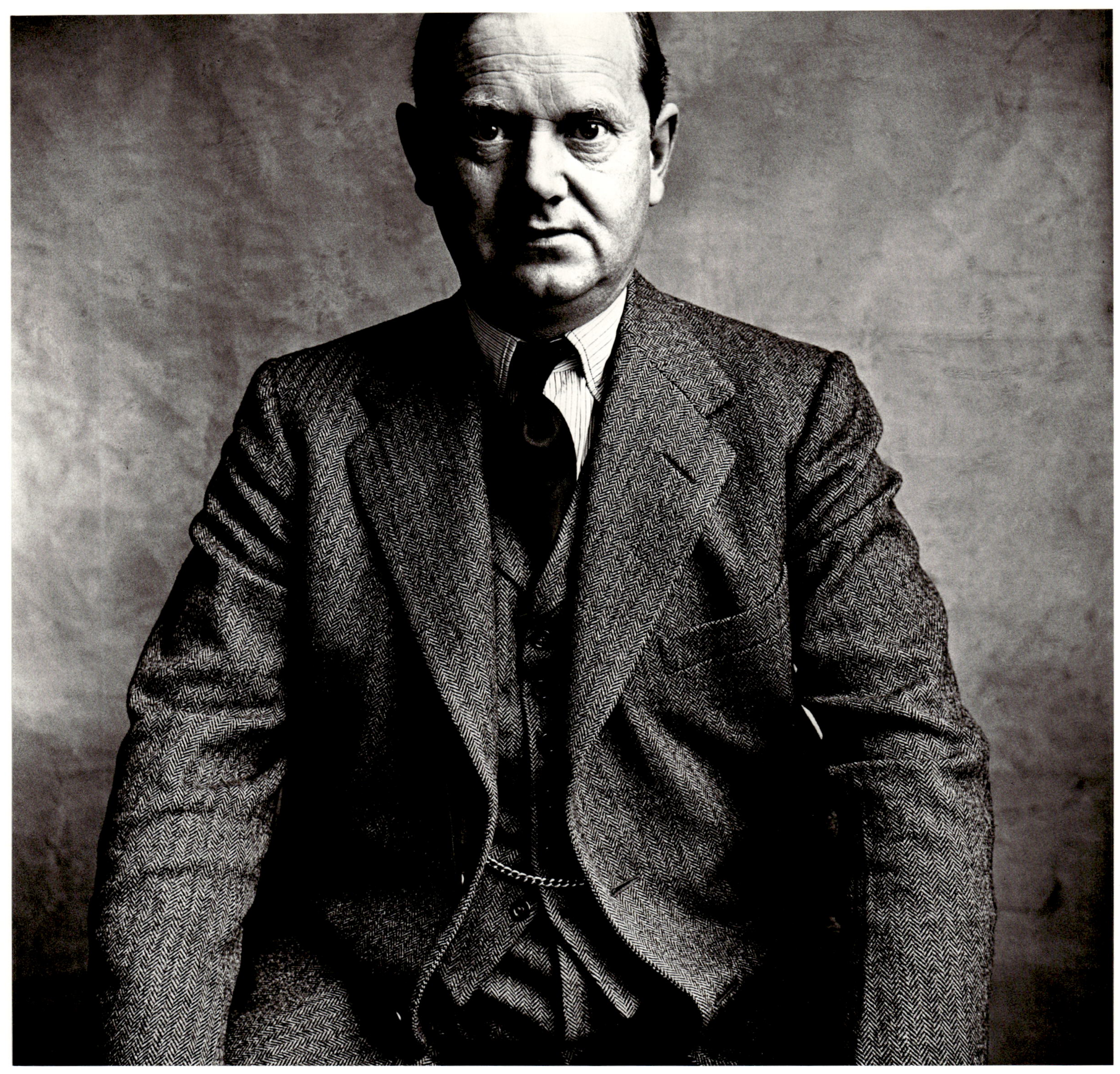

22. **Evelyn Waugh.** London, 1950

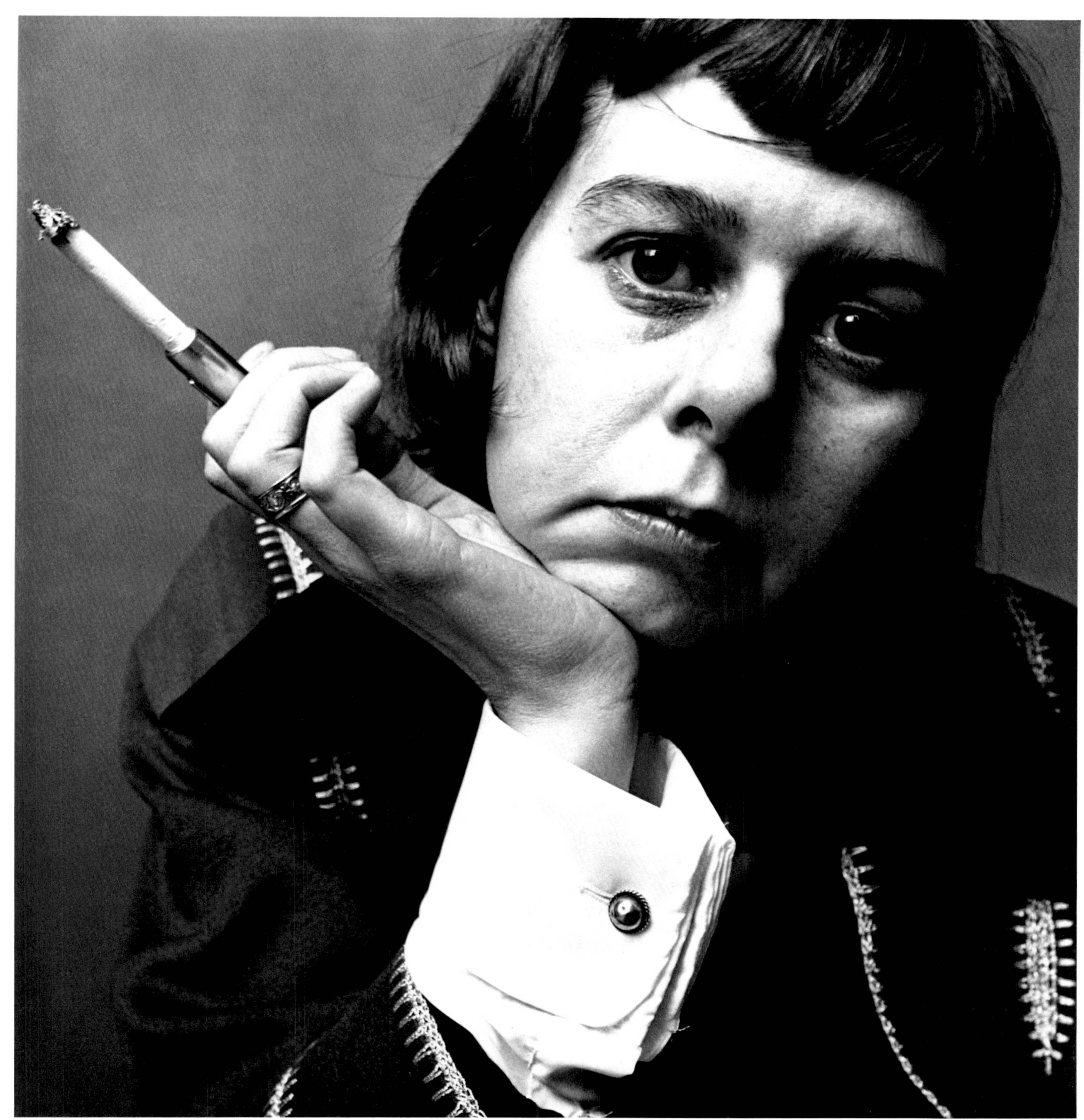

23. Carson McCullers. New York, 1950

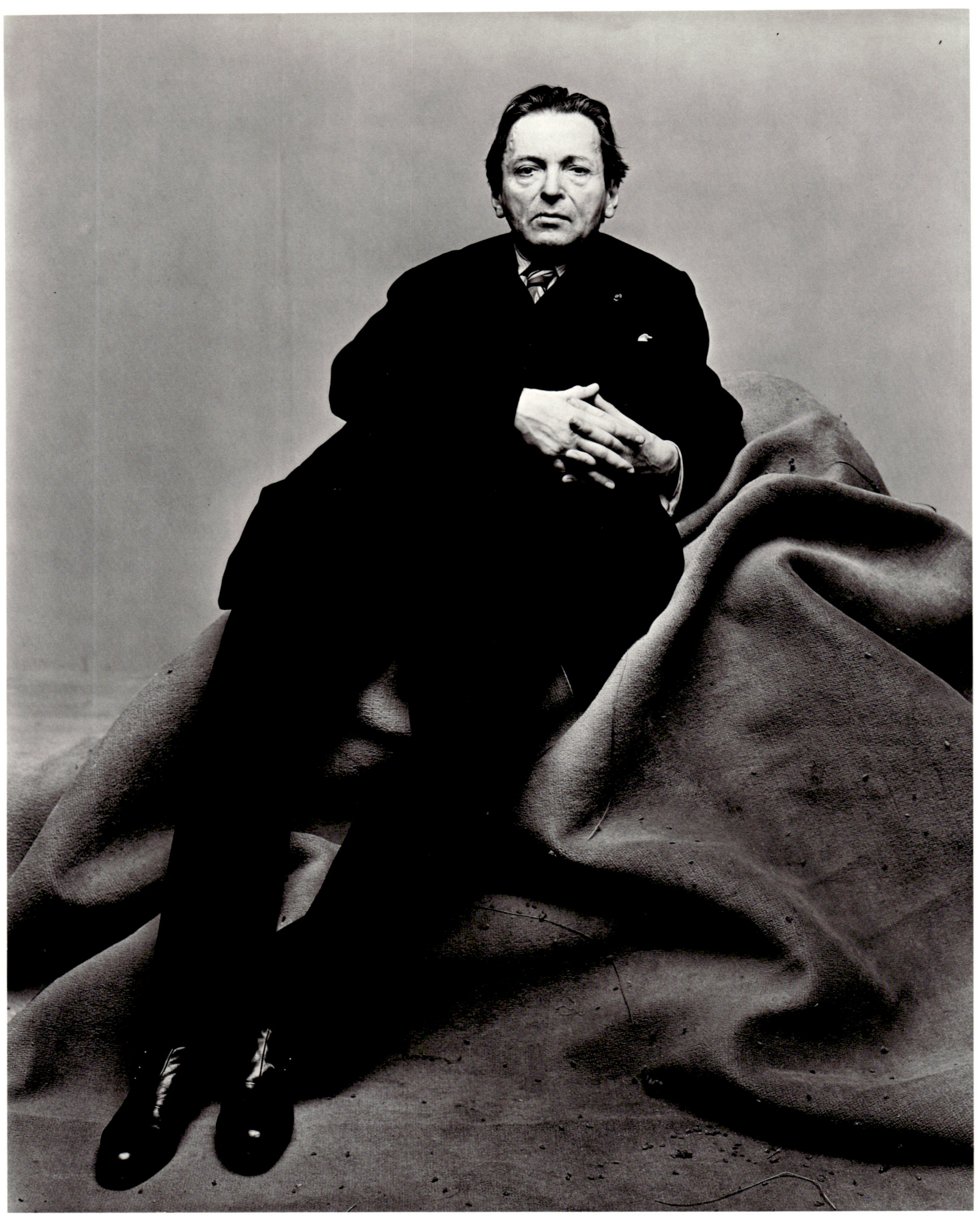

24. Georges Enesco. New York, 1948

25. C. Day Lewis. London, 1950

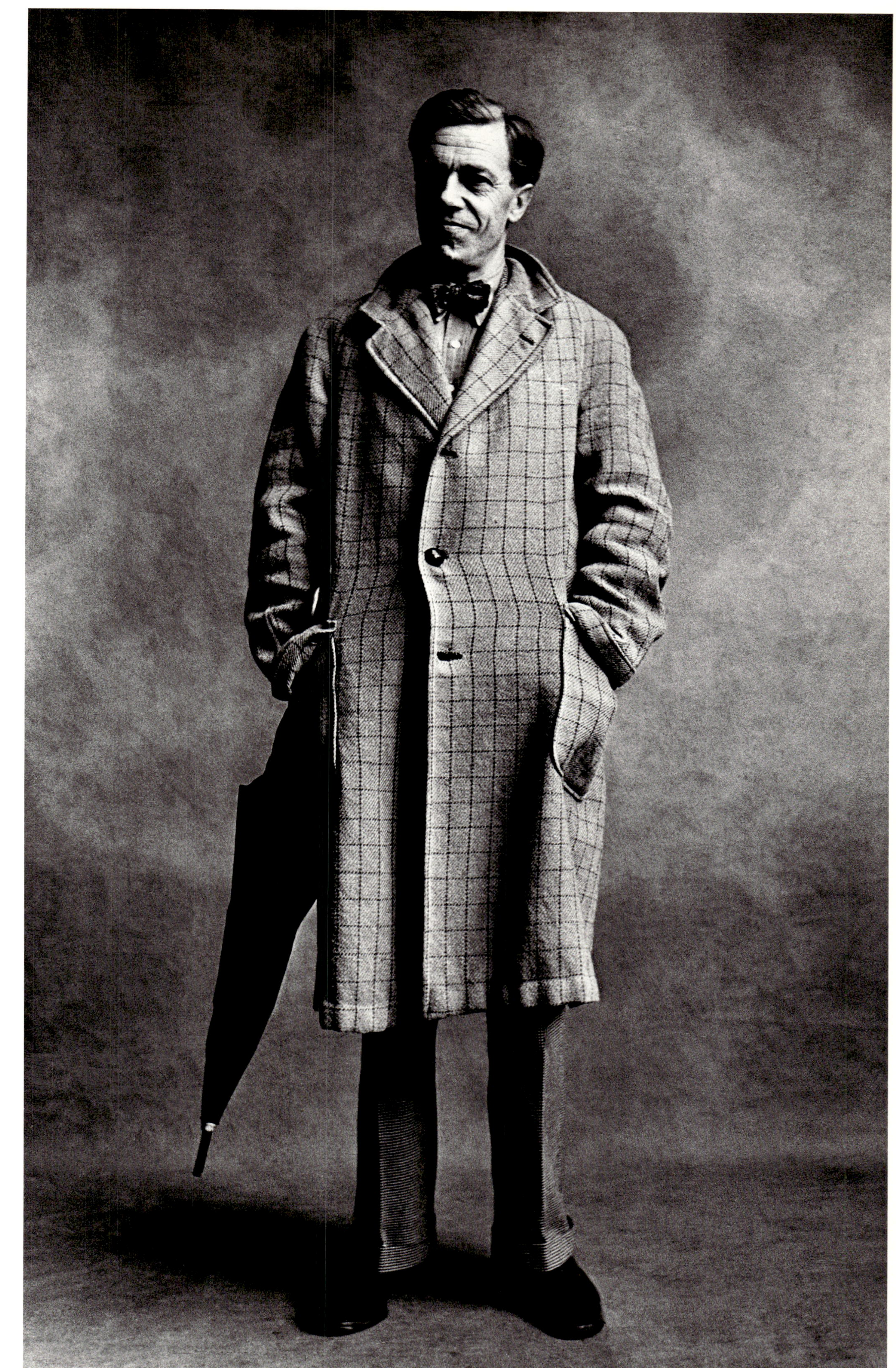

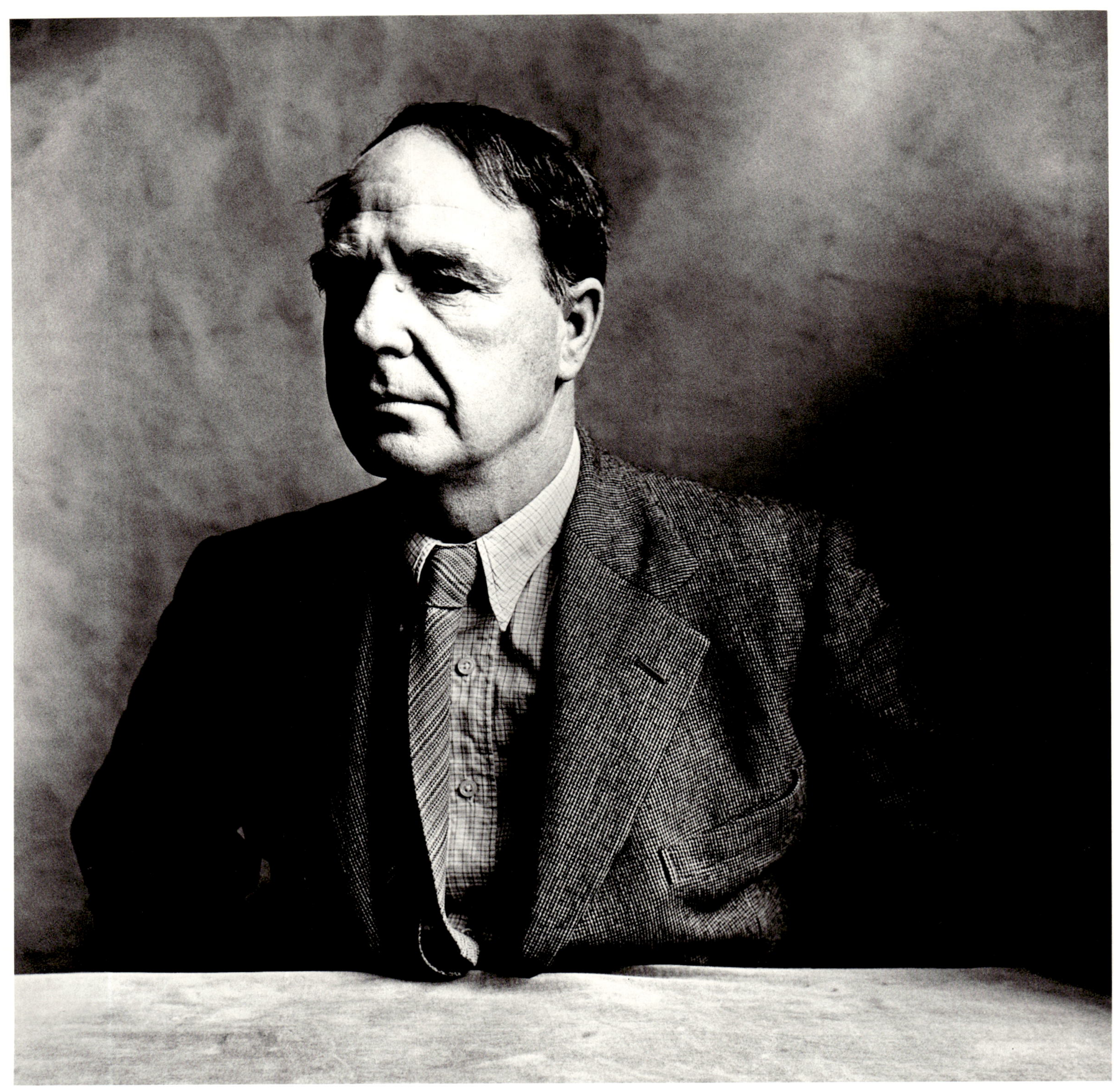

26. **Henry Moore**. London, 1950

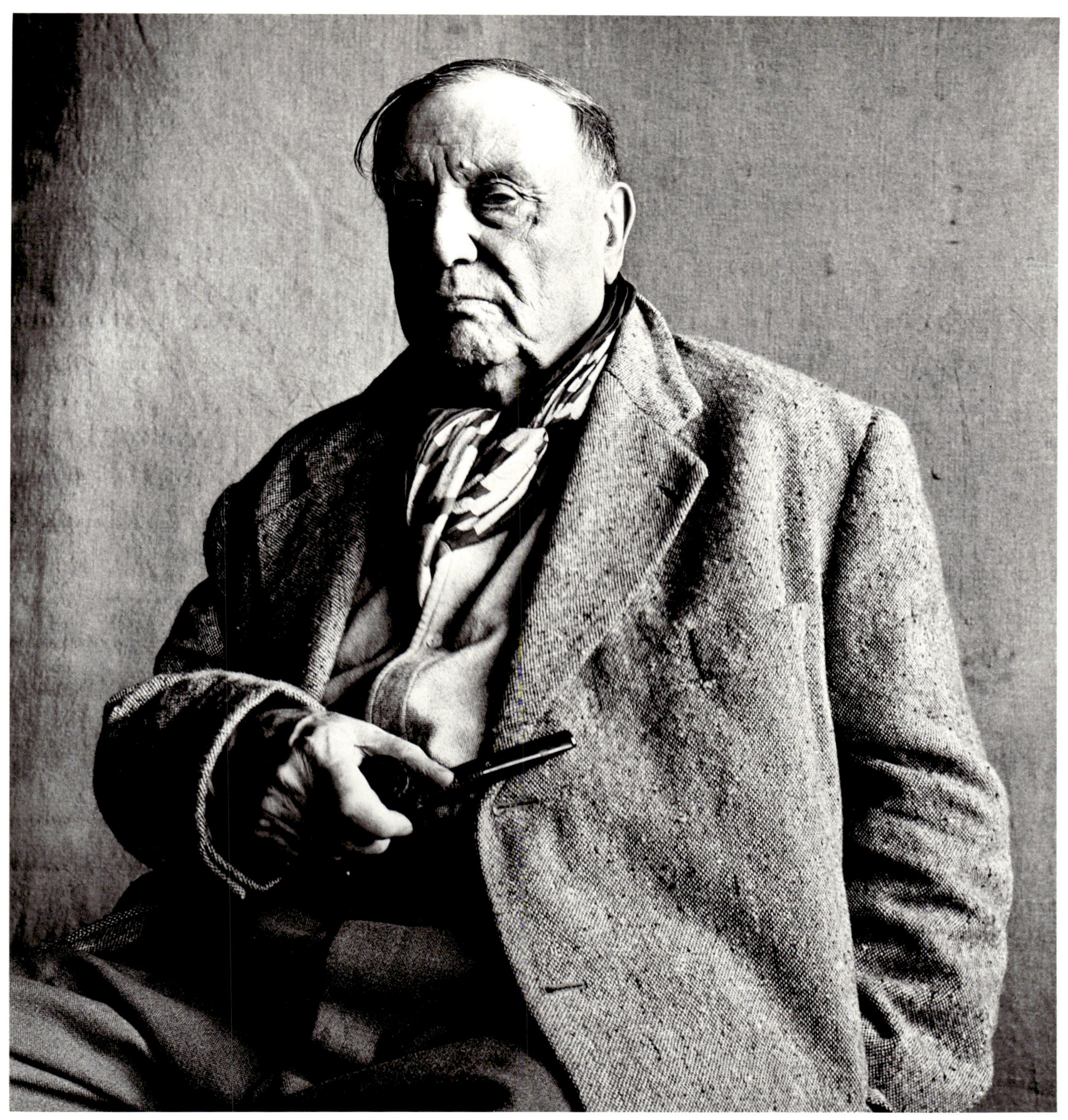

27. **Maurice de Vlaminck**. Normandy, France, 1951

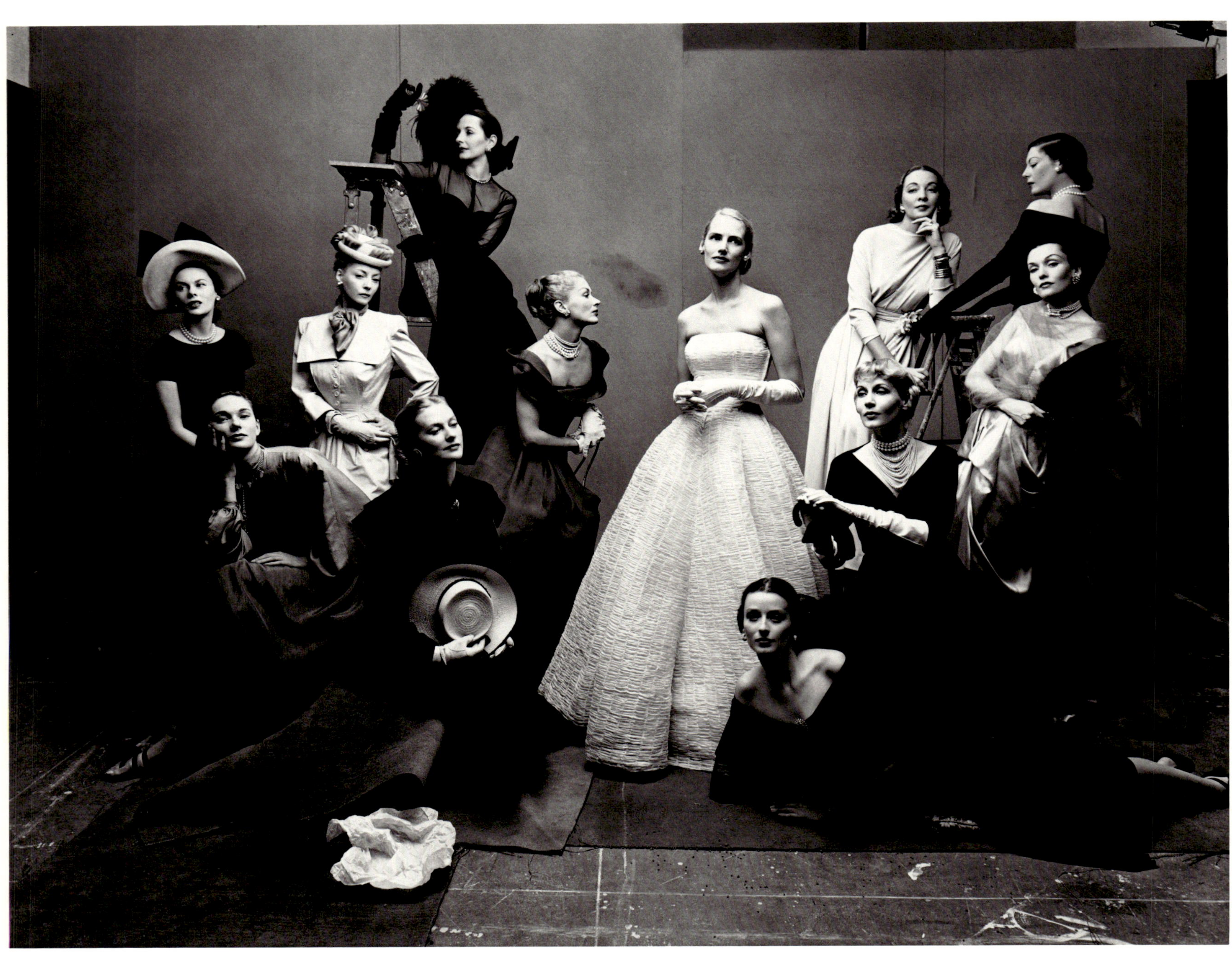

28. **Twelve Most Photographed Models**. New York, 1947

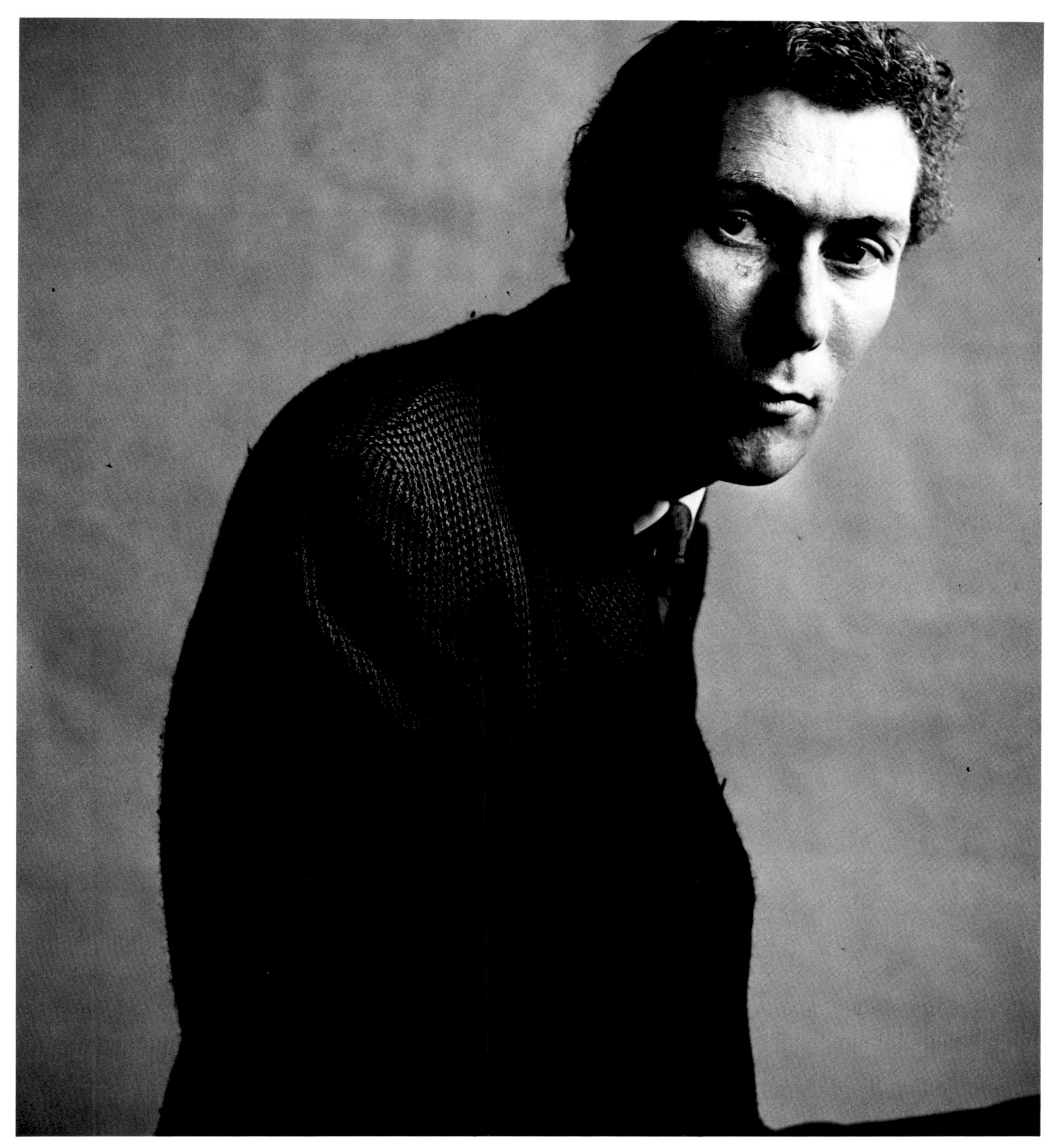

29. John Osborne. London, 1958

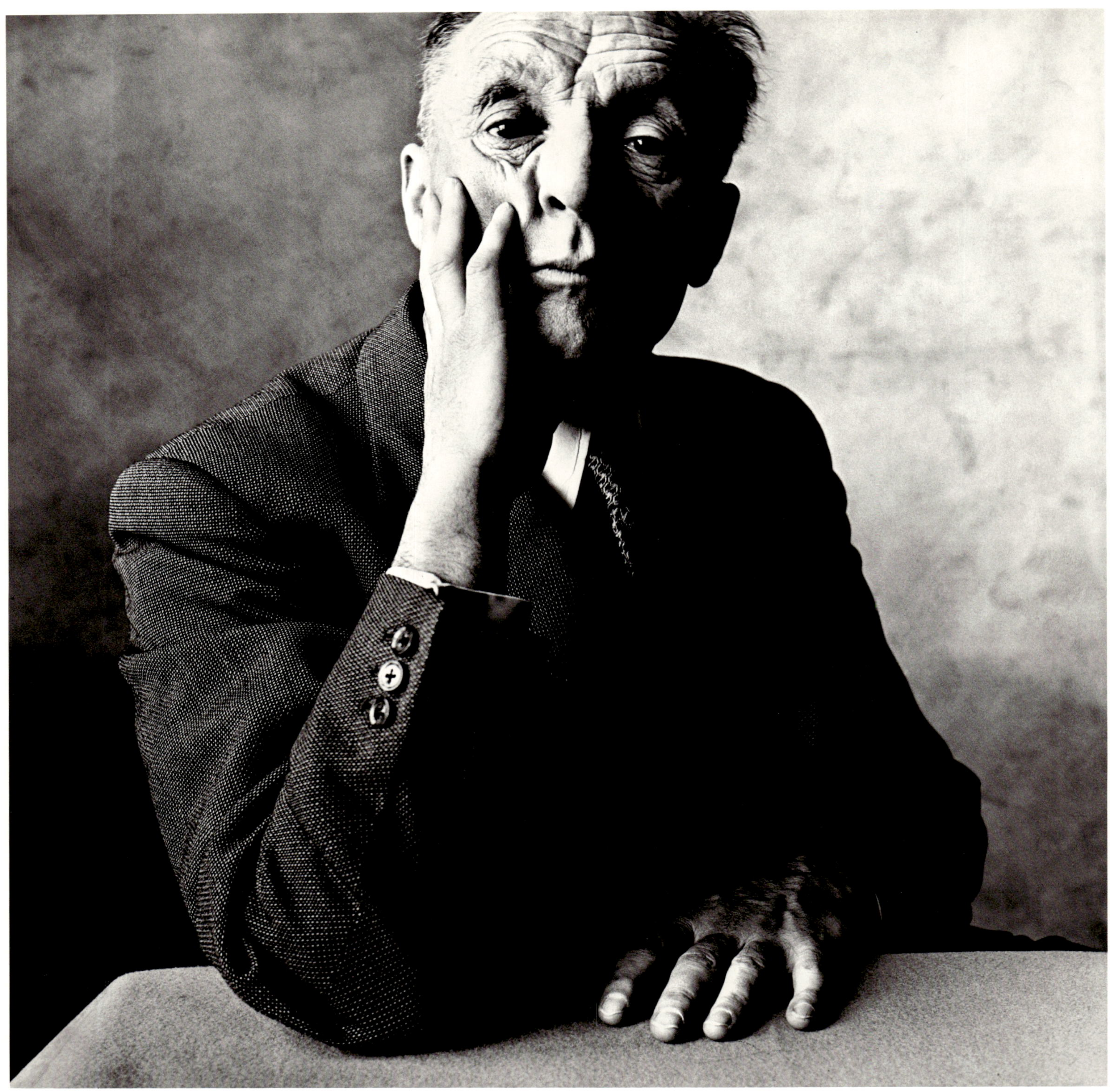

30. Joyce Cary. New York, 1951

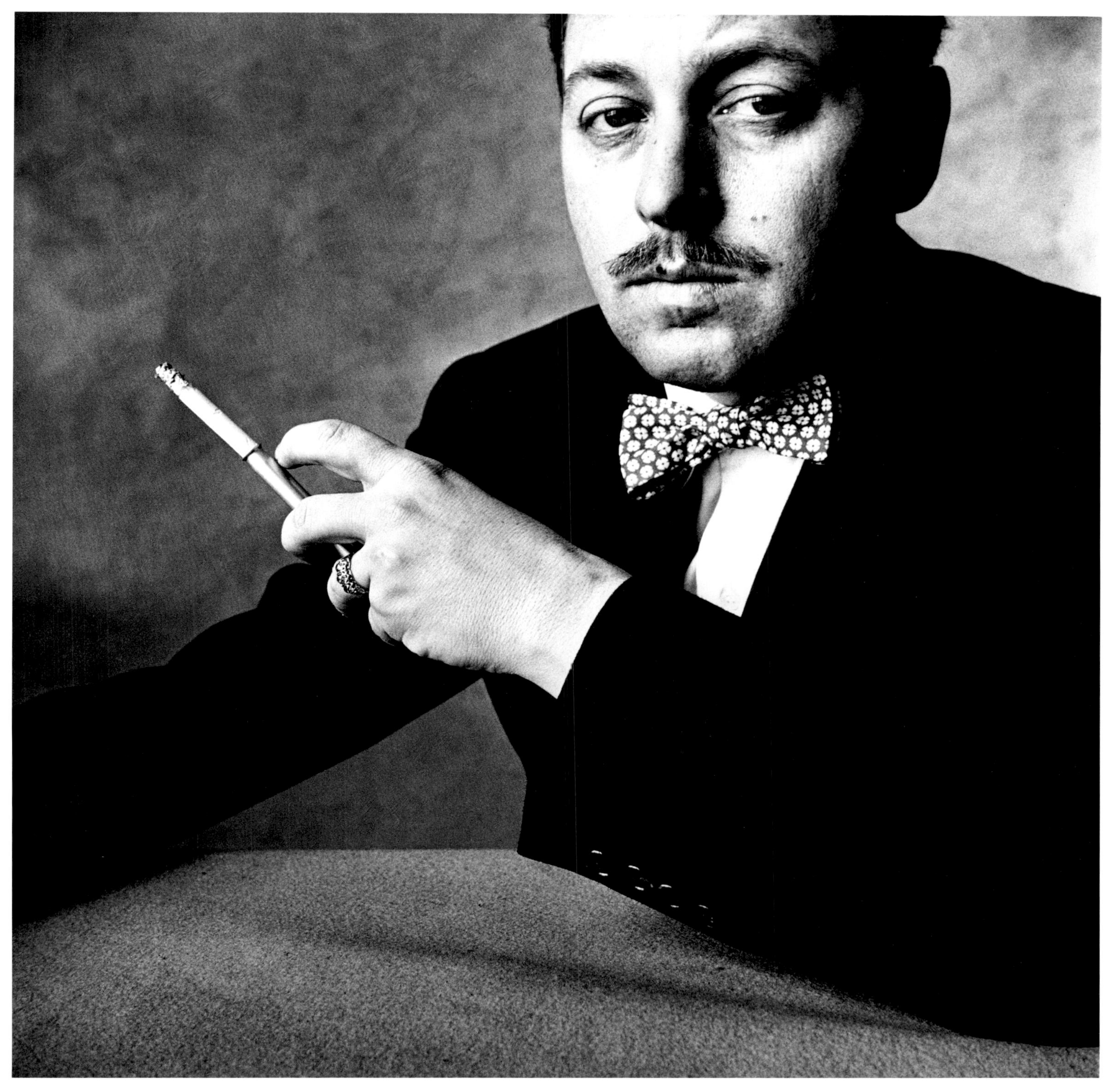

31. Tennessee Williams. New York, 1951

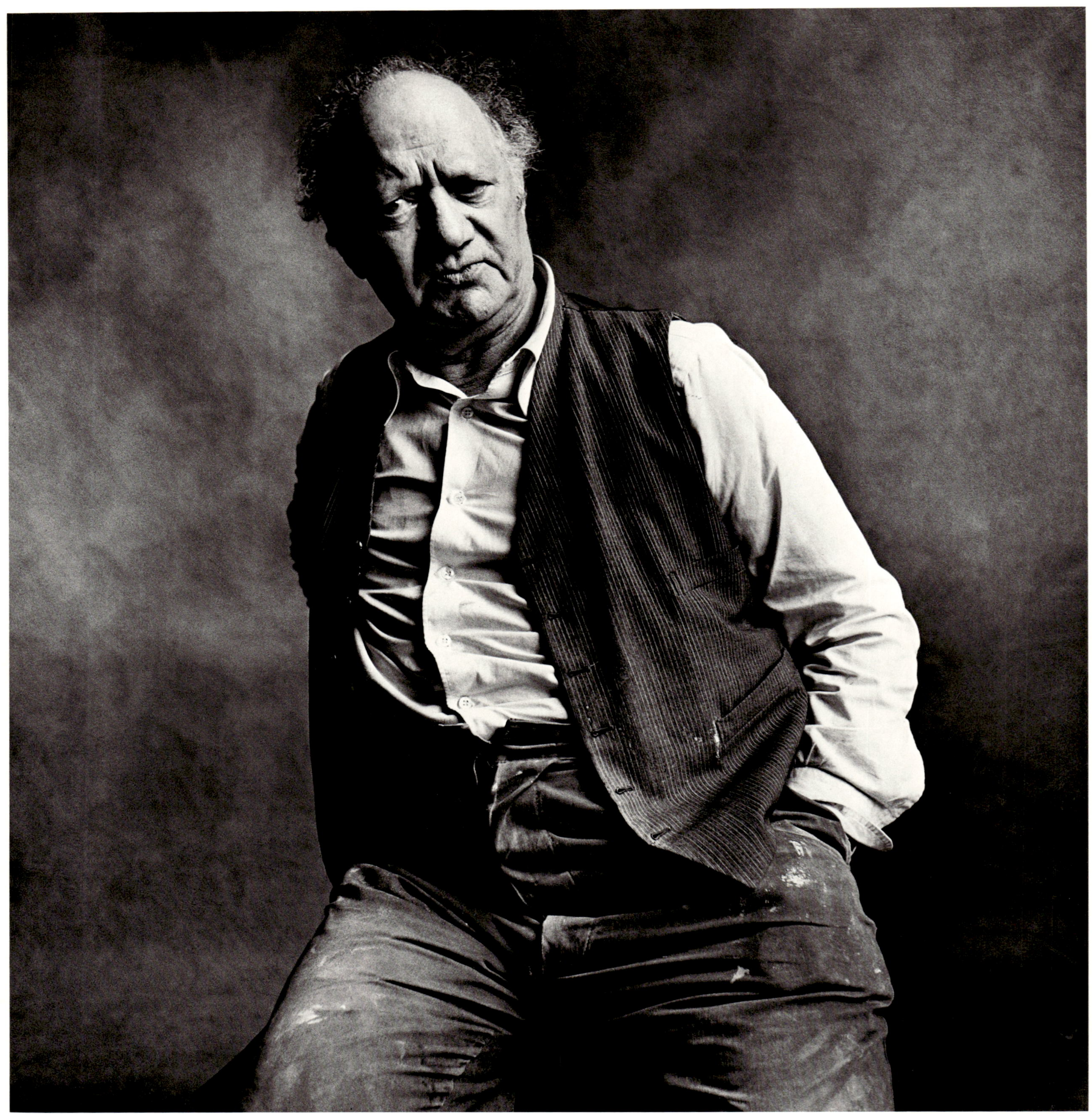

32. **Sir Jacob Epstein**. London, 1950

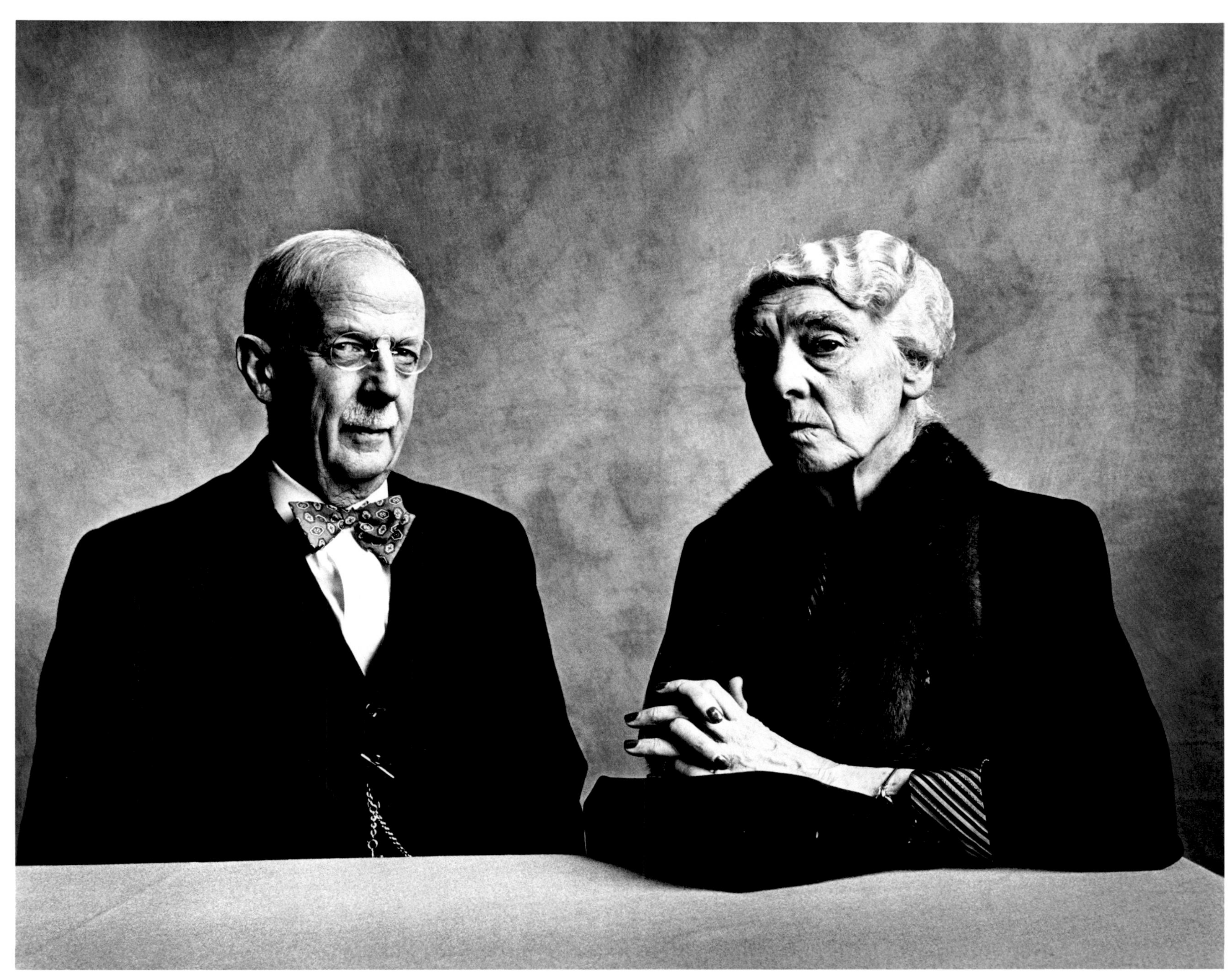

33. Dr. and Mrs. Gilbert H. Grosvenor. Washington, D.C., 1951

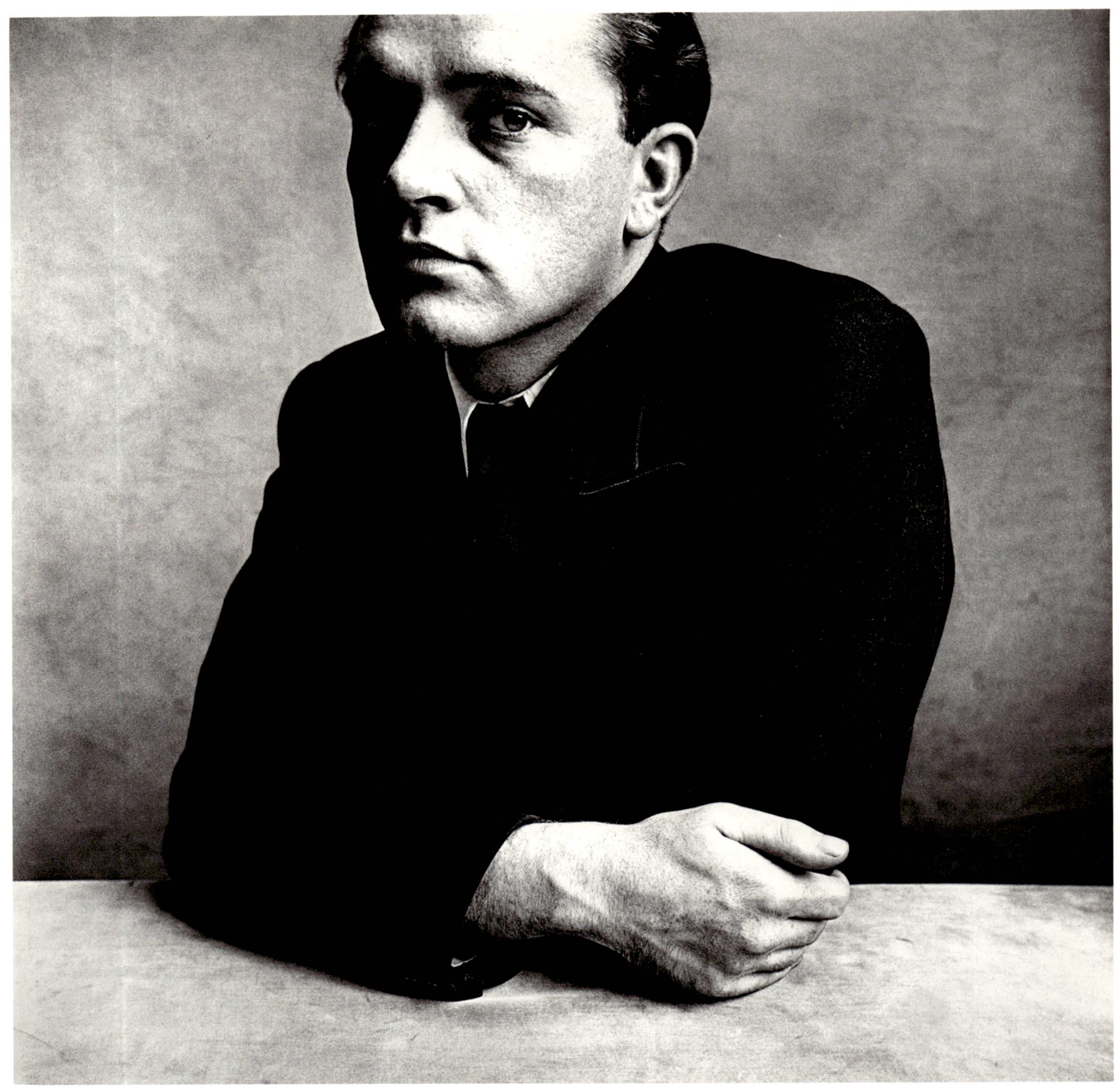

34. **Richard Burton**. London, 1950

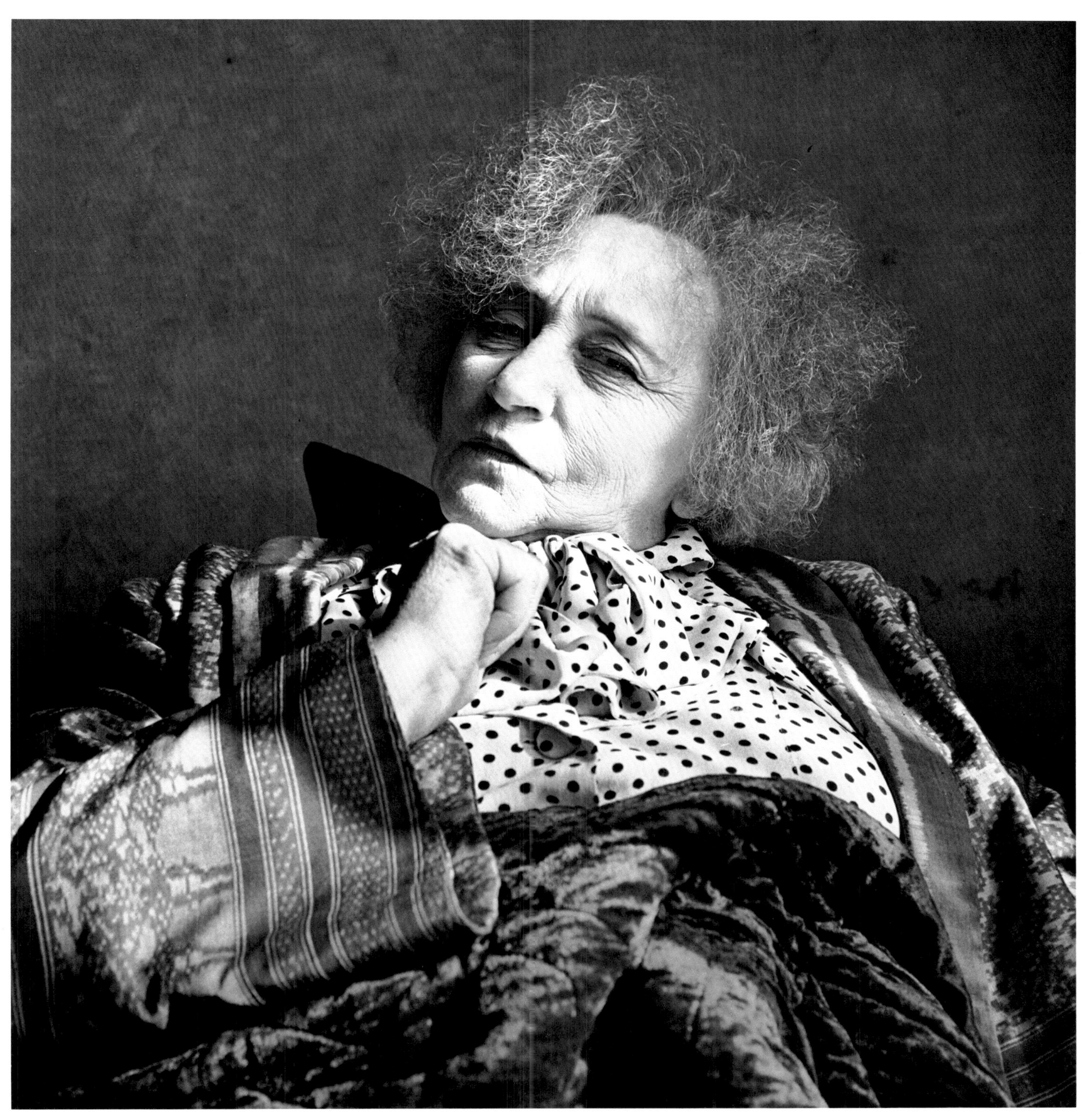

35. Colette. Paris, 1951

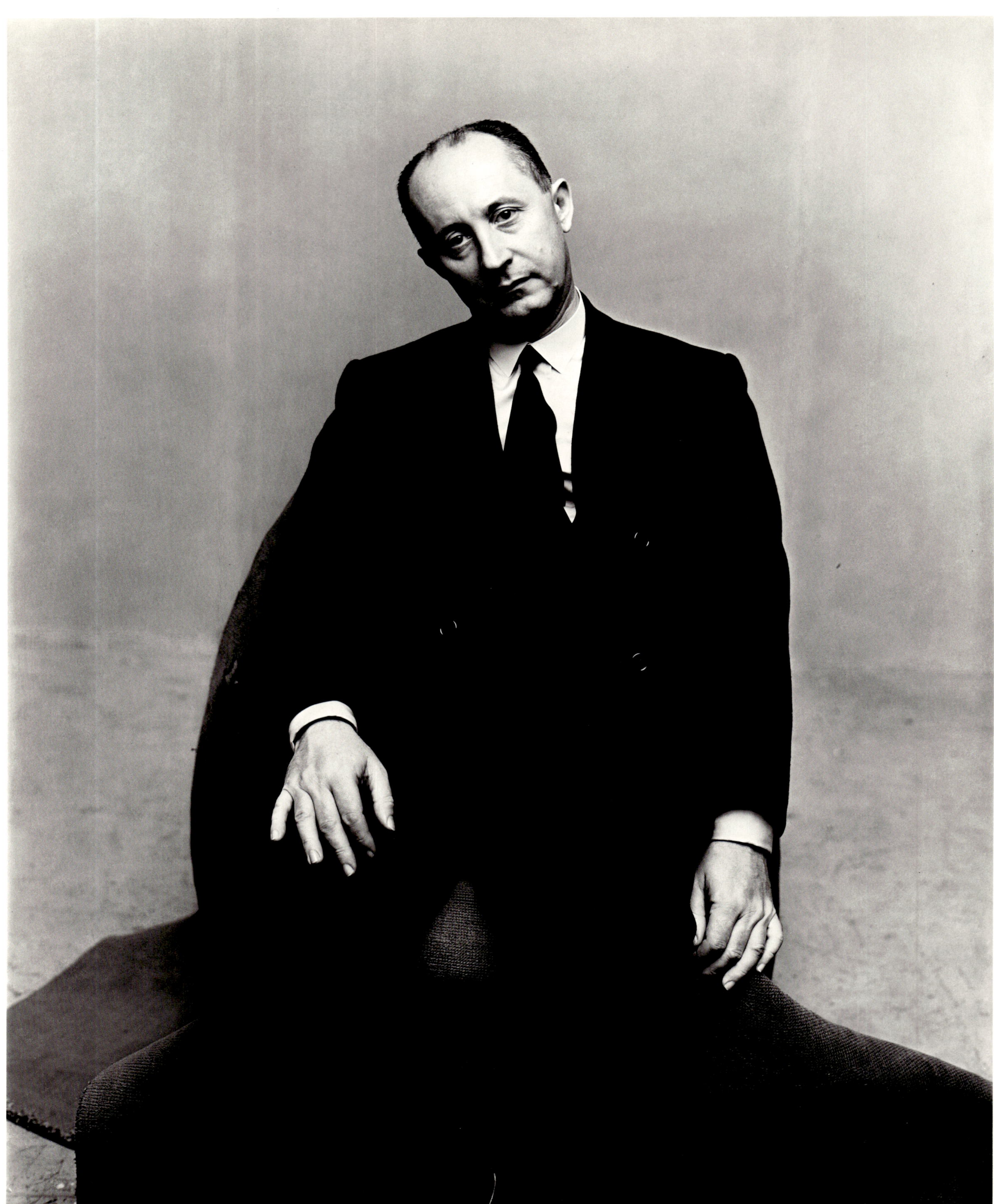

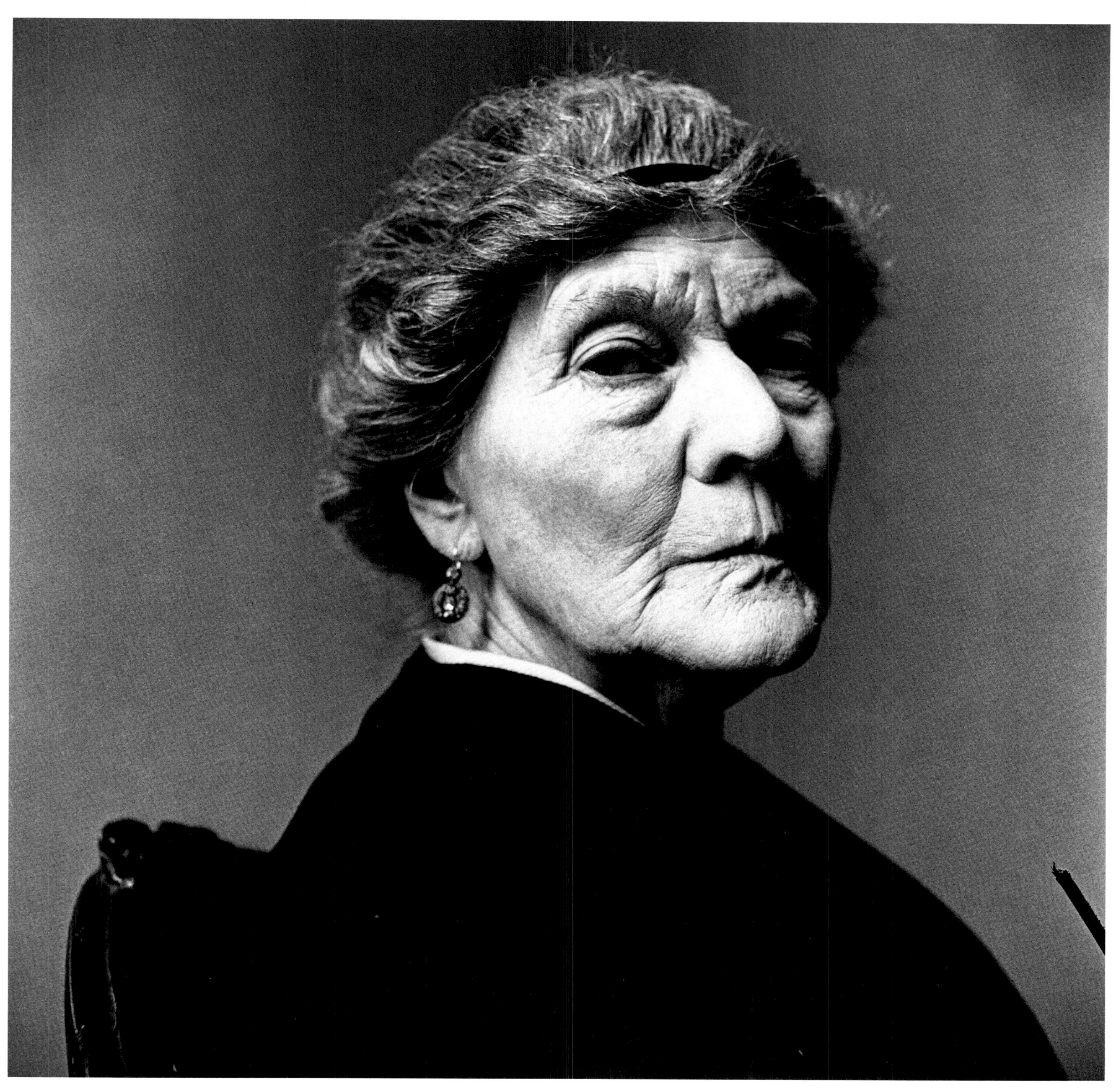

36. Christian Dior. New York, 1947

37. Ivy Compton Burnett. London, 1958

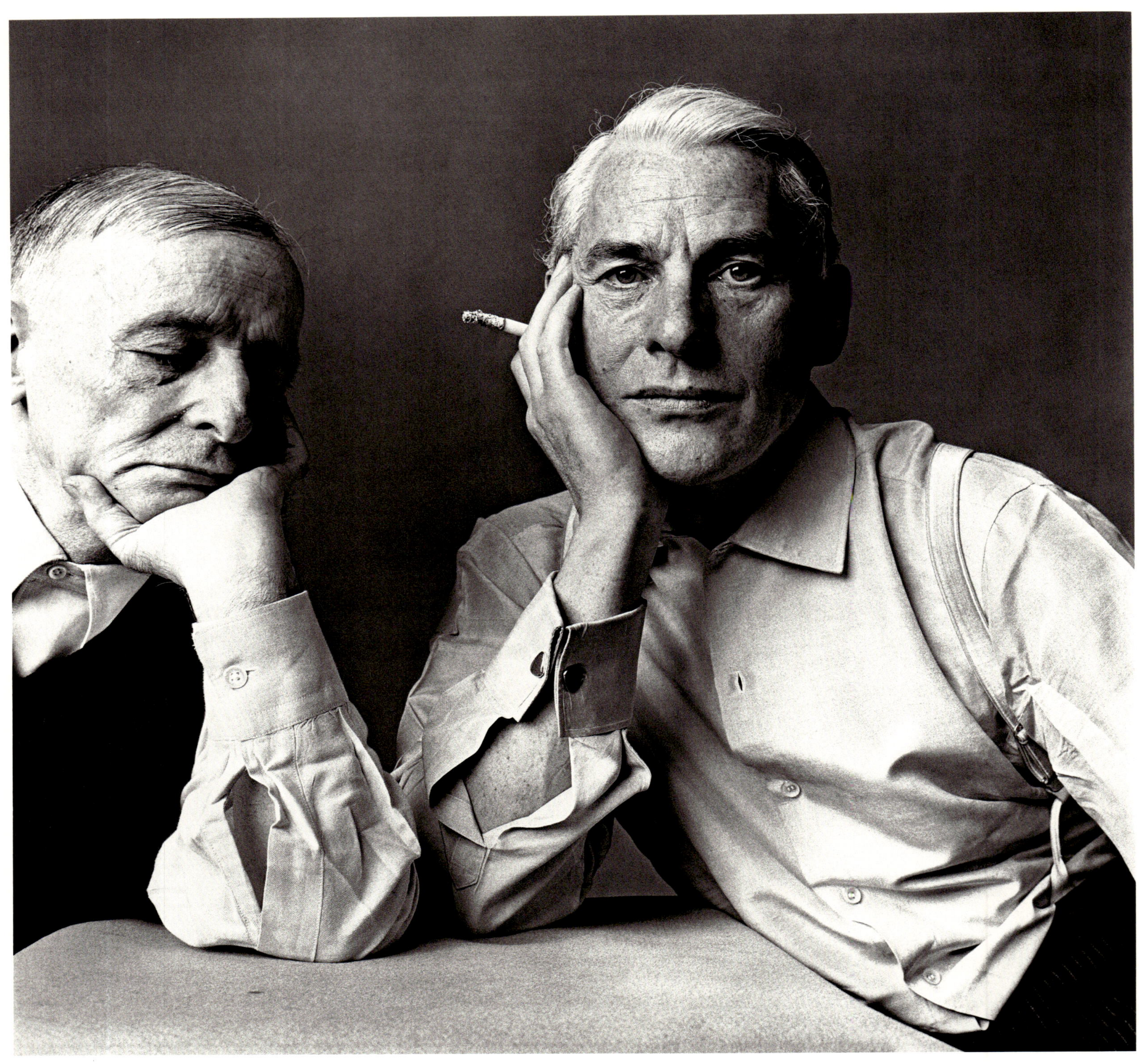

38. Frederick Kiesler and Willem de Kooning. New York, 1960. Platinum-palladium print, 1982

39. Mrs. Amory Carhart. New York, 1947

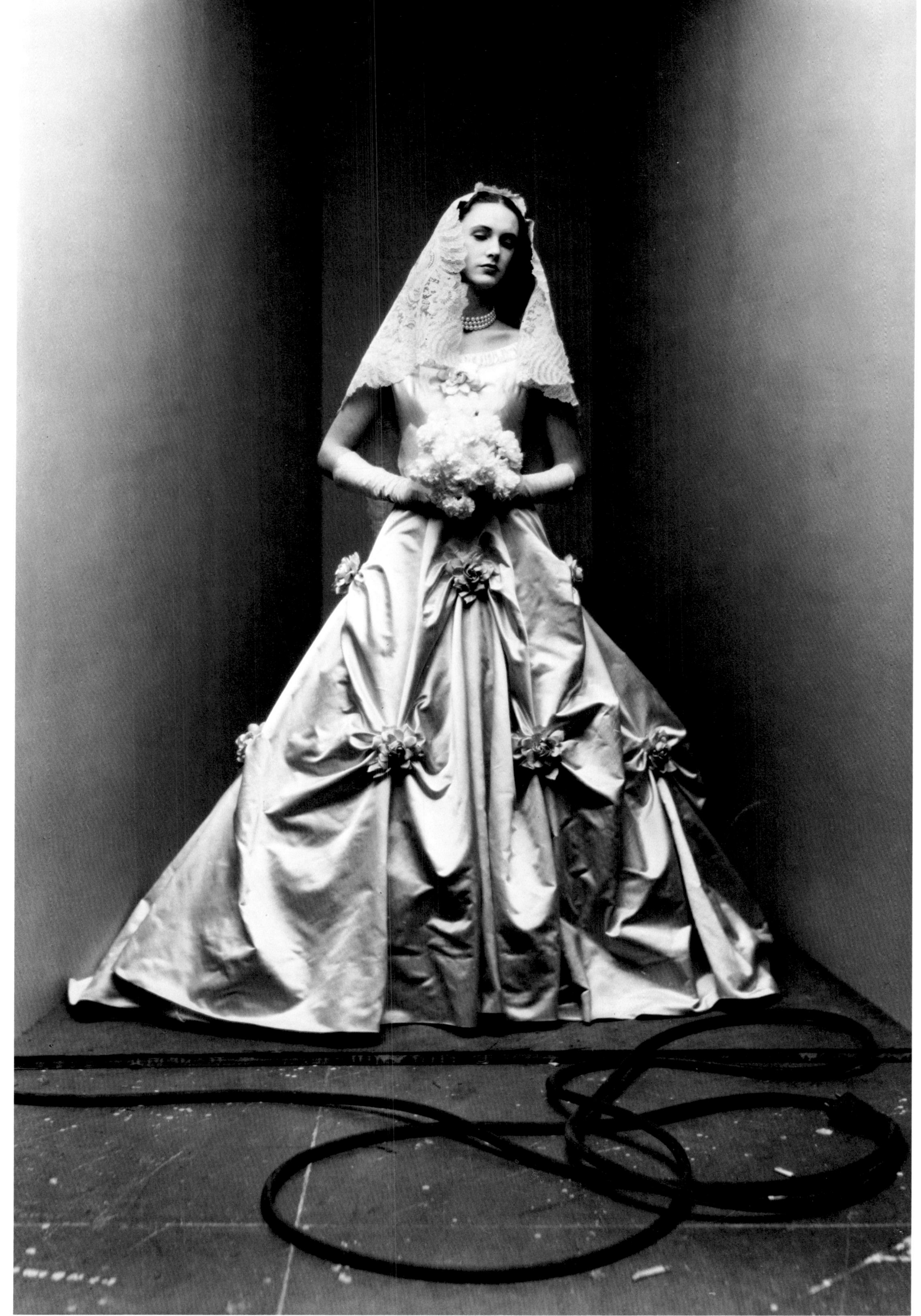

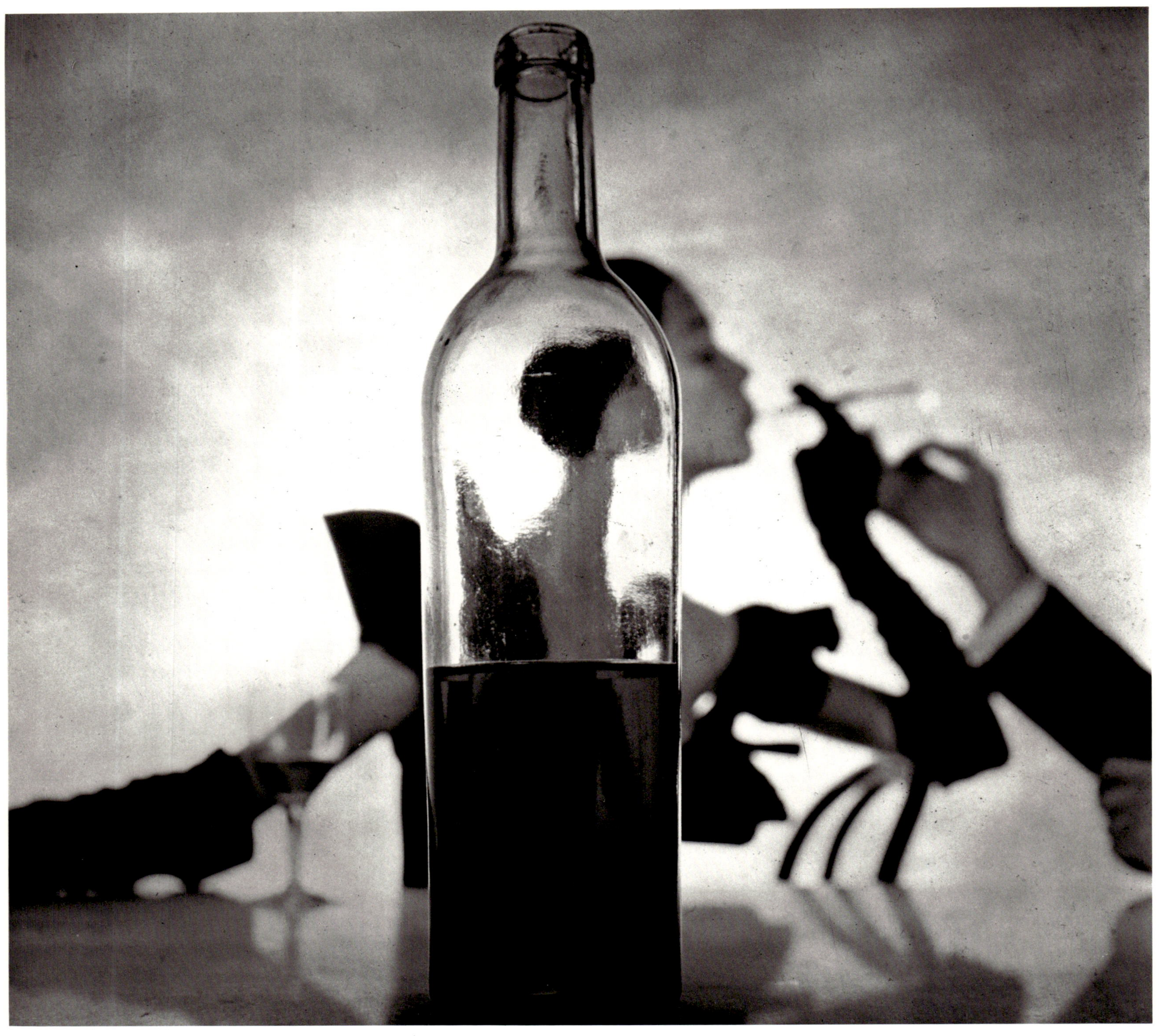

40. **Man Lighting Girl's Cigarette** (Jean Patchett). New York, 1949. Platinum-palladium print, 1977

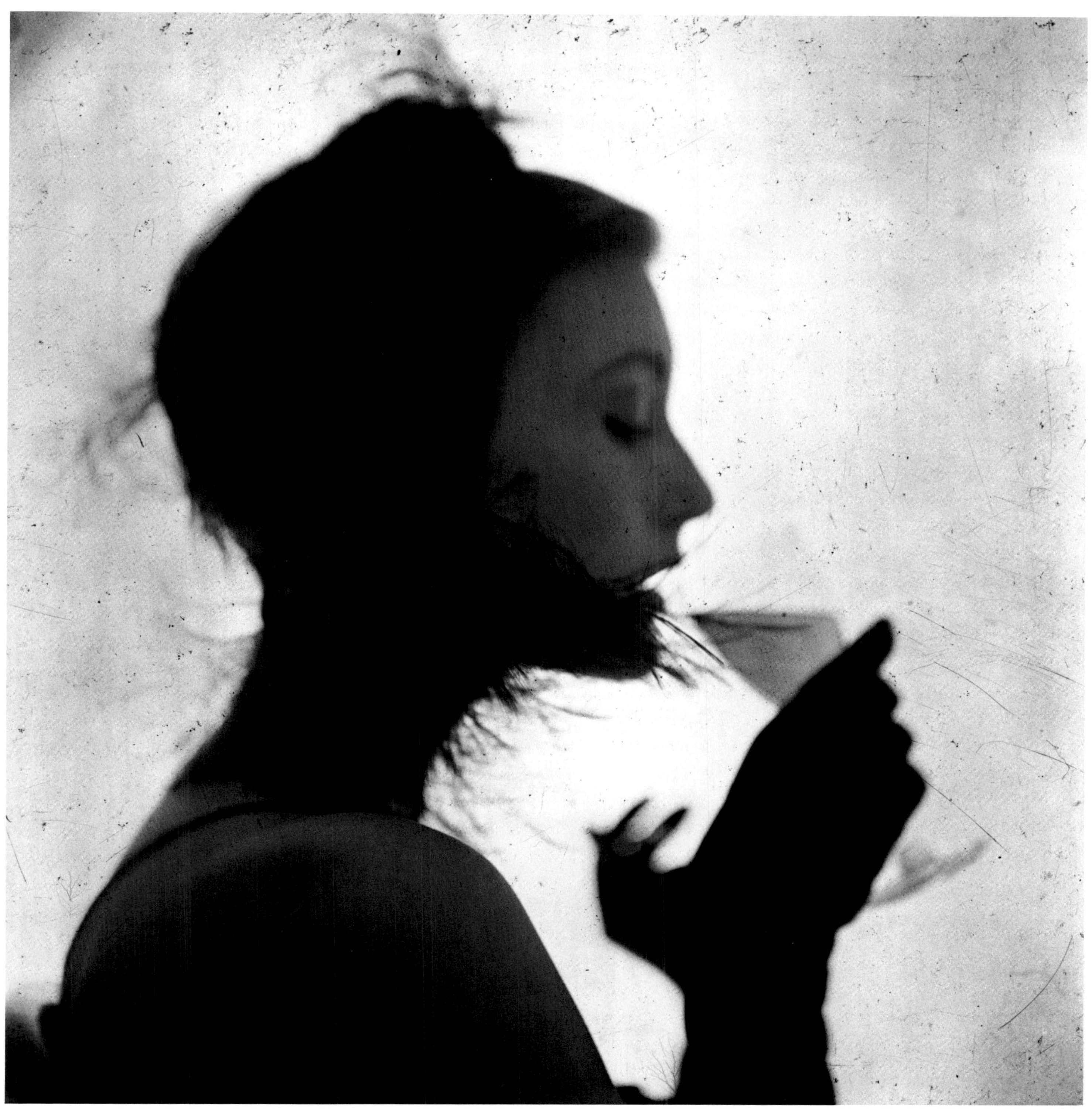

41. **Girl Drinking** (Mary Jane Russell). New York, 1949. Platinum-palladium print, 1979

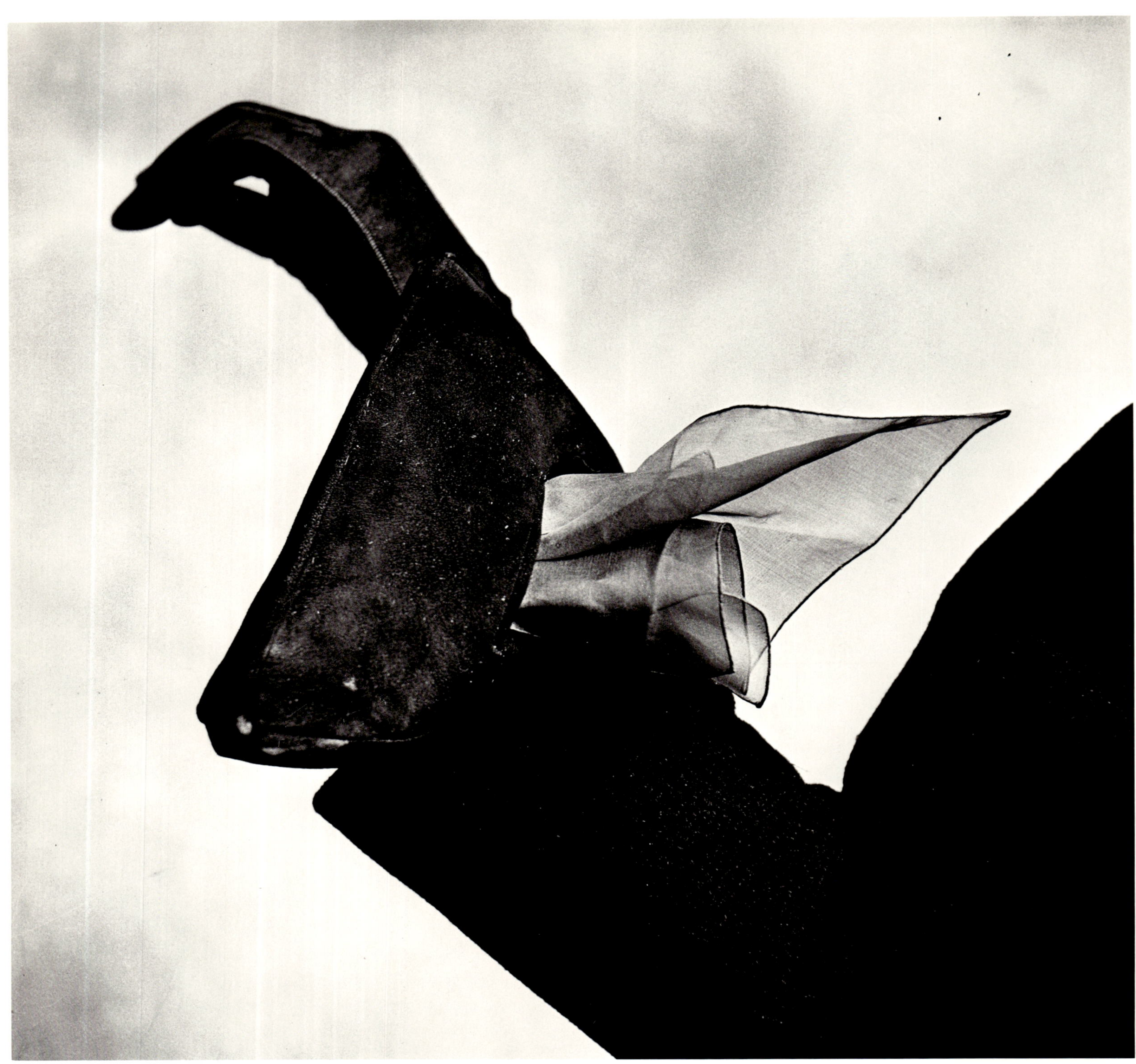

42. Kerchief-Glove. New York, 1950

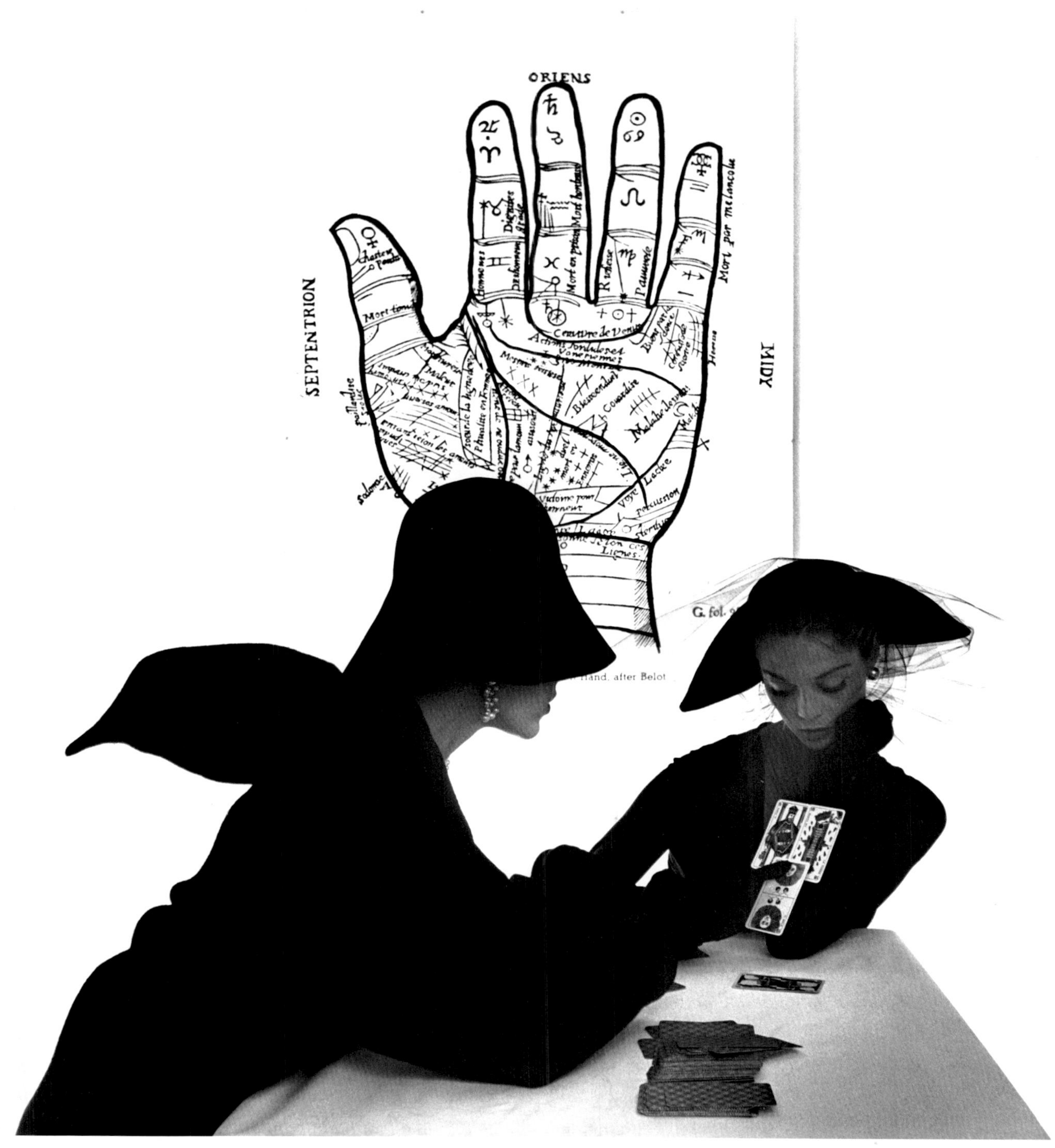

43. The Tarot Reader. New York, 1949

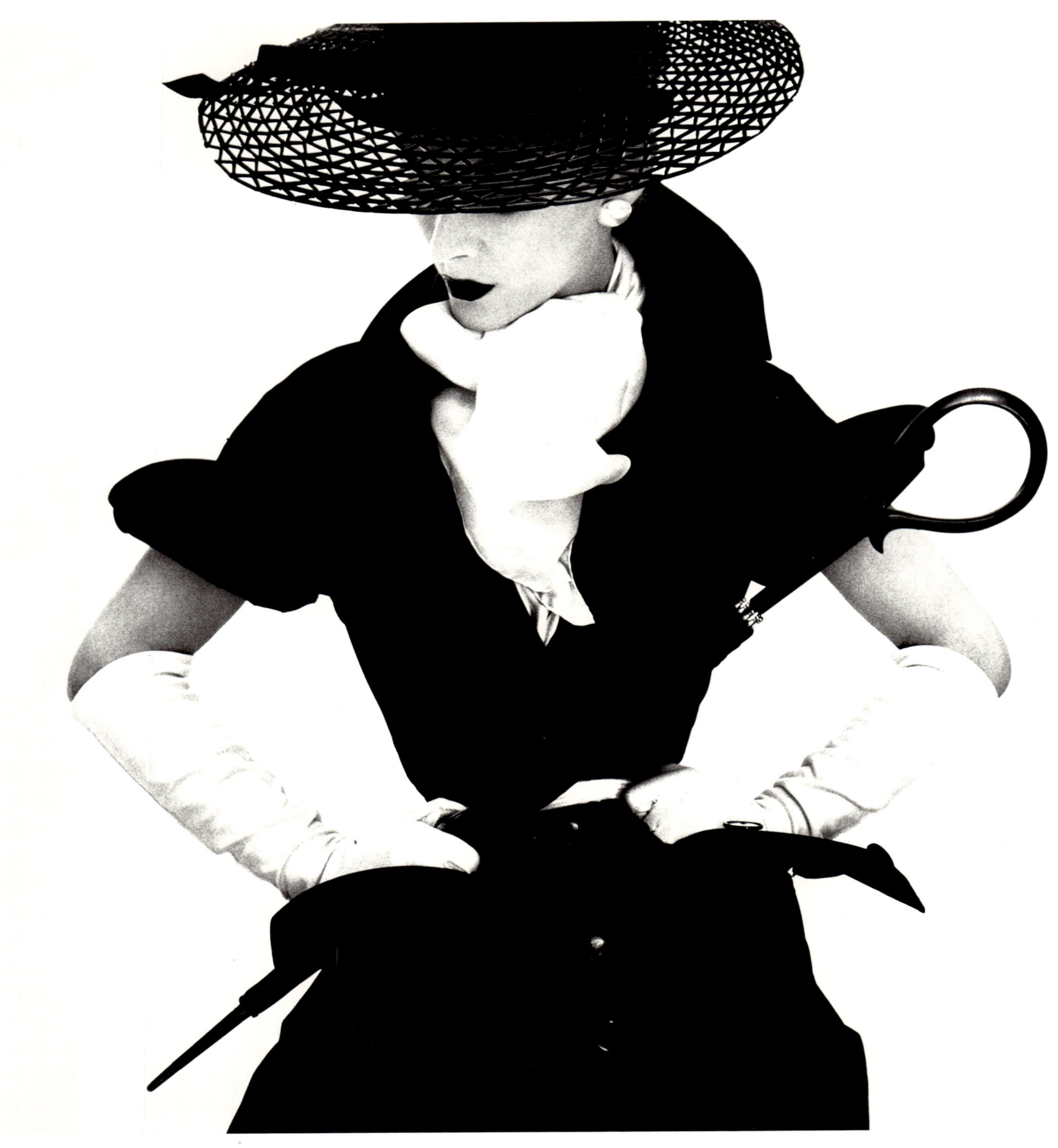

44. **Woman with Umbrella** (Lisa Fonssagrives-Penn). New York, 1950

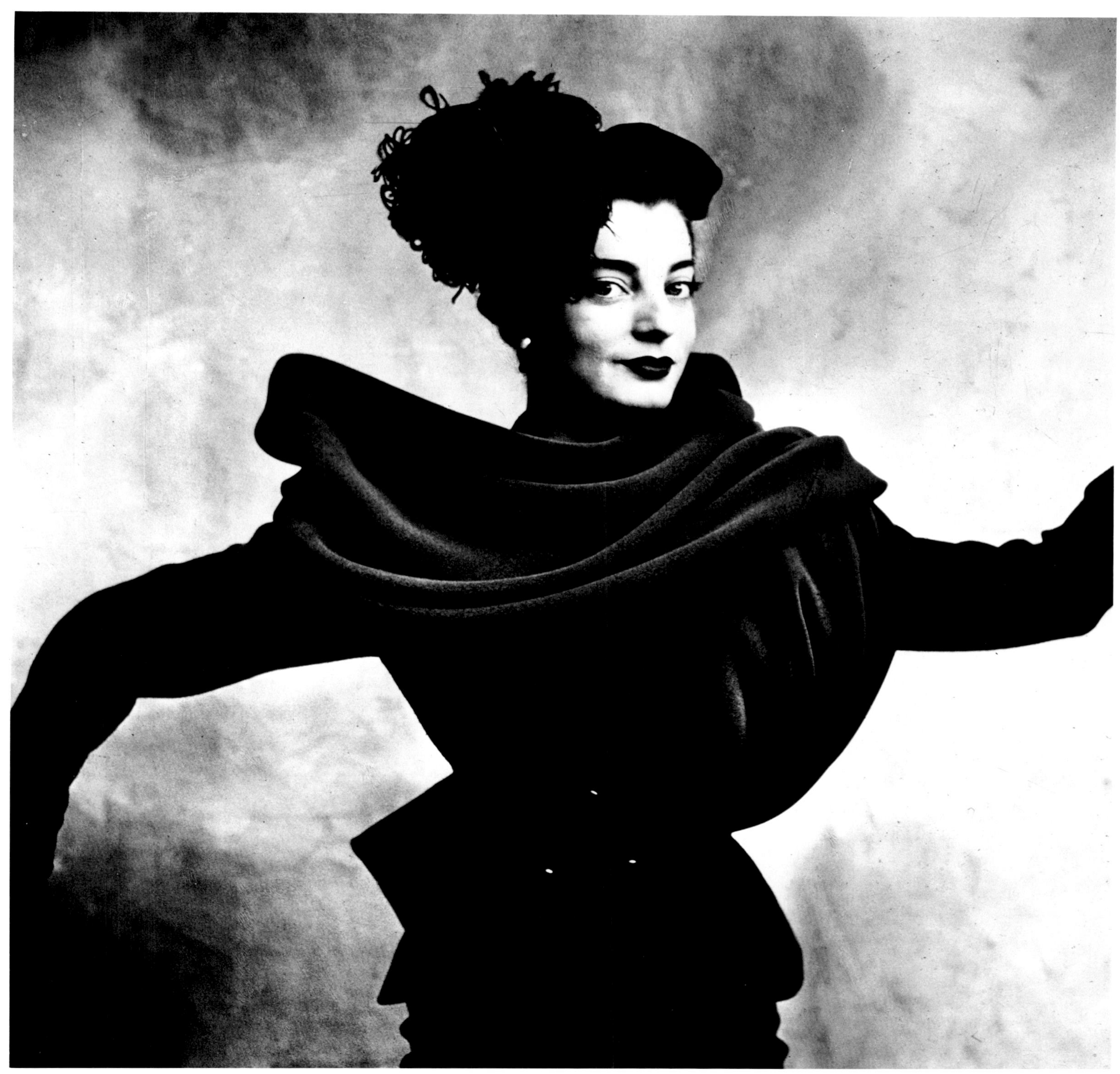

45. Régine (Balenciaga Suit). Paris, 1950

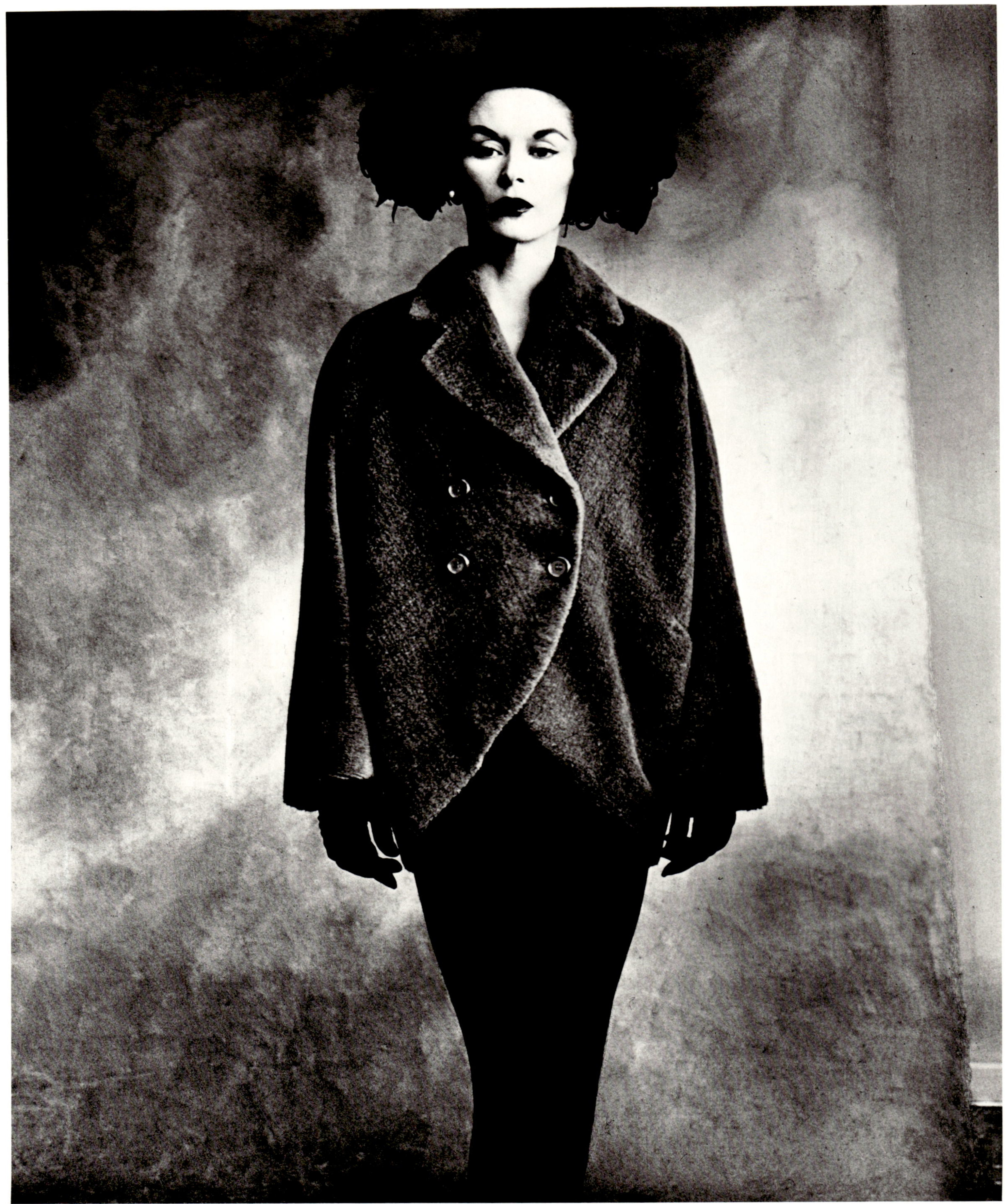

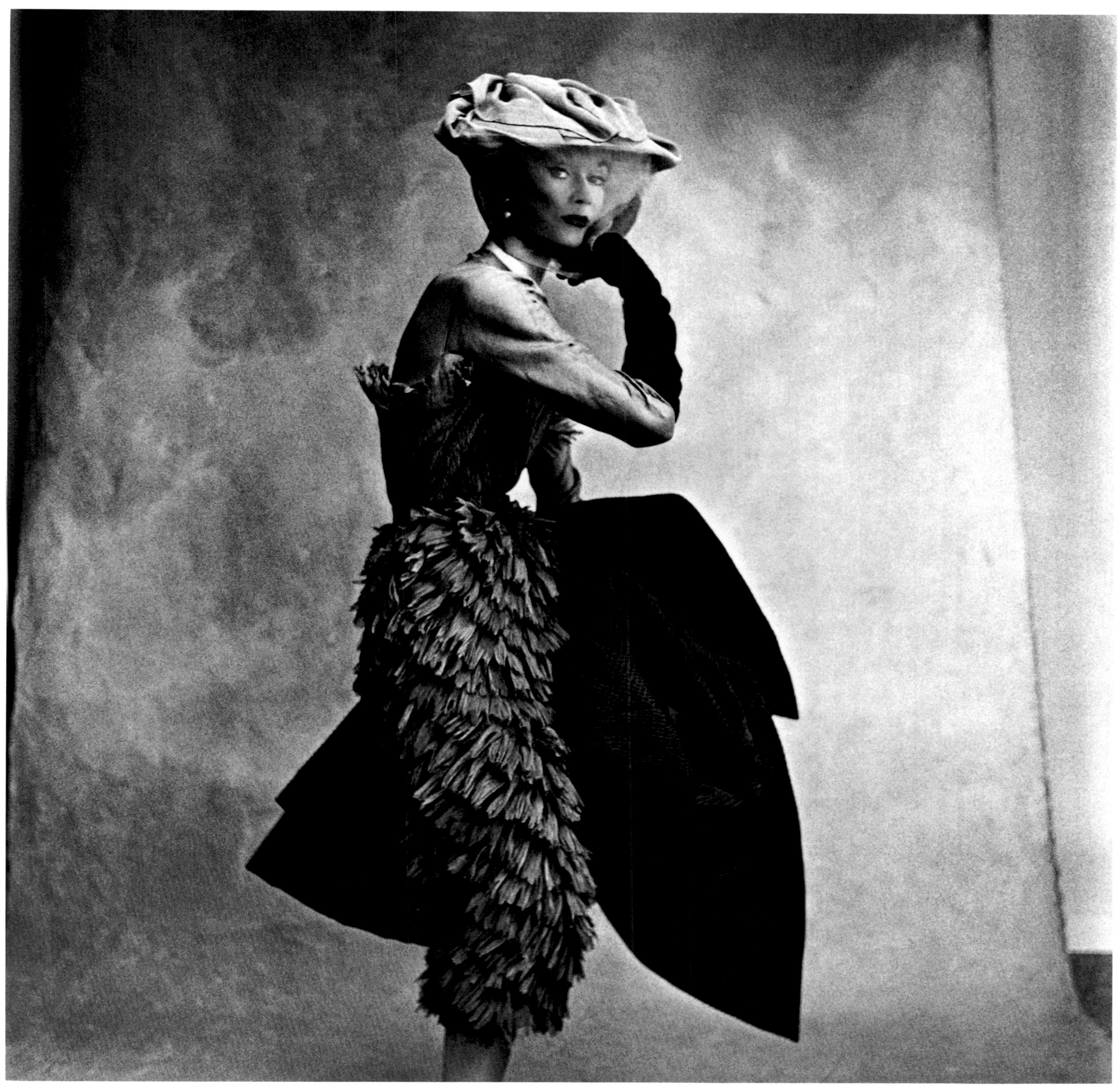

46. Woman in Balenciaga Coat (Lisa Fonssagrives-Penn). Paris, 1950

47. Cocoa-colored Balenciaga Dress (Lisa Fonssagrives-Penn). Paris, 1950. Platinum-palladium print, 1979

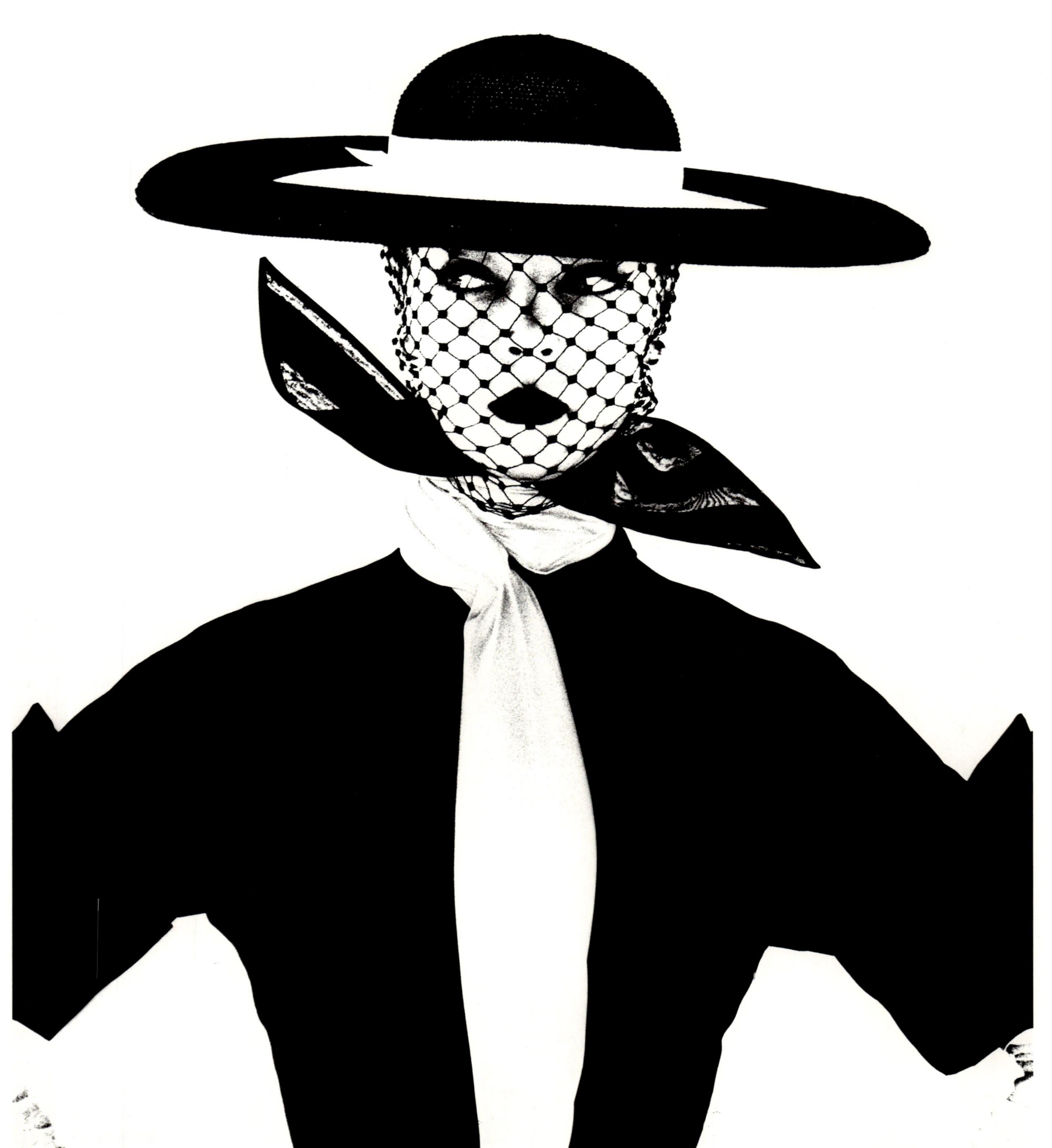

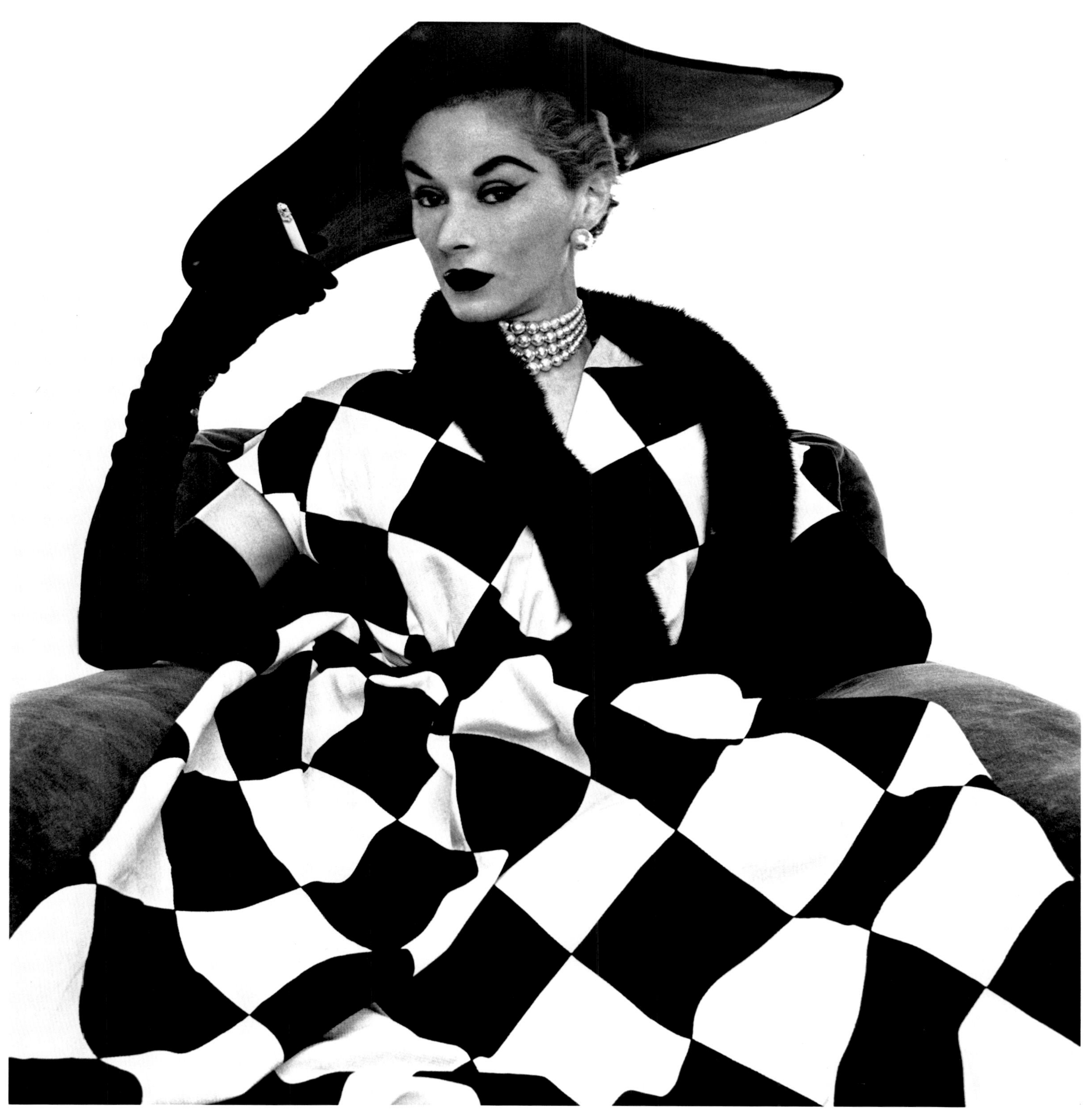

48. Black-and-white *Vogue* Cover (Jean Patchett). New York, 1950. Platinum-palladium print, 1968

49. Harlequin Dress (Lisa Fonssagrives-Penn). New York, 1950. Platinum-palladium print, 1979

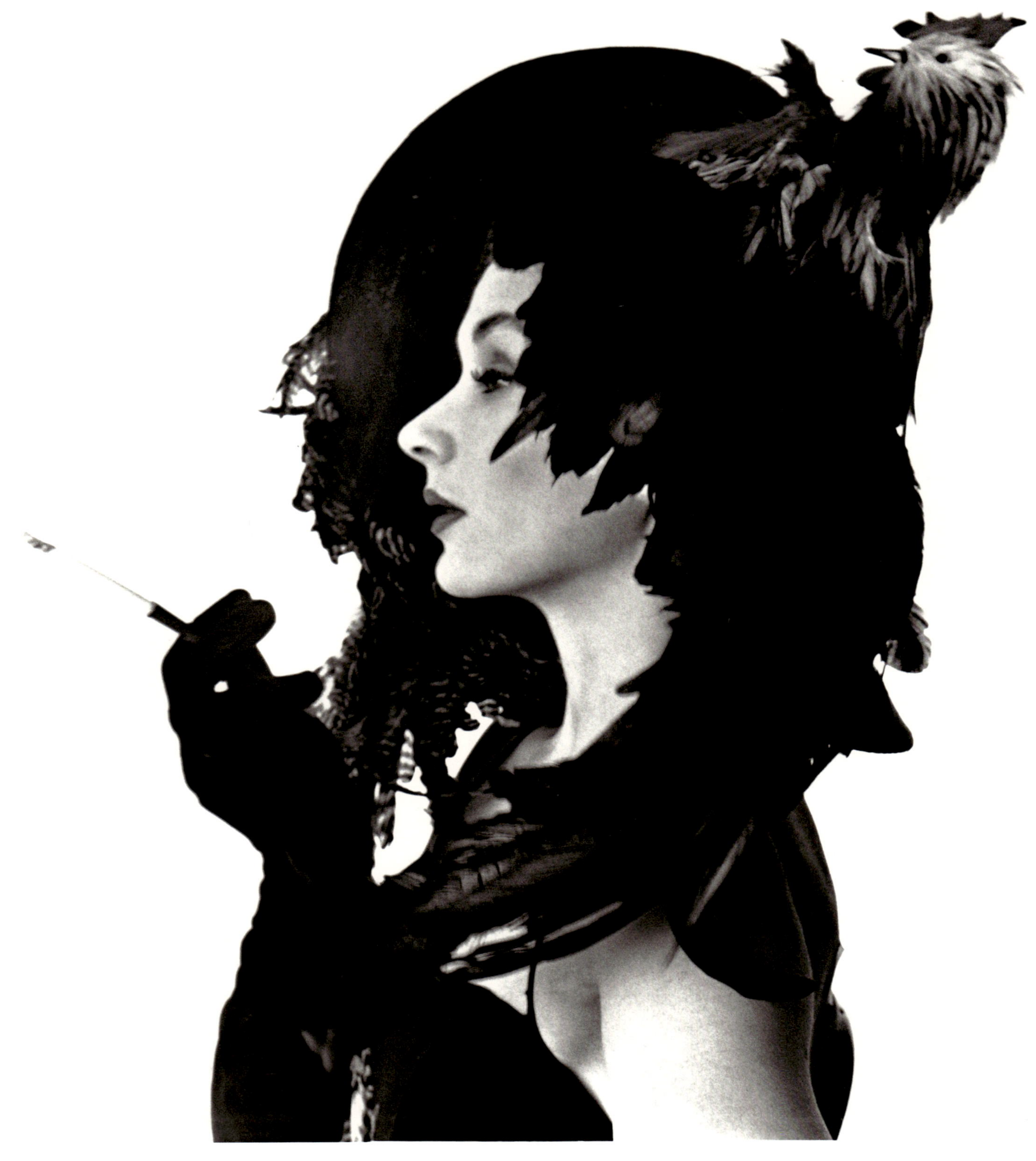

50. **Woman in Chicken Hat** (Lisa Fonssagrives-Penn). New York, c. 1949. Platinum-palladium print, 1983

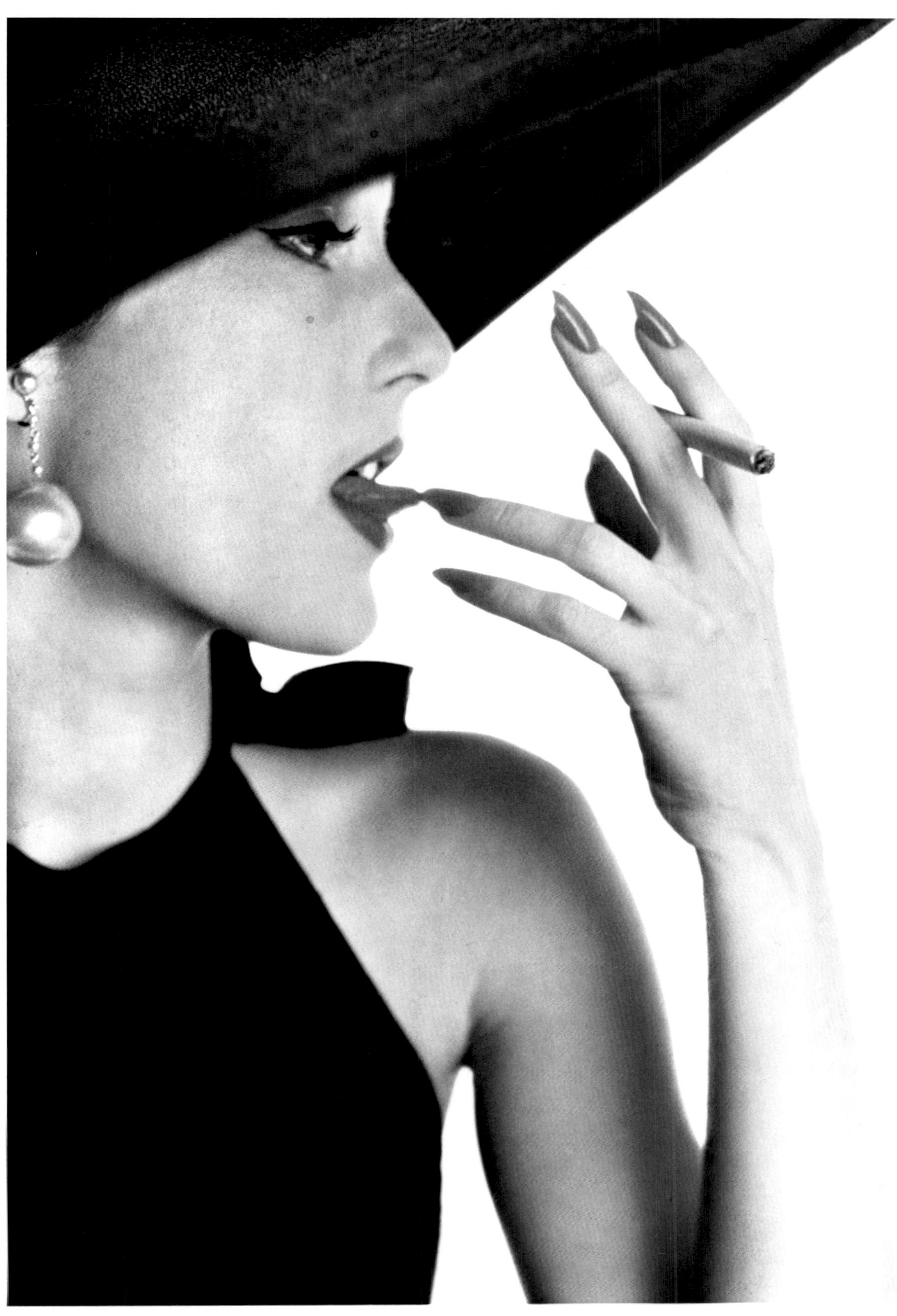

51. **Woman with Tobacco on Her Tongue** (Mary Jane Russell). New York, 1951

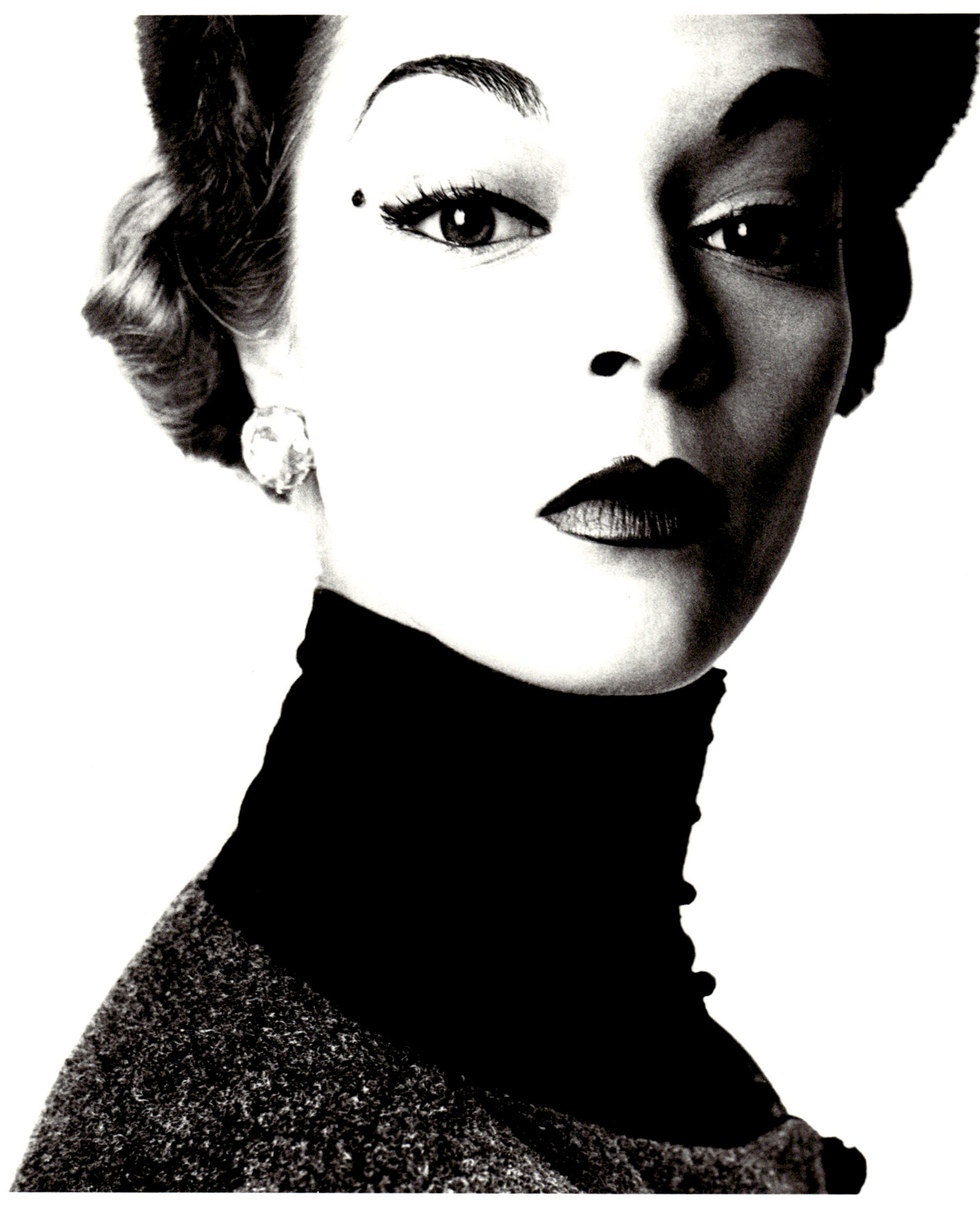

52. Woman with Long Black Neck (Jean Patchett). New York, c. 1951

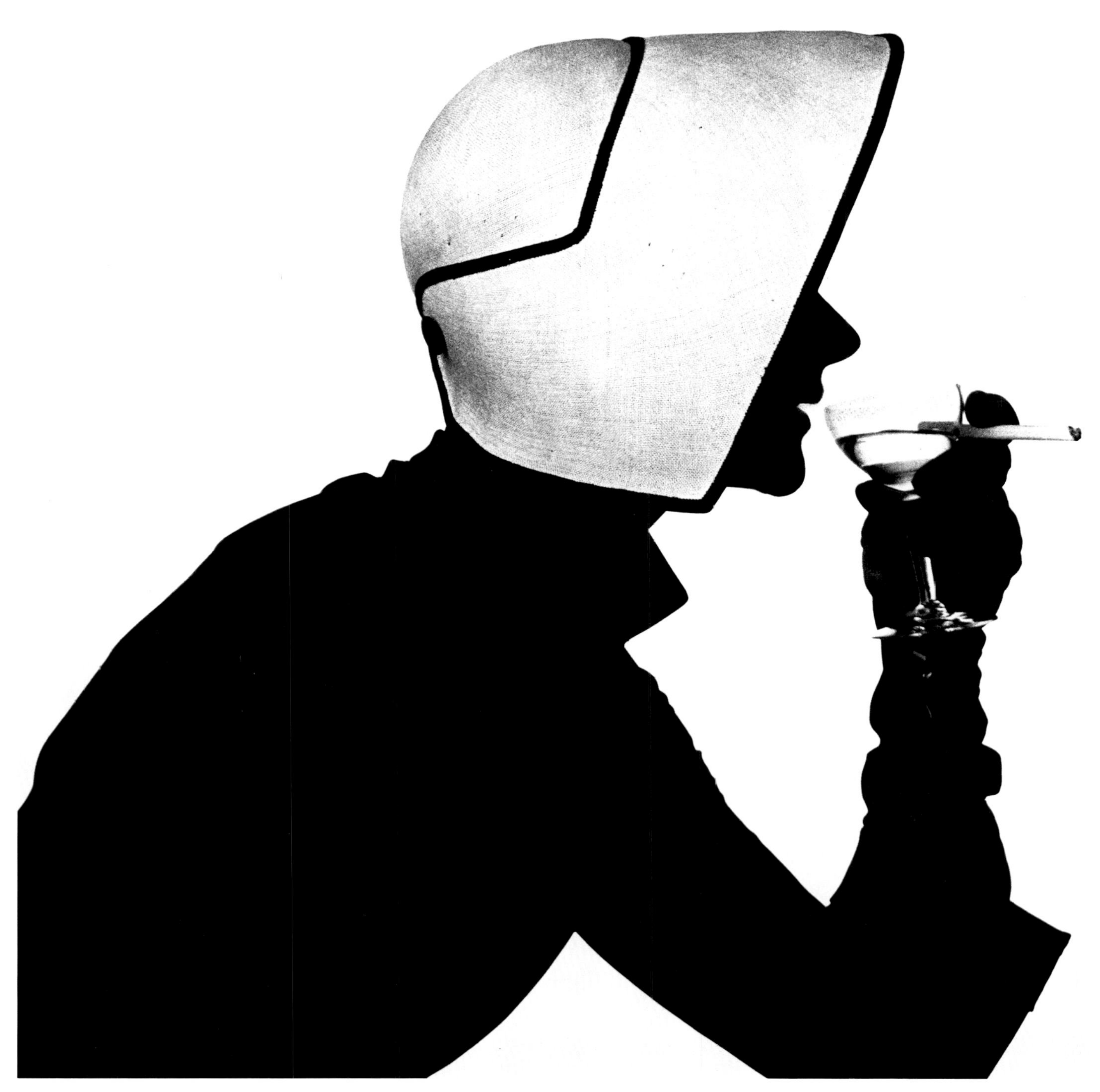

53. **Woman in Dior Hat with Martini.** (Lisa Fonssagrives-Penn). New York, 1952

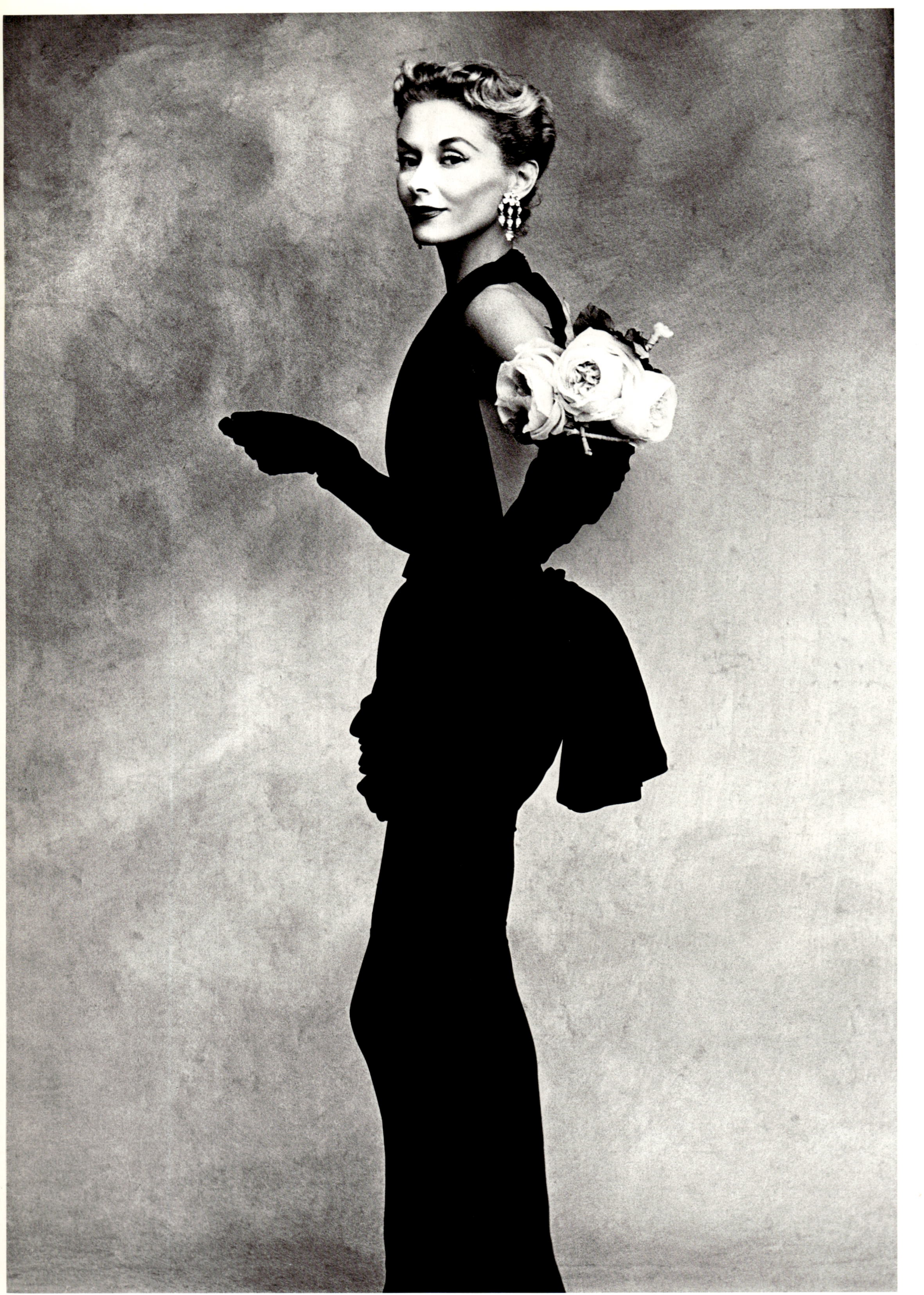

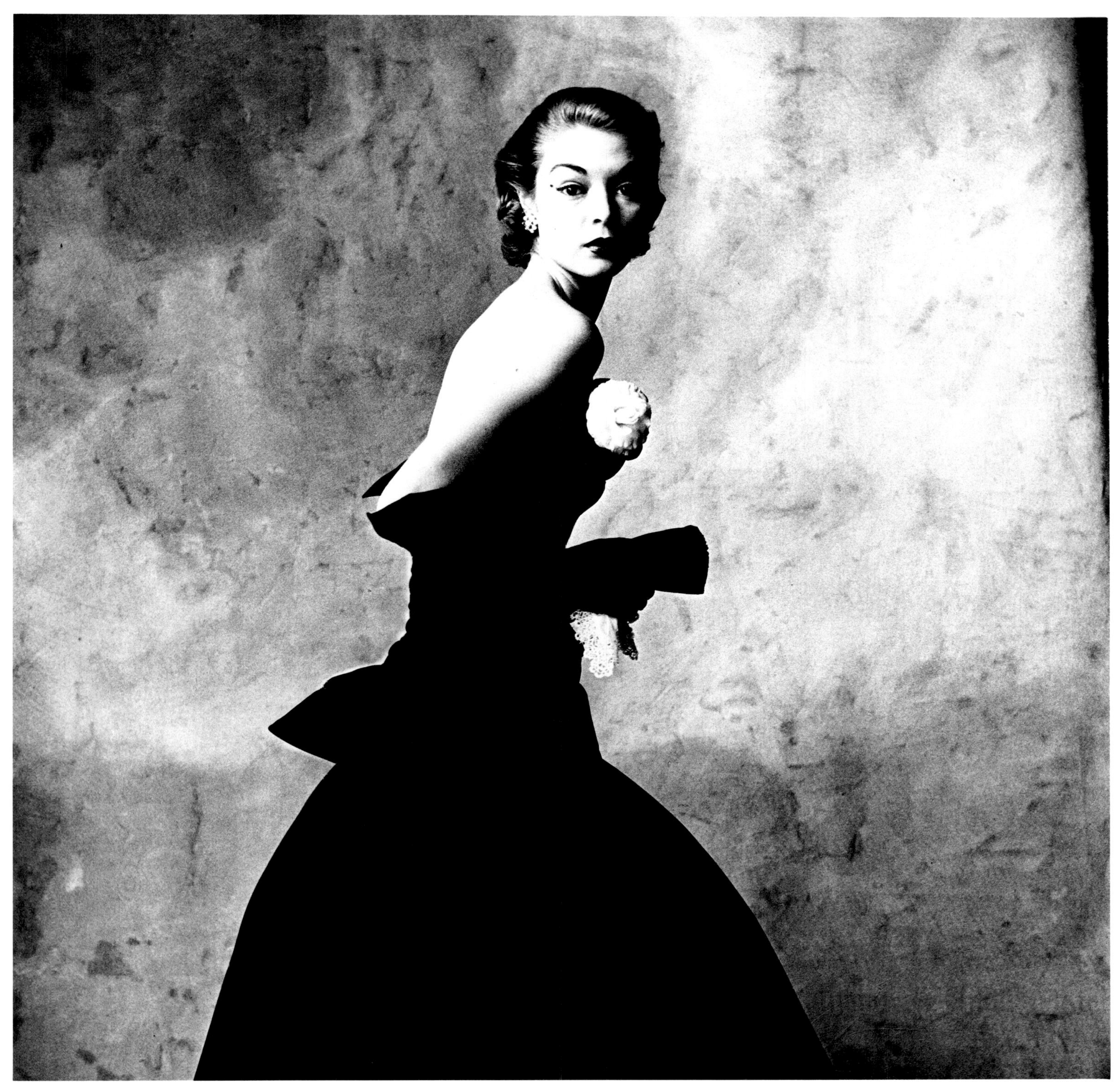

54. Woman with Roses (Lisa Fonssagrives-Penn). Paris, 1950

55. Woman with Handkerchief (Jean Patchett). New York, c. 1951

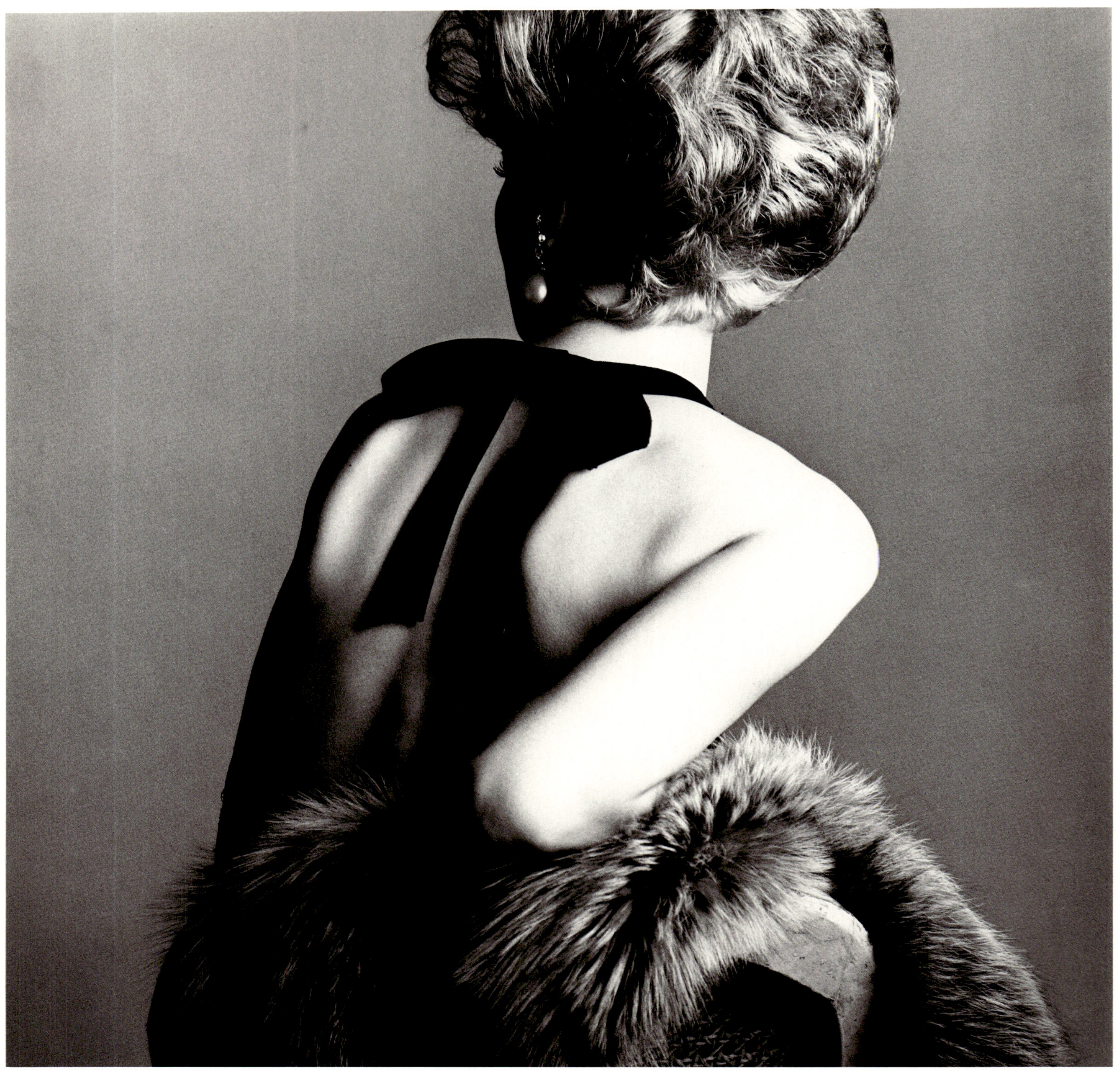

56. **Woman with Bare Back. New York, 1961**

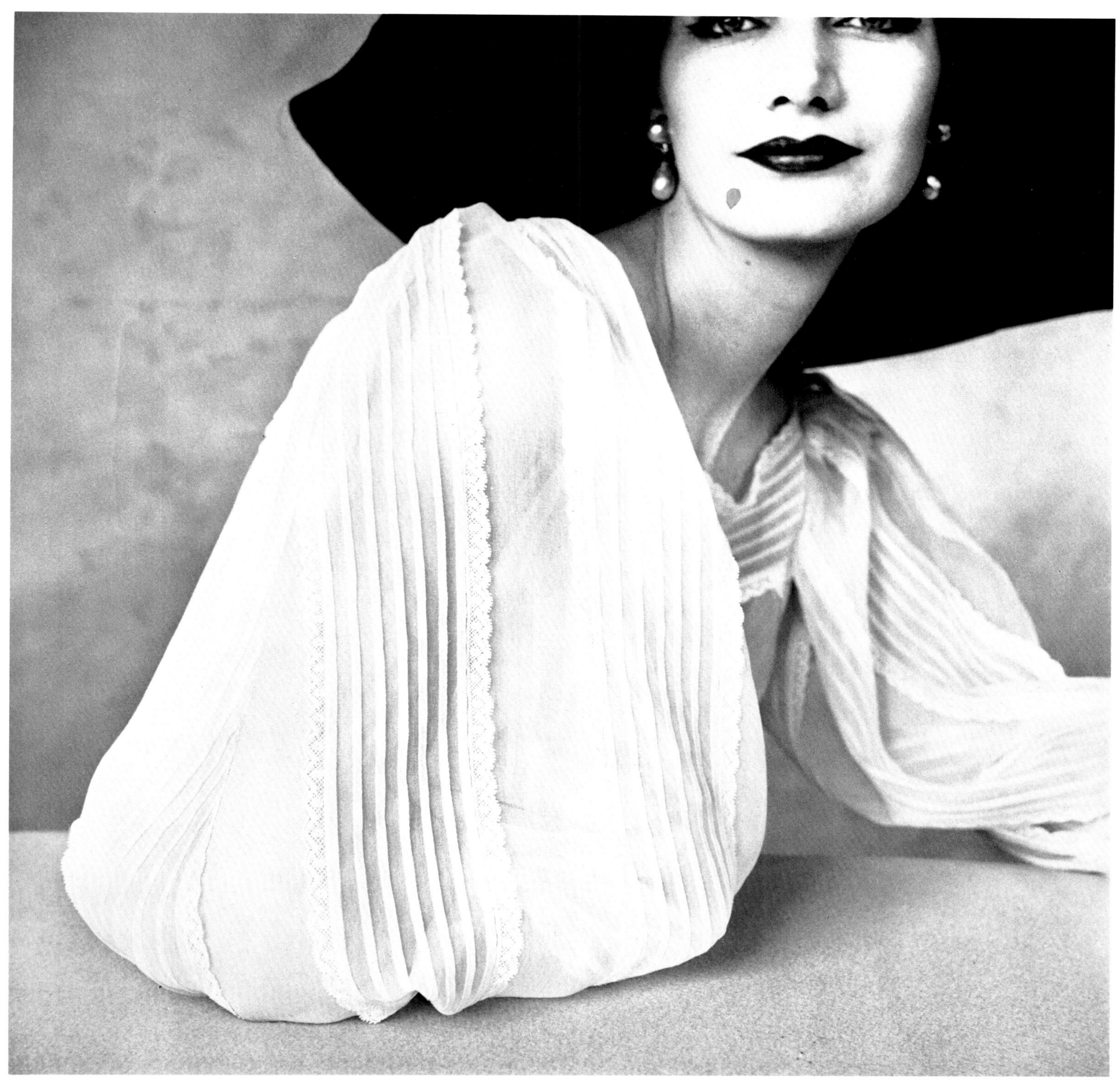

57. Large Sleeve (Sunny Harnett). New York, 1951

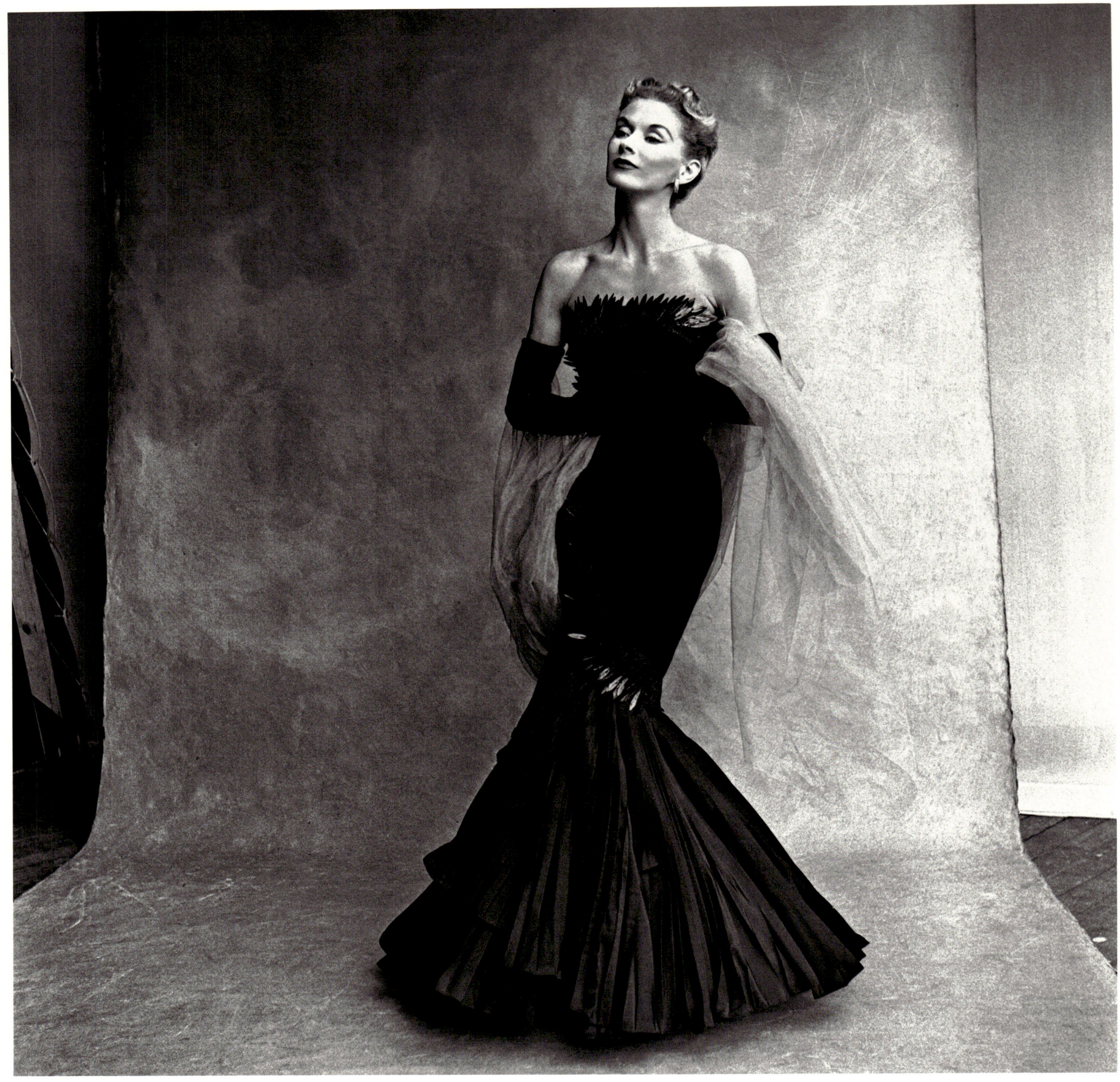

58. **Rochas Mermaid Dress** (Lisa Fonssagrives-Penn). Paris, 1950. Platinum-palladium print, 1979

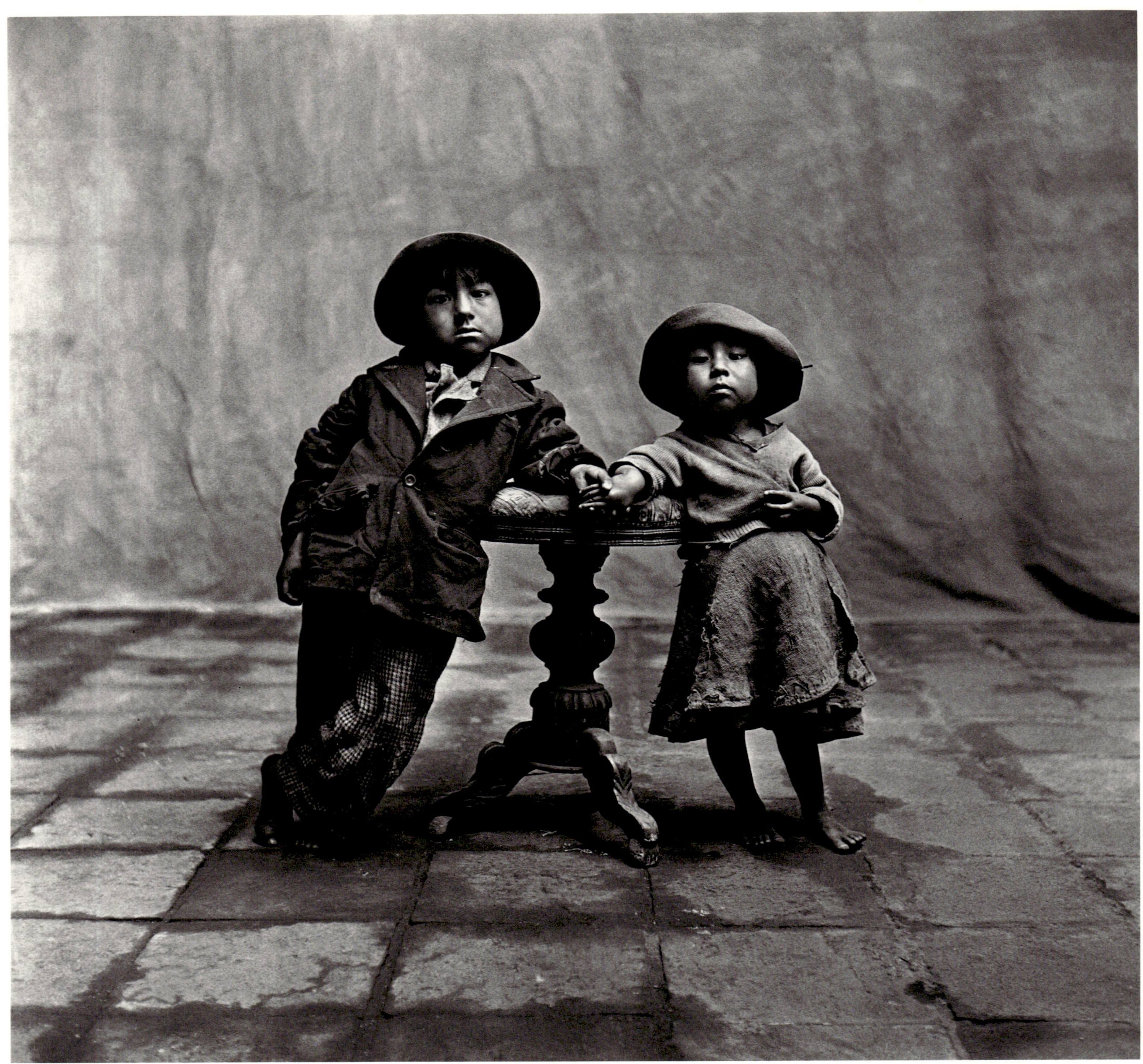

59. **Mountain Children. Cuzco, 1948. Platinum-palladium print, 1976–77**

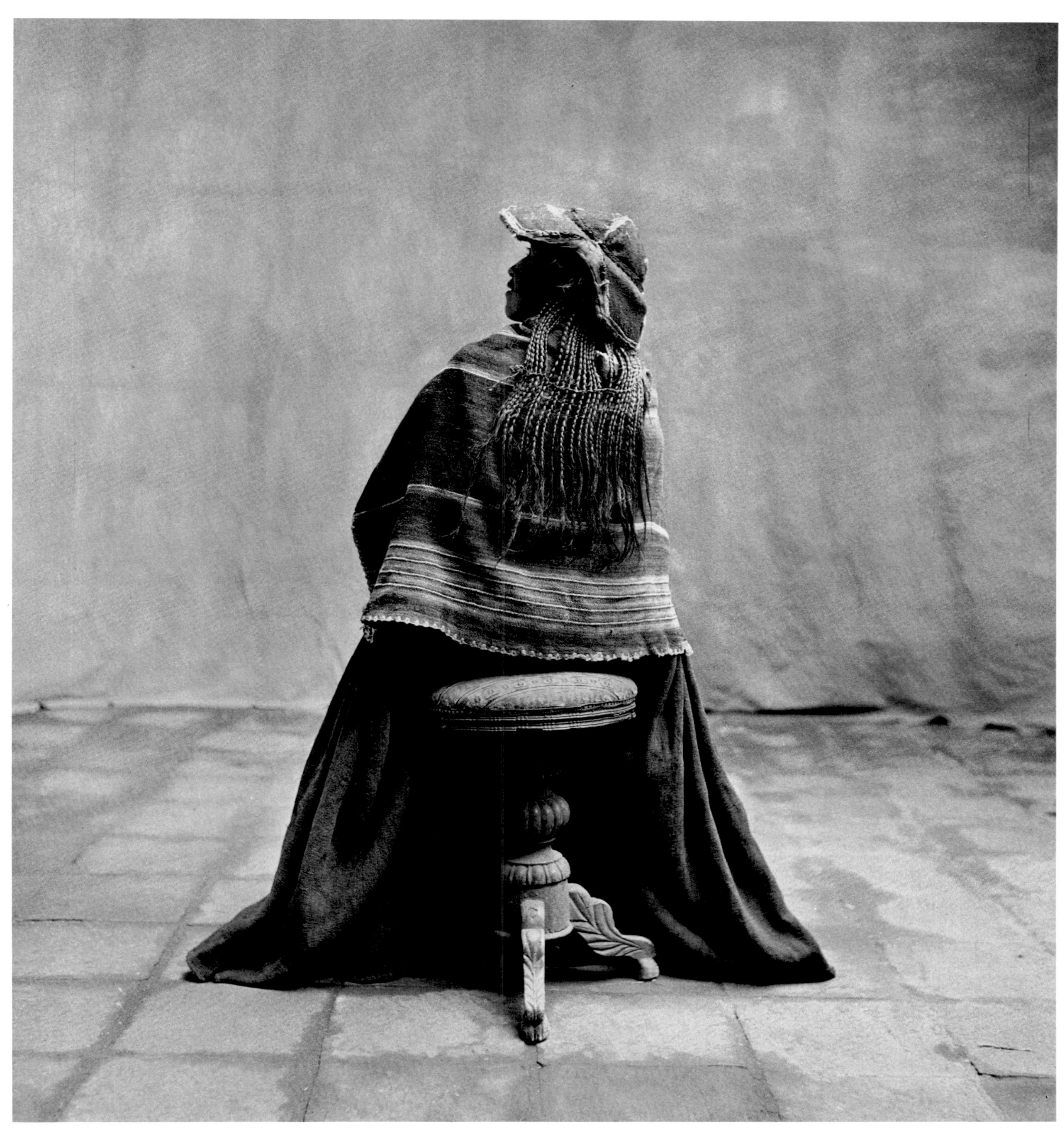

60. Woman with Braided Hair. Cuzco, 1948

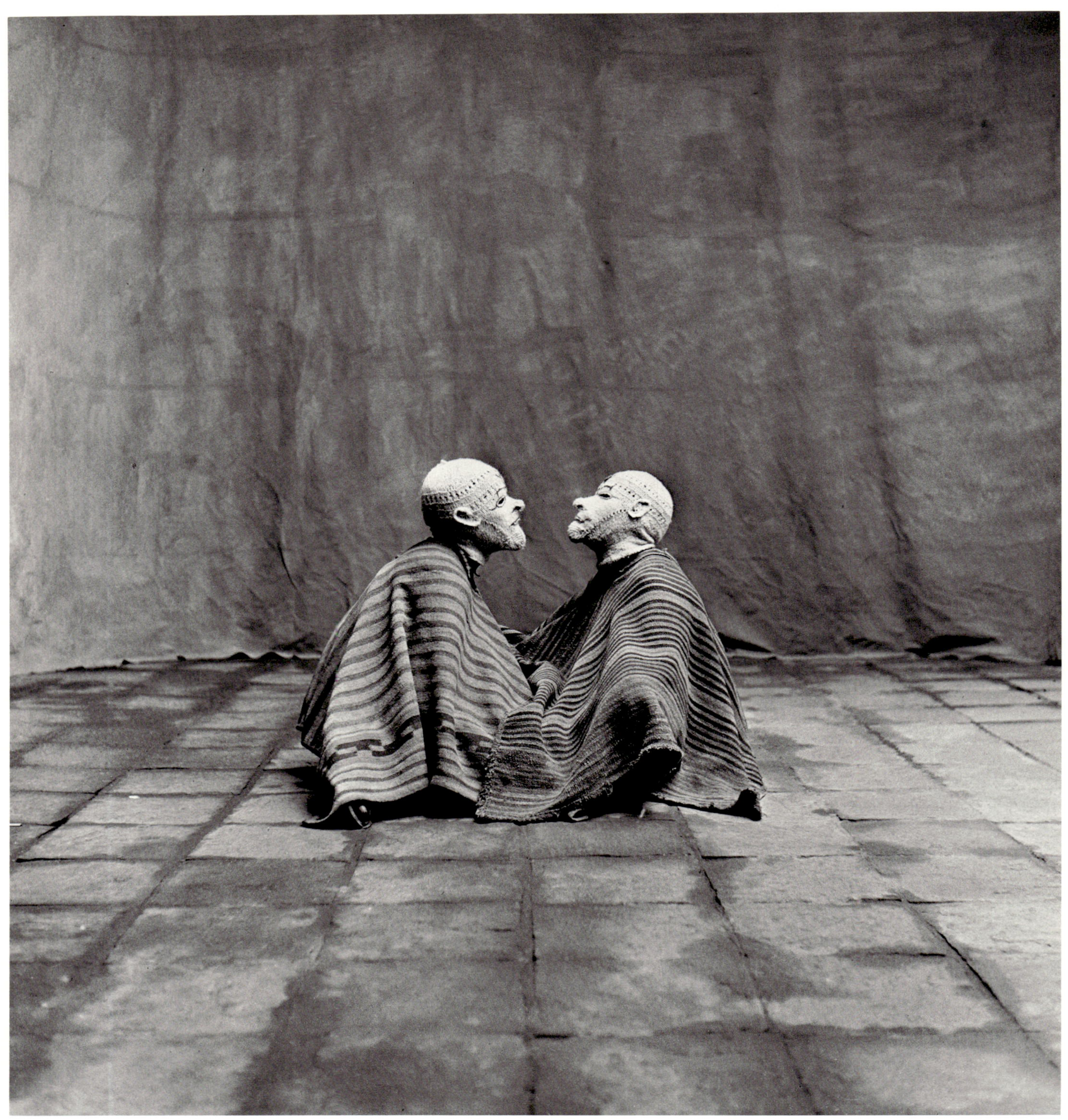

61. Two Men in White Masks. Cuzco, 1948

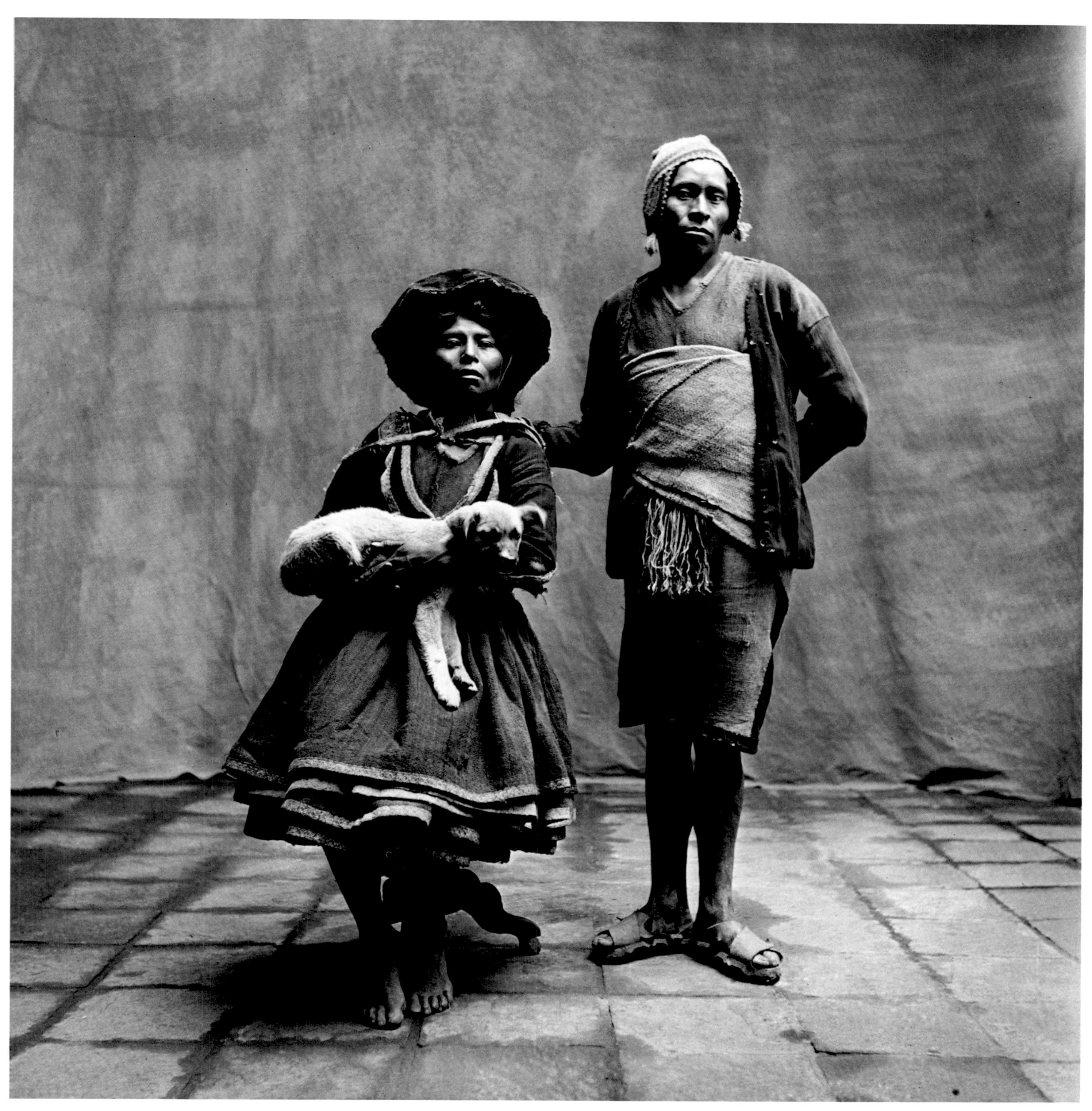

62. **Couple with Dog. Cuzco, 1948**

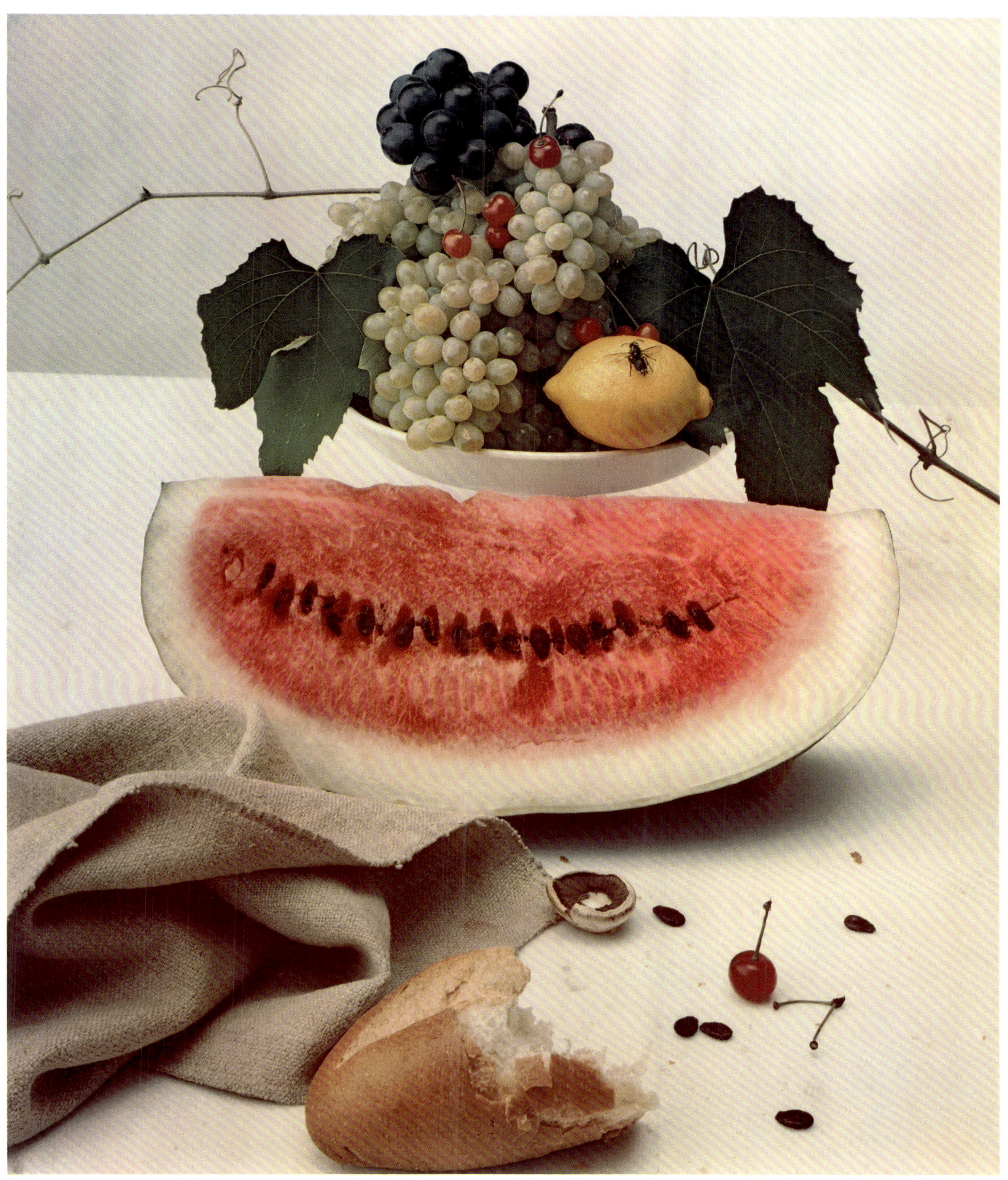

63. **Still Life with Watermelon**. New York, 1947. Dye-transfer print, c. 1959

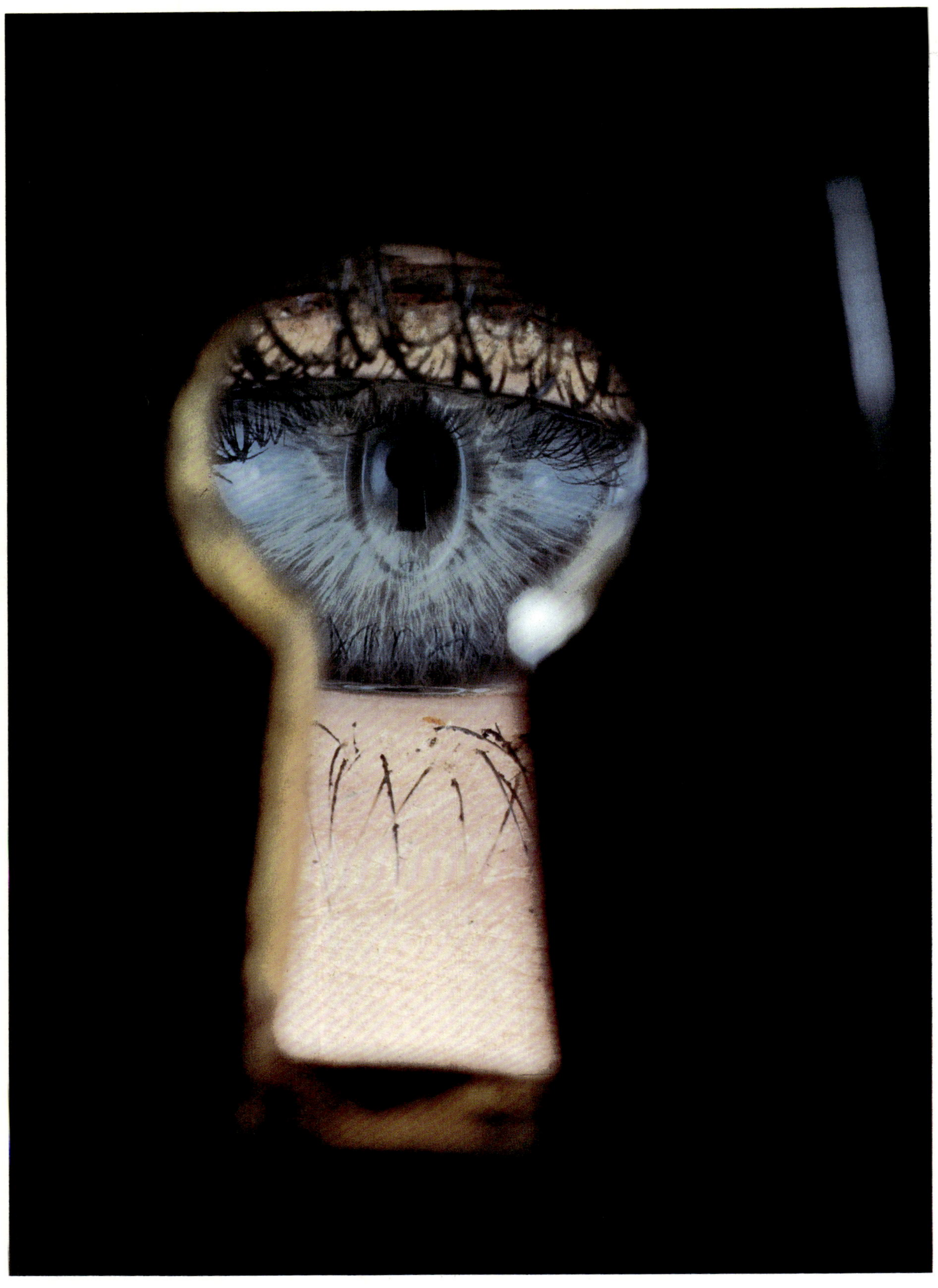

64. Eye in Keyhole. New York, 1953. Reproduced from Kodachrome transparency

65. Faucet Dripping Diamonds. New York, 1963. Reproduced from Kodachrome transparency

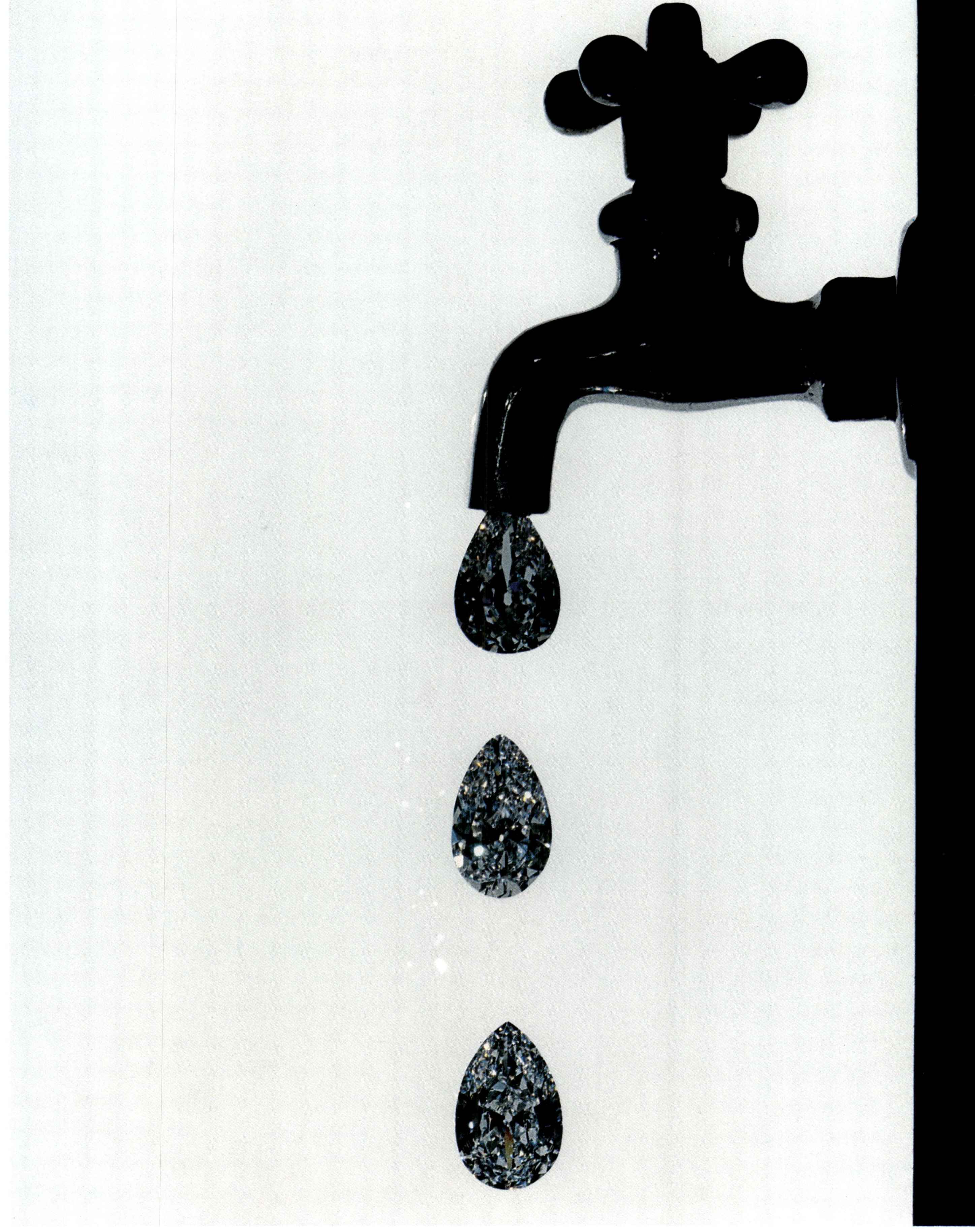

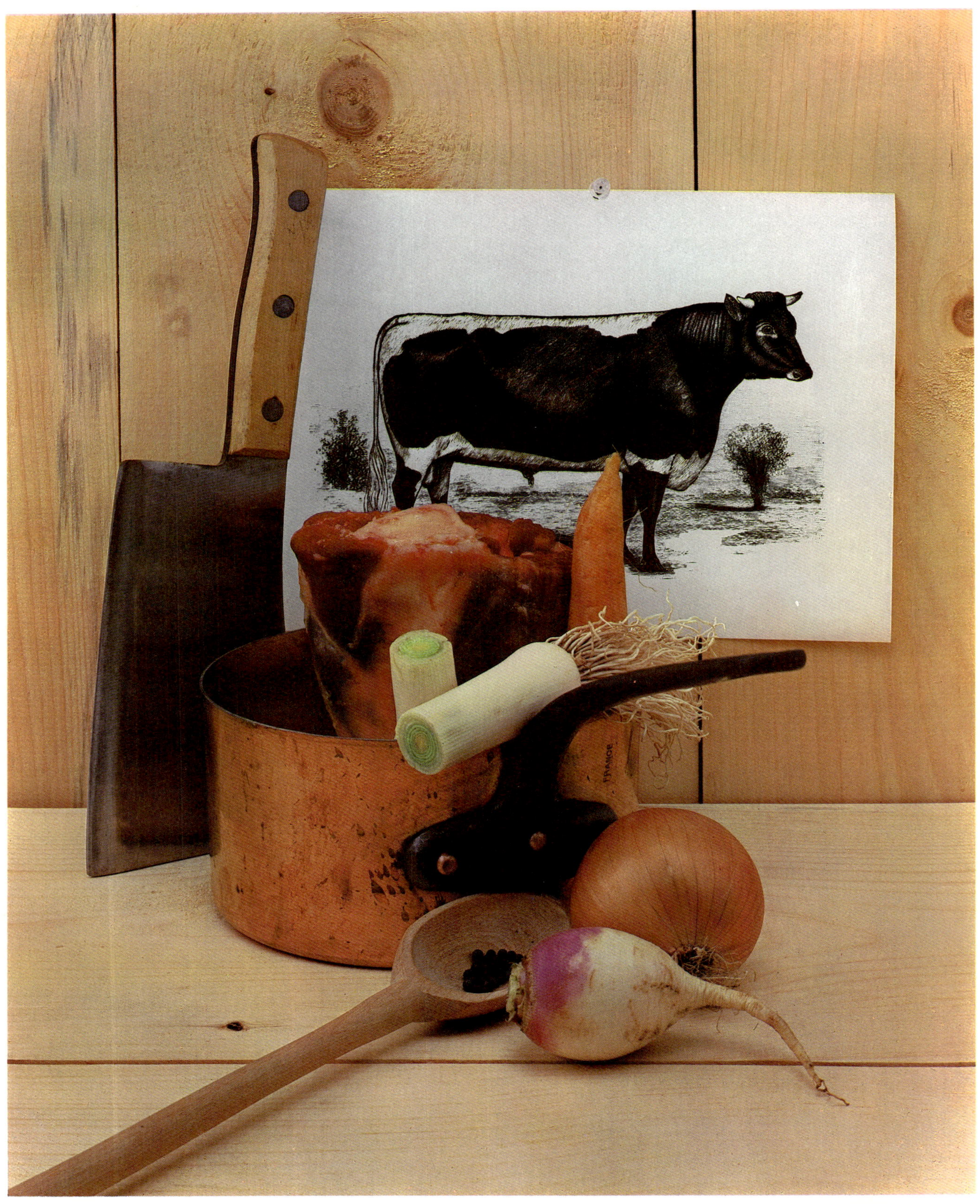

66. **Beef Still Life.** New York, 1943. Dye-transfer print, 1983

67. **Salad Ingredients.** New York, 1947. Reproduced from Kodachrome transparency

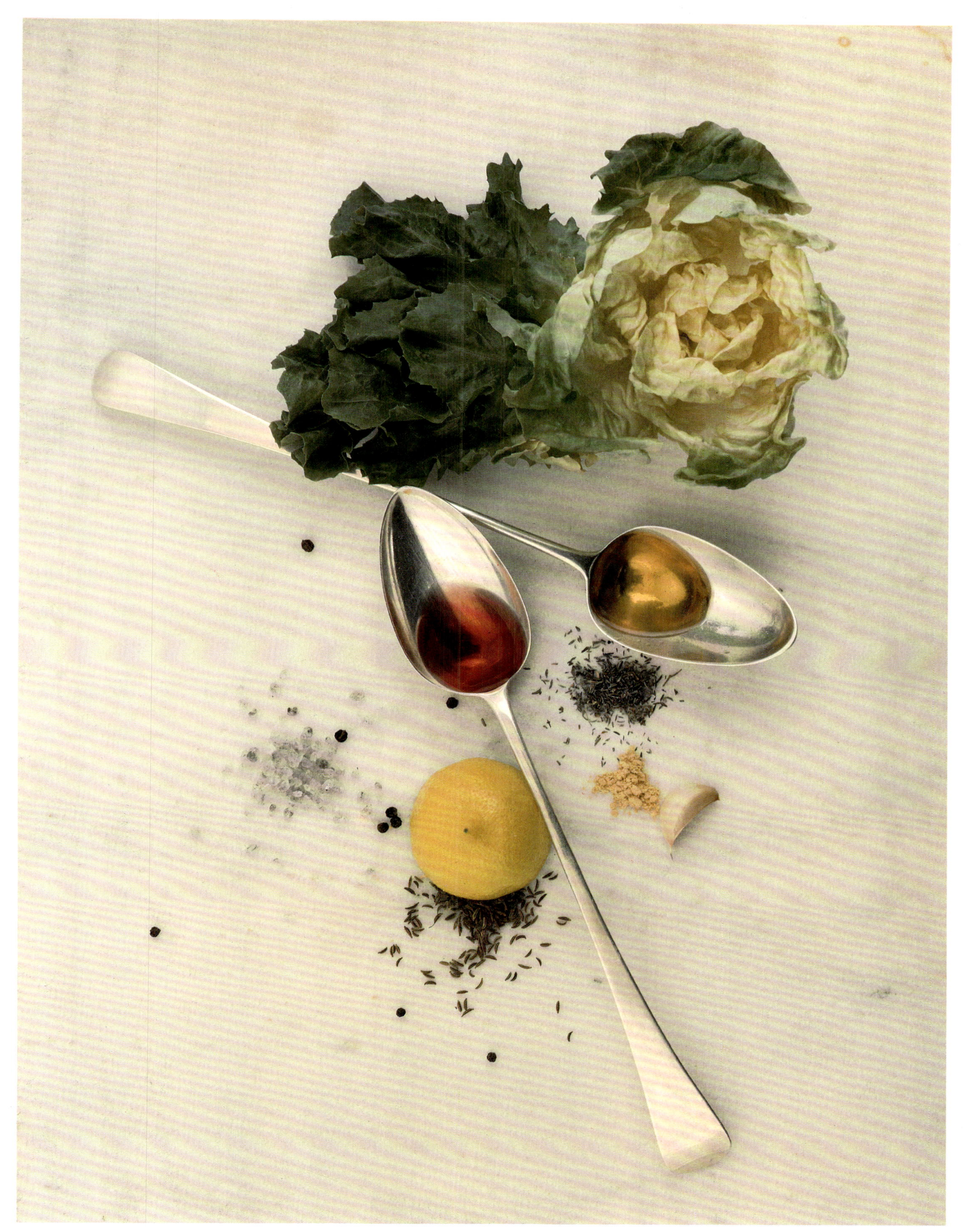

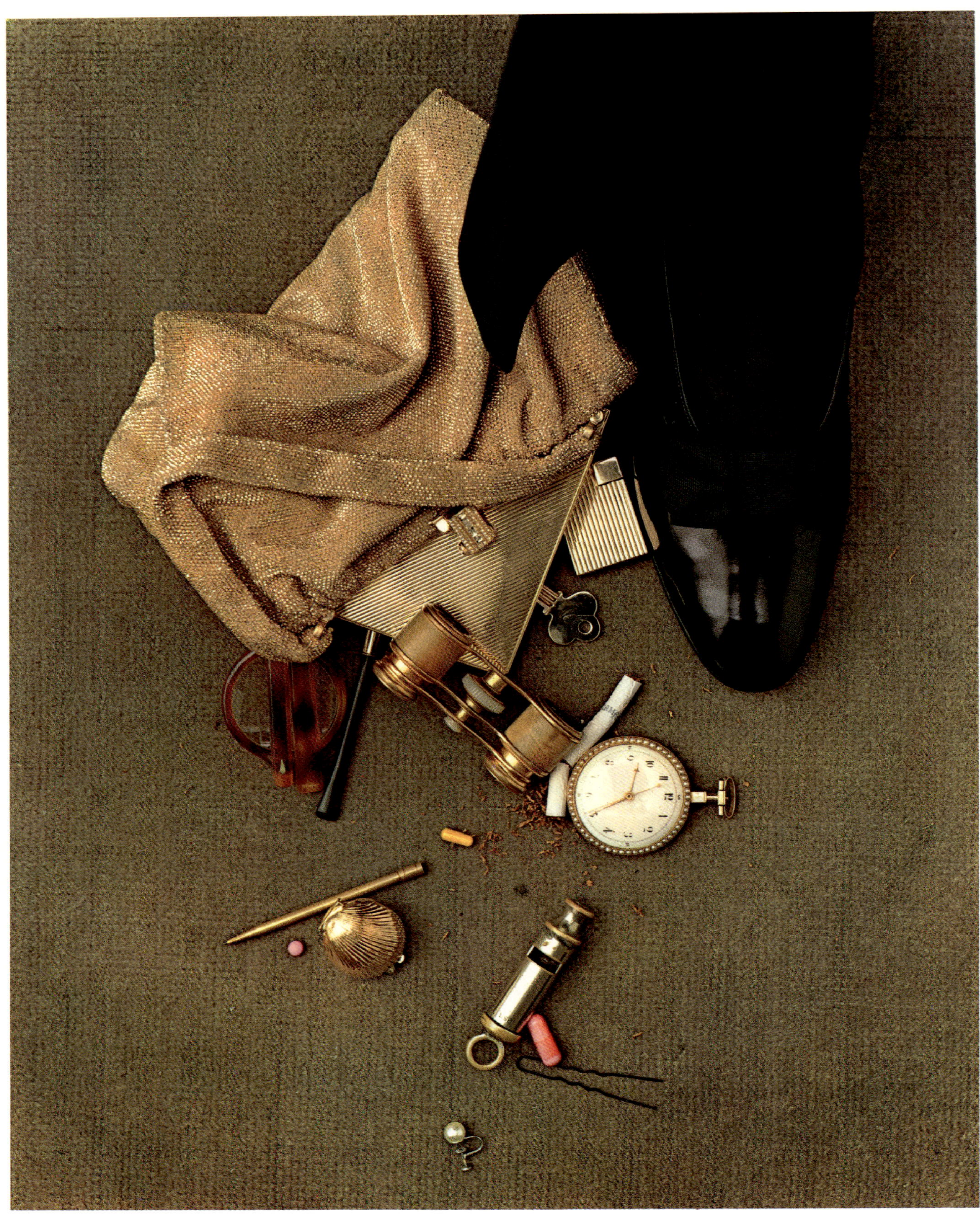

68. **Theater Accident.** New York, 1947. Dye-transfer print, 1984

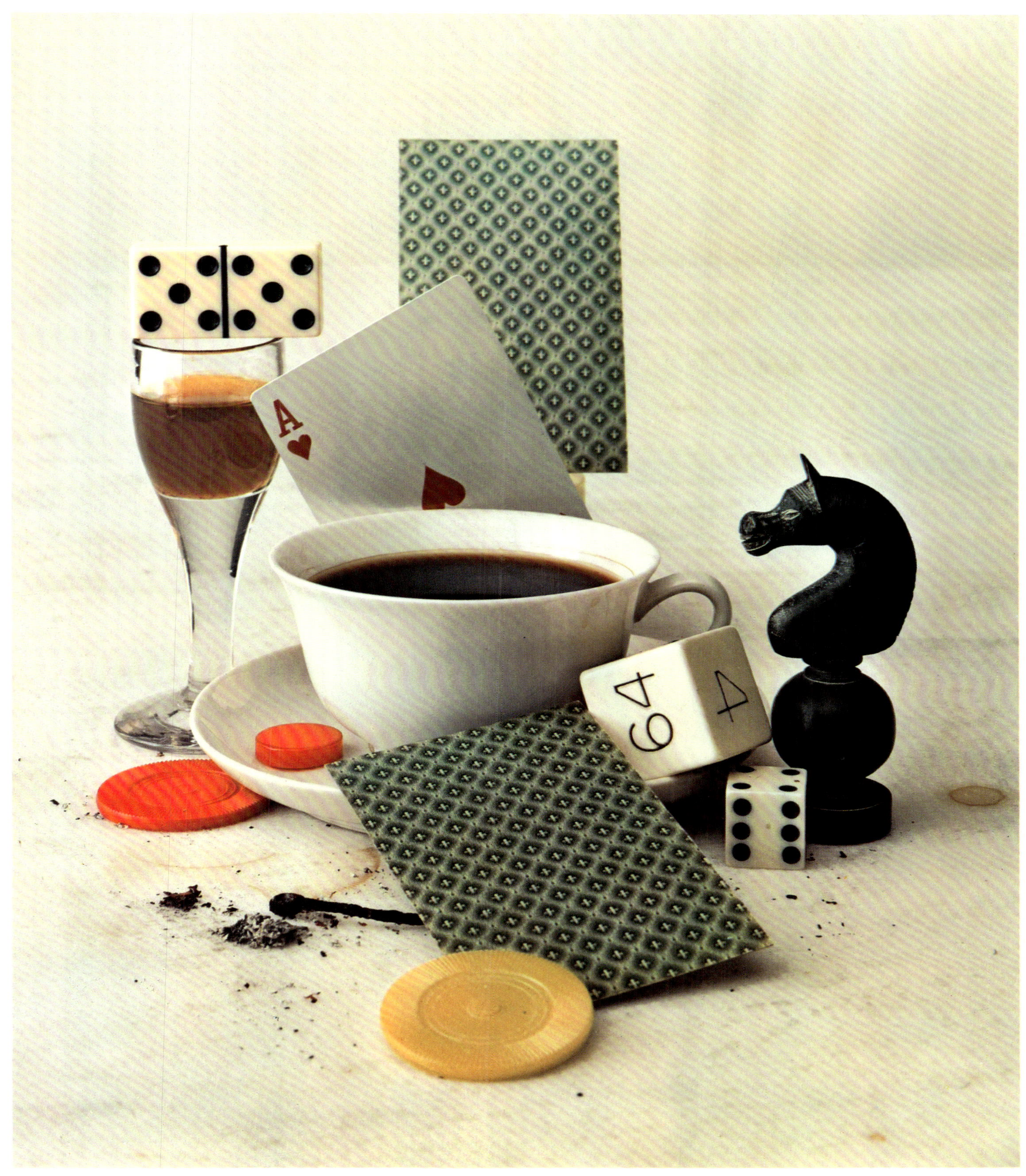

69. **After-dinner Games**. New York, 1947. Dye-transfer print, c. 1959

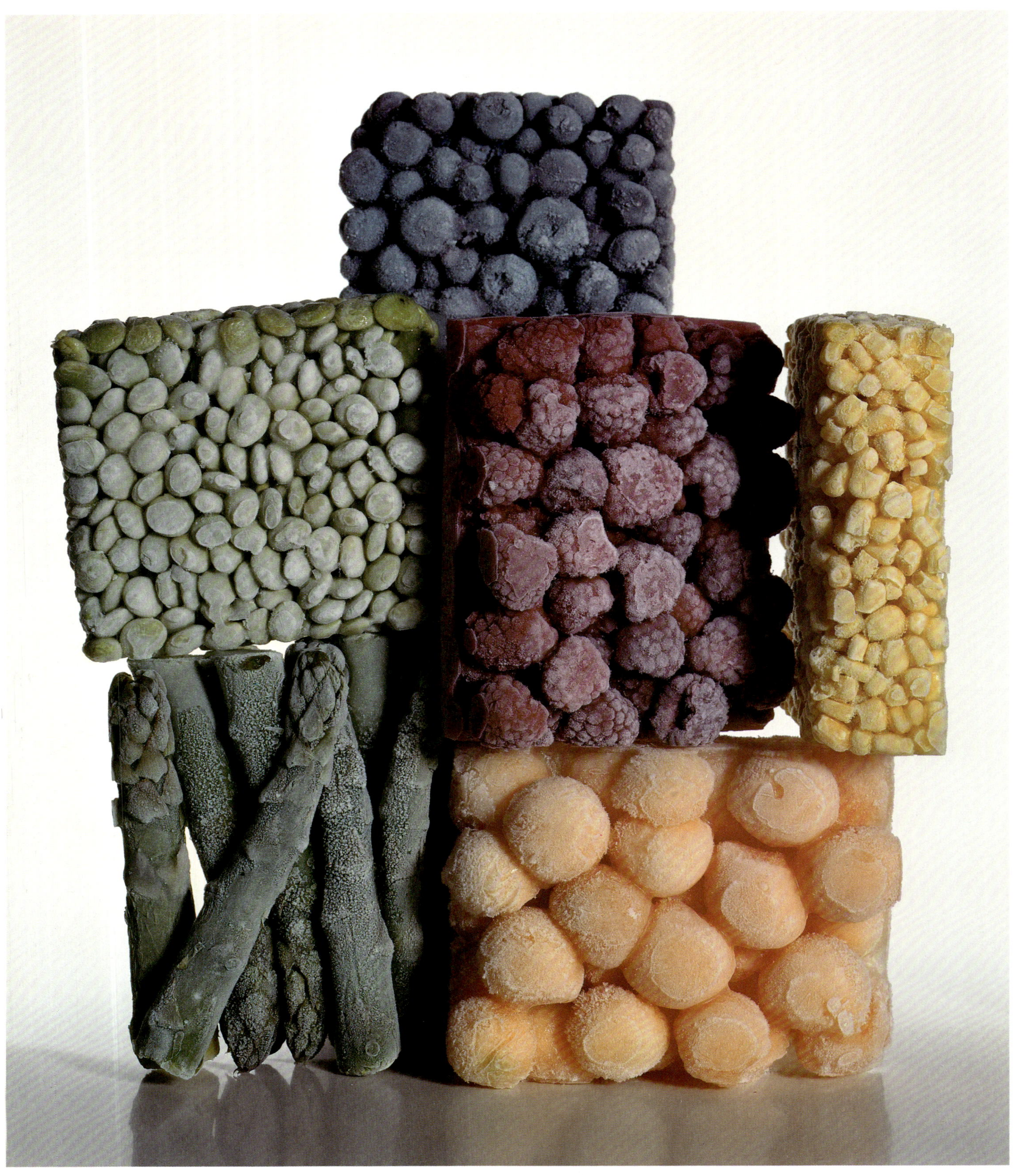

70. **Frozen Foods**. New York, 1977. Reproduced from Ektachrome transparency

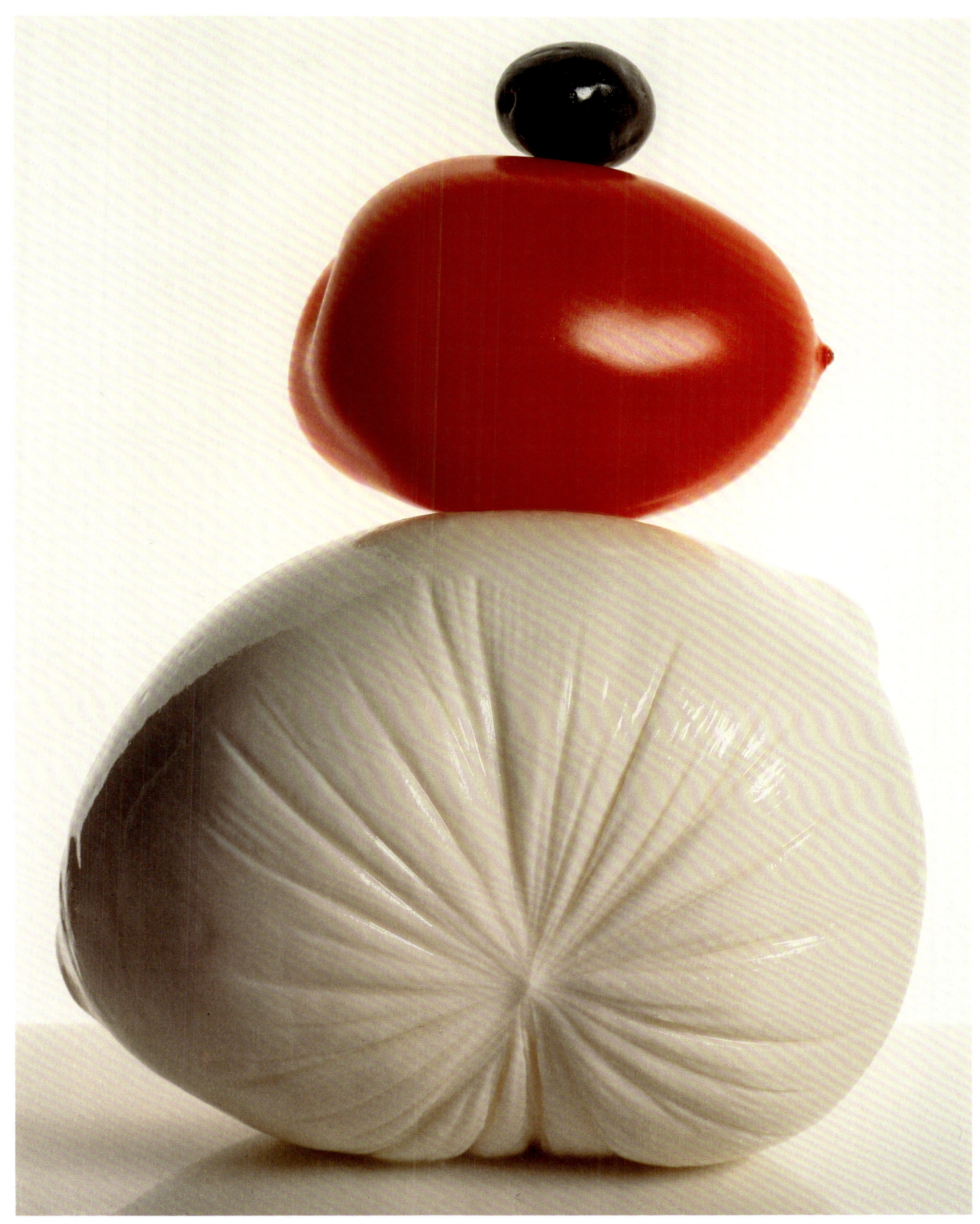

71. Italian Still Life. New York, 1981. Reproduced from Ektachrome transparency

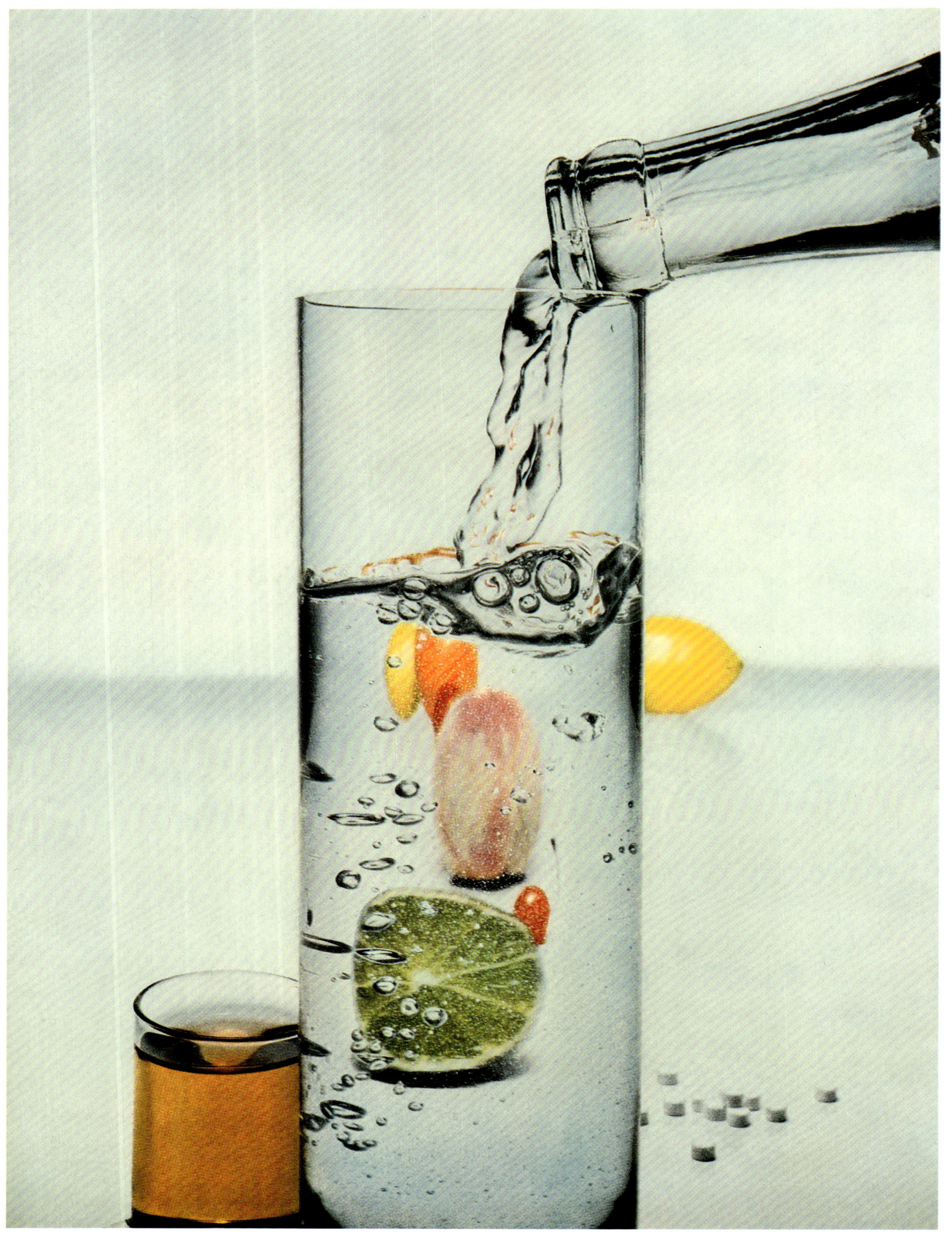

72. Low-calorie Drink. New York, 1953. Reproduced from tear sheet

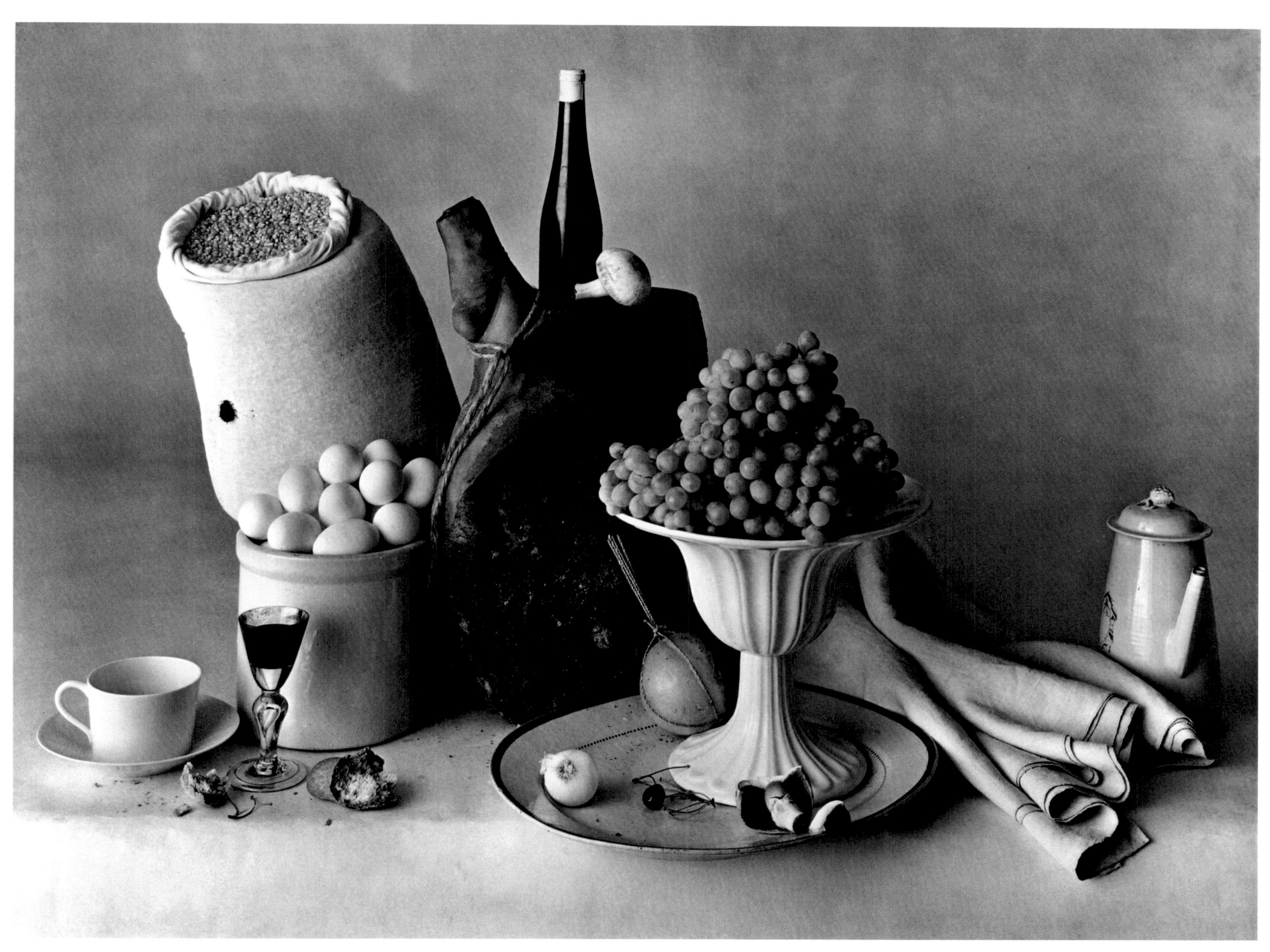

73. Still Life with Food. New York, 1947. Platinum-palladium print, 1978

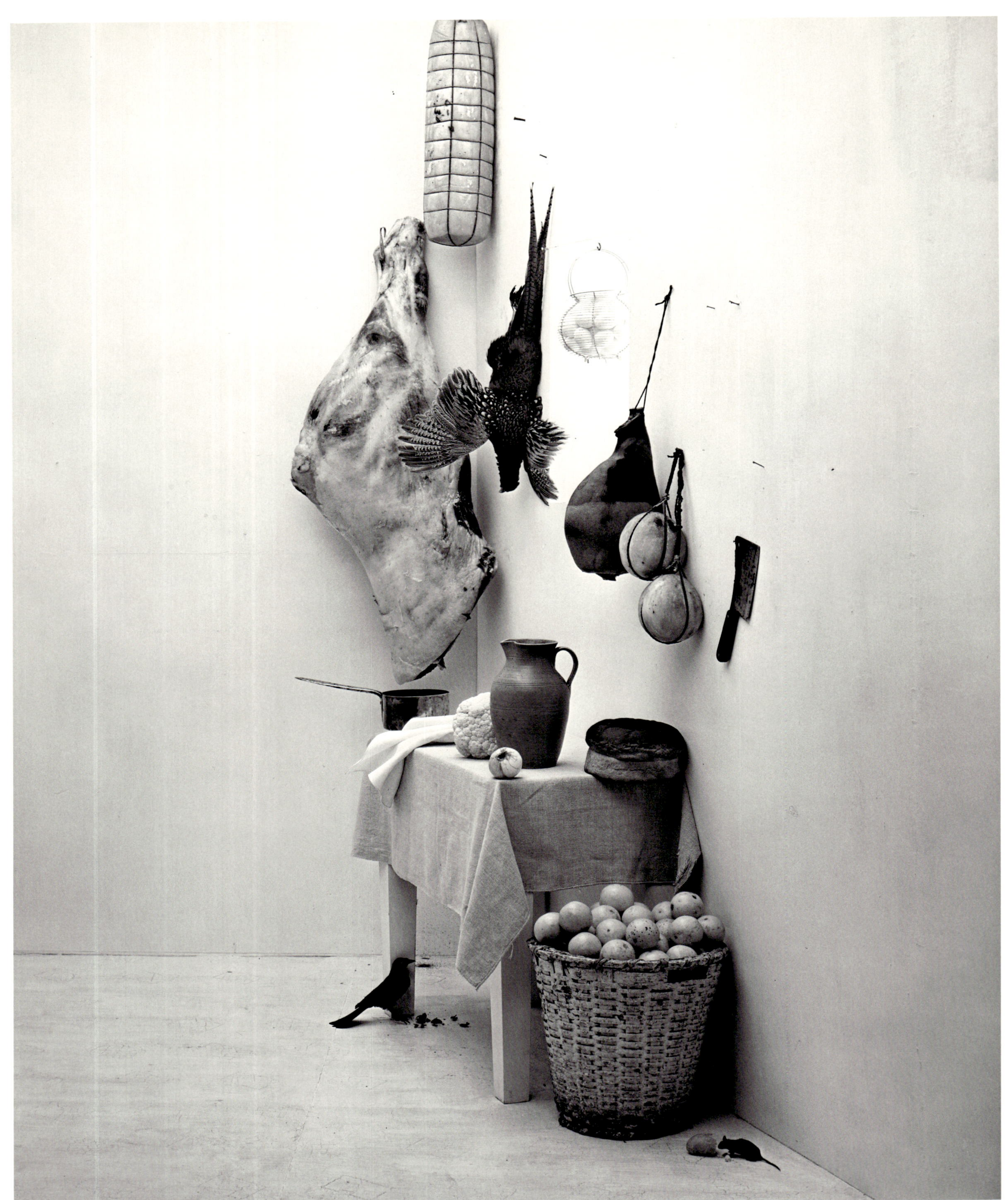

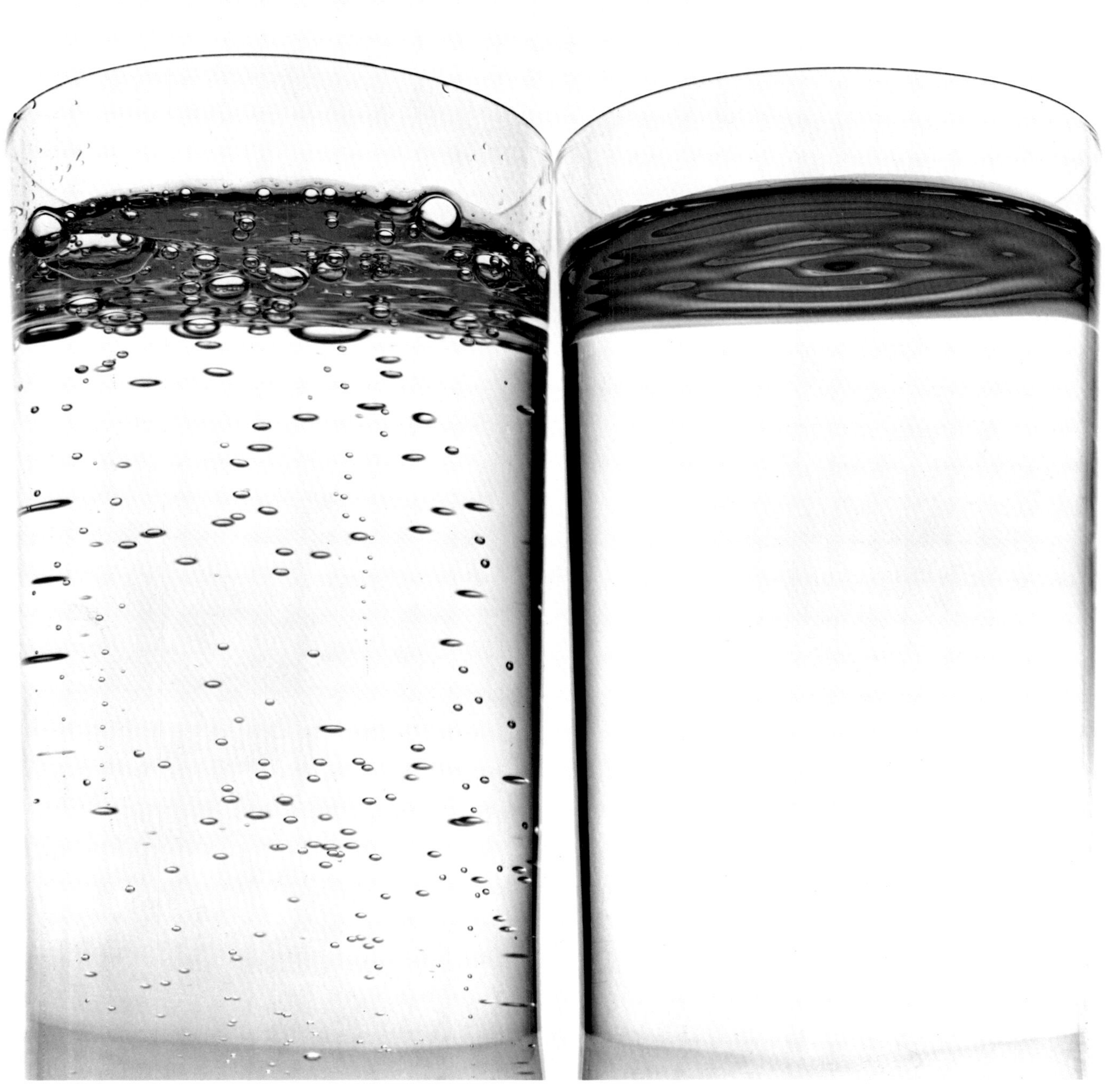

74. Vermeer Still Life (with Mouse). New York, 1947

75. Two Glasses of Water. New York, 1970

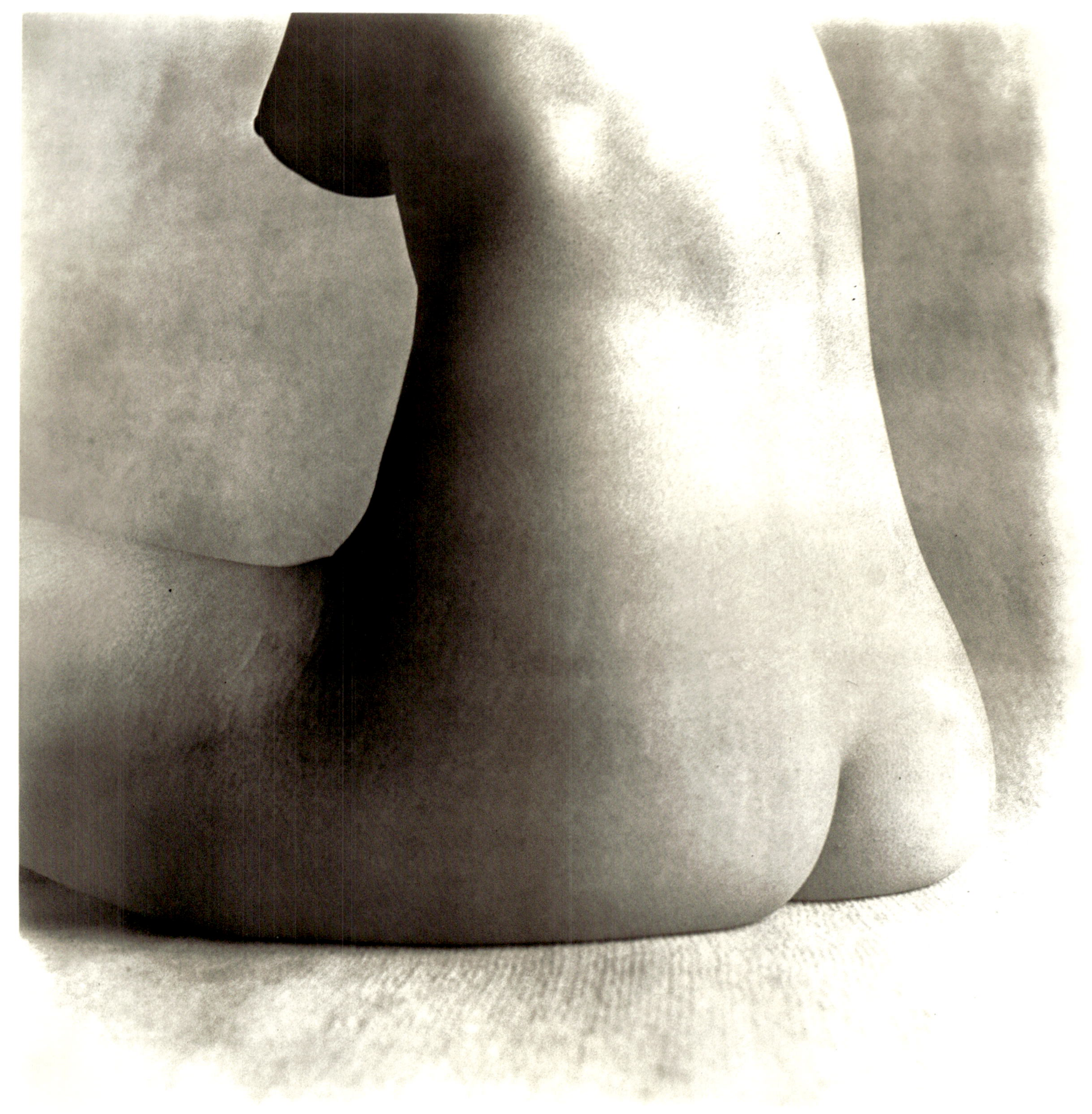

76. Nude 16. New York, 1949–50

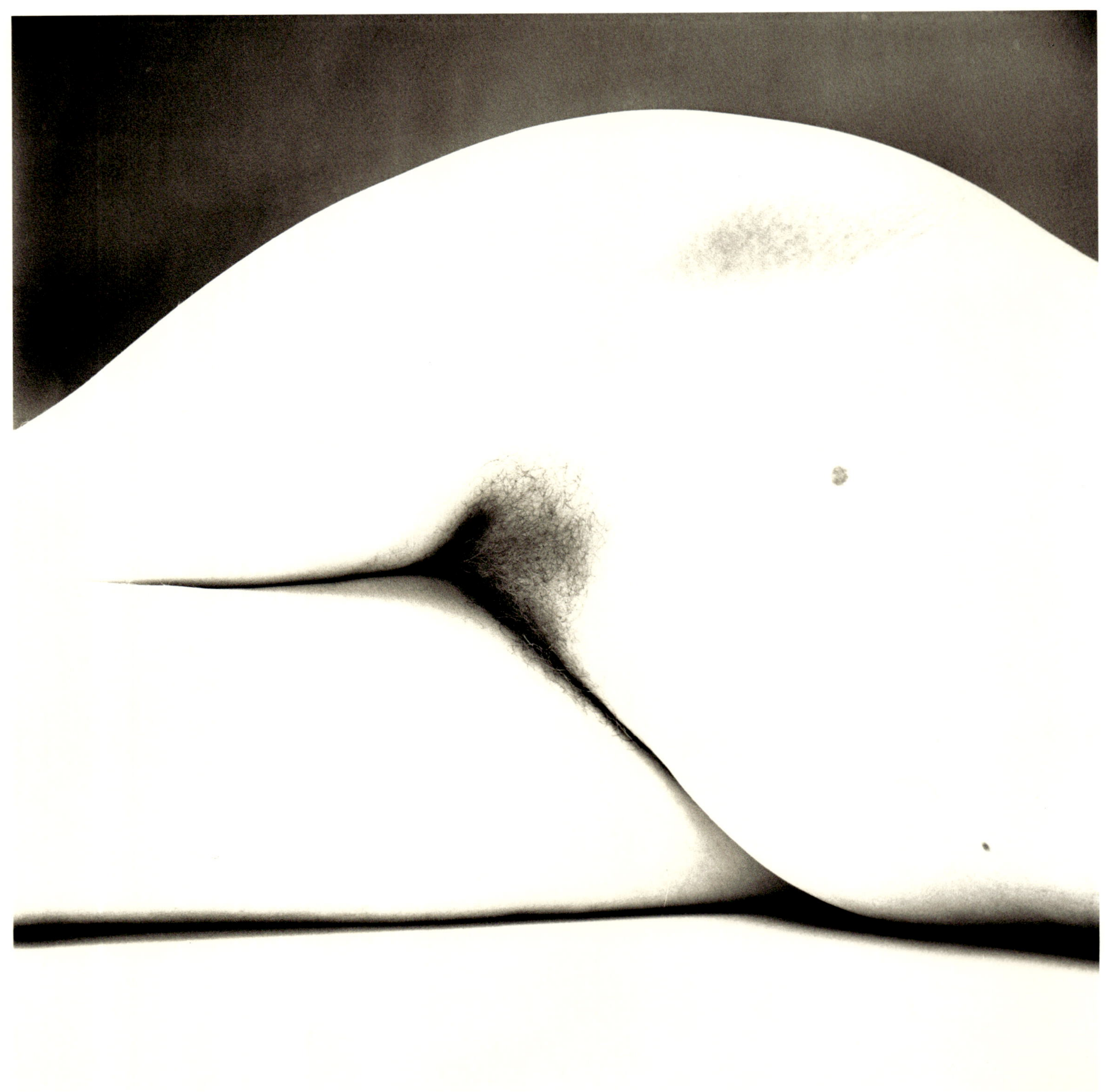

77. **Nude 65**. New York, 1949–50

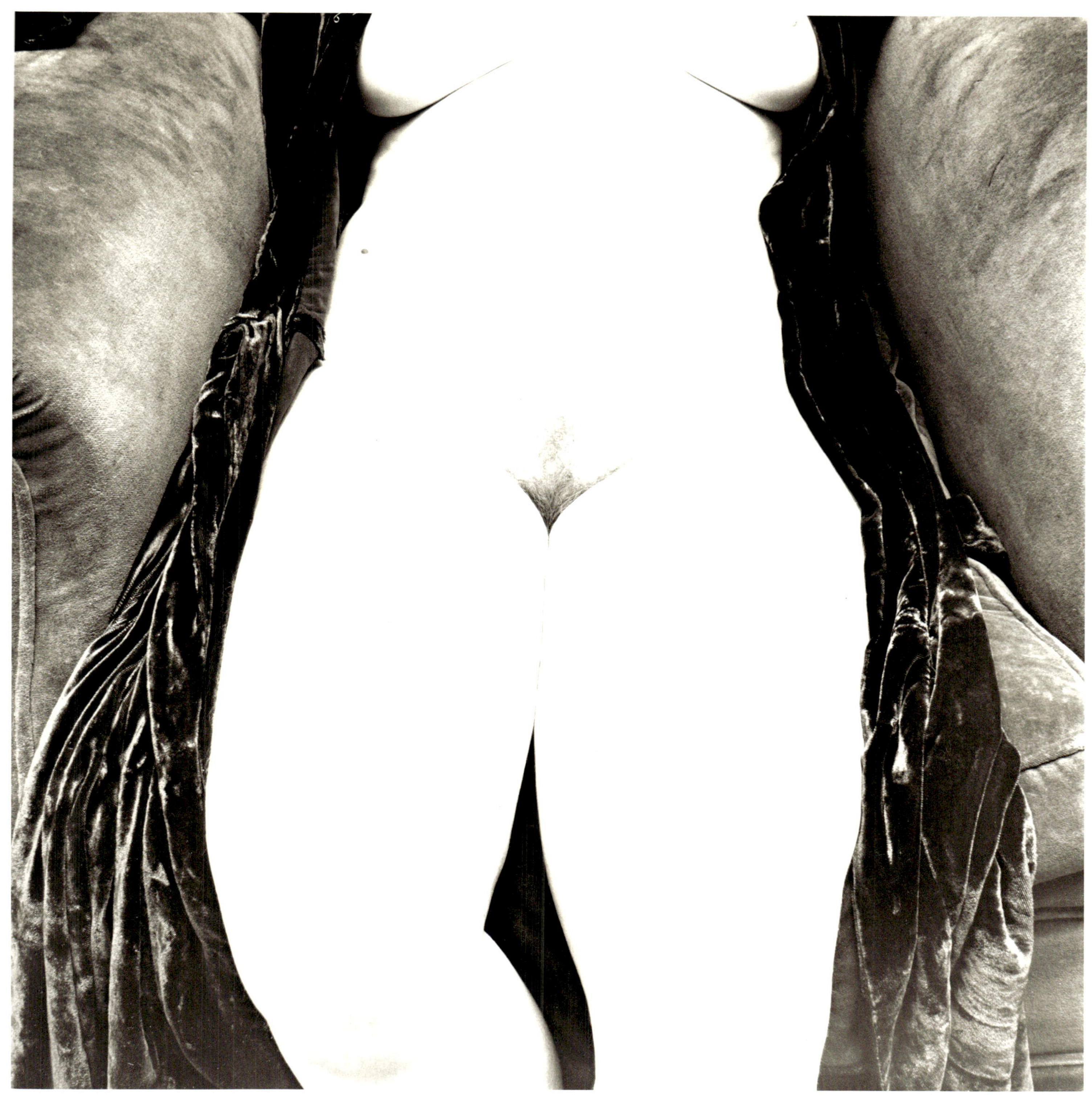

78. **Nude 119**. New York, 1949–50

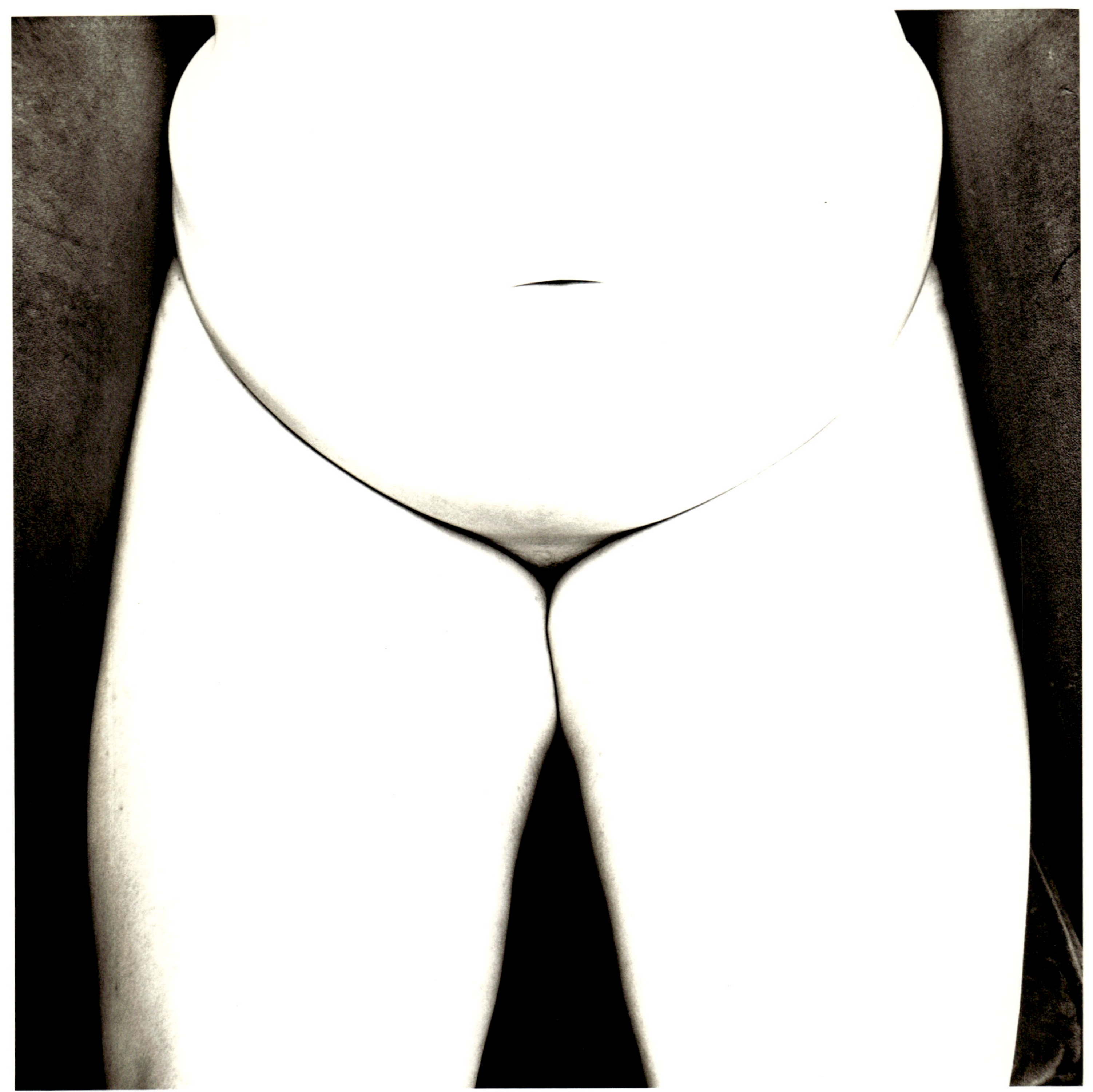

79. **Nude 92**. New York, 1949–50

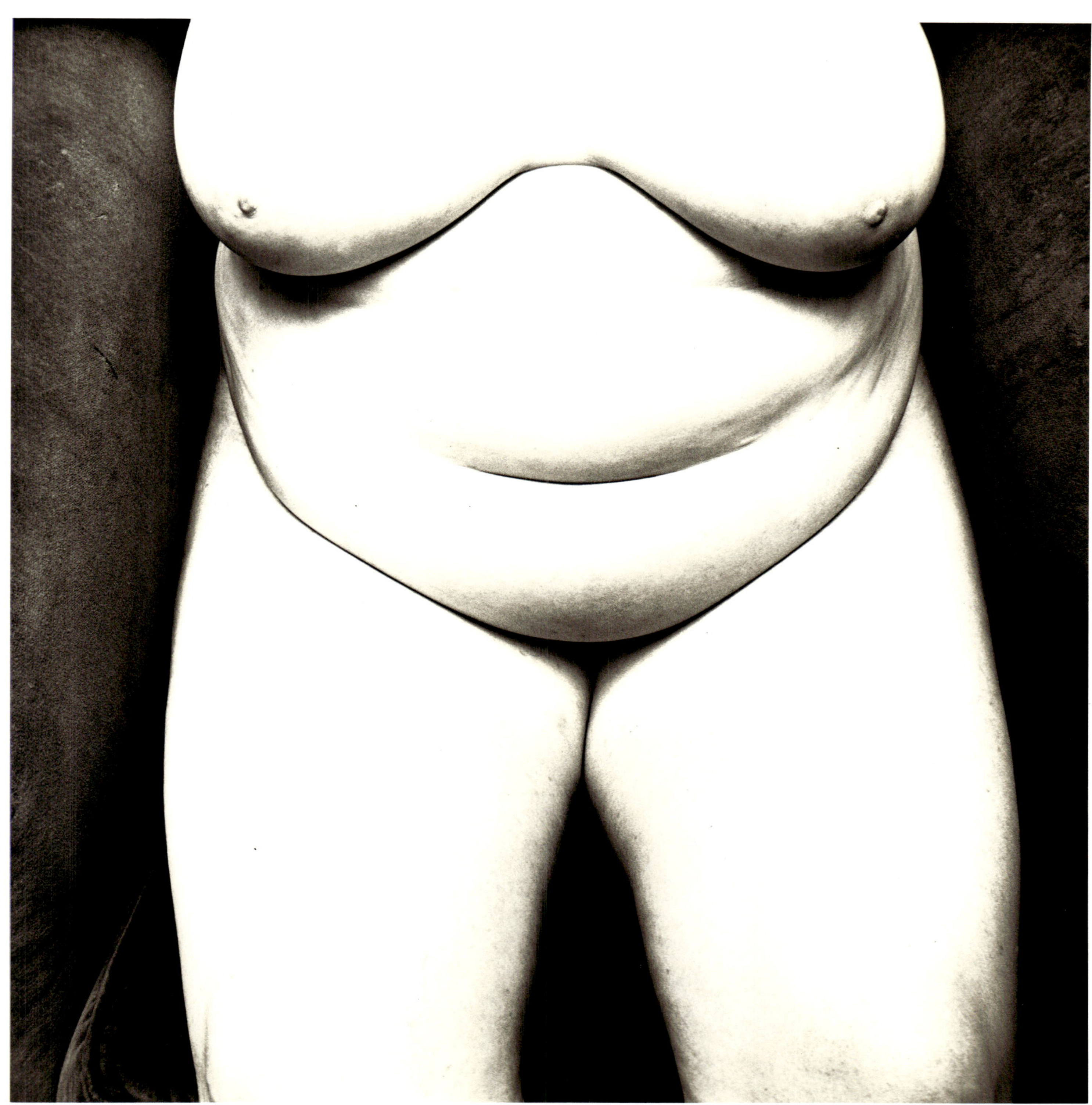

30. **Nude 89**. New York, 1949–50

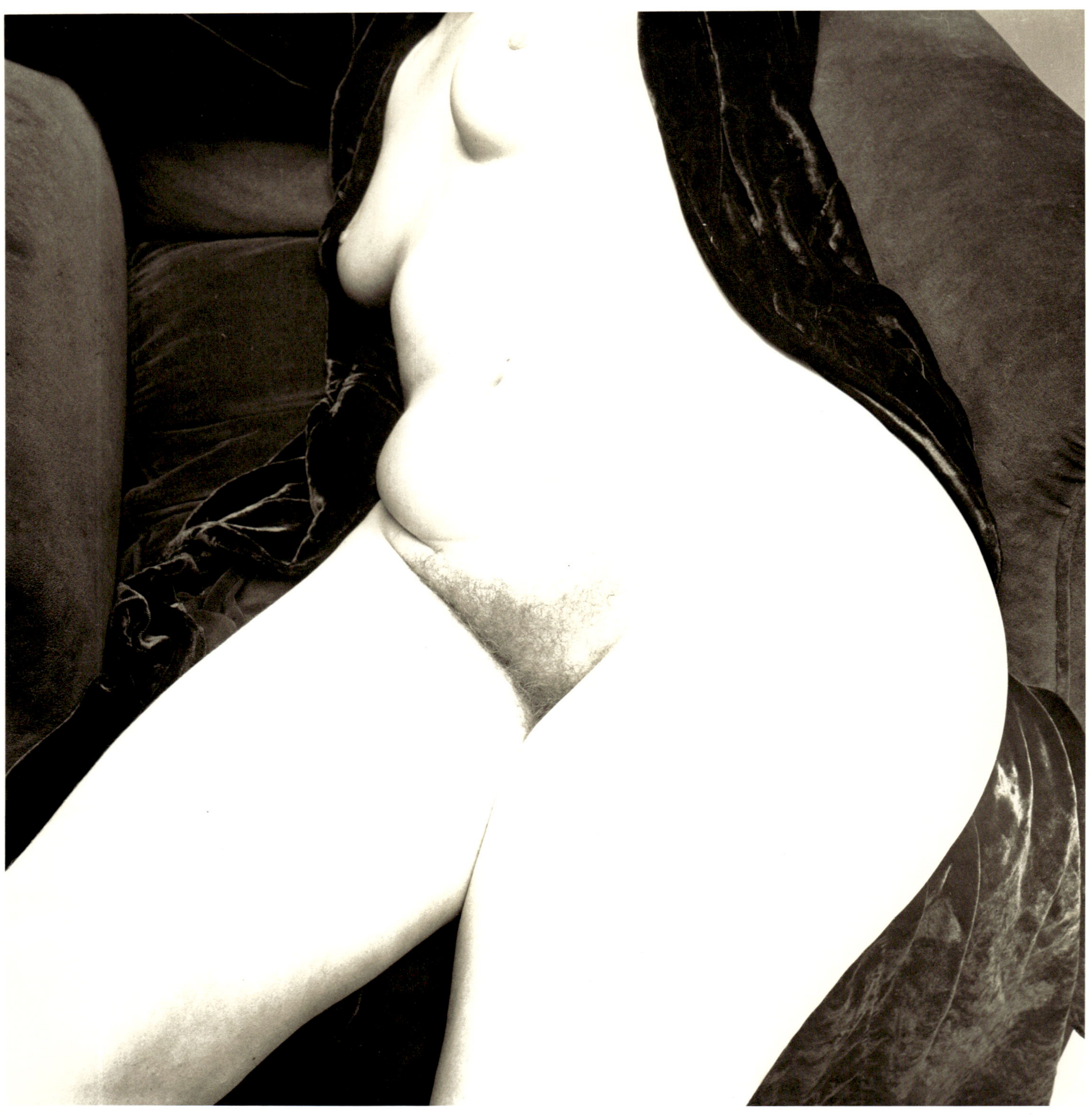

81. Nude 130. New York, 1949–50

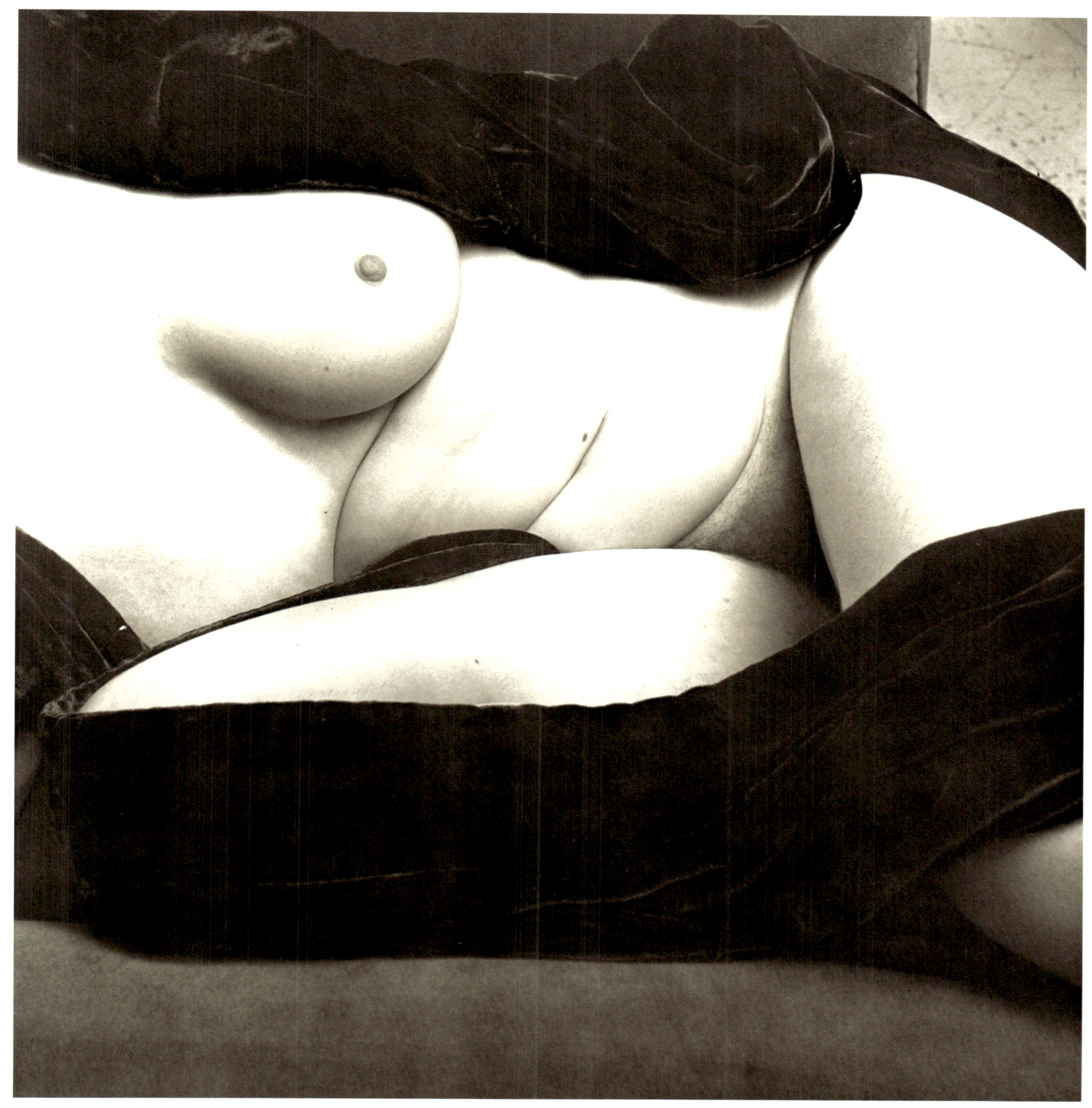

82. Nude 140. New York, 1949–50

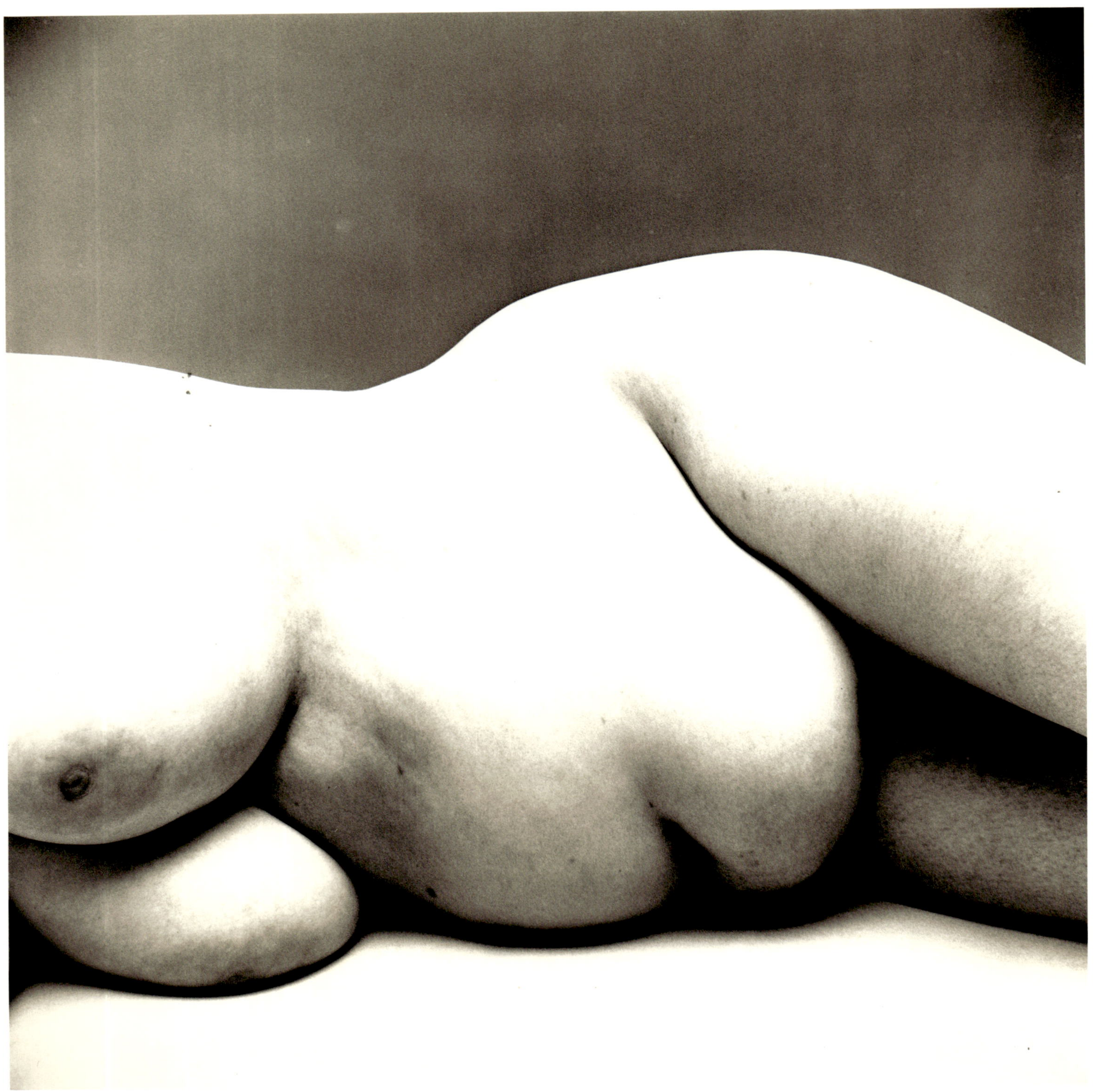

83. Nude 99. New York, 1949–50

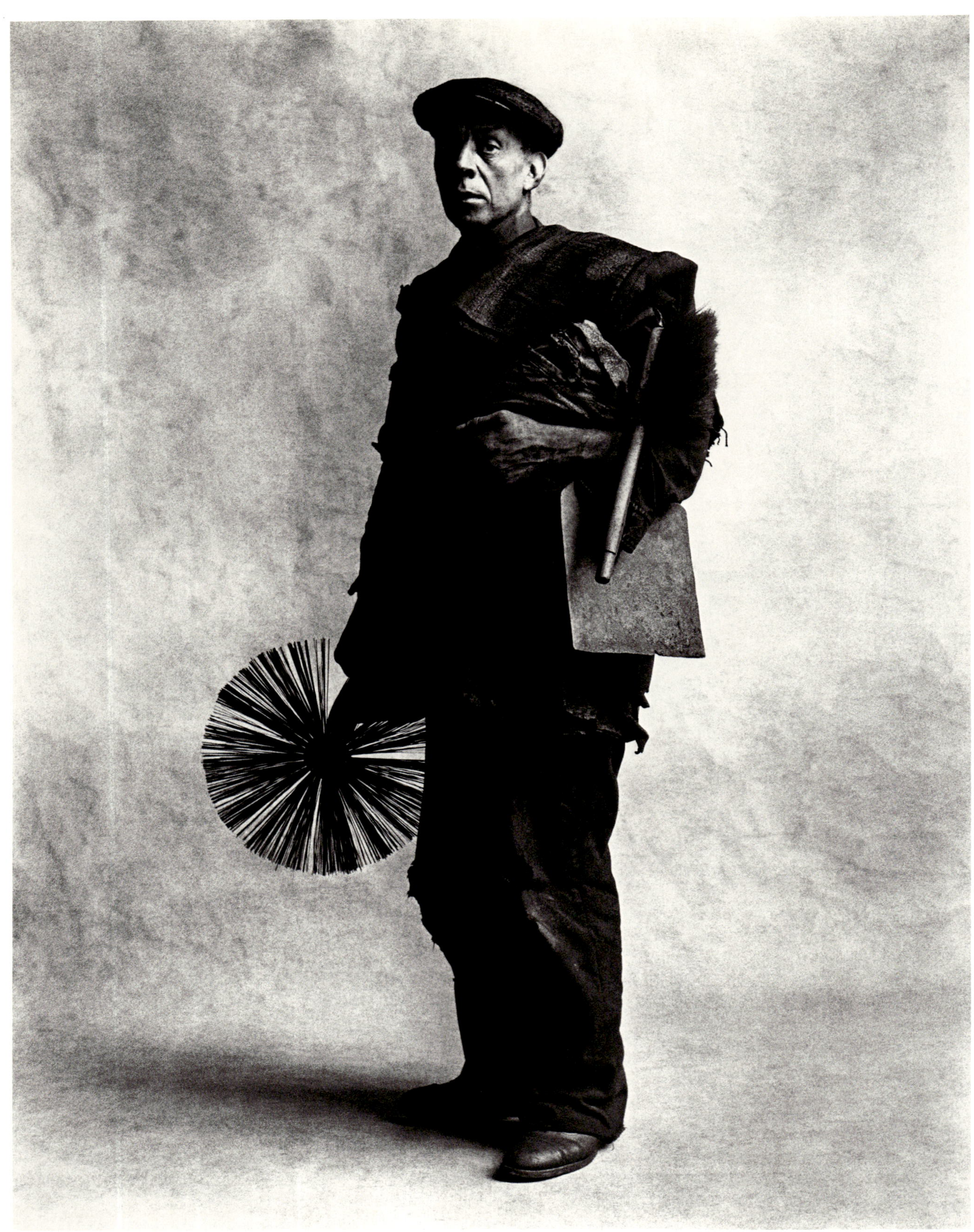

84. **Chimney Sweep**. London, 1950. Platinum-palladium print, 1976

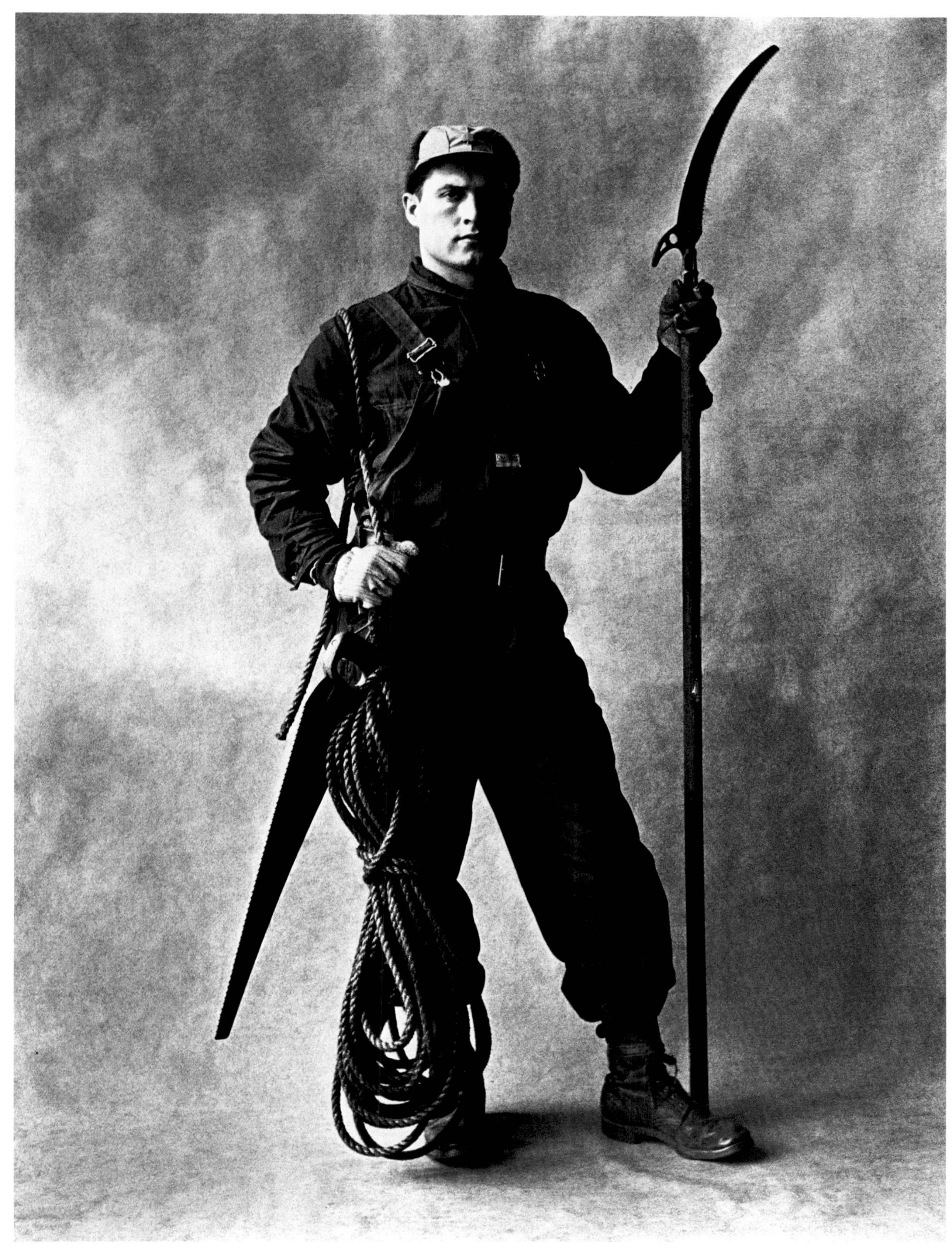

85. **Tree Pruner**. New York, 1951. Platinum-palladium print, 1972

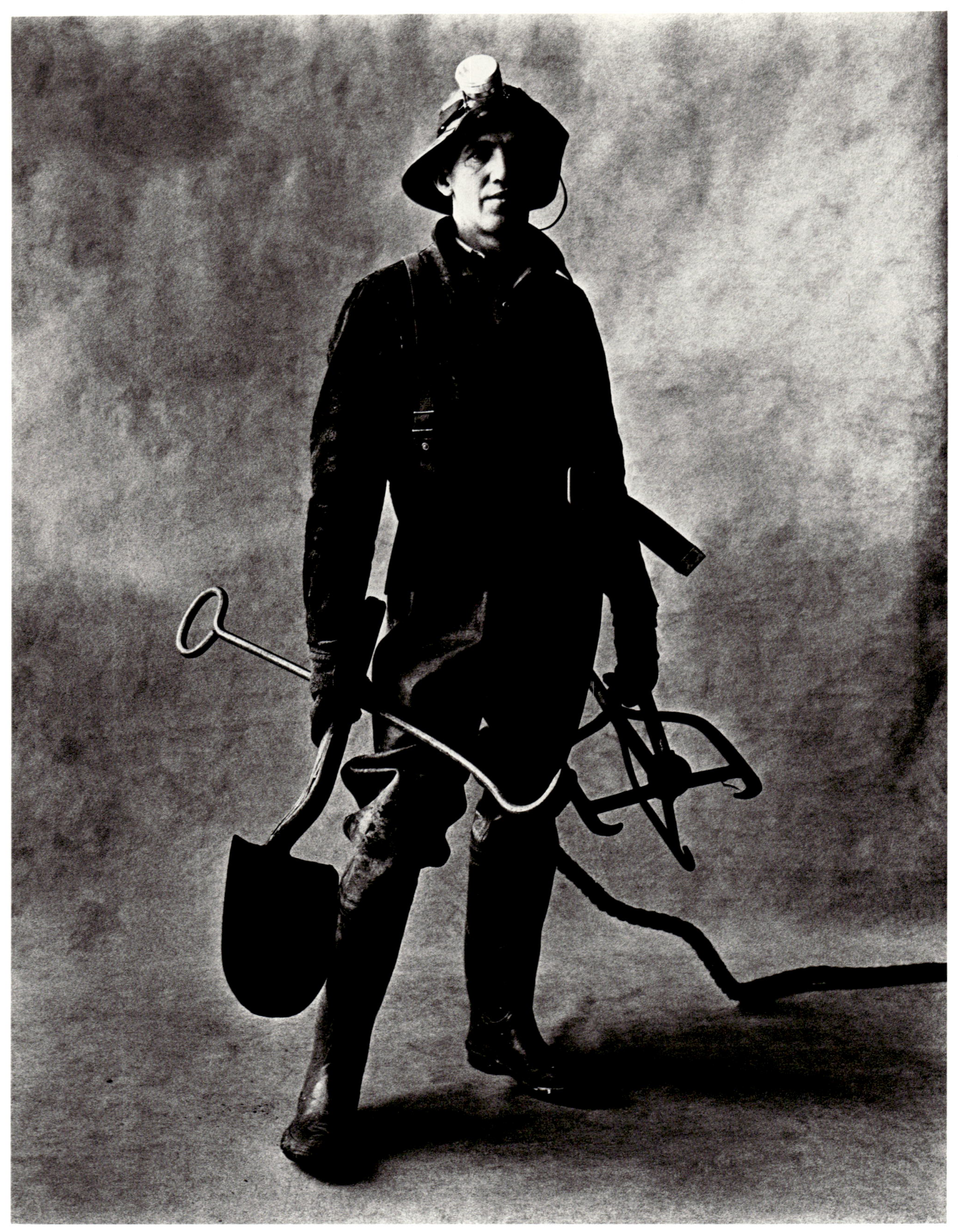

86. **Sewer Cleaner**. New York, 1951. Platinum-palladium print, 1976

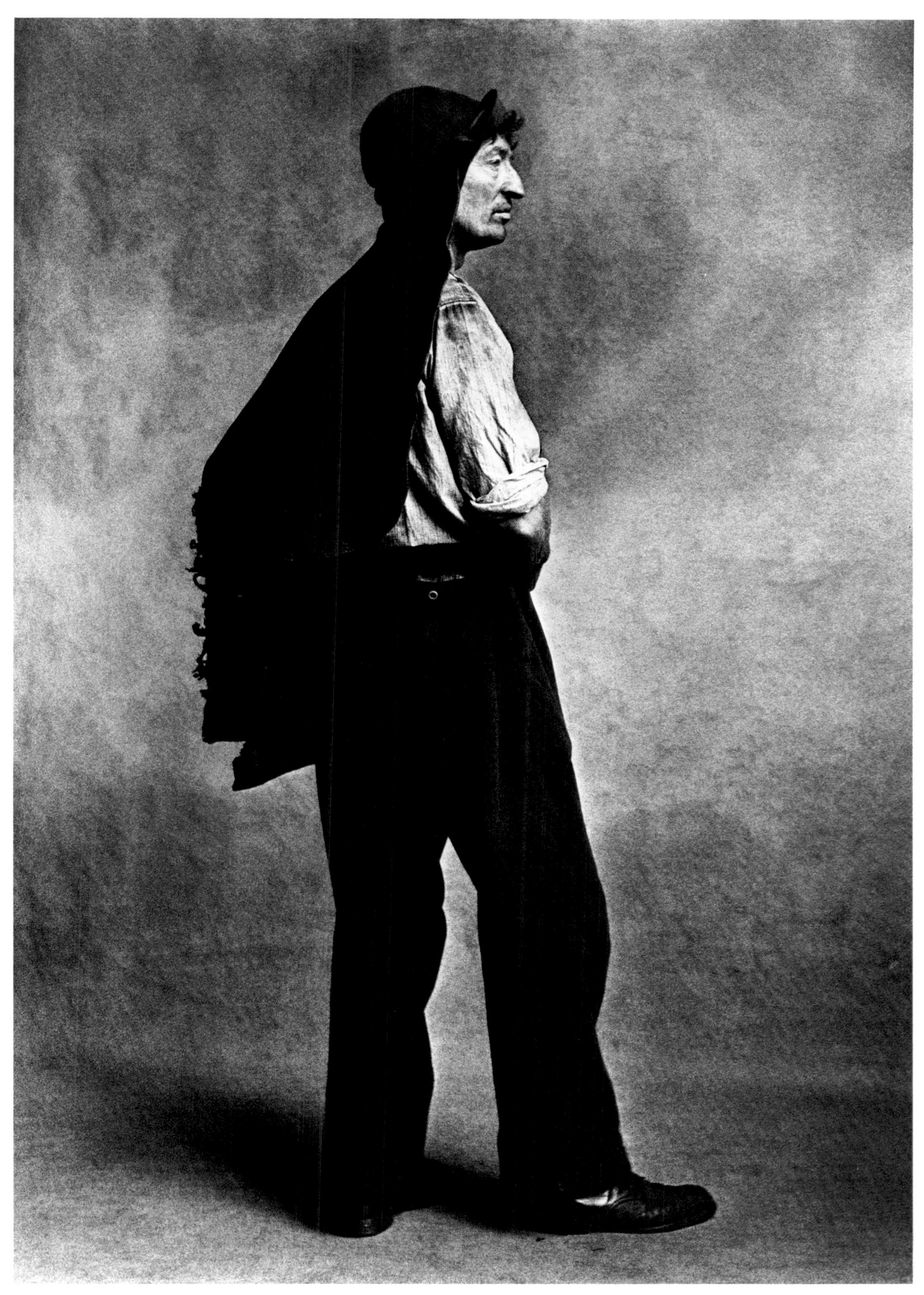

87. **Coal Man**. London, 1950. Platinum-palladium print, 1976

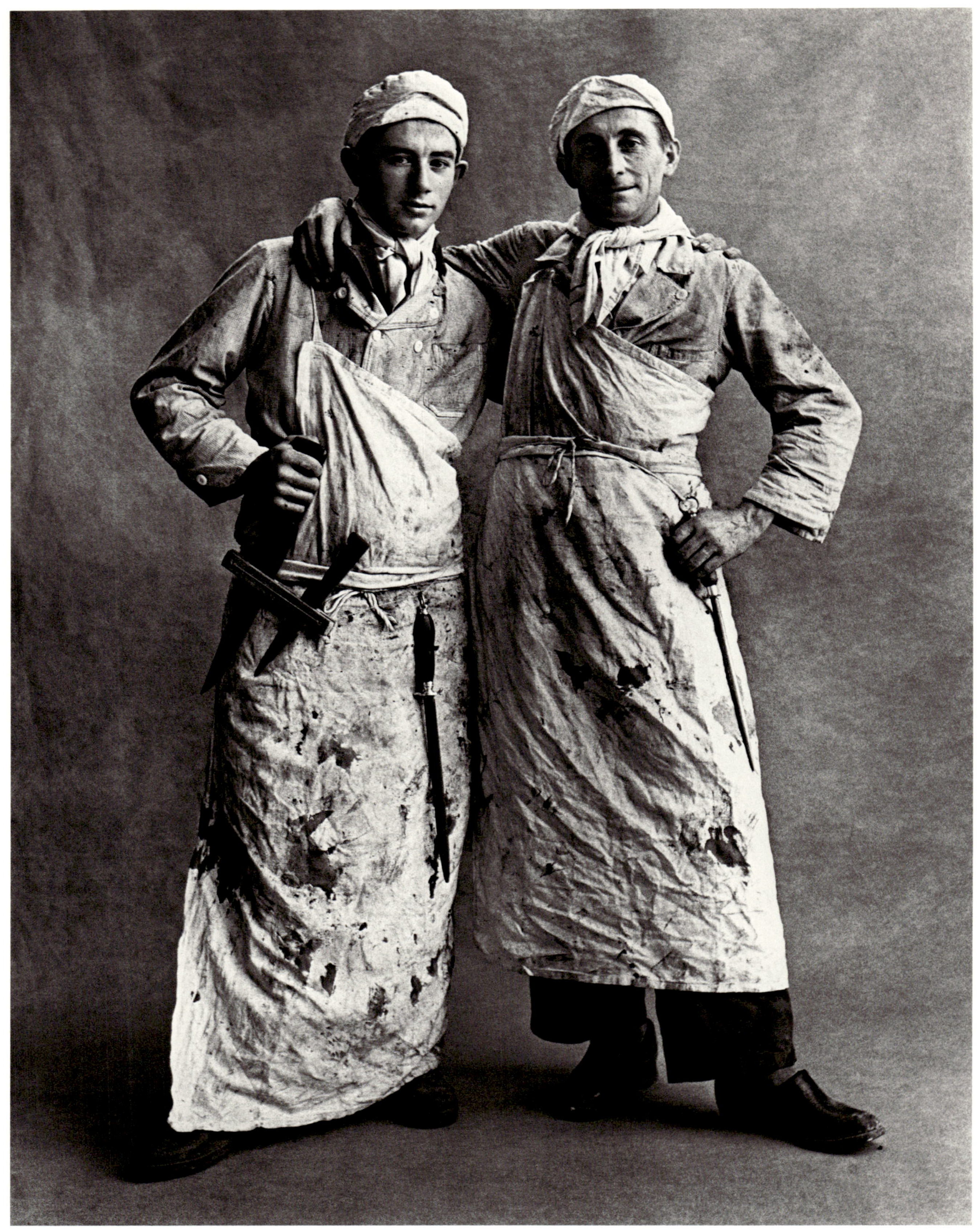

88. **Bouchers**. Paris, 1950. Platinum-palladium print, 1976

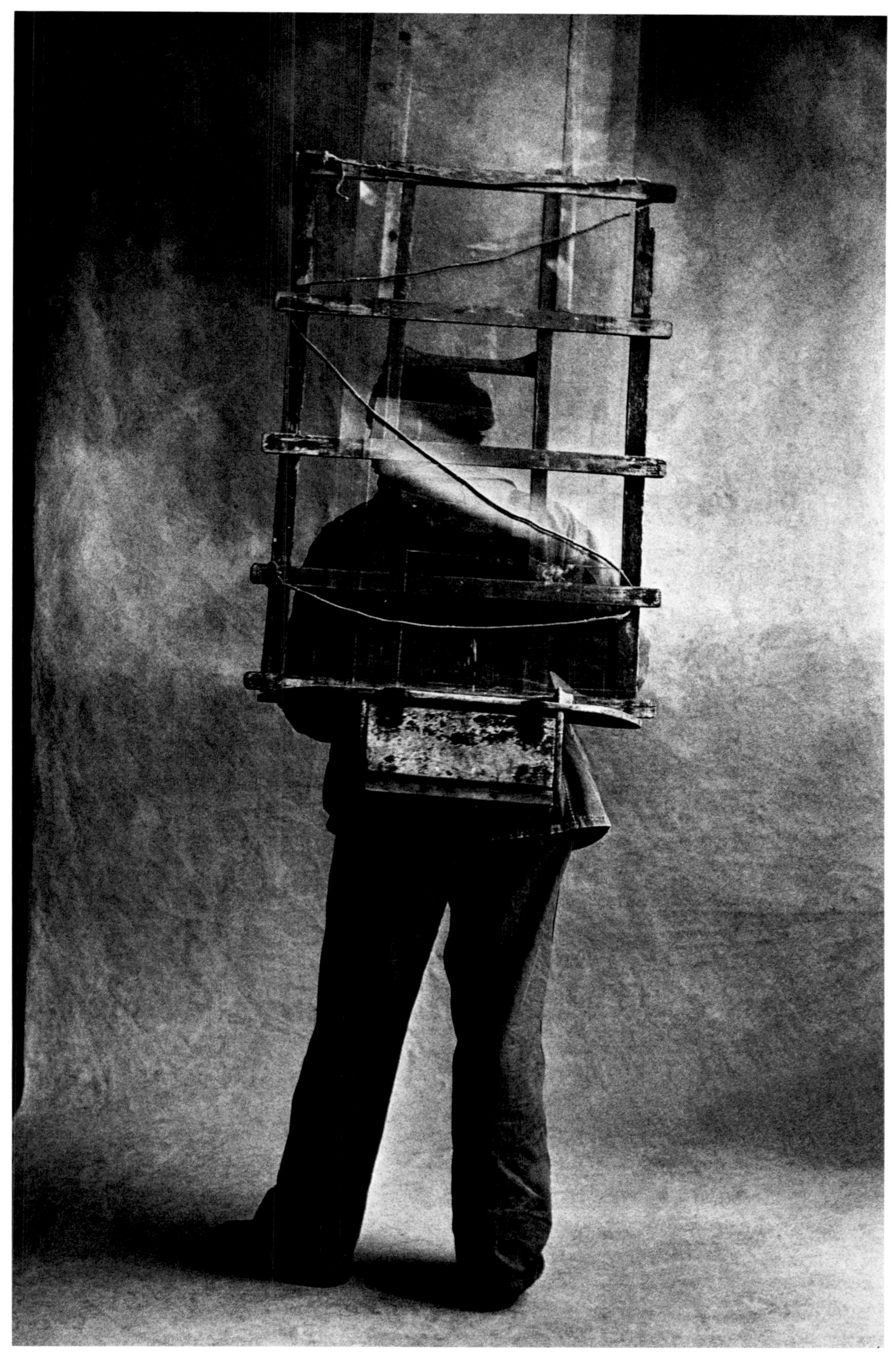

89. **Vitrier.** Paris, 1950. Platinum-palladium print, 1976

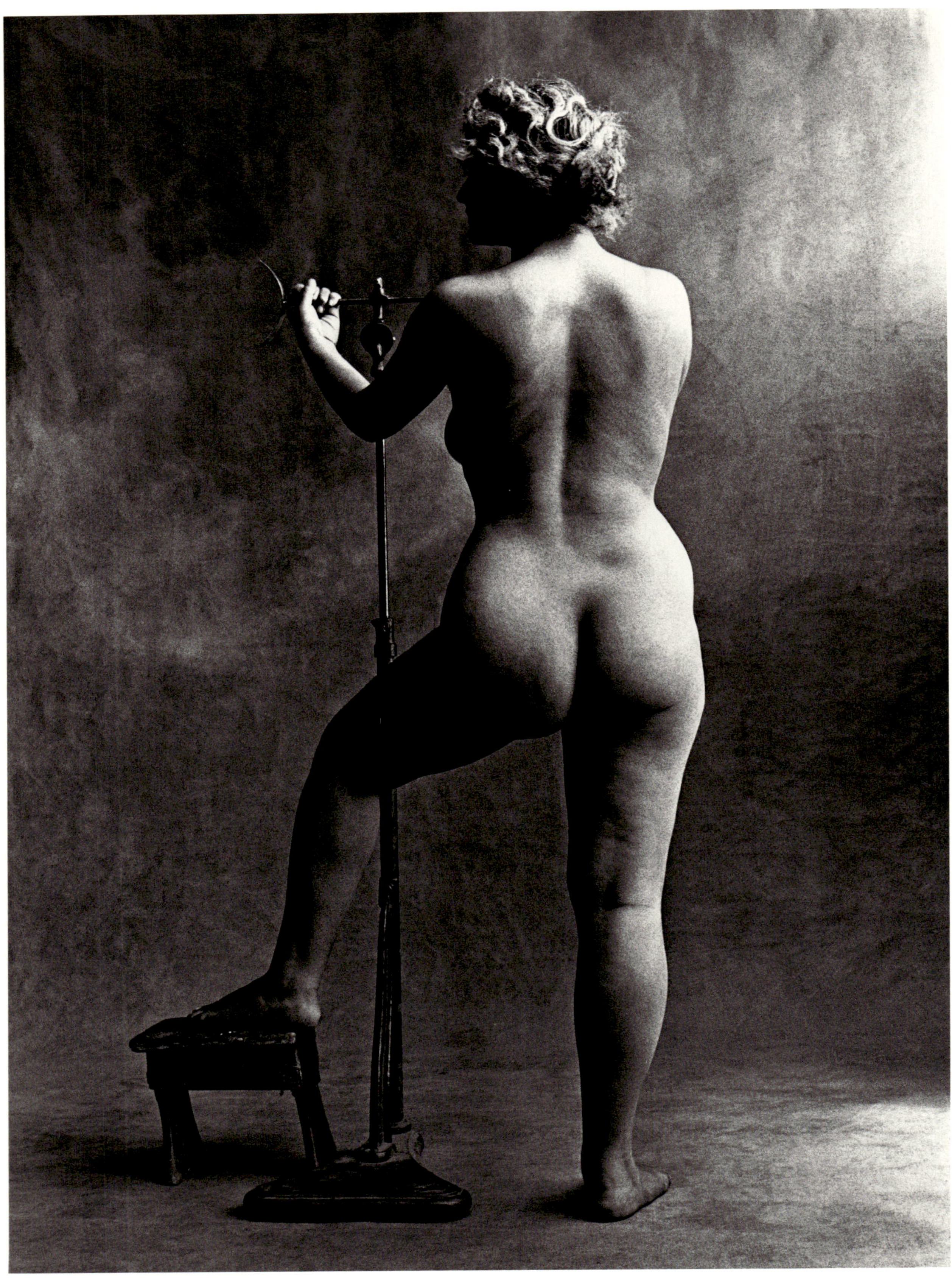

90. **Sculptor's Model**. Paris, 1950. Platinum-palladium print, 1980

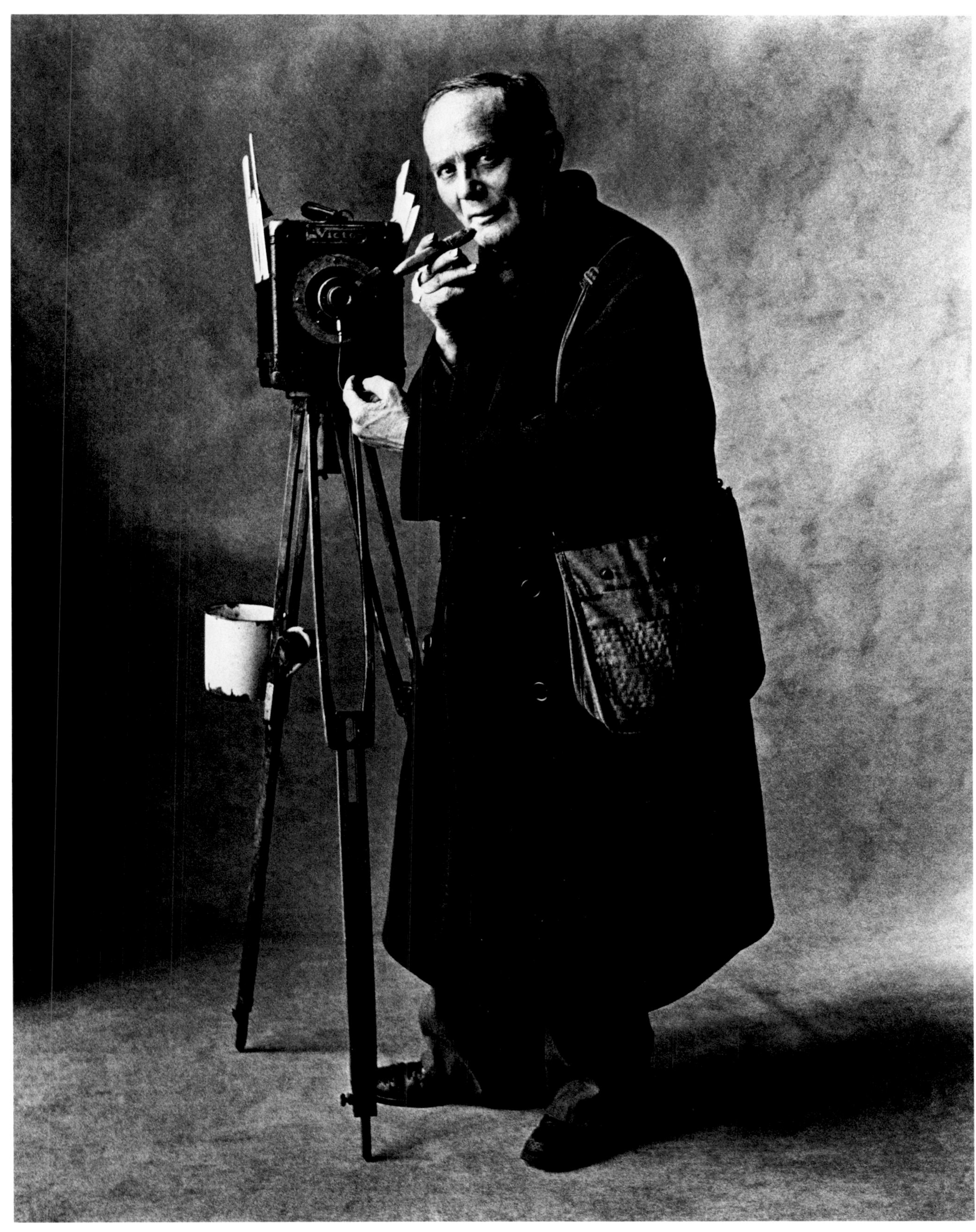

91. **Street Photographer.** New York, 1951. Platinum-palladium print, 1976

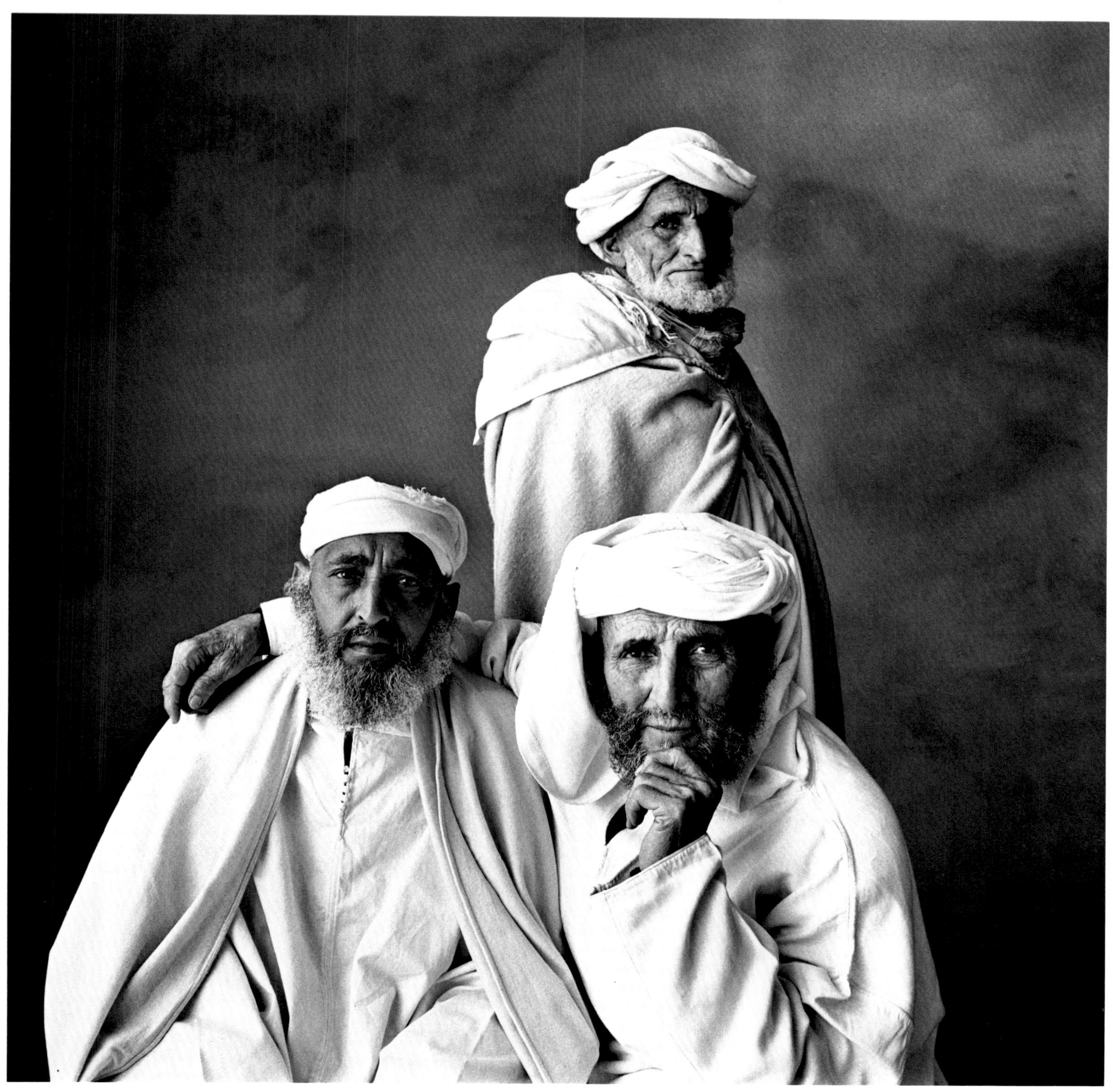

92. **Three Village Elders**. Khenifra, Morocco, 1971

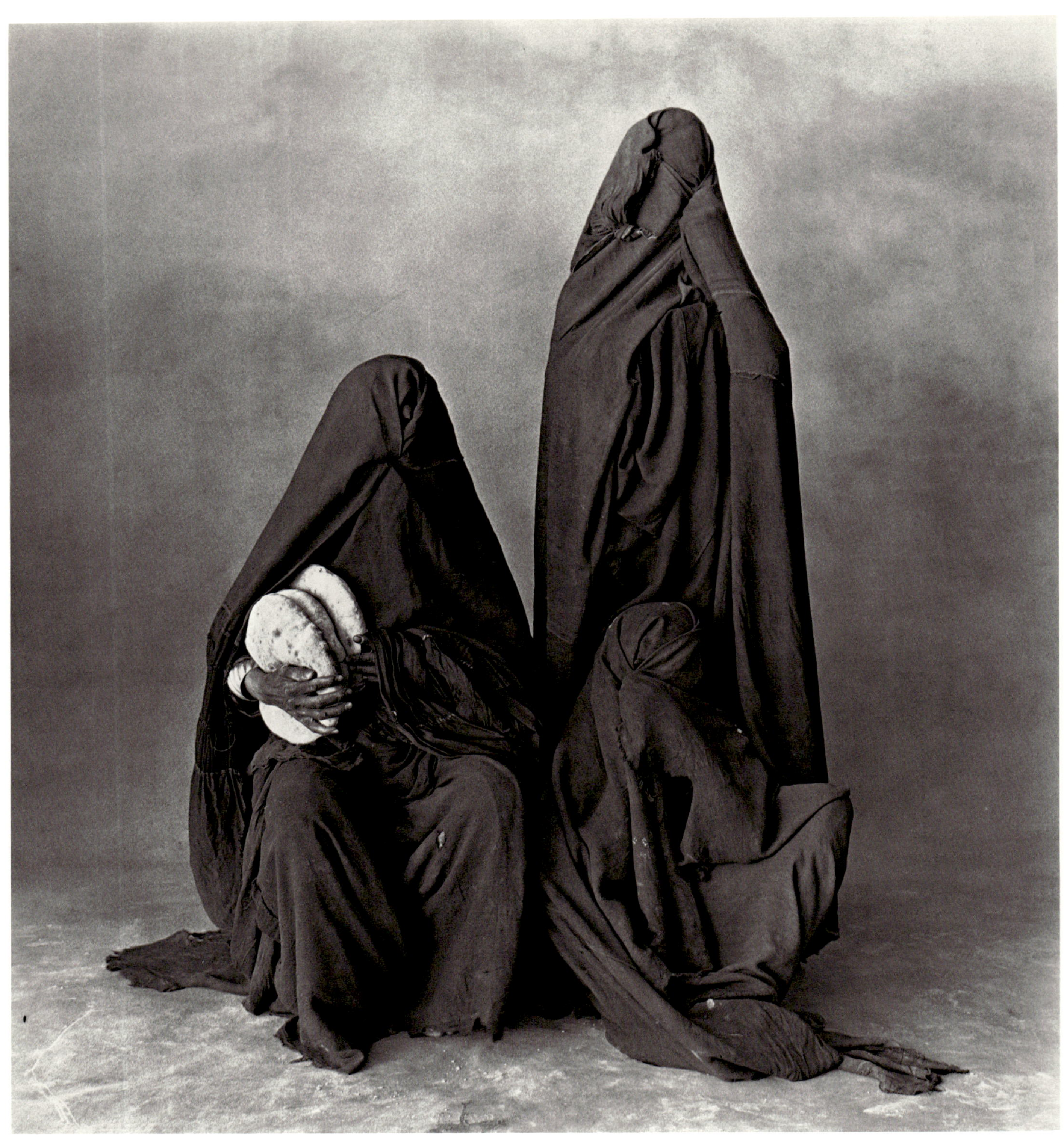

93. **Three Women of Rissani.** Morocco, 1971. Platinum-palladium print, 1978

94. **Two Guedras.** Goulimine, Morocco, 1971. Platinum-palladium print, 1977

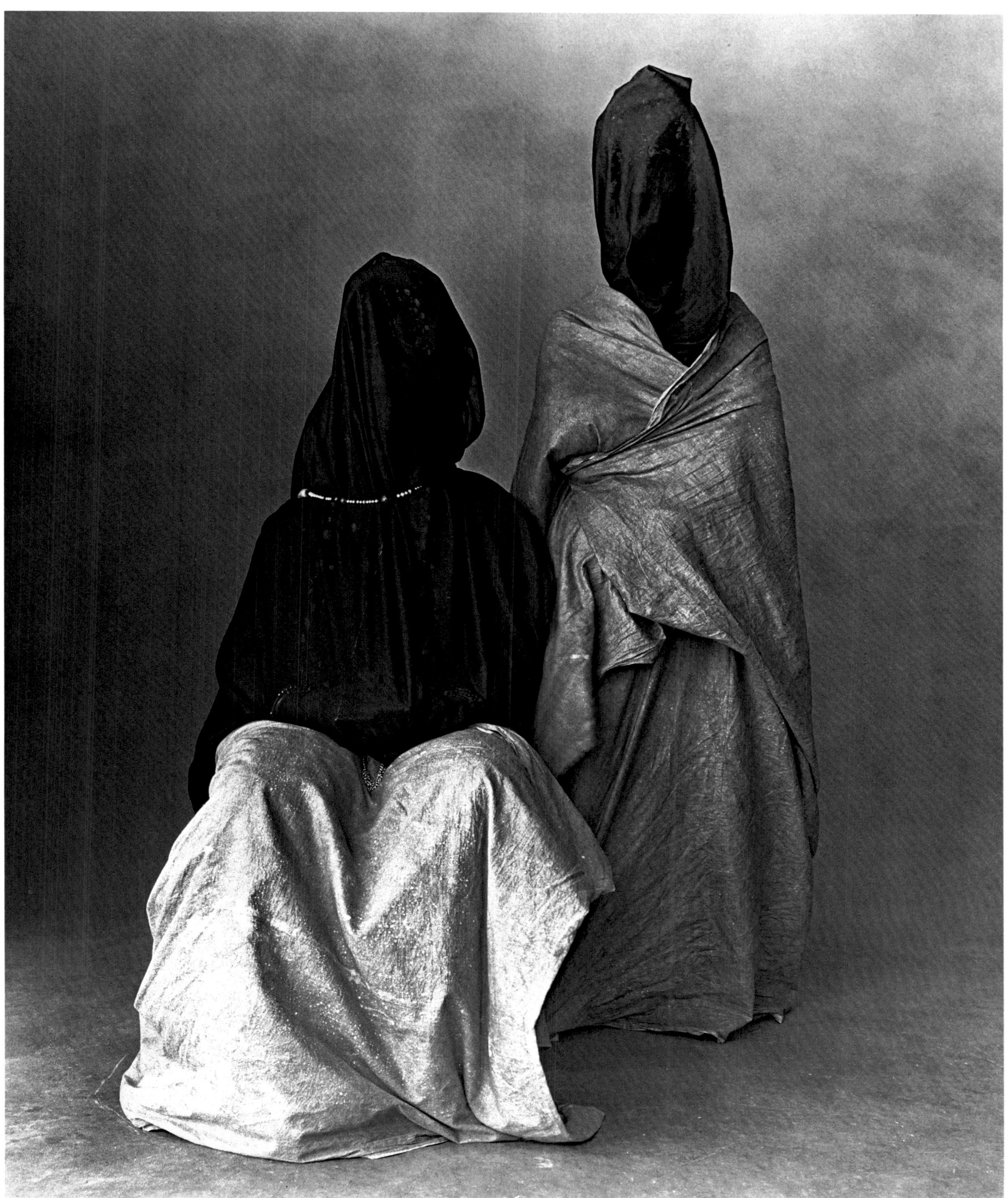

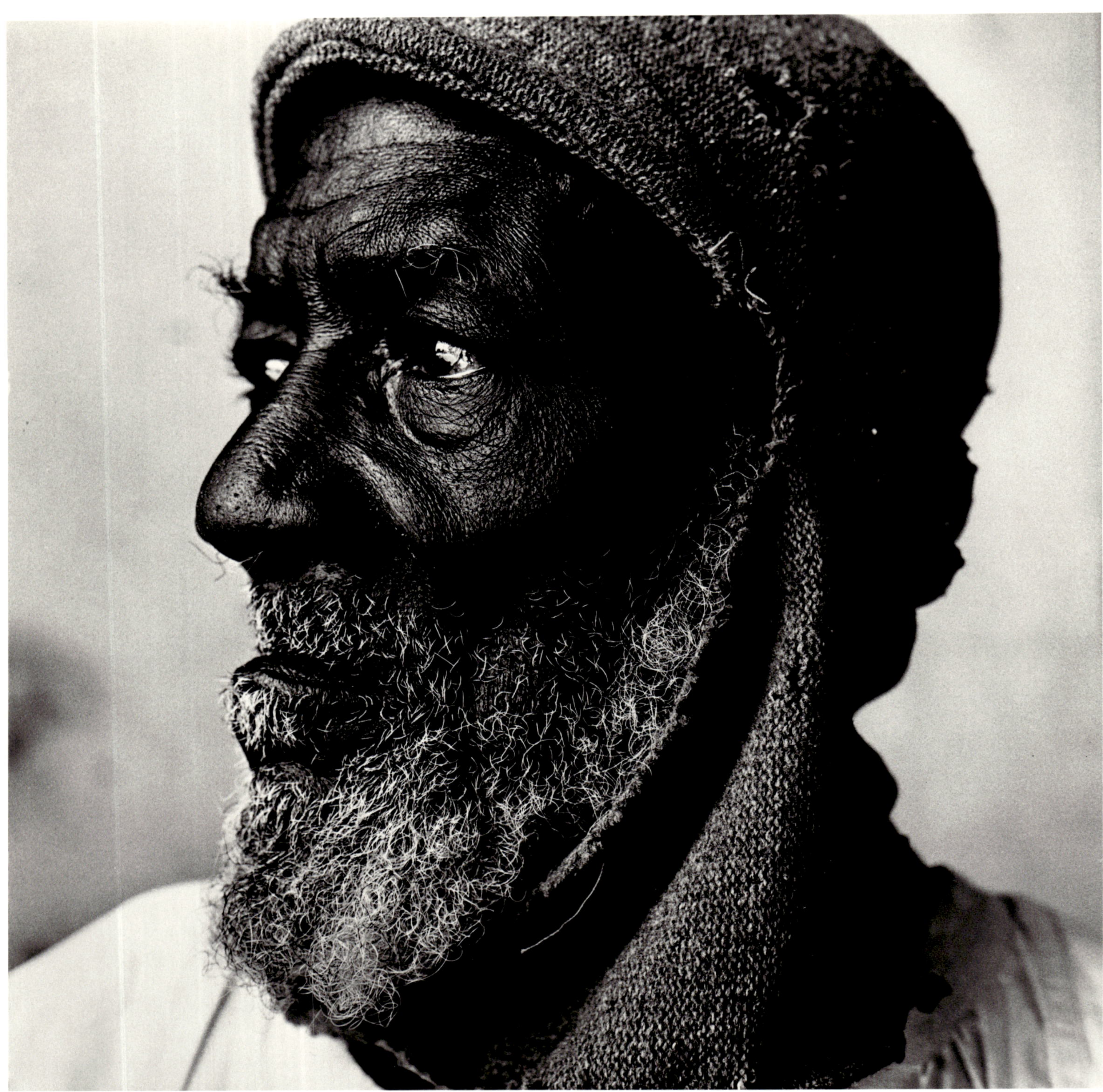

95. **Old Man**. Dahomey, 1967

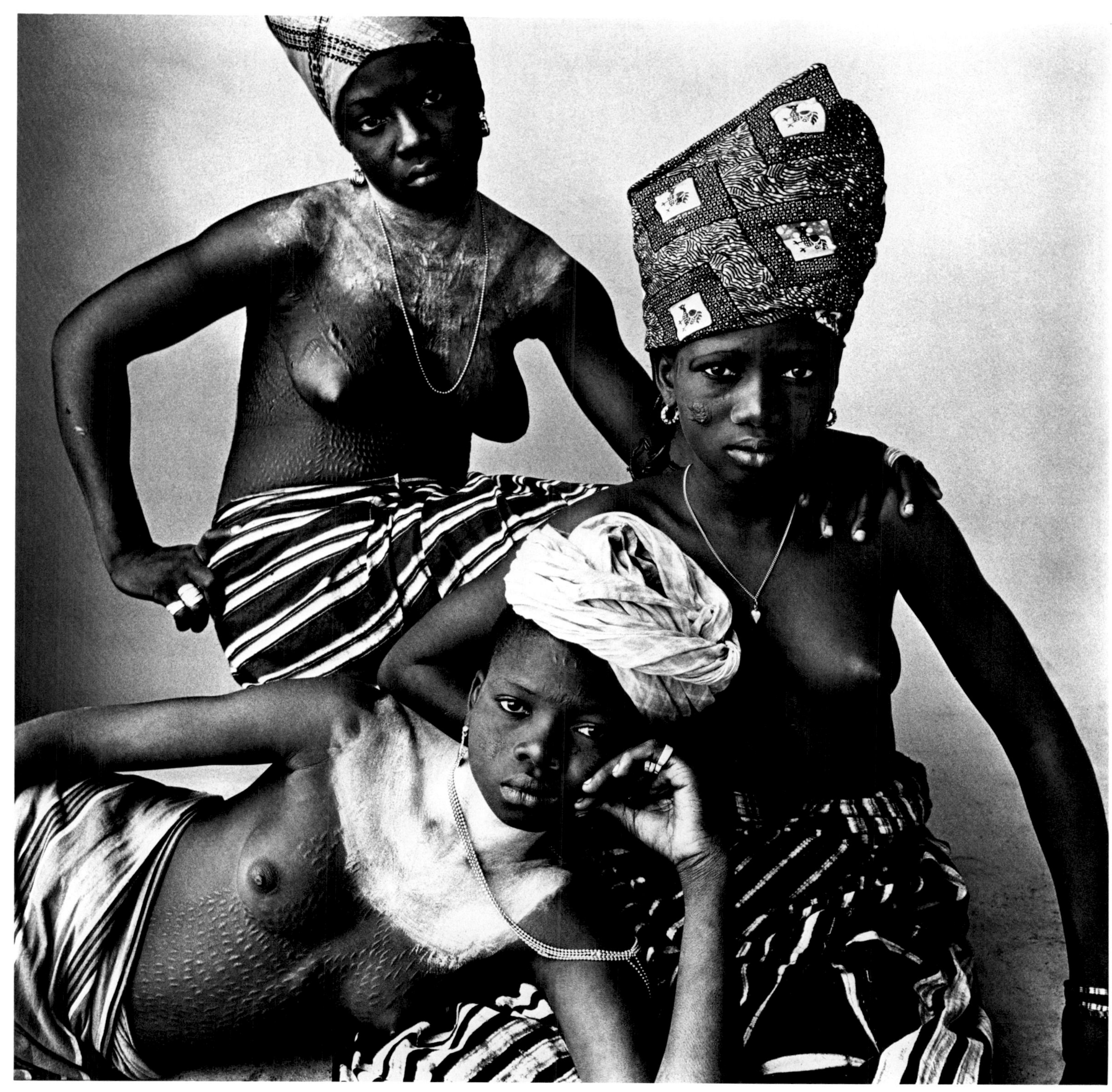

96. **Three Girls, One Reclining. Dahomey, 1967. Platinum-palladium print, 1980**

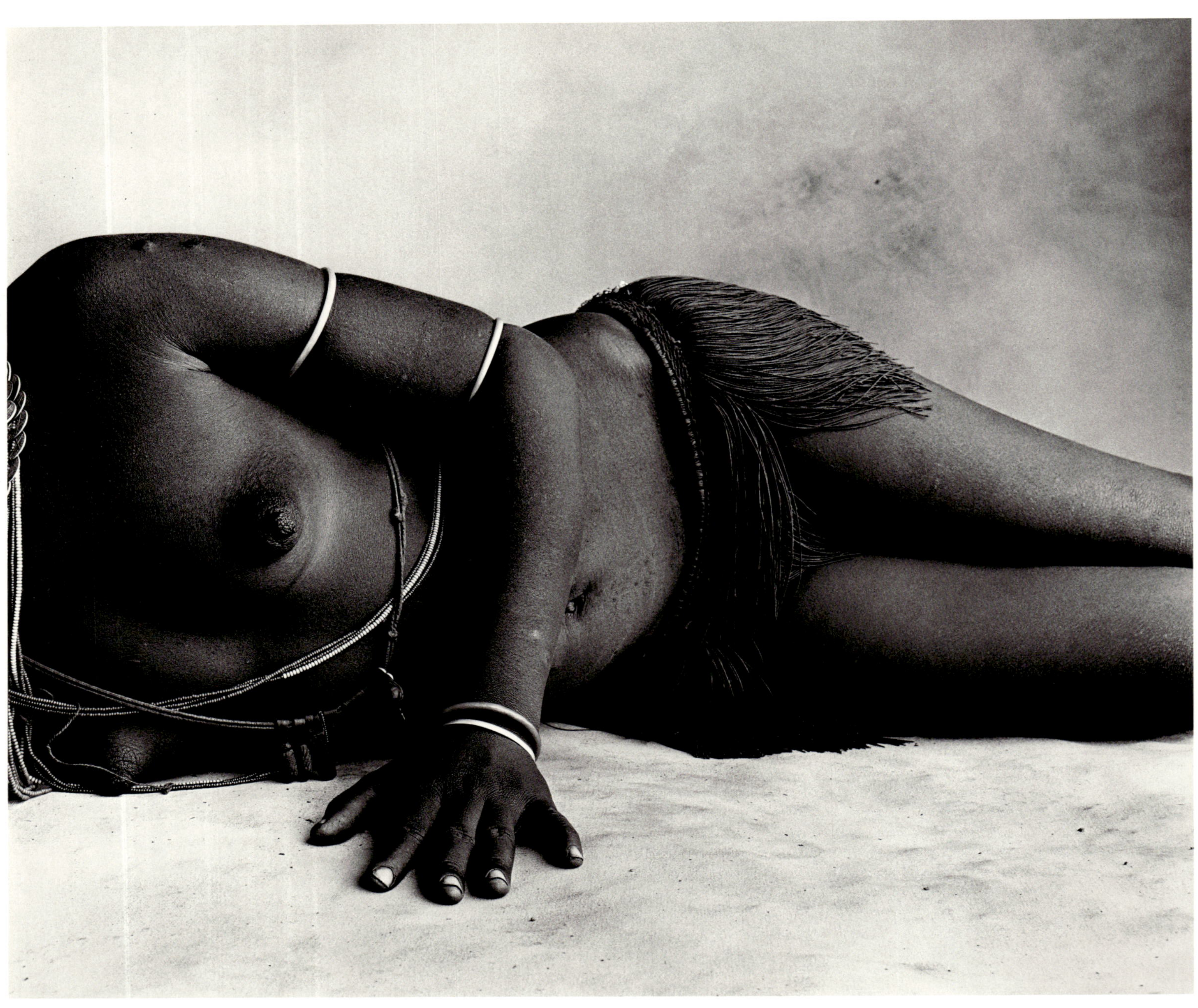

97. Chieftain's Wife. Cameroon, 1969

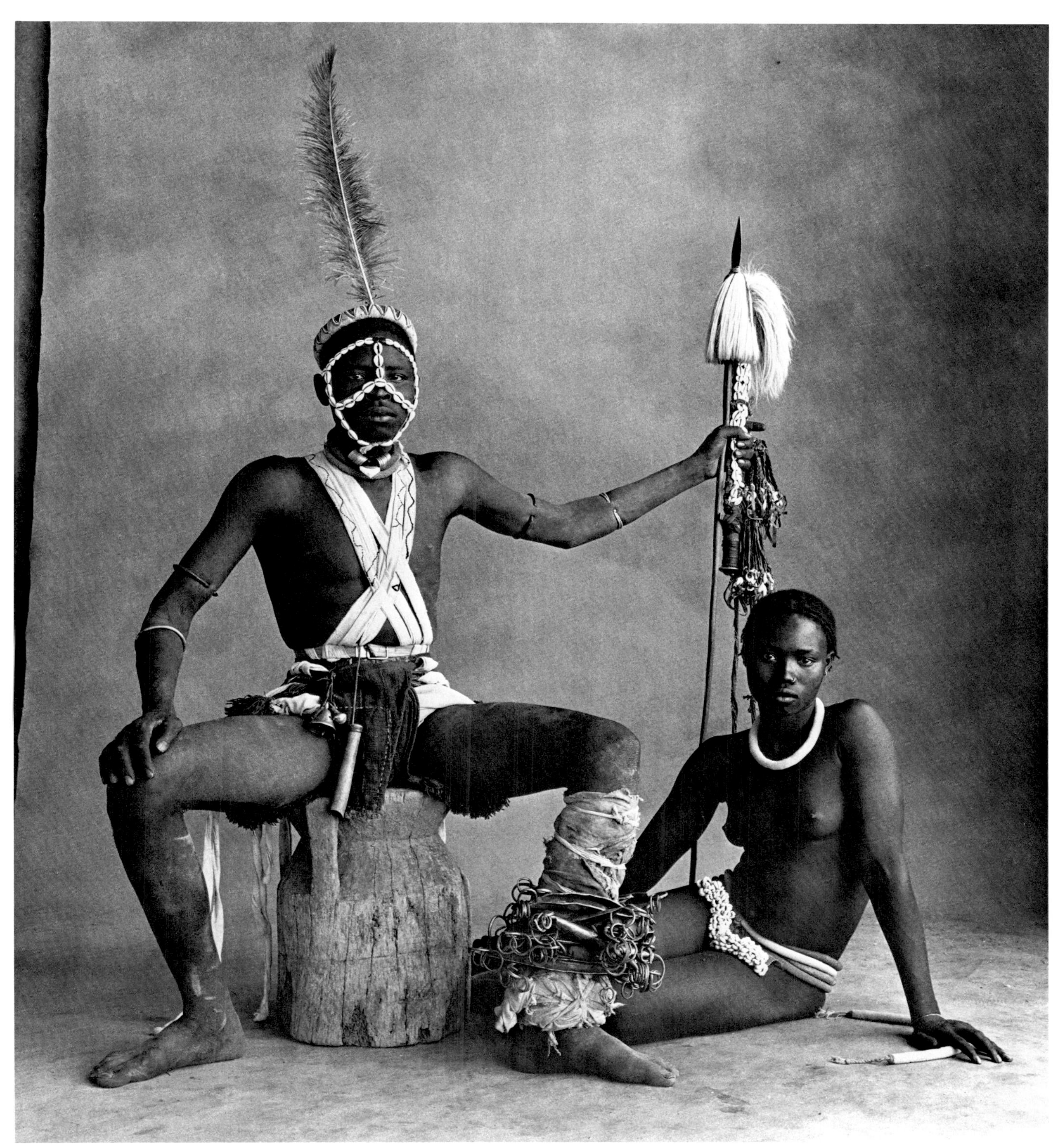

98. Seated Warrior, Sitting Girl. Cameroon, 1969. Platinum-palladium print, 1979

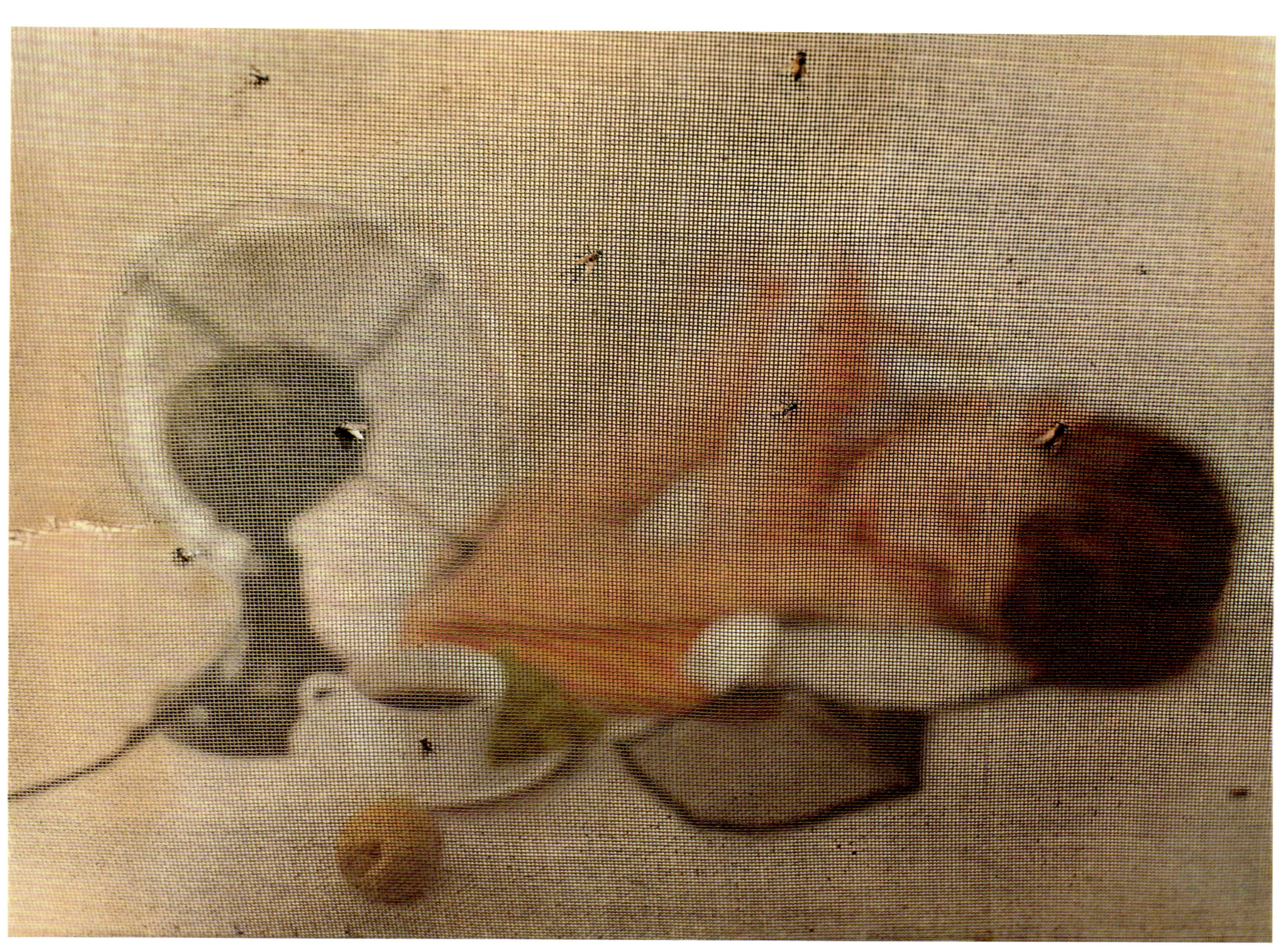

99. Summer Sleep. New York, 1949. Dye-transfer print, c. 1959

100. Lipstick Brush. New York, 1959. Reproduced from tear sheet

101. Contact Lens. New York, 1981. Reproduced from Ektachrome transparency

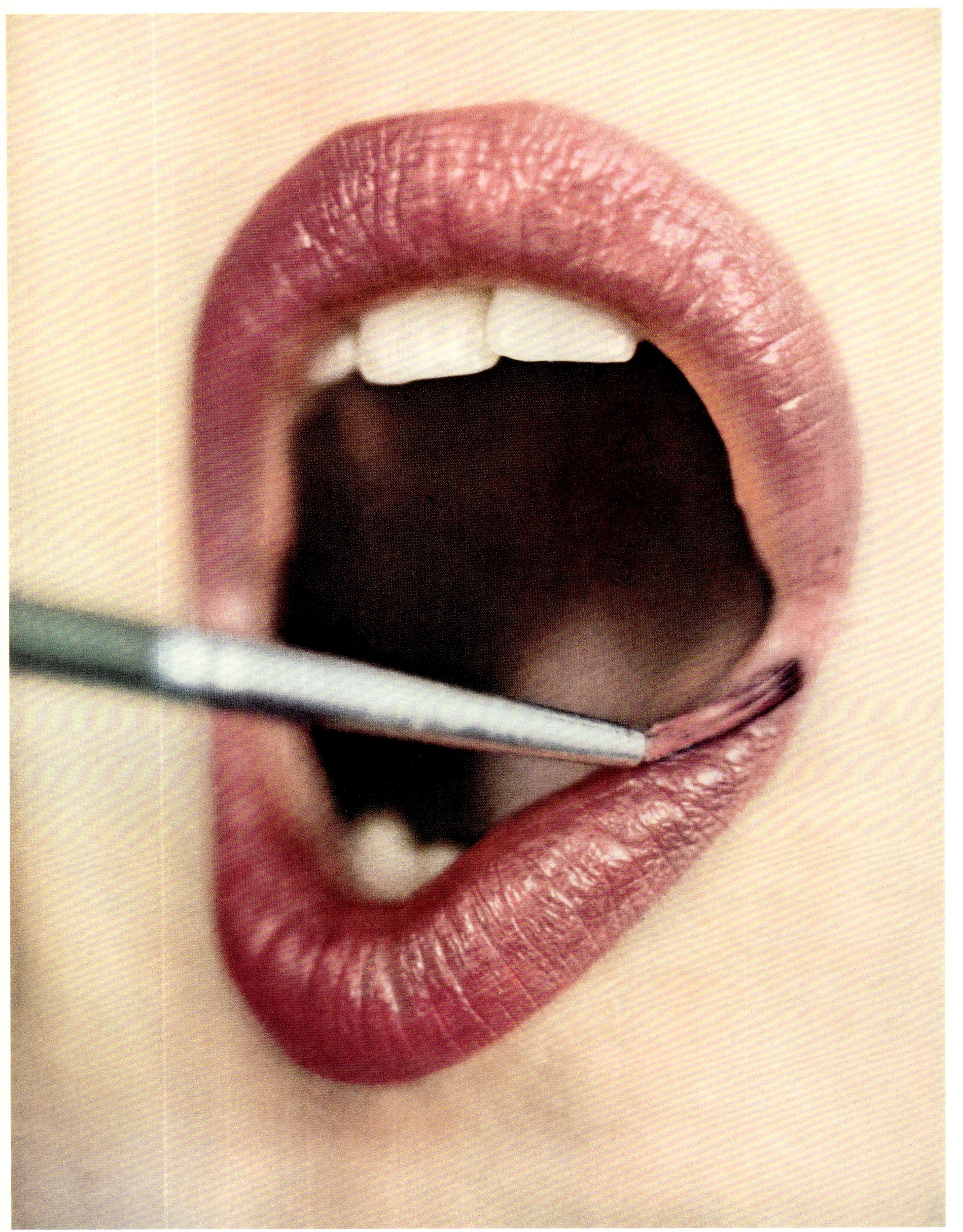

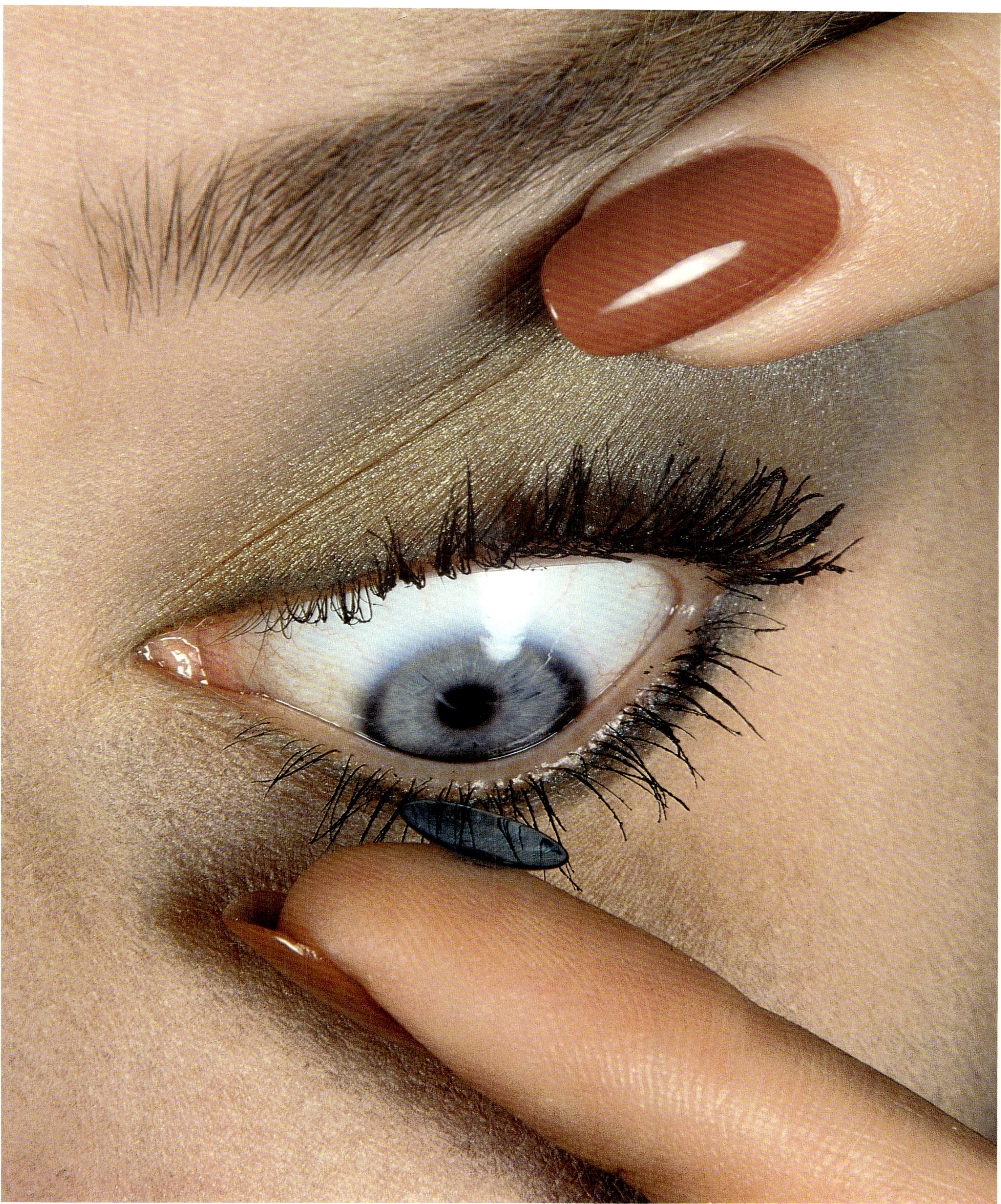

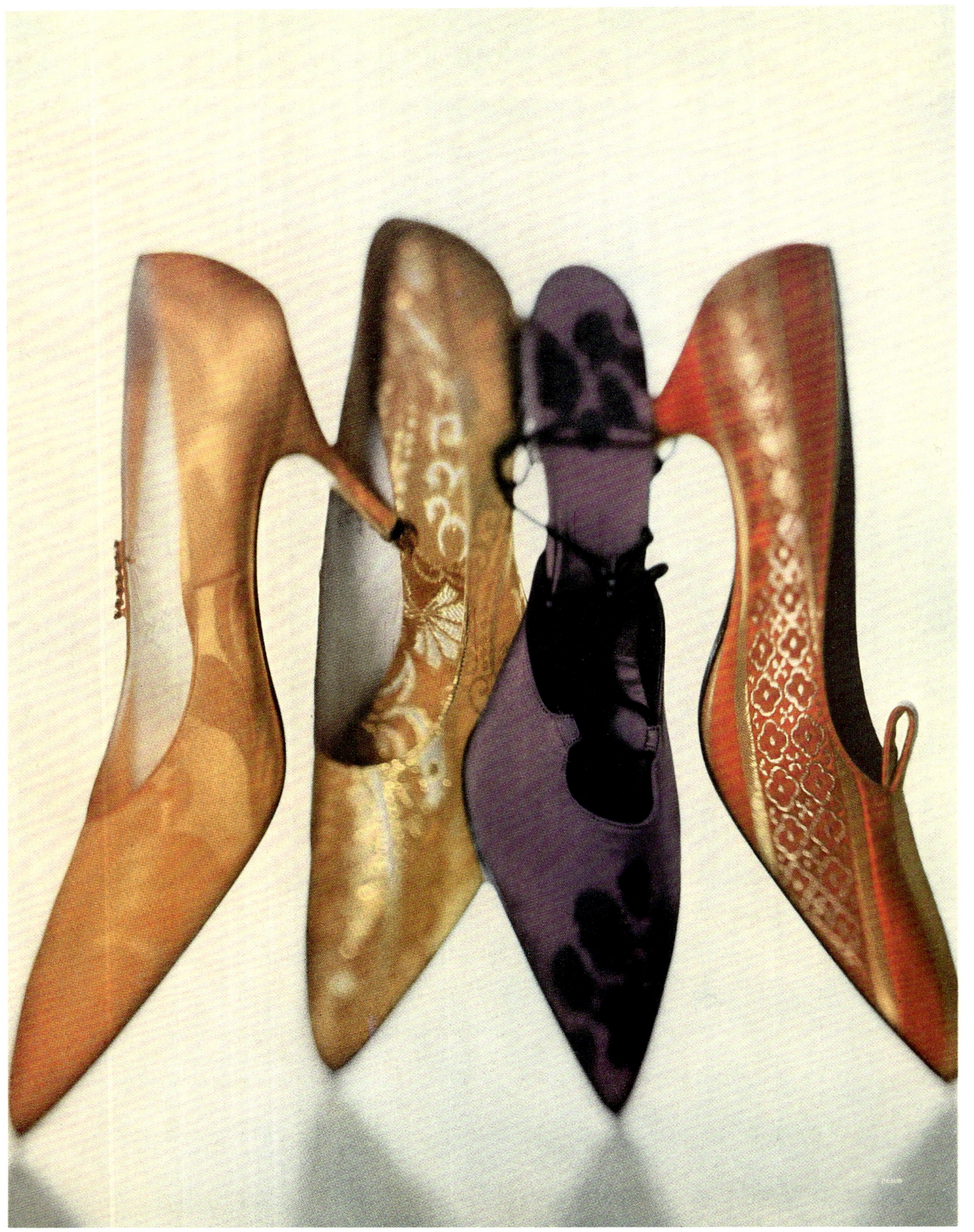

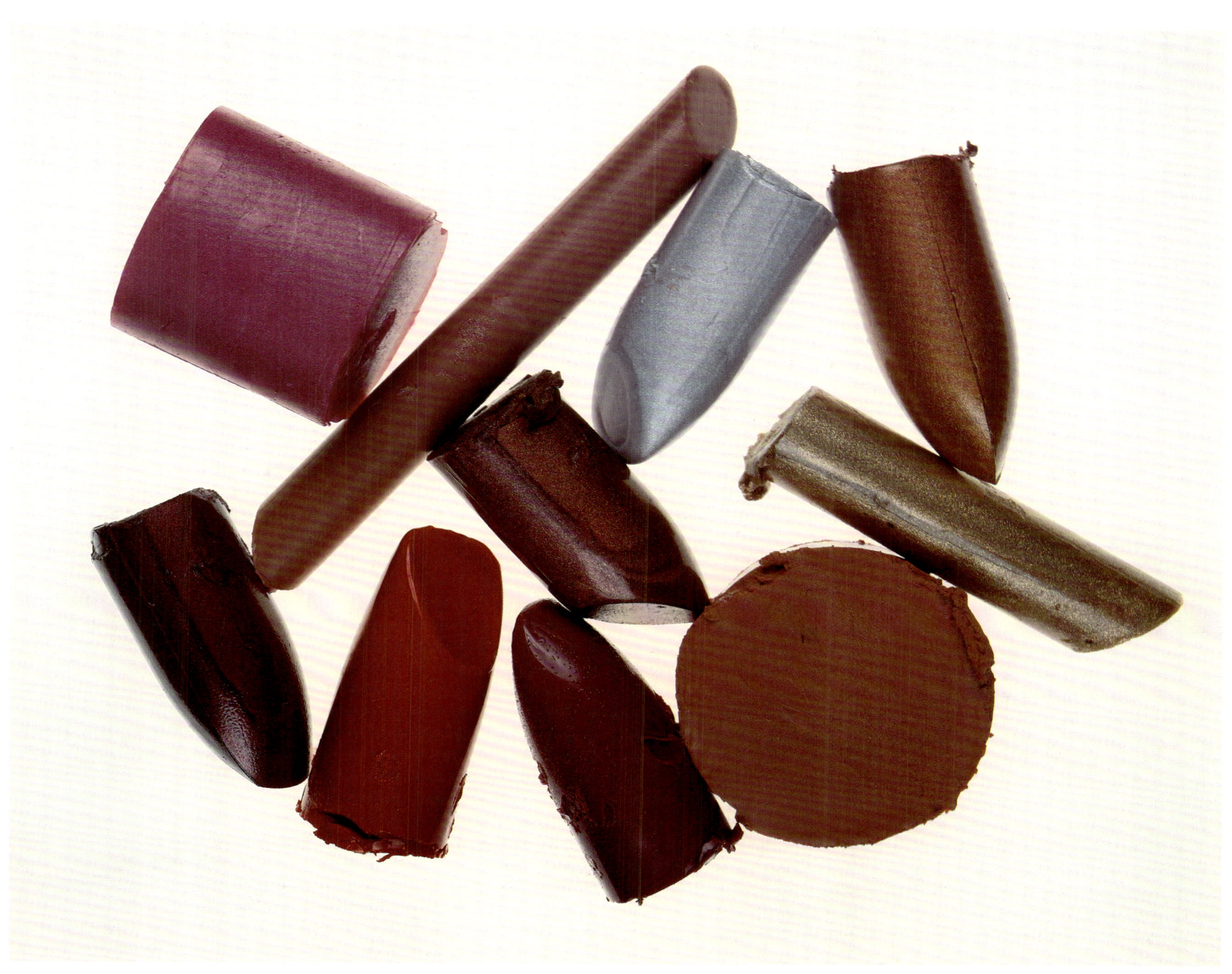

102. **Four Shoes**. New York, 1959. Reproduced from tear sheet

103. **Lipstick Chunks**. New York, 1982. Reproduced from Ektachrome transparency

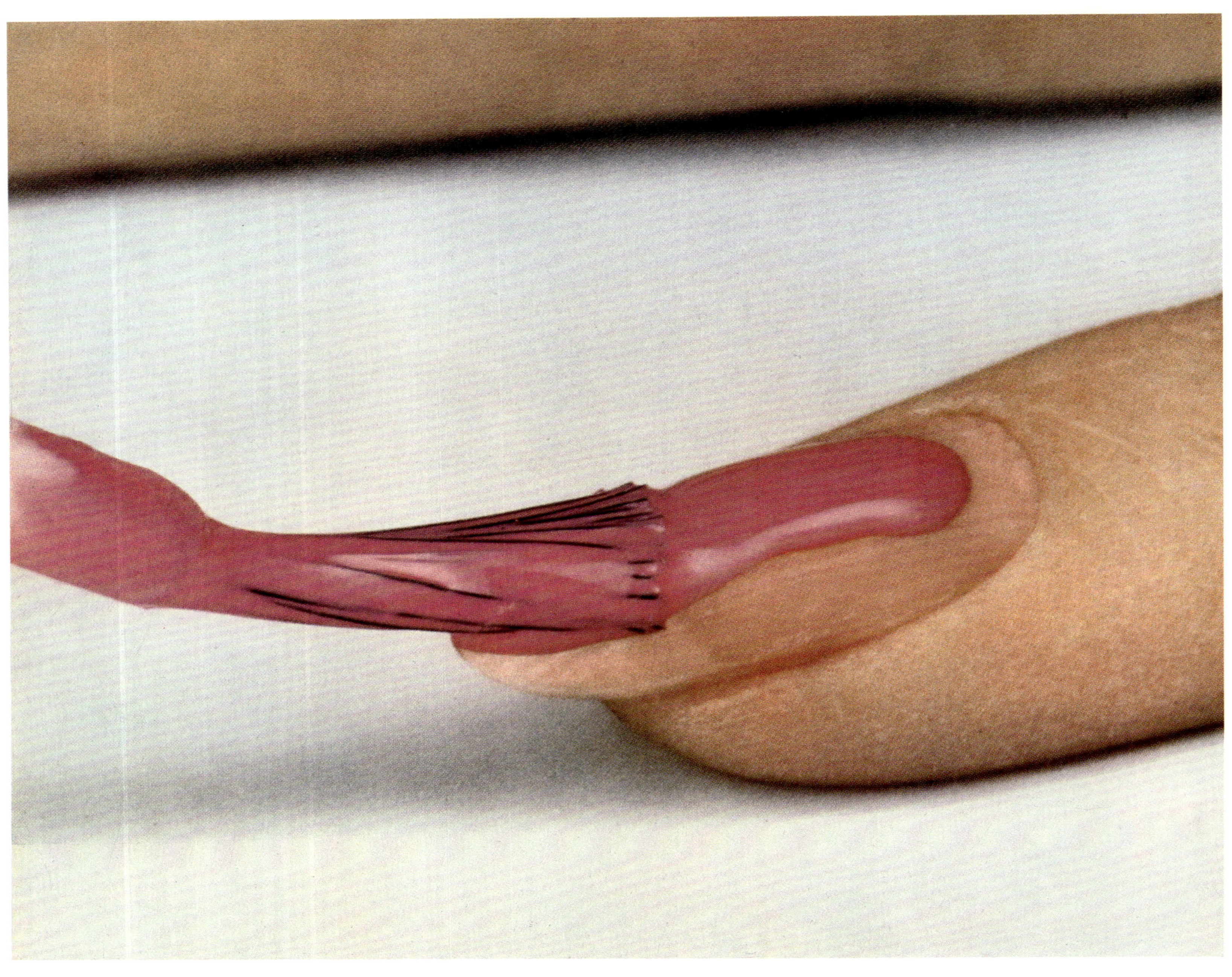

104. **Nail Polish**. New York, 1959. Reproduced from tear sheet

105. **Woman with Sun Block**. New York, 1966. Reproduced from Ektachrome transparency

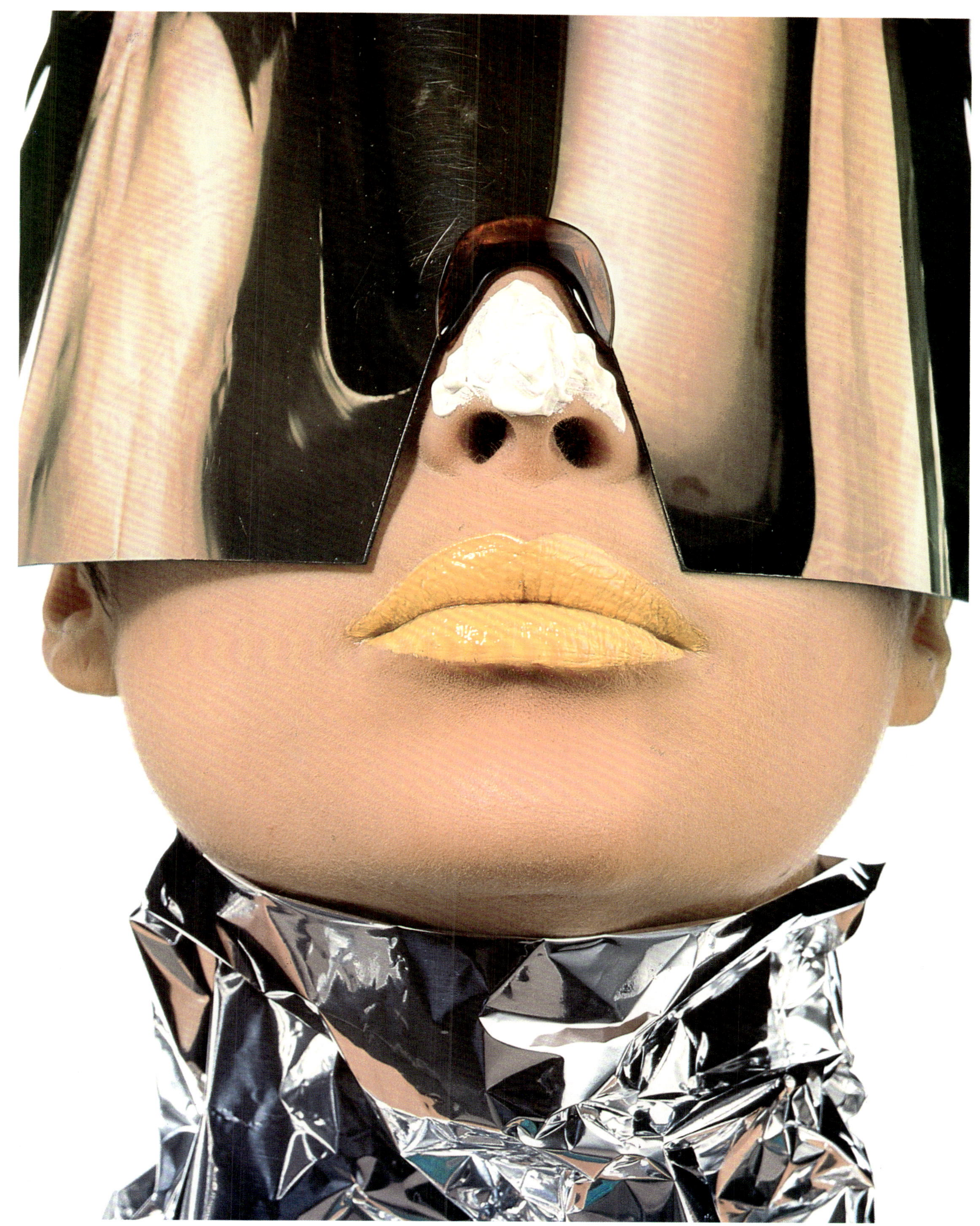

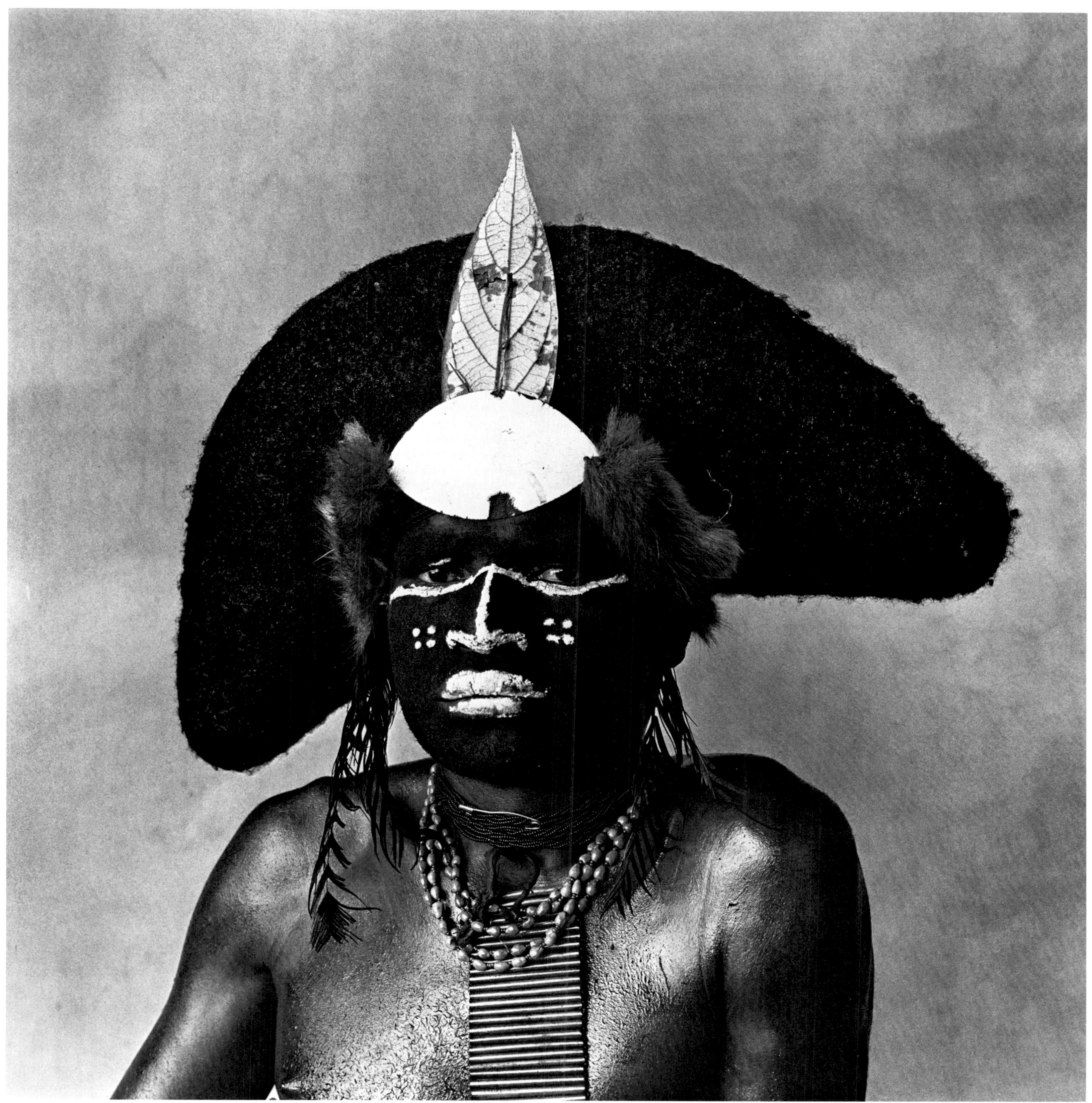

106. Enga Warrior. New Guinea, 1970. Platinum-palladium print, 1977

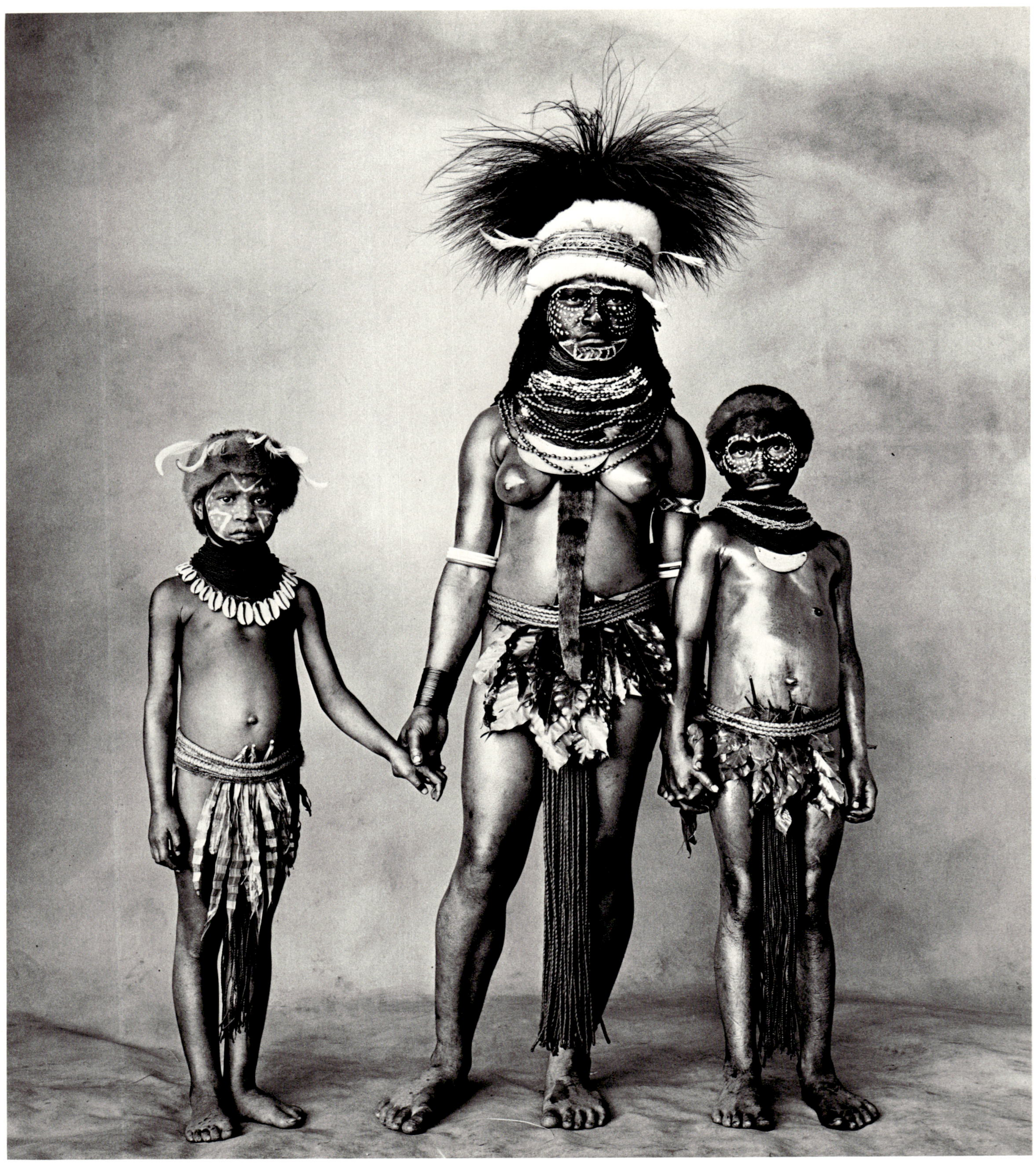

107. **Enga Woman and Two Young Girls**. New Guinea, 1970

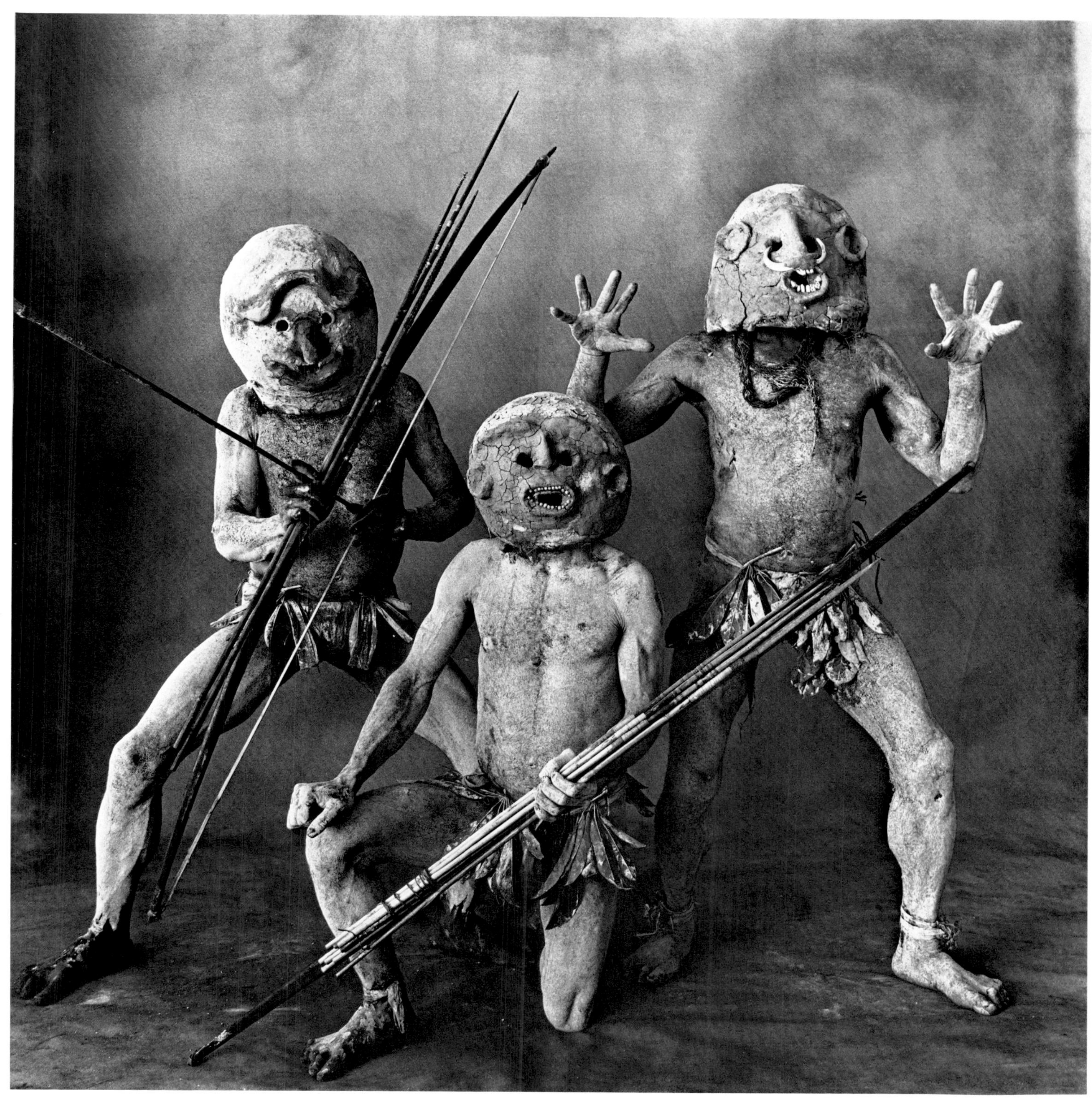

108. **Three Asaro Mud Men**. New Guinea, 1970. Platinum-palladium print, 1976

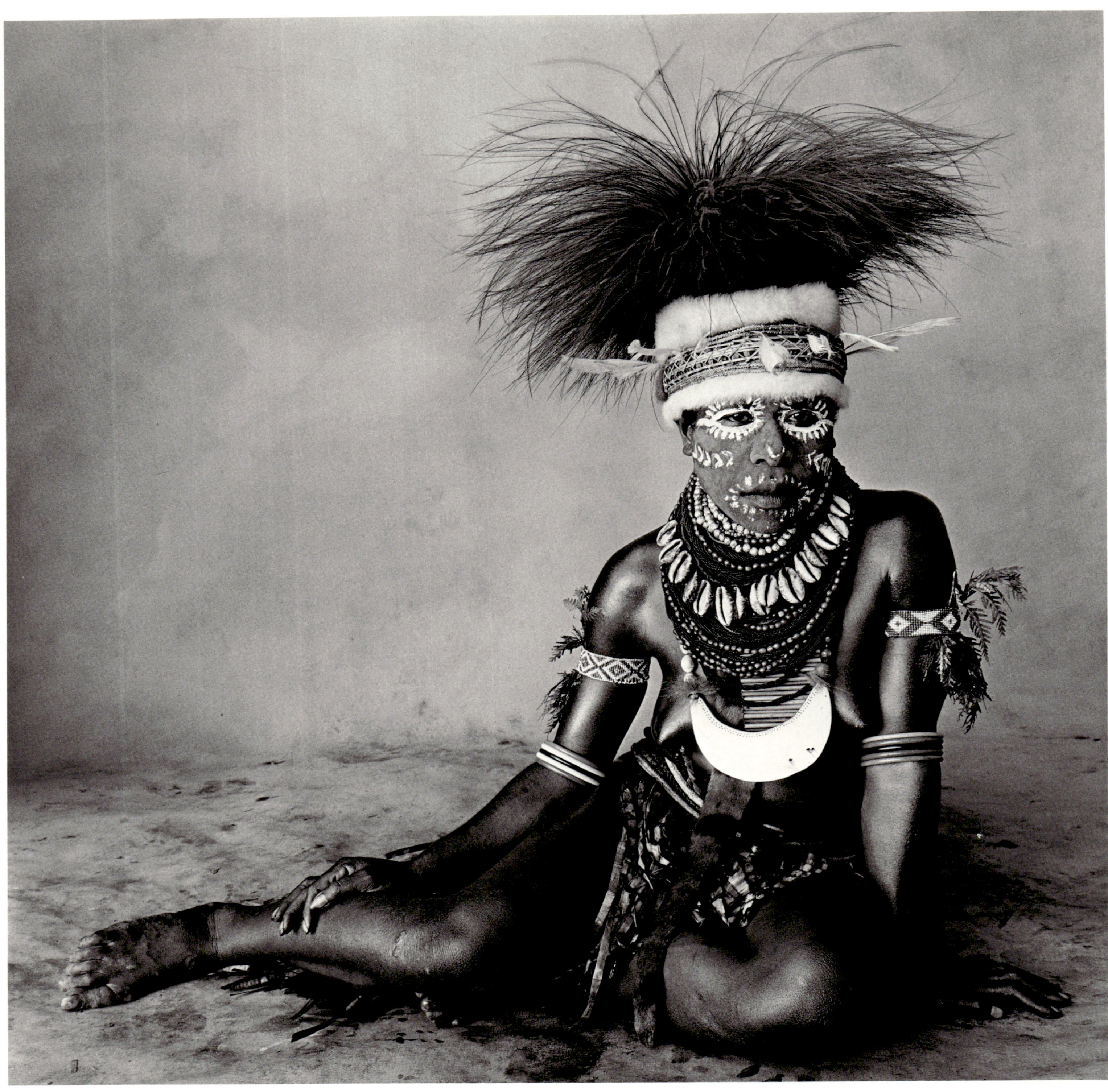

109. Sitting Woman. New Guinea, 1970

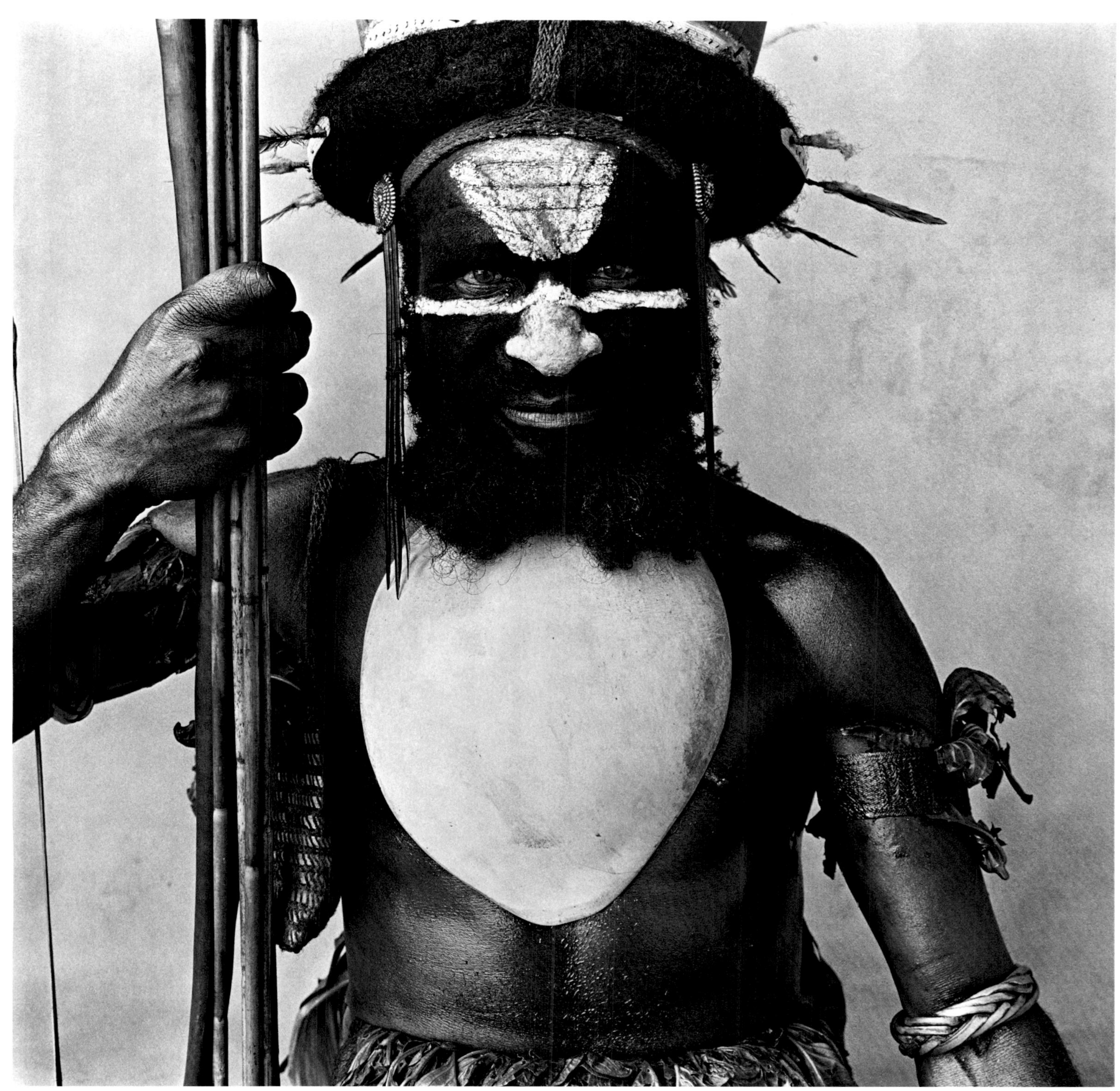

110. **Tambul Warrior**. New Guinea, 1970. Platinum-palladium print, 1979

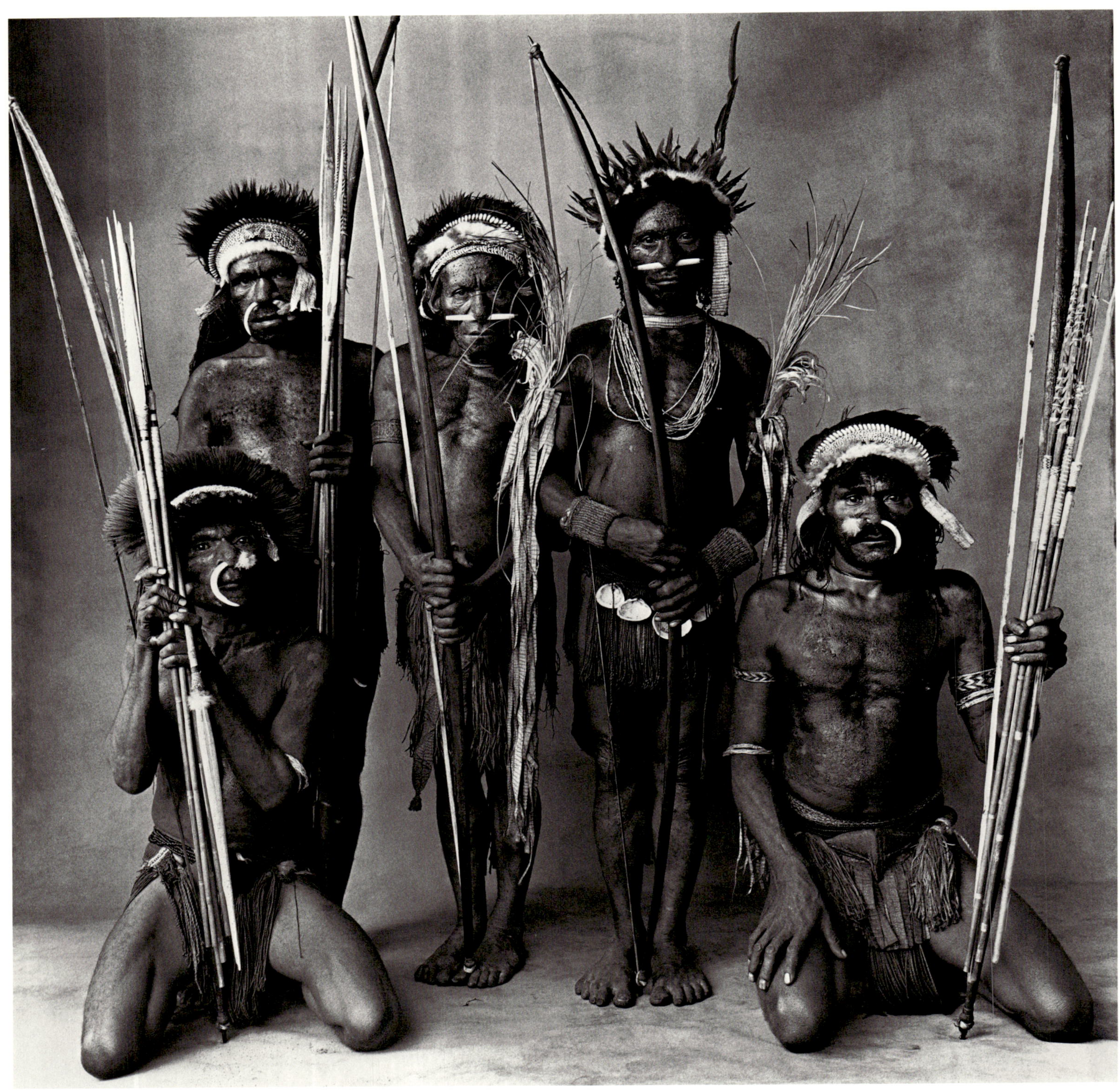

111. **Five Okapa Warriors**. New Guinea, 1970. Platinum-palladium print, 1977

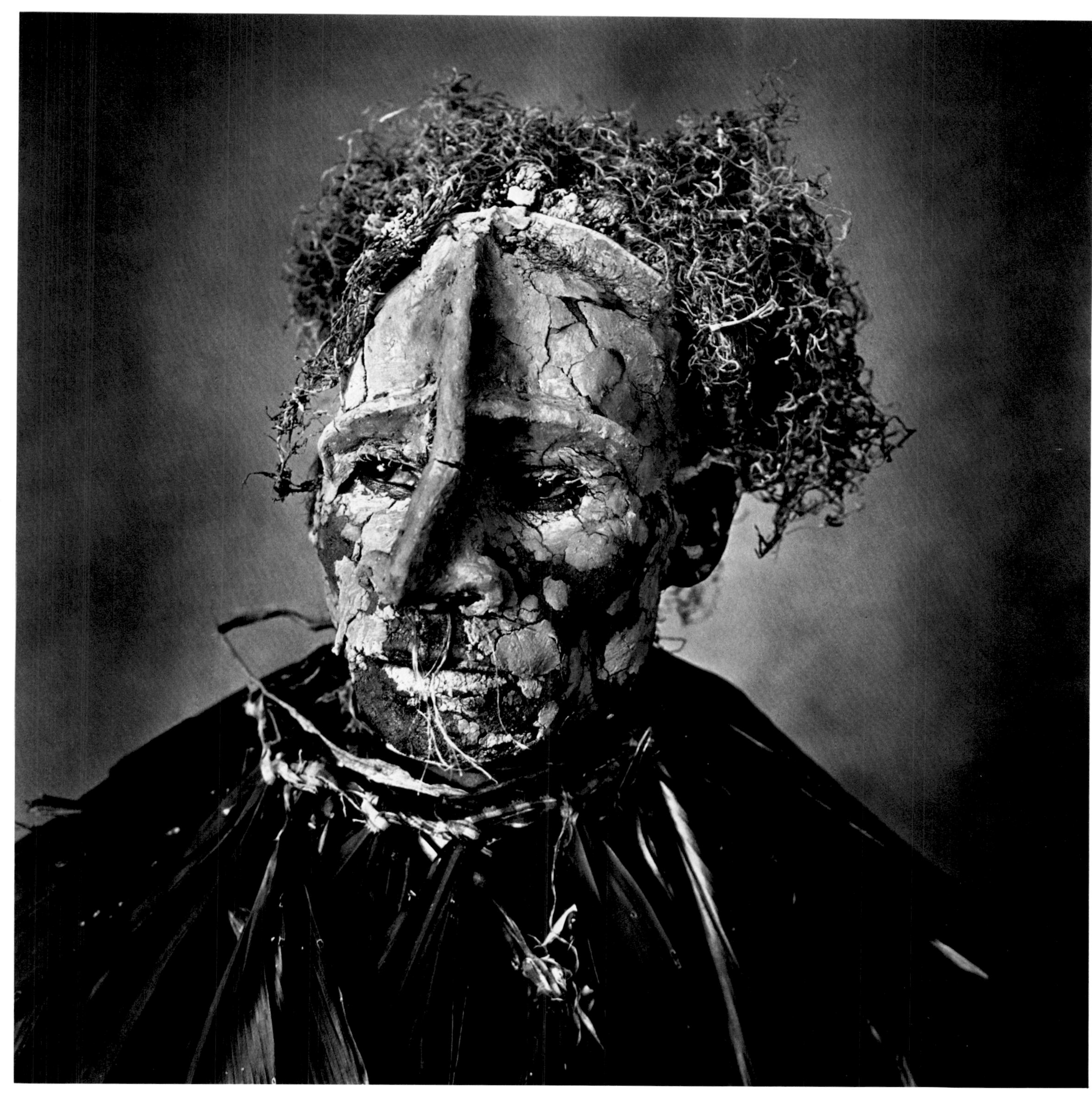

112. **Man with Pink Face.** New Guinea, 1970. Platinum-palladium print, 1978

113. **Cigarette 17.** New York, 1972. Platinum-palladium print

114. **Cigarette 8.** New York, 1972. Platinum-palladium print

115. **Cigarette 69.** New York, 1972. Platinum-palladium print

116. **Cigarette 123.** New York, 1972. Platinum-palladium print

117. **Cigarette 34.** New York, 1972. Platinum-palladium print

118. **Cigarette 37.** New York, 1972. Platinum-palladium print

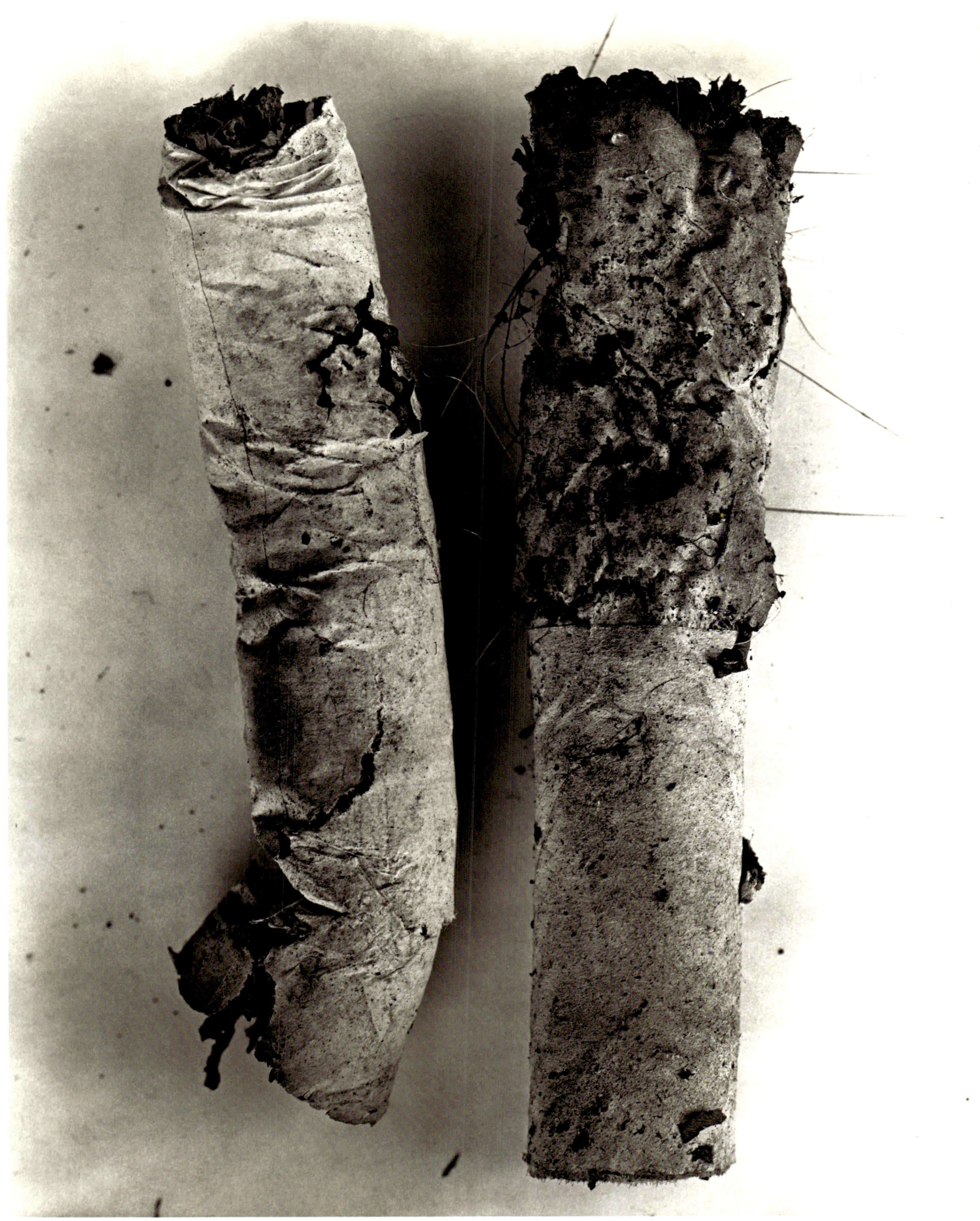

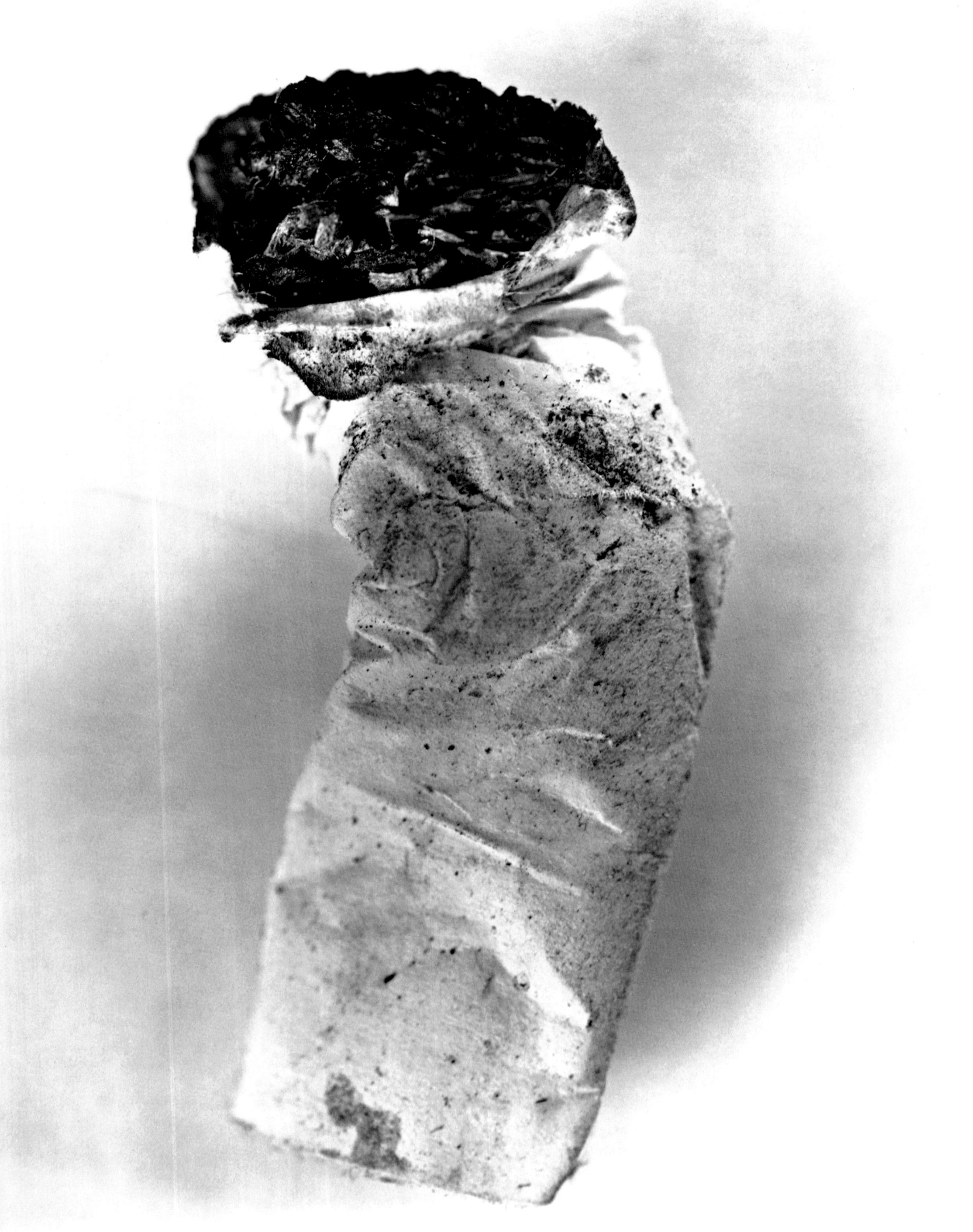

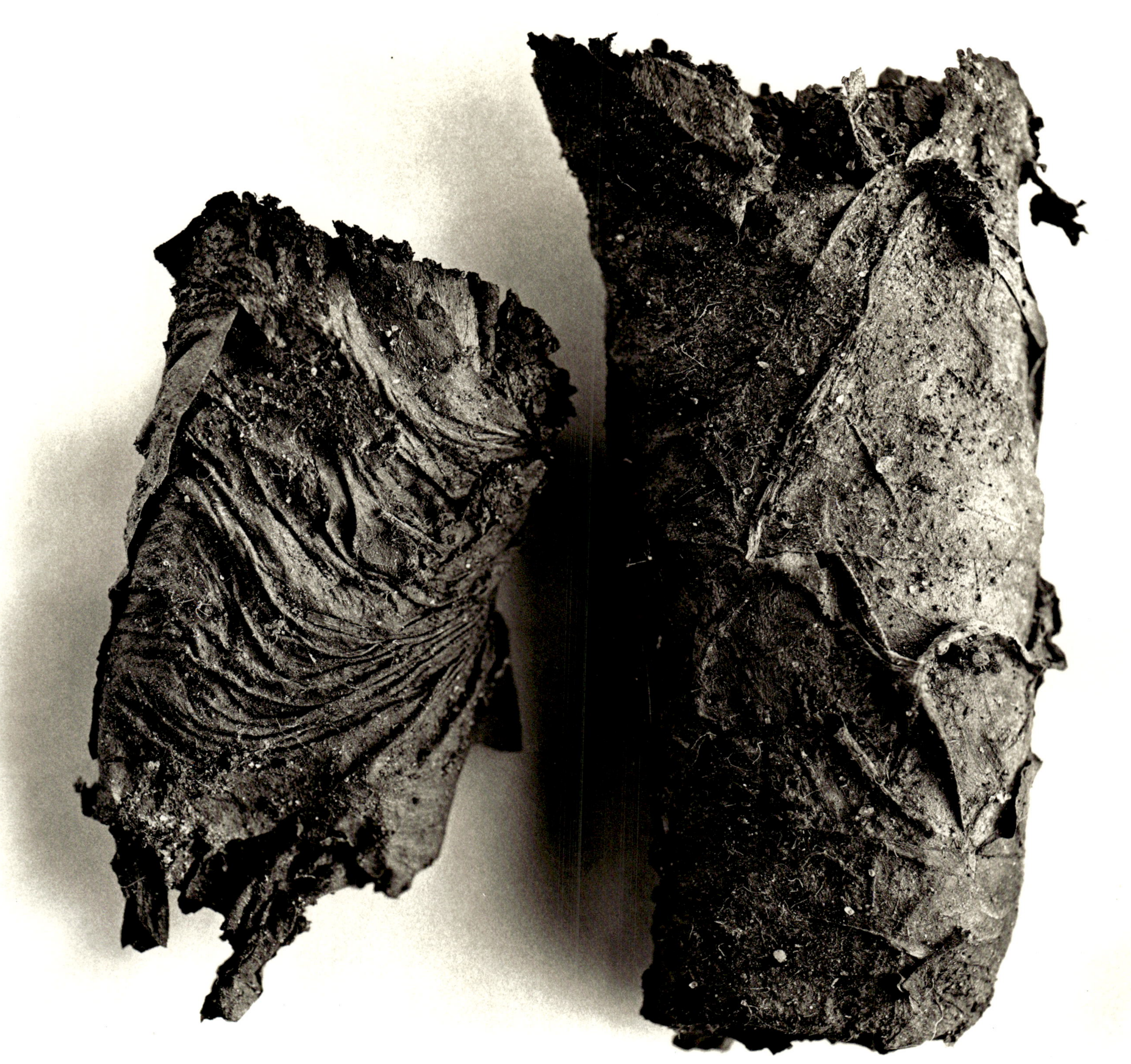

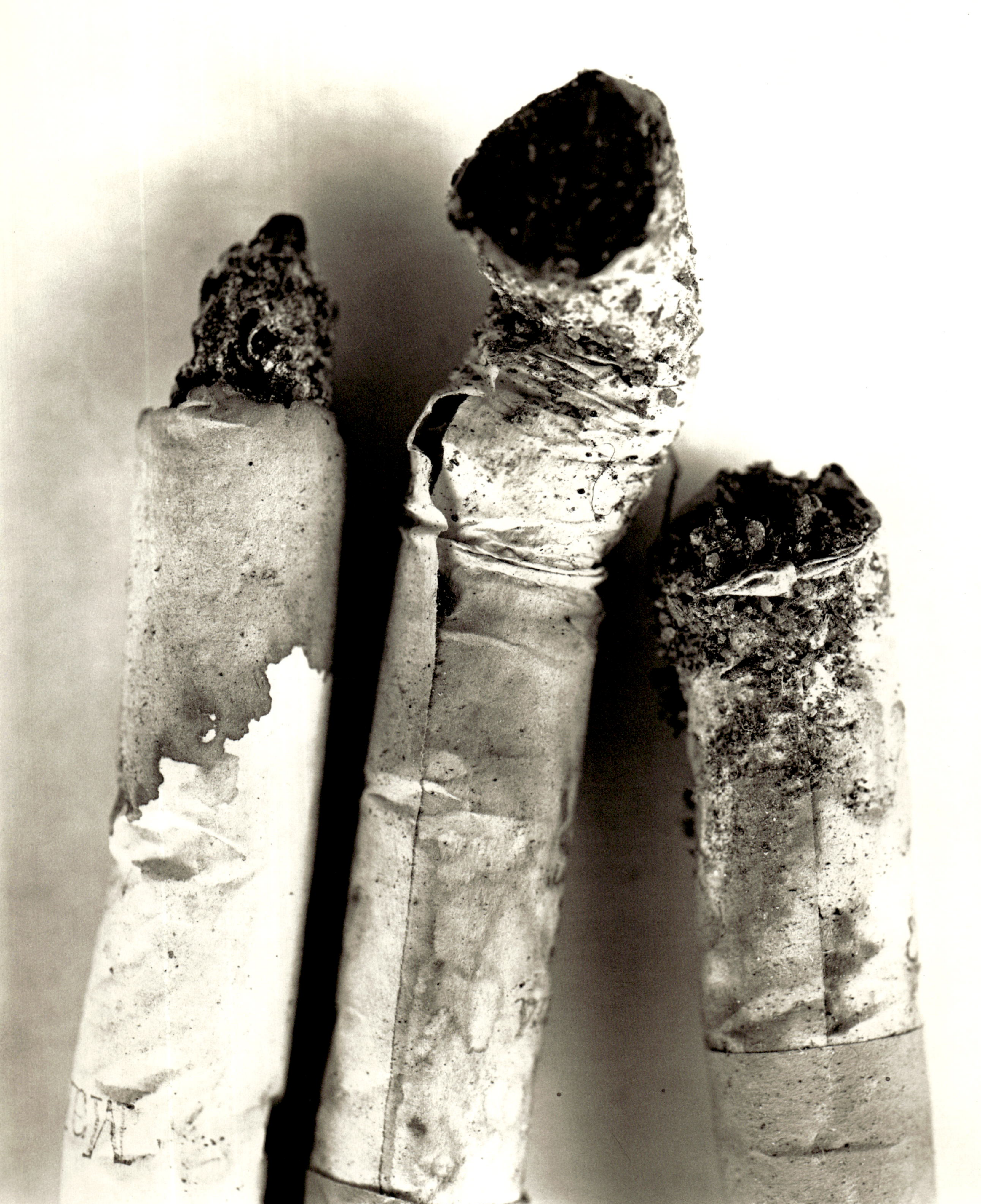

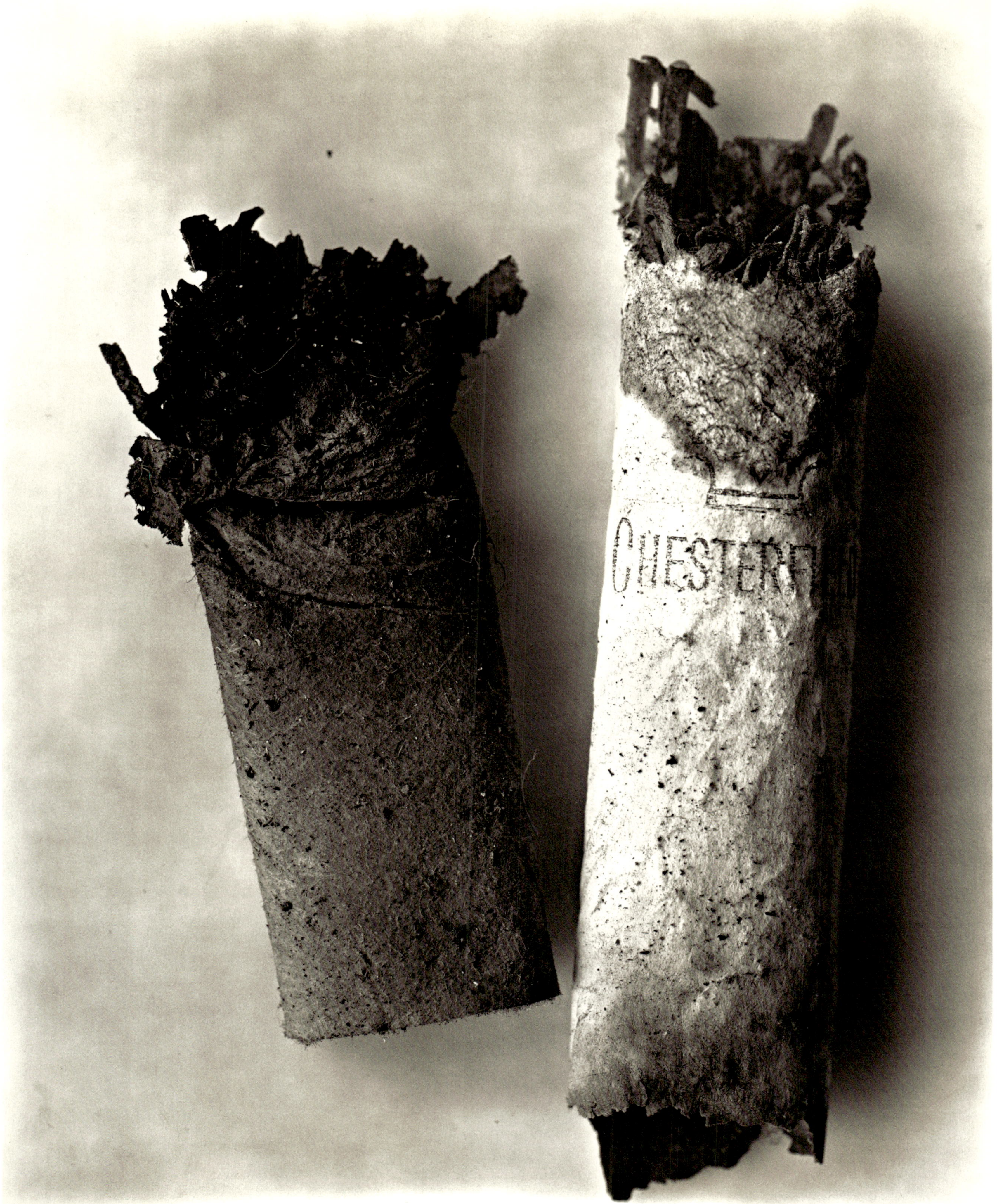
CHESTERF

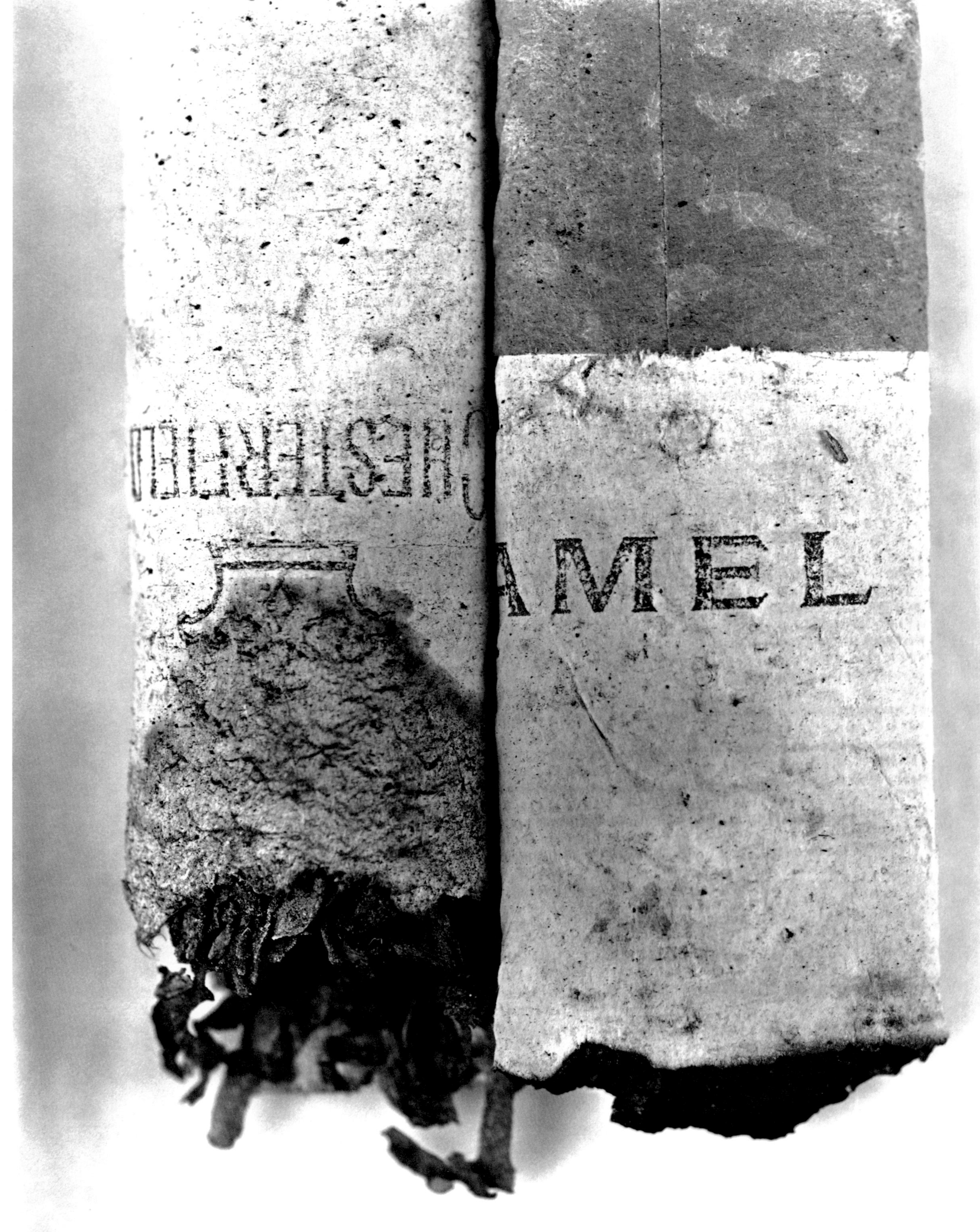

CHESTERFIELD
CAMEL

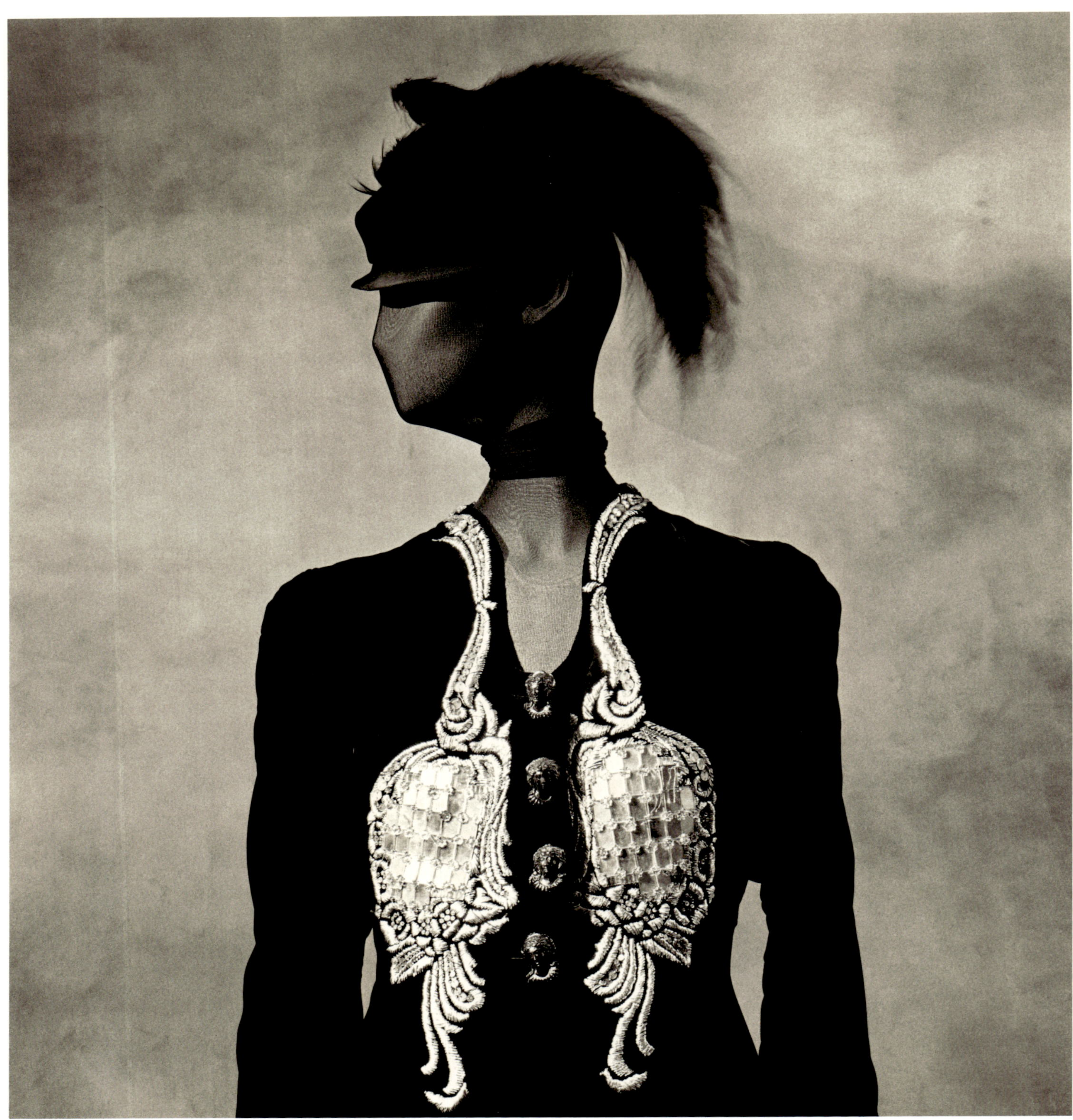

119. **Schiaparelli Jacket with Tinsel and Glass. New York, 1974. Platinum-palladium print**

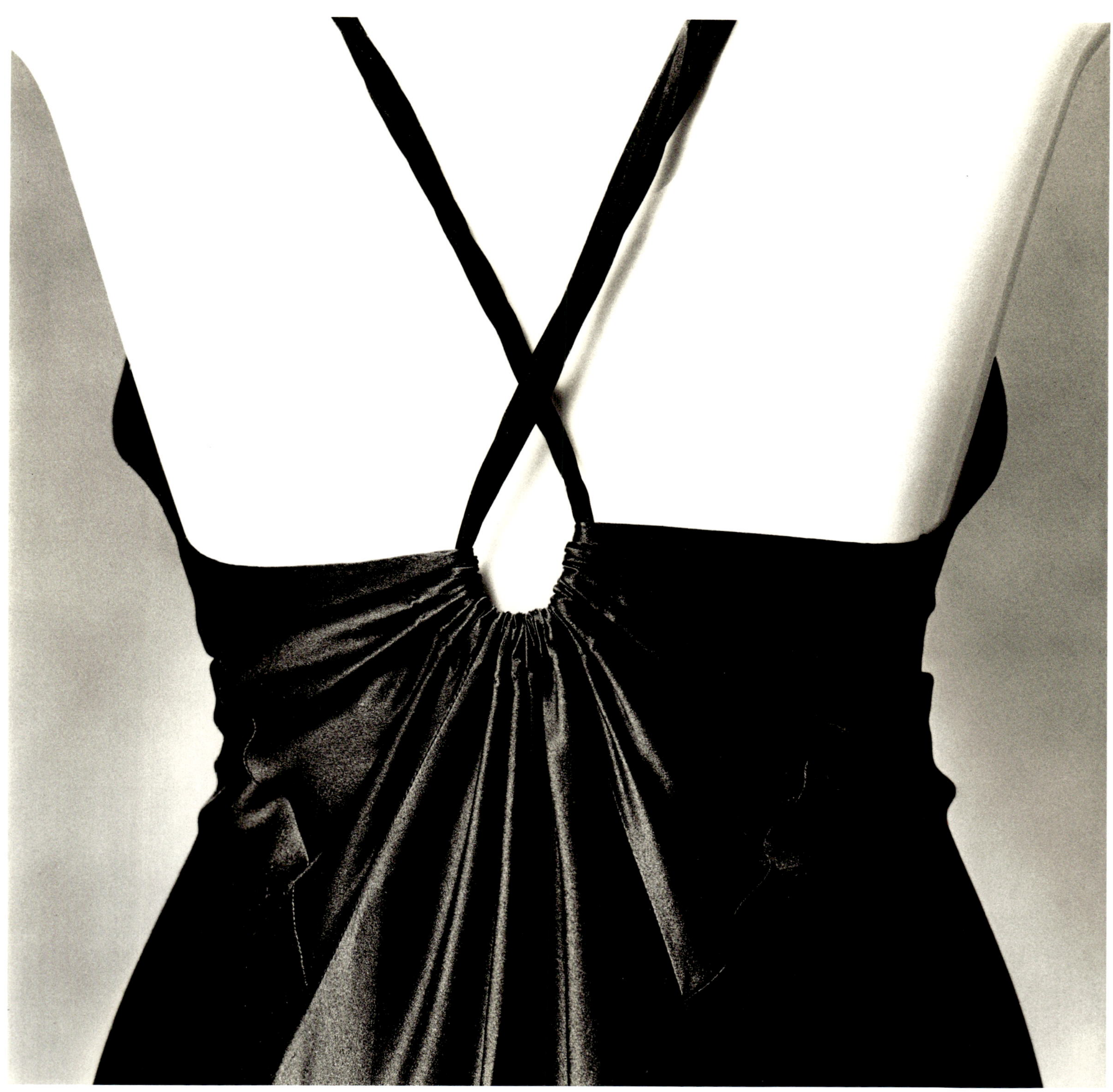

120 Vionnet Harness Dress. New York, 1974

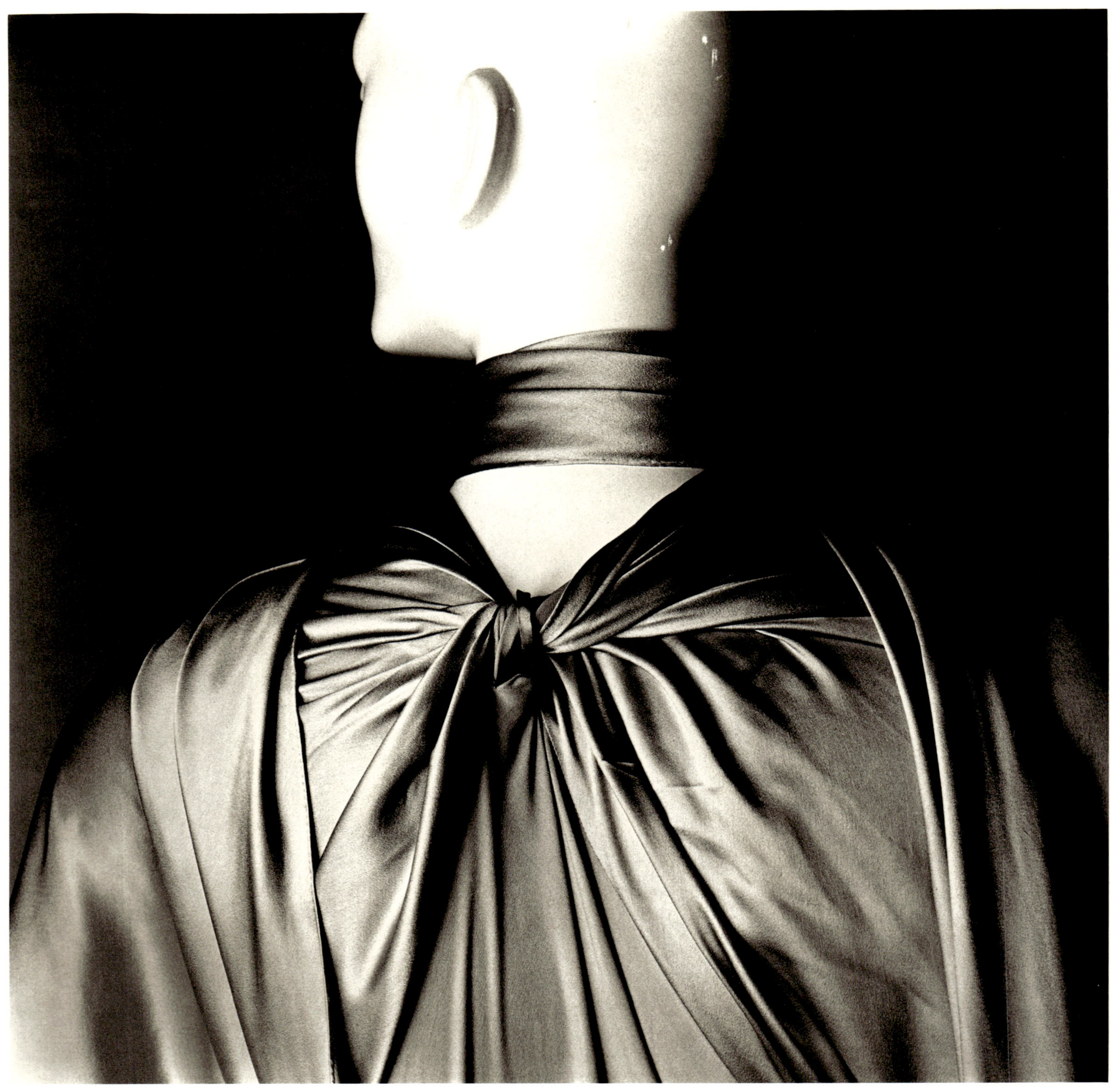

121. **Vionnet Back Tie**. New York, 1974. Platinum-palladium print

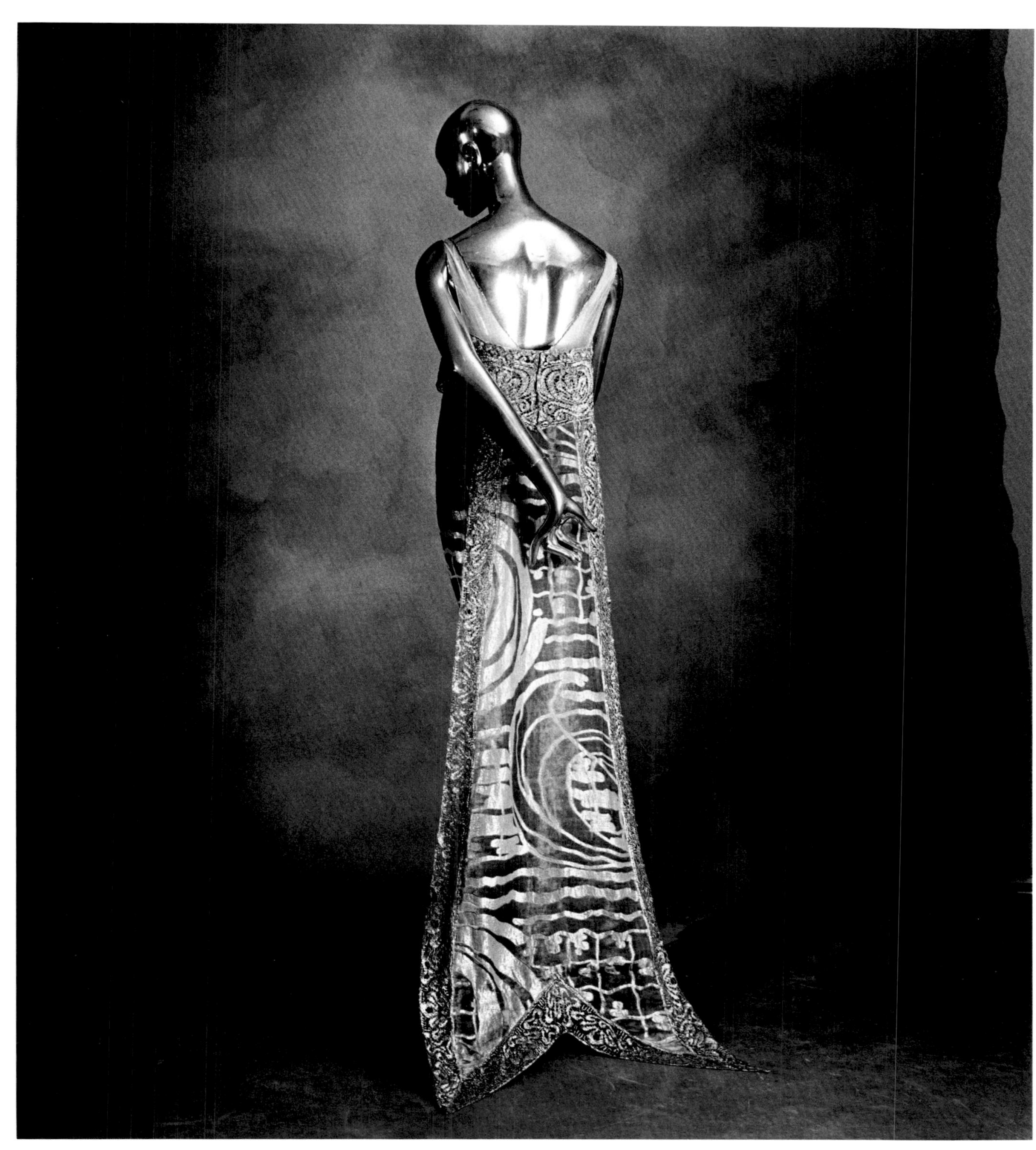

122. Callot Swallowtail Dress. New York, 1974. Platinum-palladium print

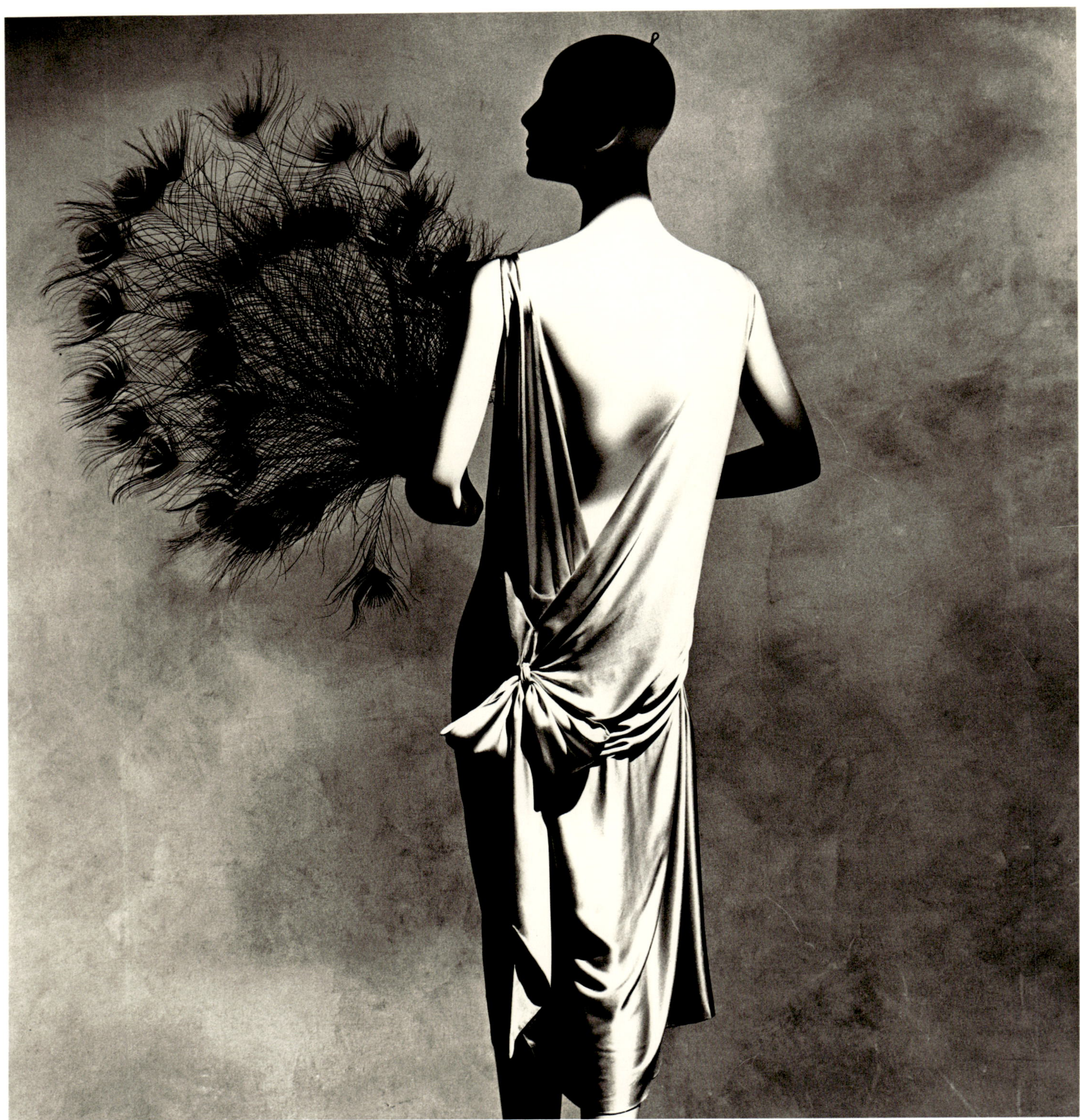

123. Vionnet Dress with Fan. New York, 1974. Platinum-palladium print

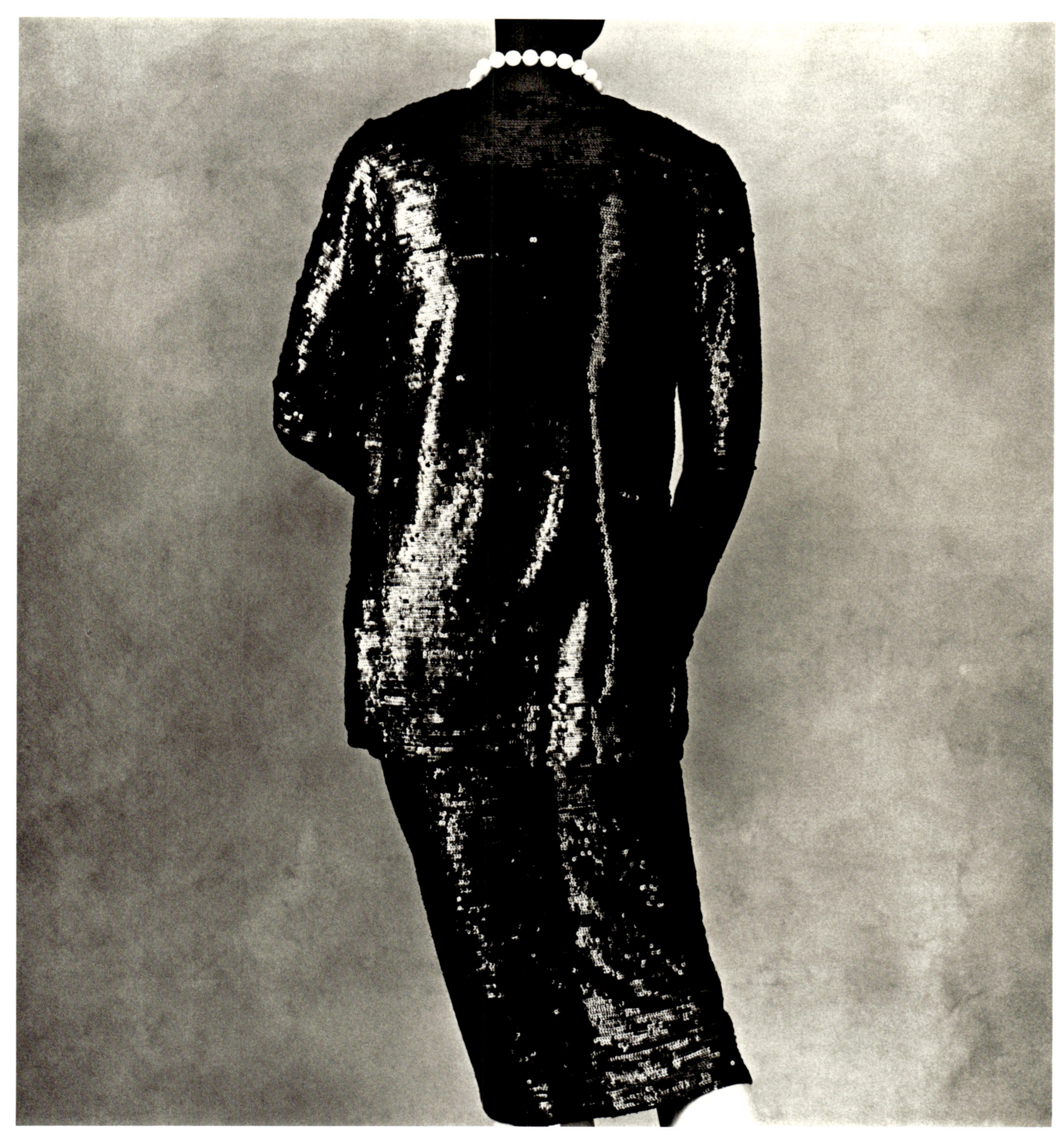

124. **Chanel Sequined Suit.** New York, 1977. Platinum-palladium print

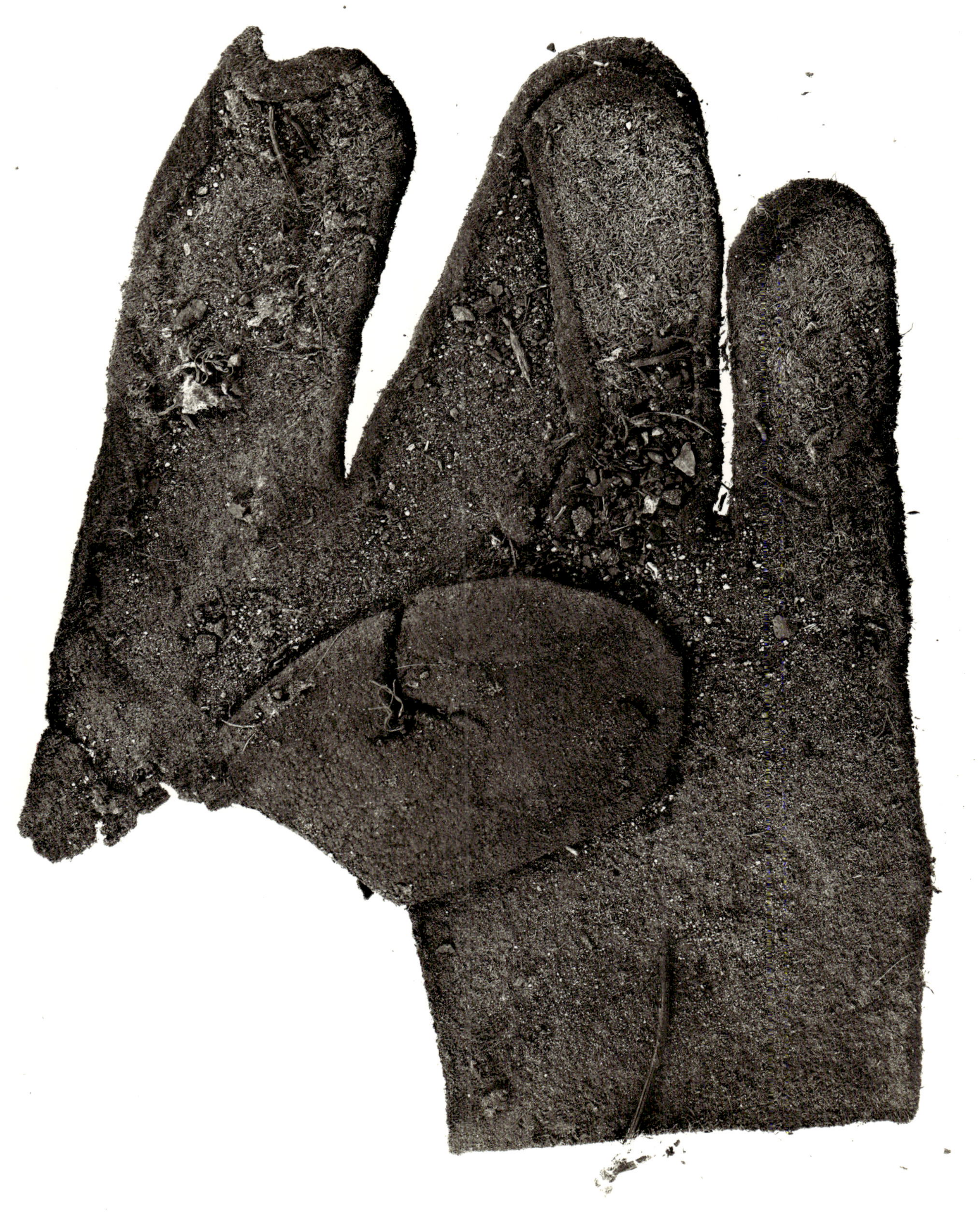

125. **Flat Glove.** New York. 1975. Platinum-palladium print

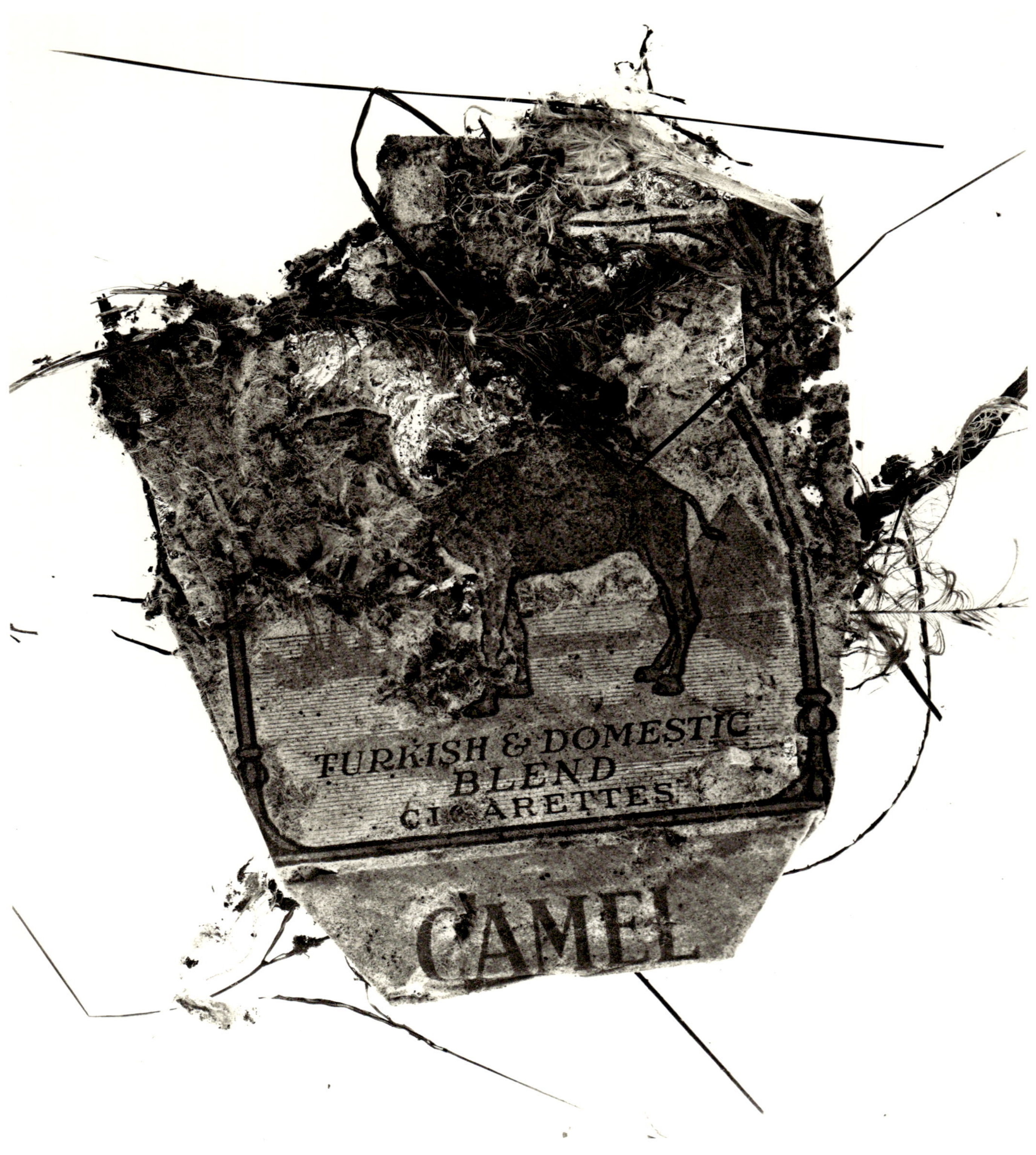

126. Camel Pack. New York, 1975. Platinum-palladium print

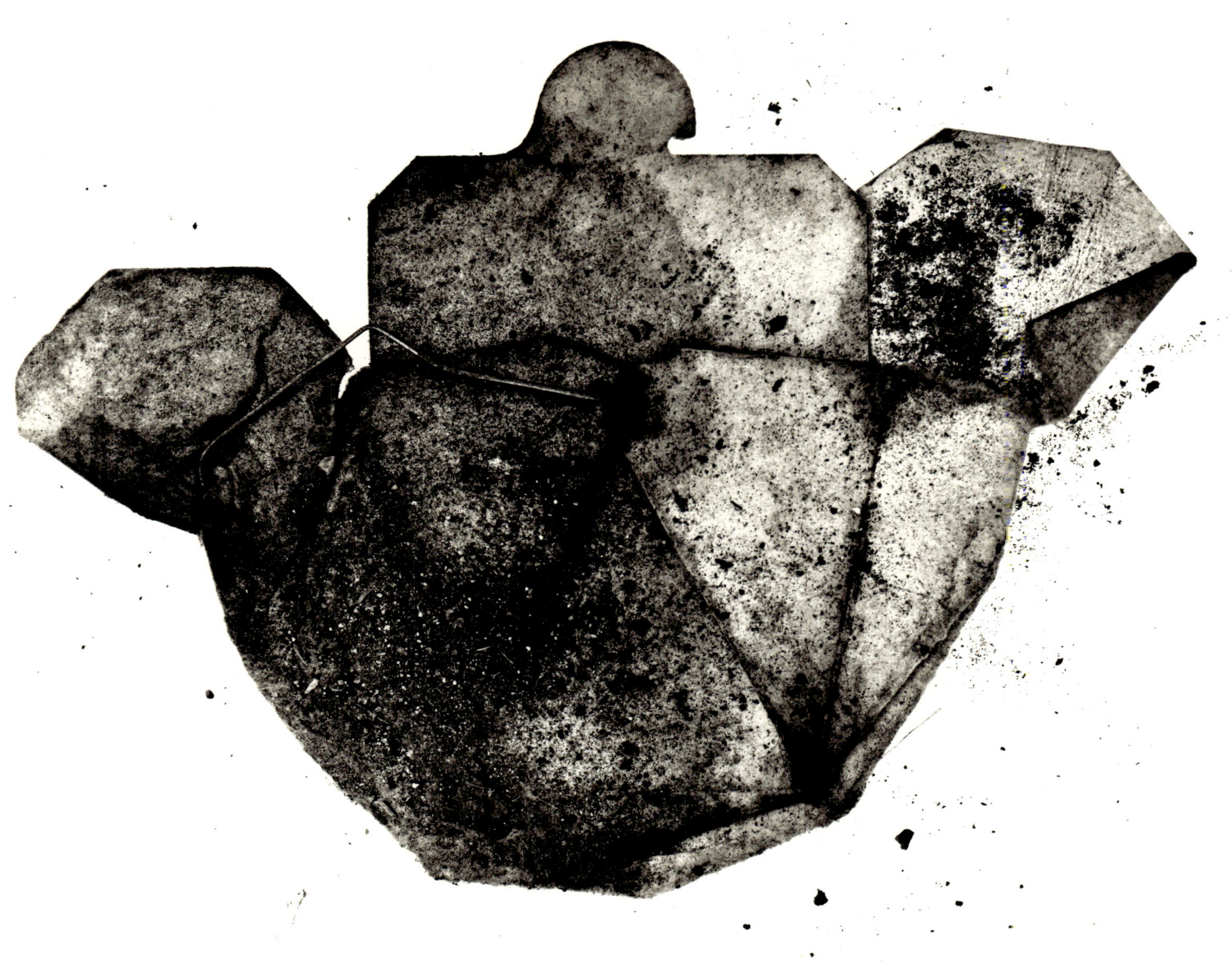

127. Deli Package. New York, 1975. Platinum-palladium print

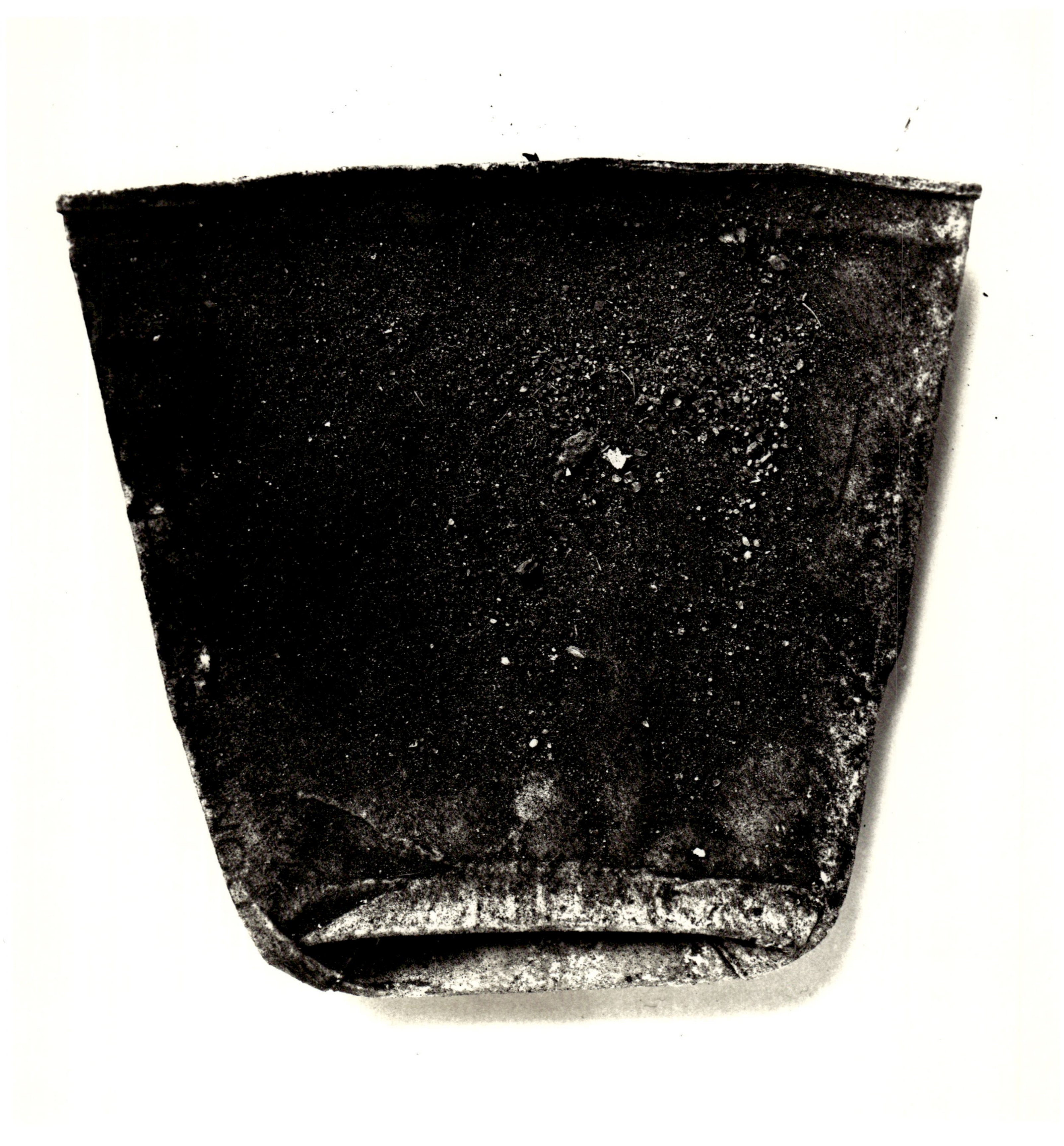

128. **Paper Cup (with Shadow)**. New York, 1975. Platinum-palladium print

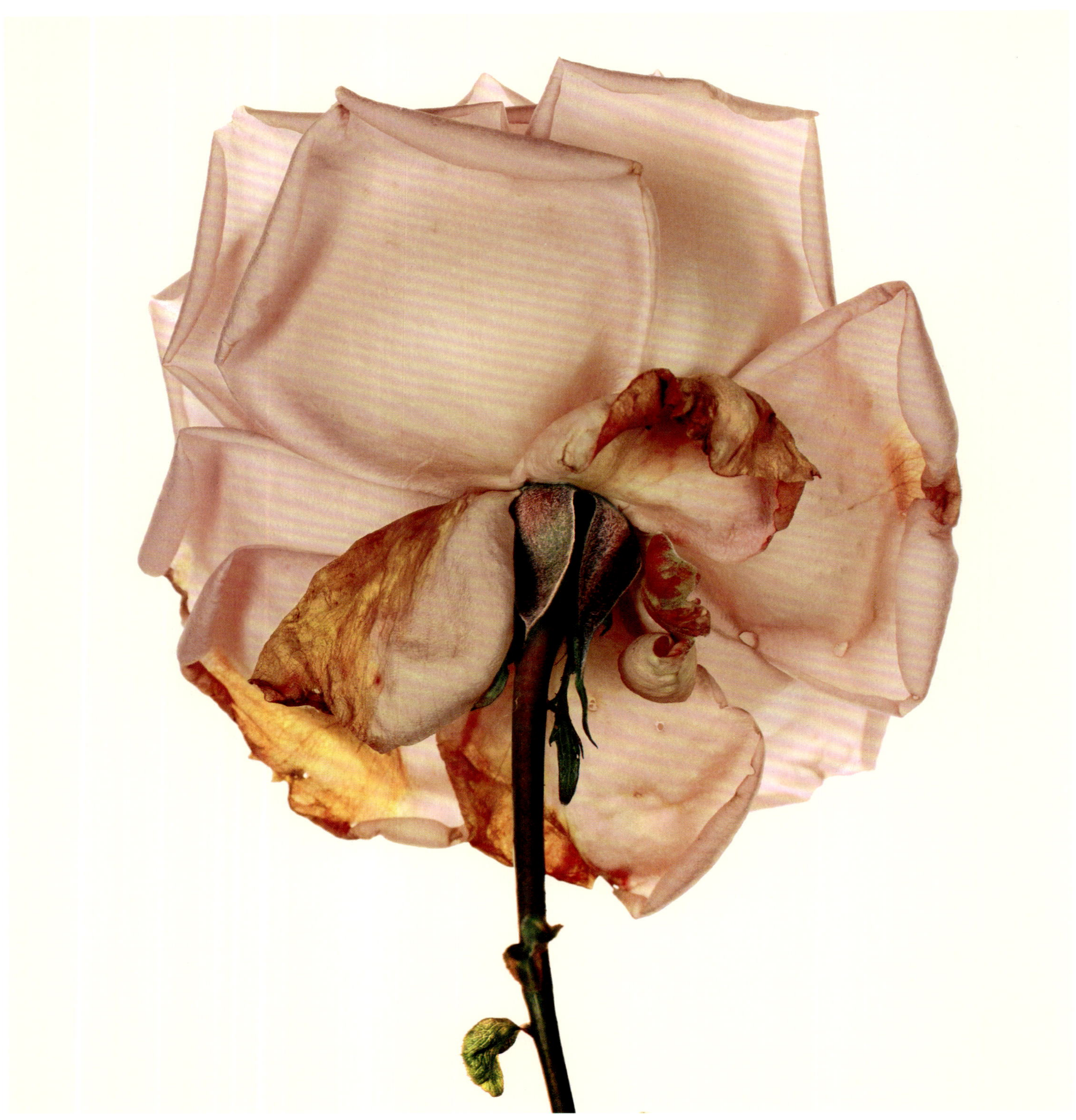

129. **Blue Moon Rose**. London, 1970. Reproduced from Ektachrome transparency

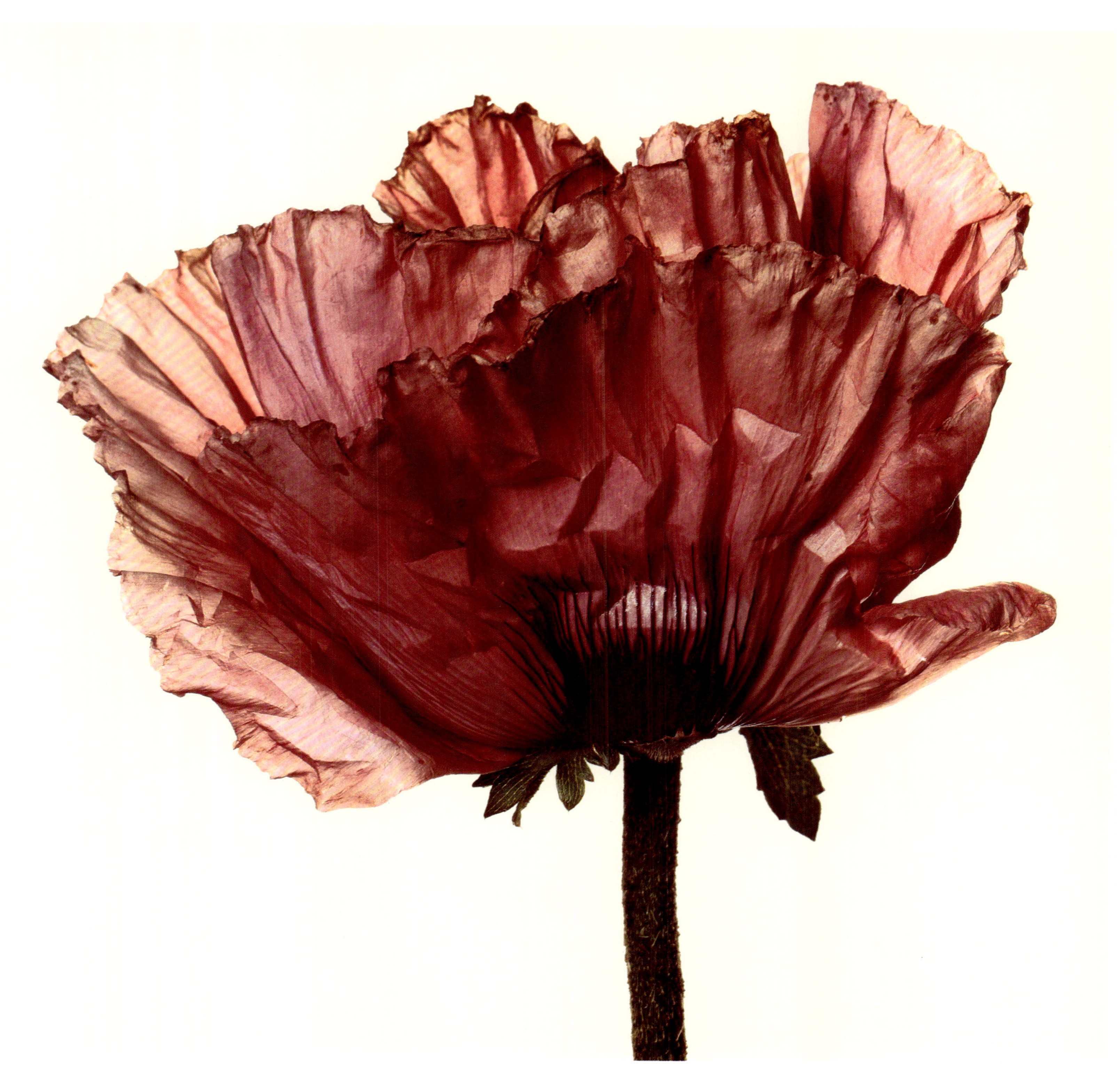

130. **Lavender Glory Poppy.** New York, 1968. Reproduced from Ektachrome transparency

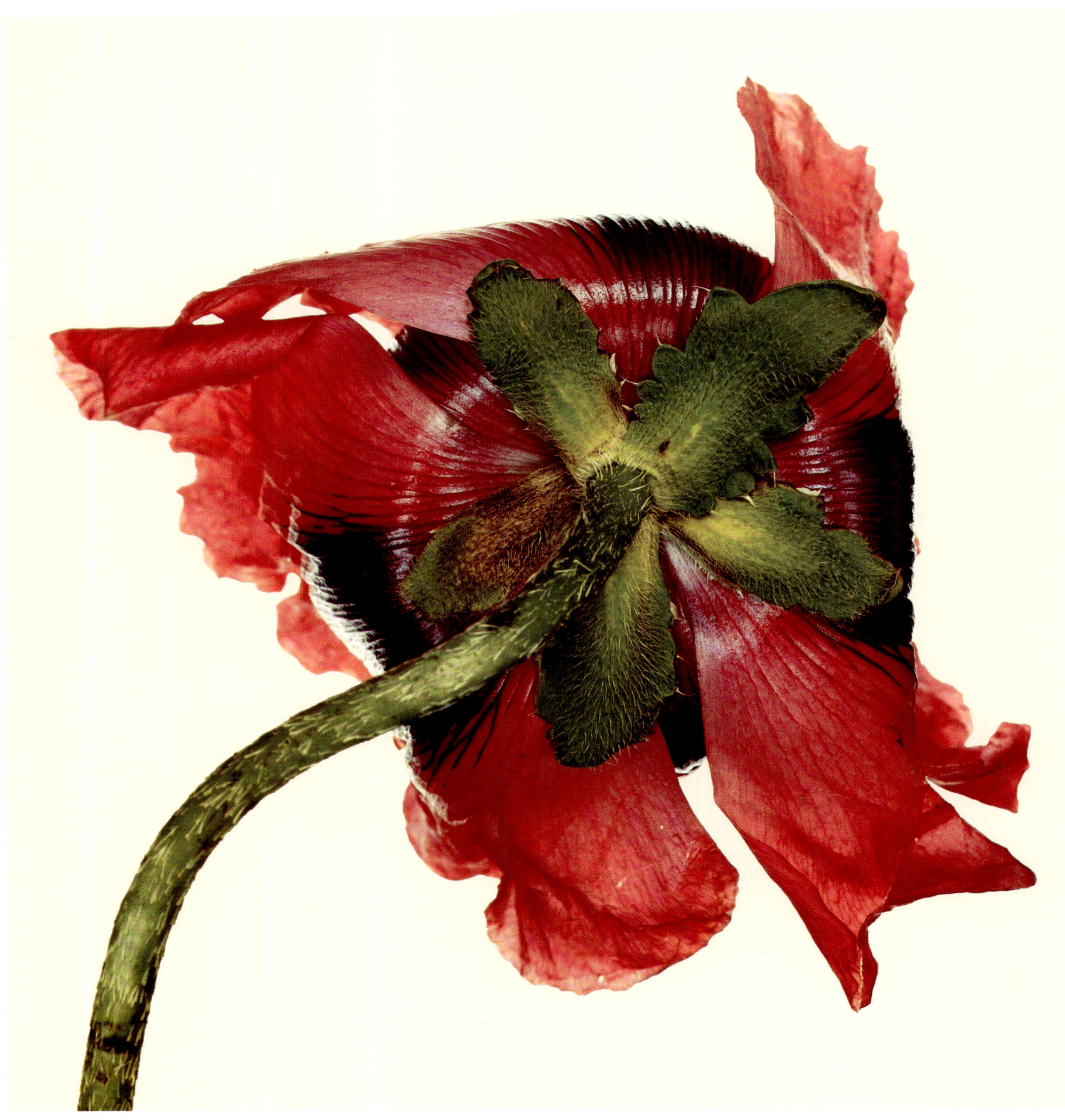

131. **Single Oriental Poppy.** New York, 1968. Reproduced from Ektachrome transparency

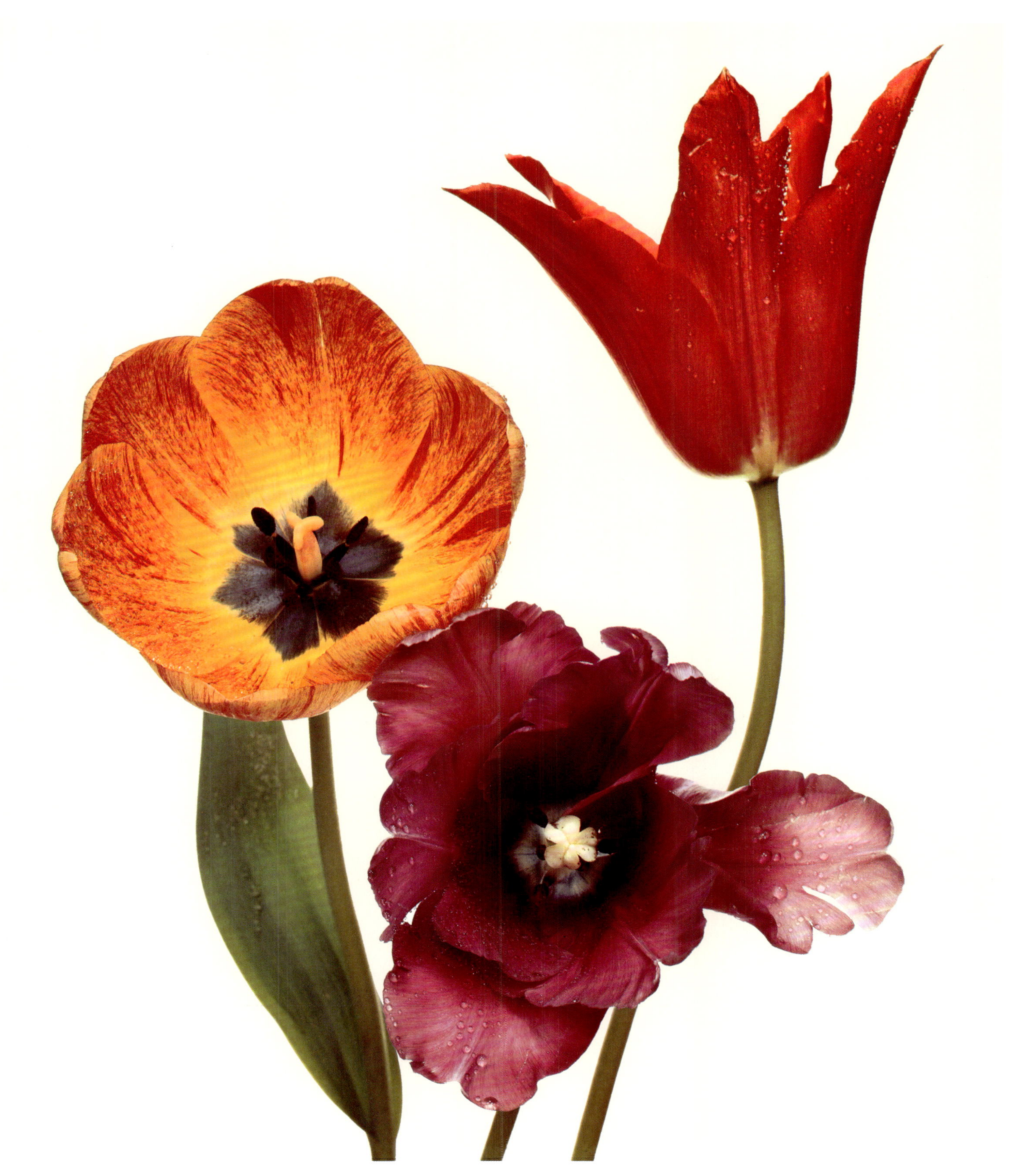

132. **Three Tulips**. New York, 1967. Reproduced from Ektachrome transparency

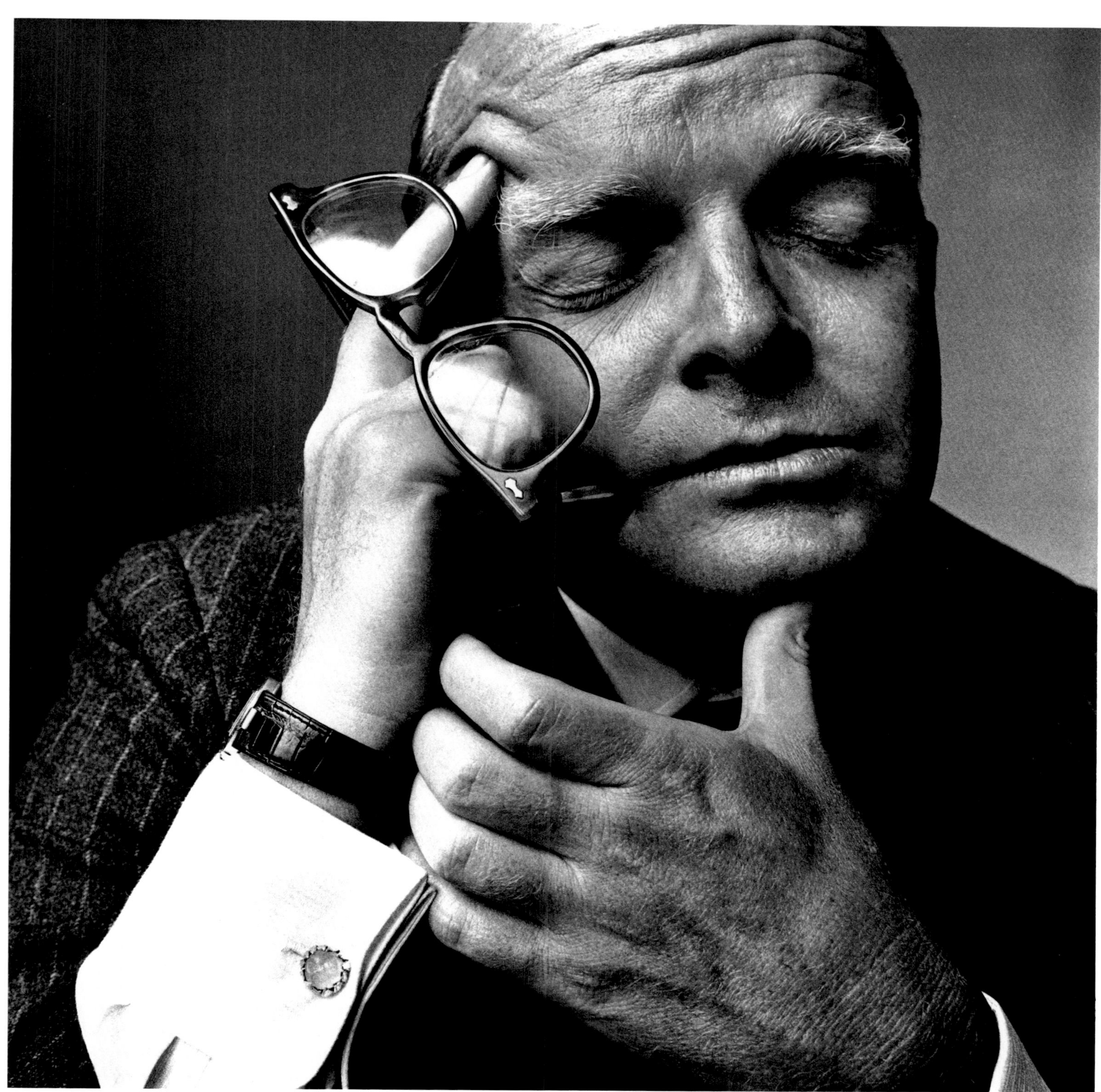

133. Truman Capote. New York, 1965

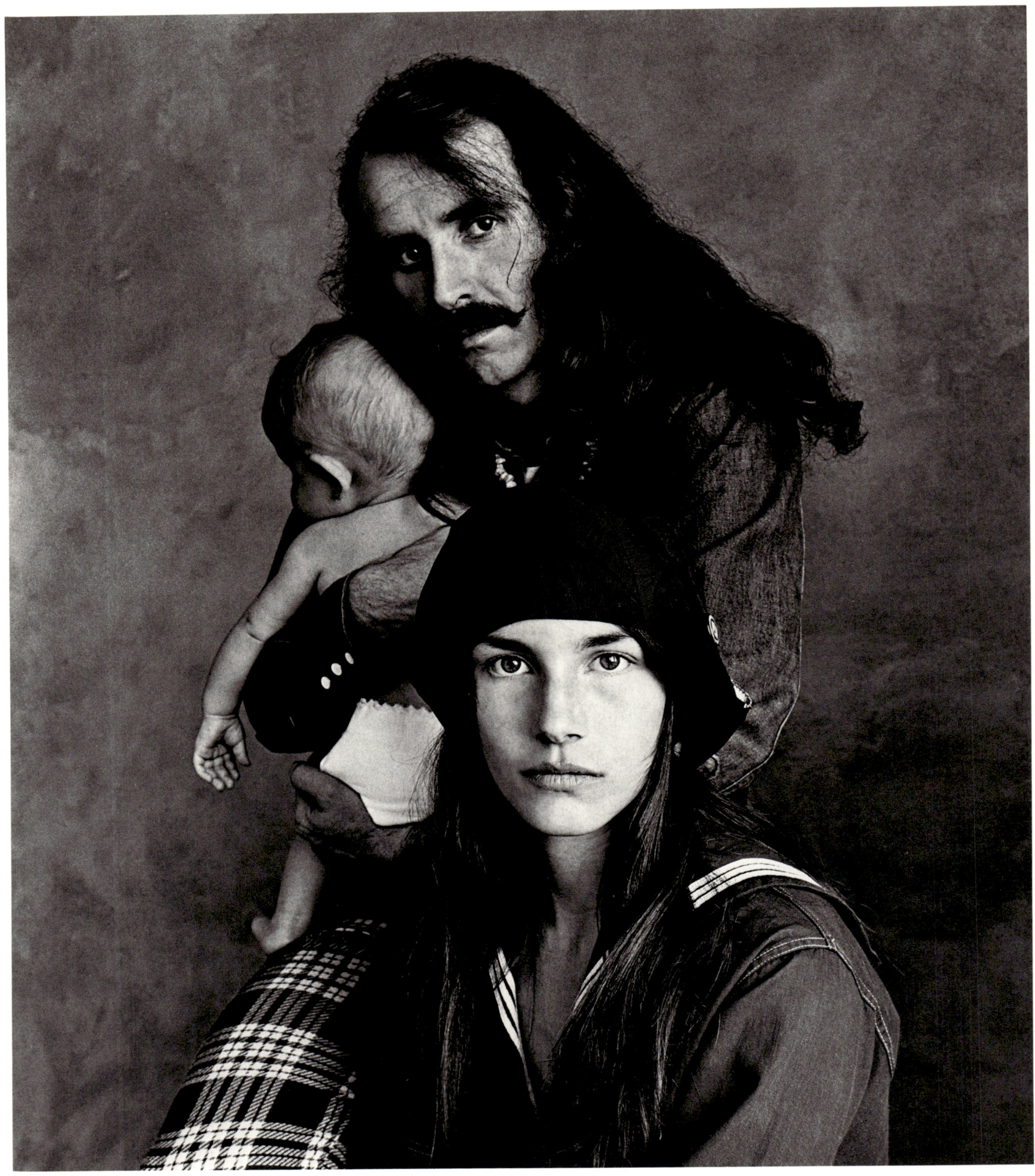

134. **Hippie Family.** San Francisco, 1967. Platinum-palladium print, 1981

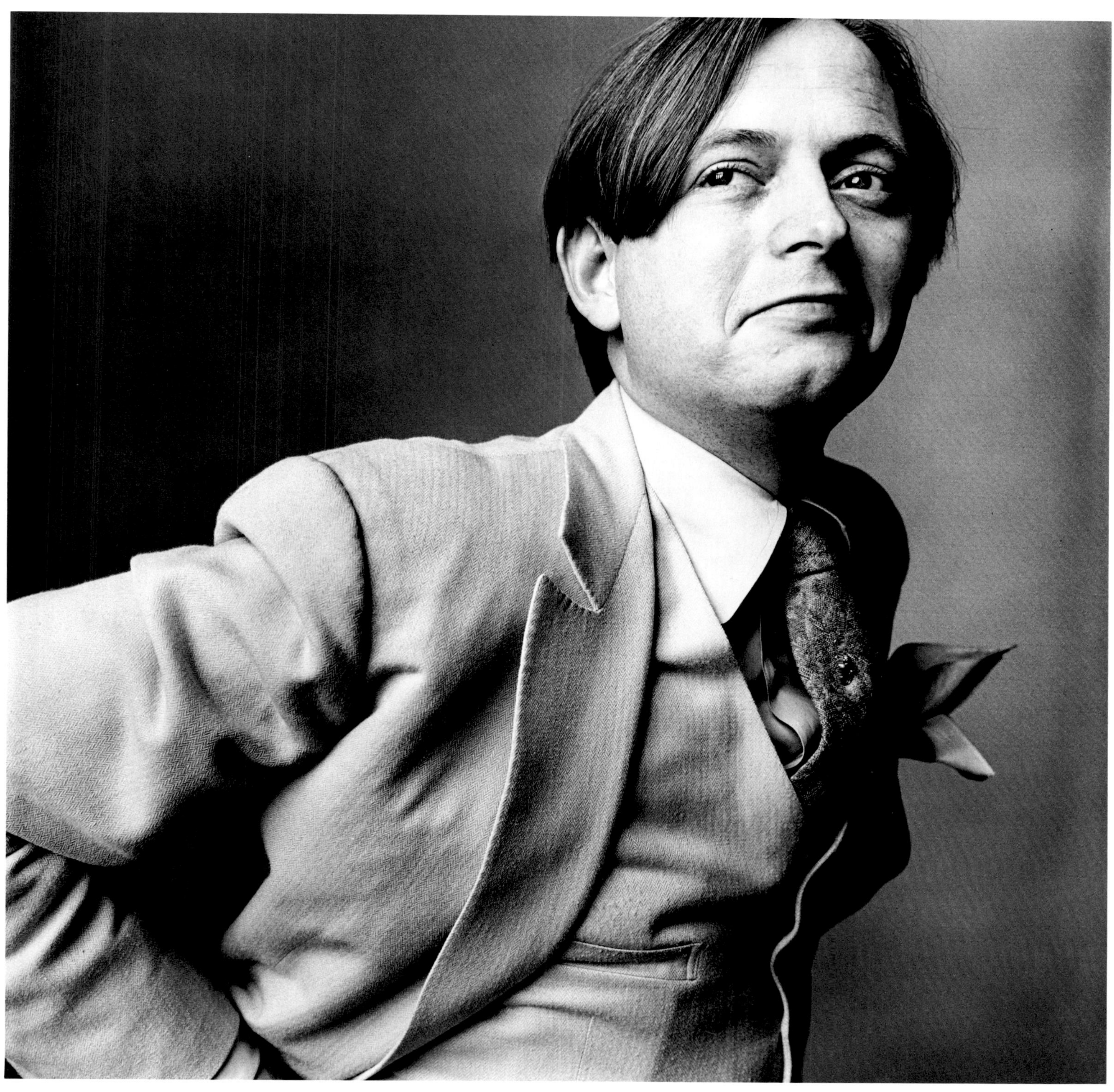

135. Tom Wolfe. New York, 1966

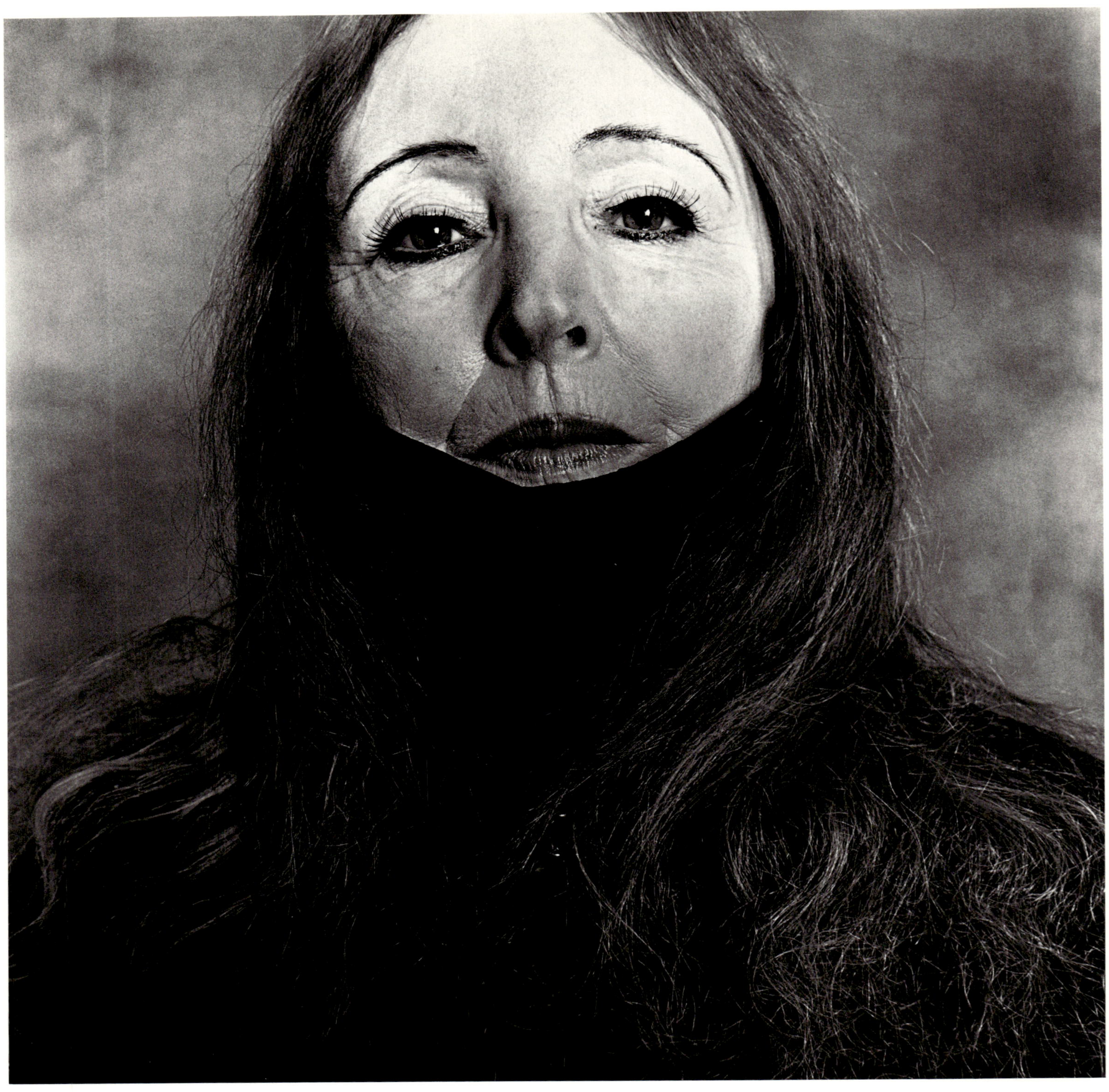

136. **Anaïs Nin**. New York, 1971. Platinum-palladium print, 1982

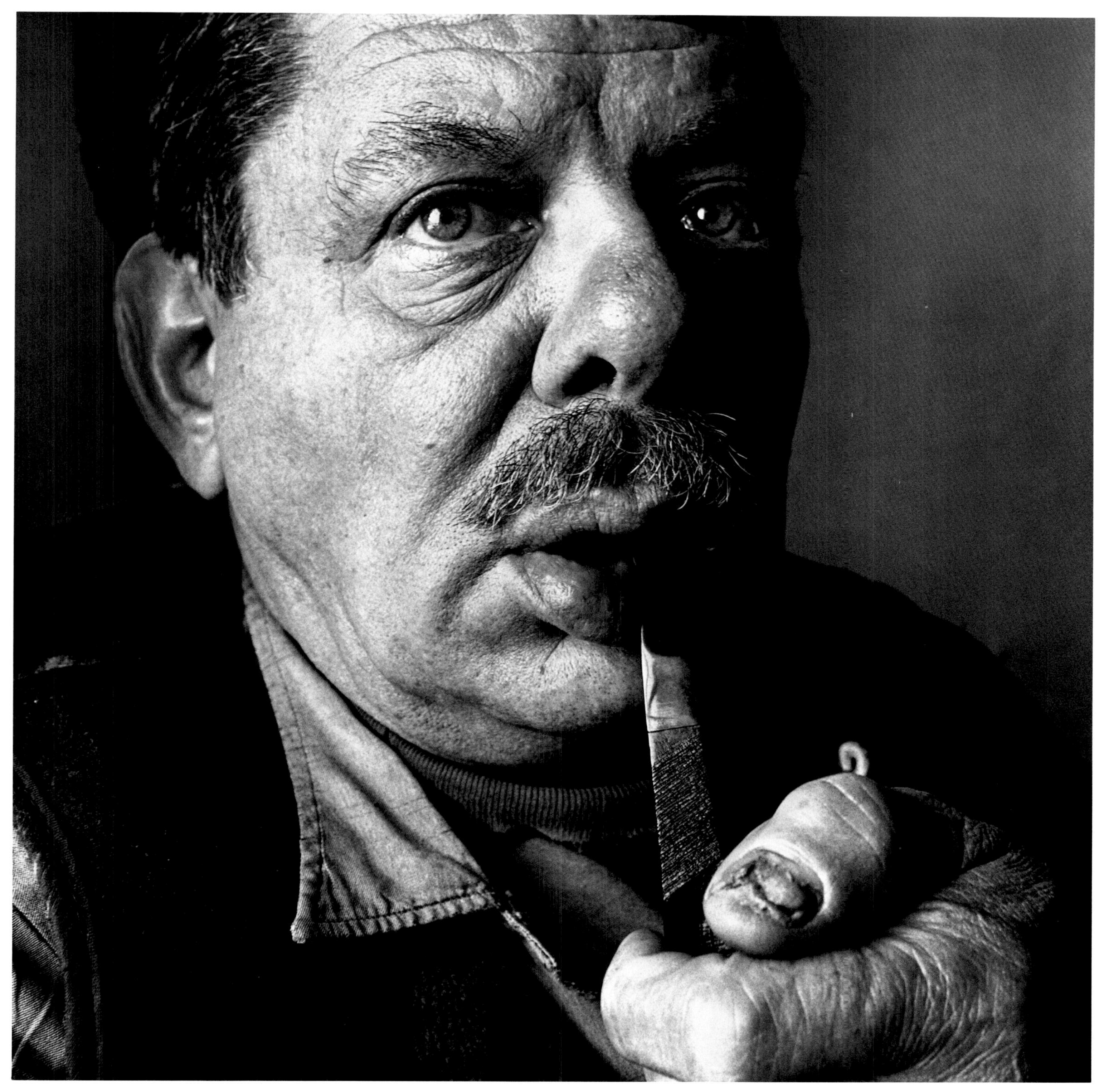

137. **David Smith**. Bolton's Landing, New York, 1964. Platinum-palladium print, 1979

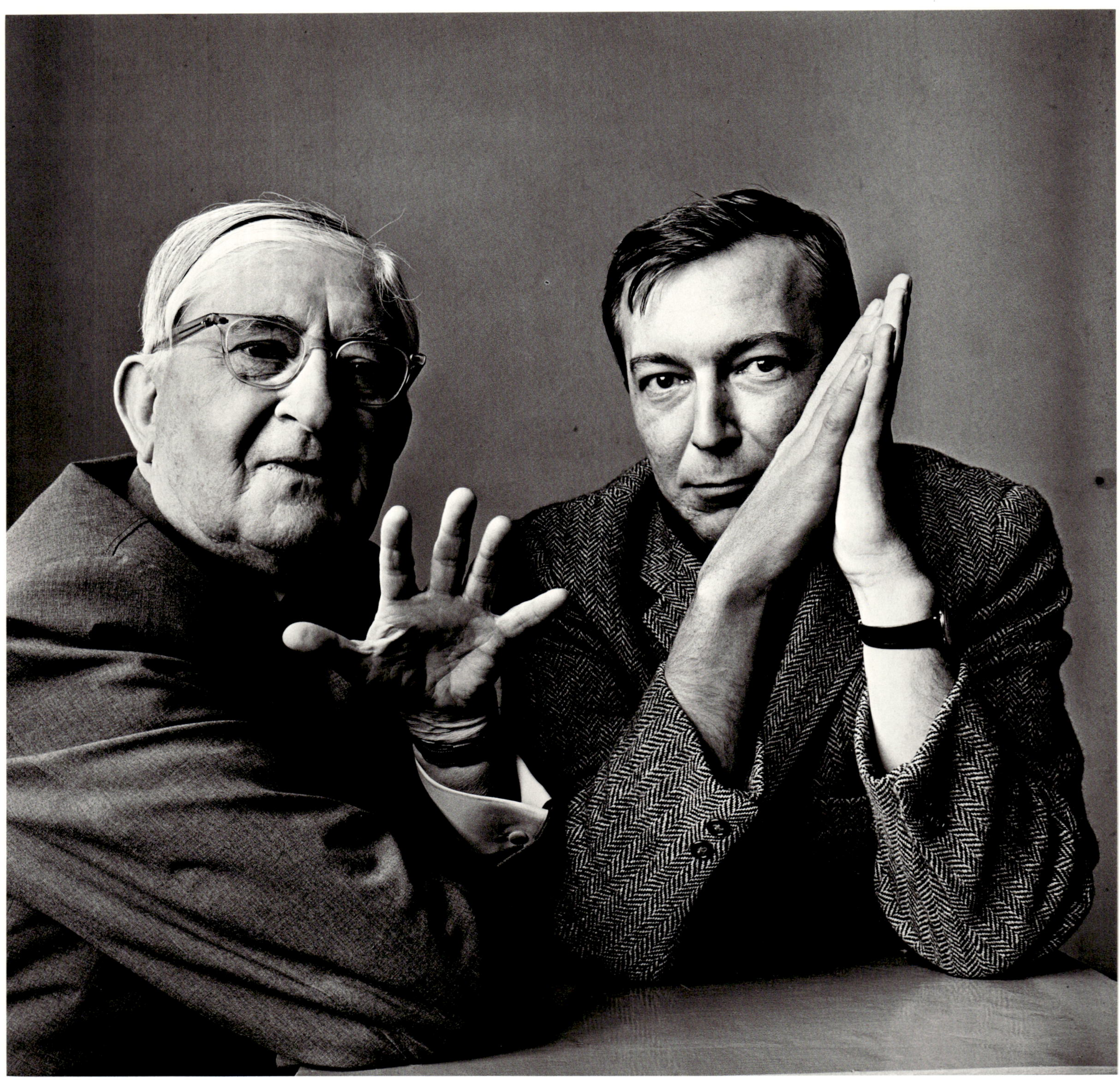

138. Josef Albers and Jasper Johns. New York, 1964

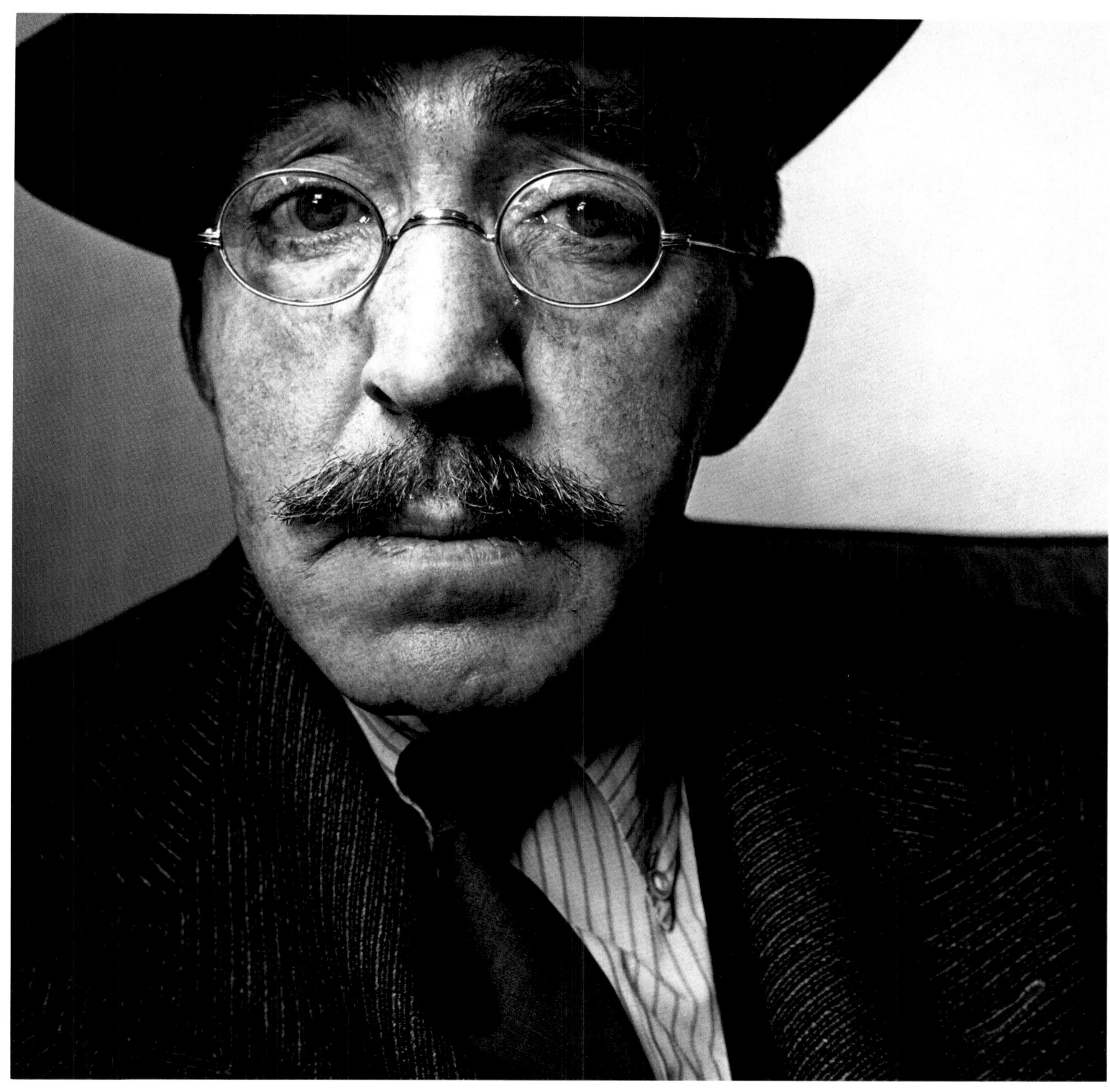

139. S. J. Perelman. New York, 1962. Platinum-palladium print, 1980

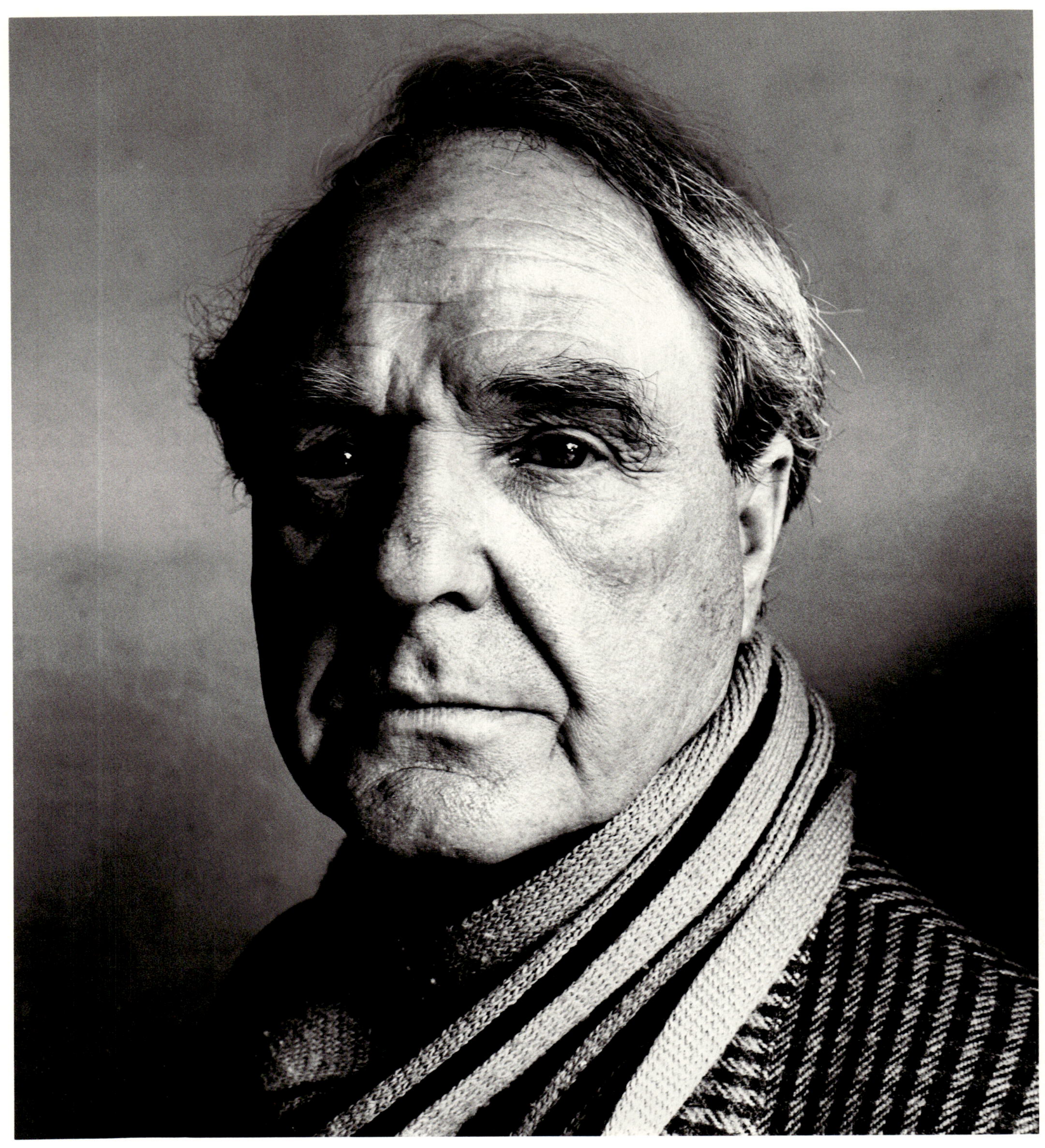

140. **Henry Moore**. Much Haddam, Hertfordshire, England, 1962

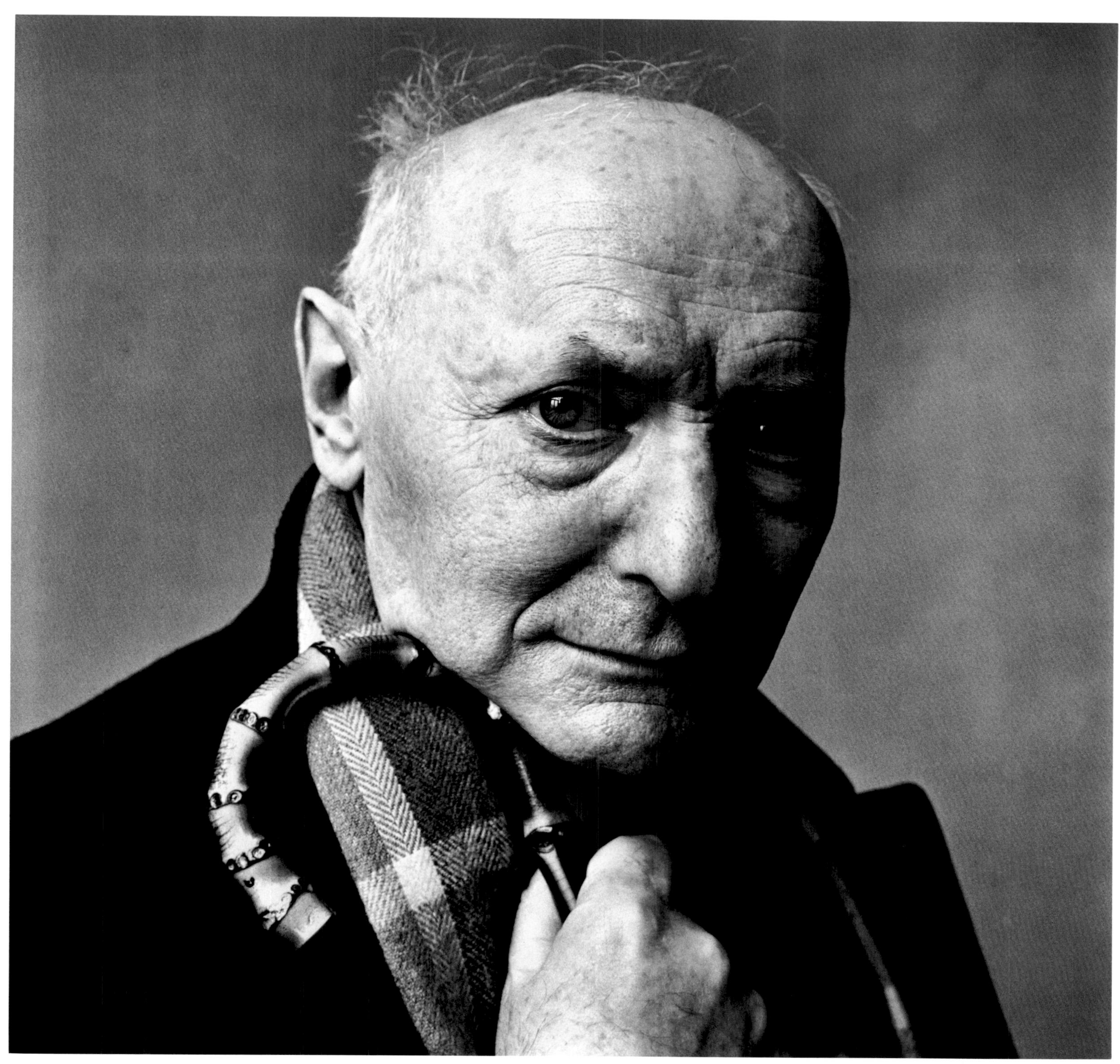

141. Isaac Bashevis Singer. New York, 1966. Platinum-palladium print, 1982

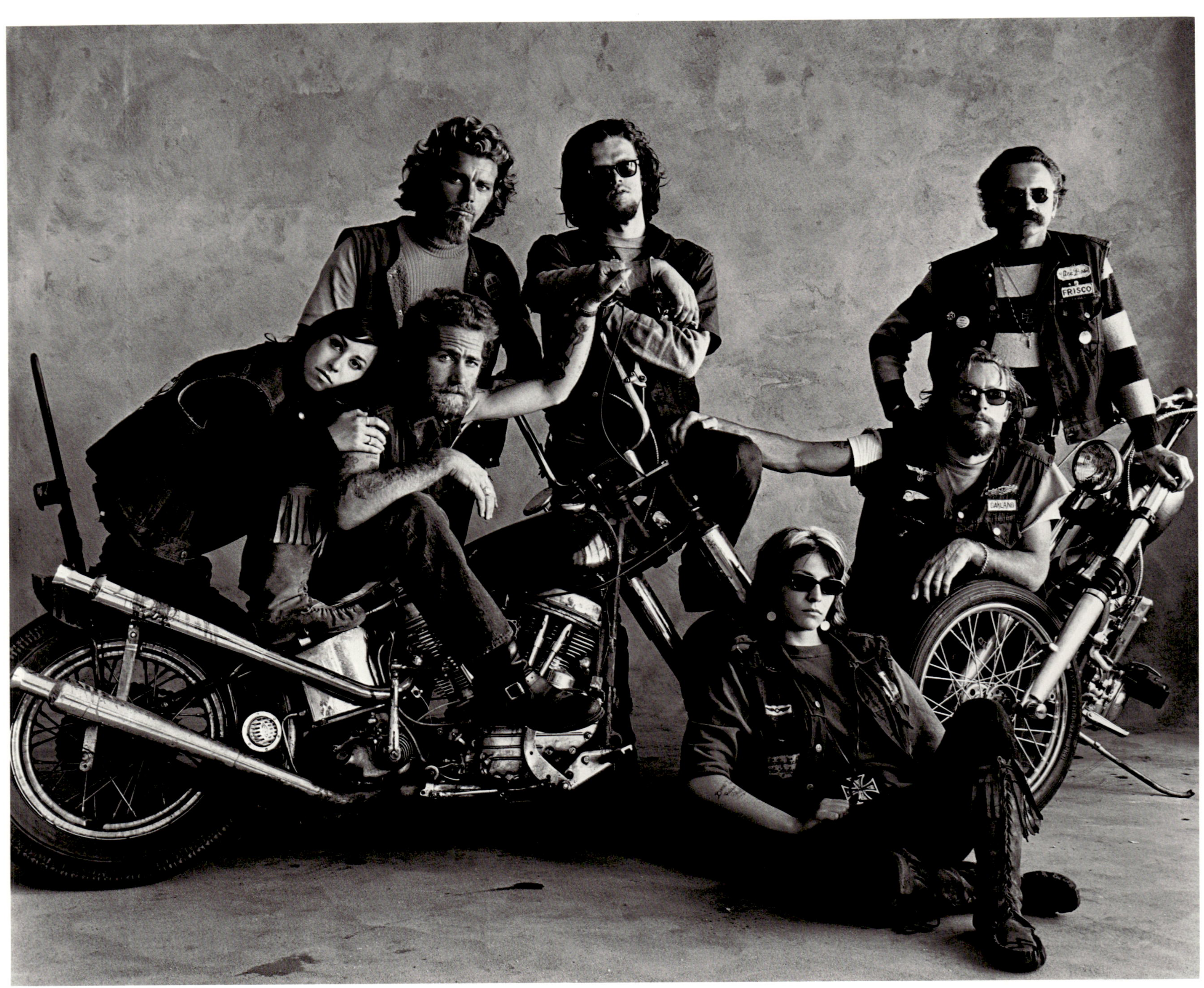

142. **Hell's Angels**. San Francisco, 1967. Platinum-palladium print, 1978

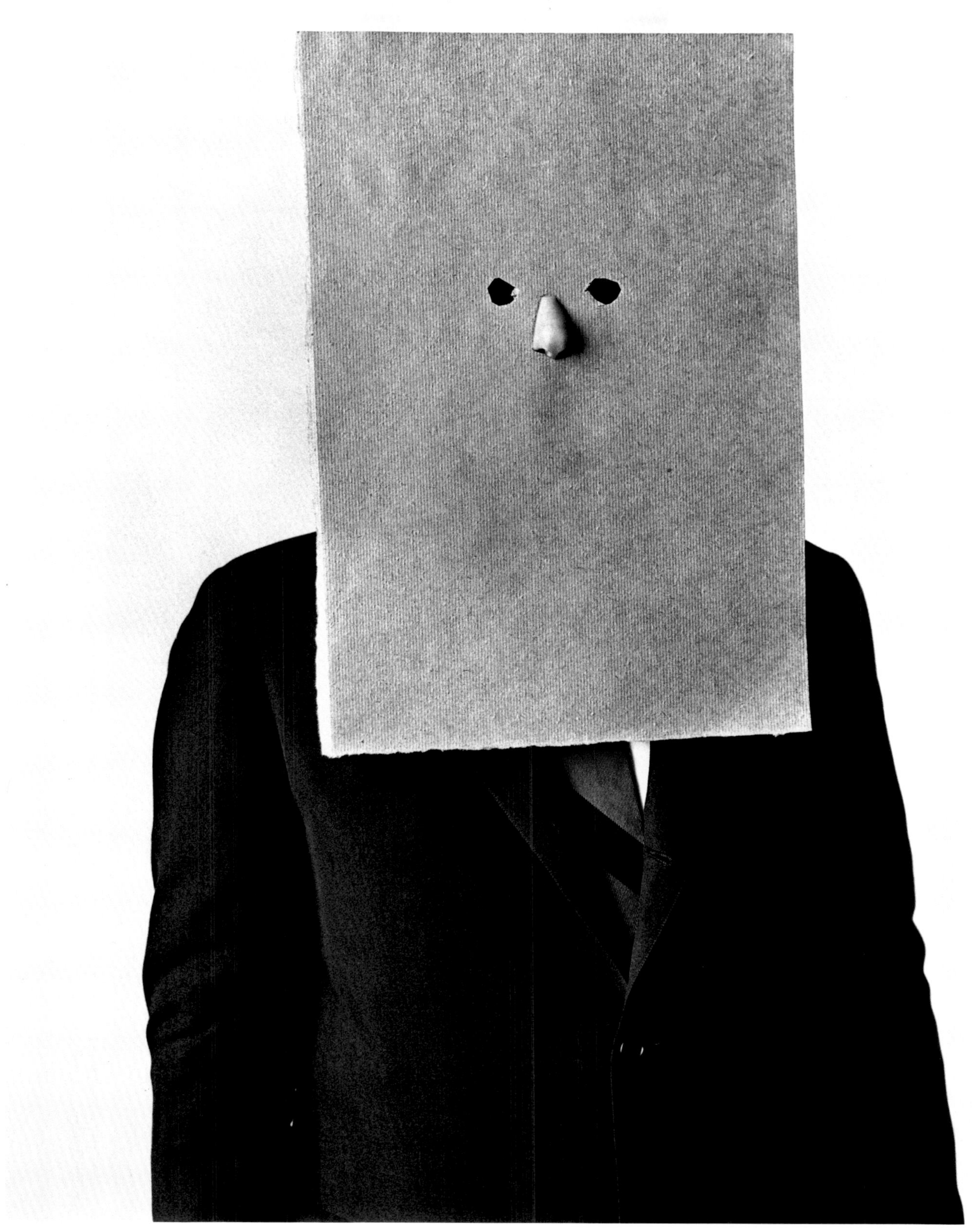

143. Saul Steinberg in Nose Mask. New York, 1966. Platinum-palladium print, 1979

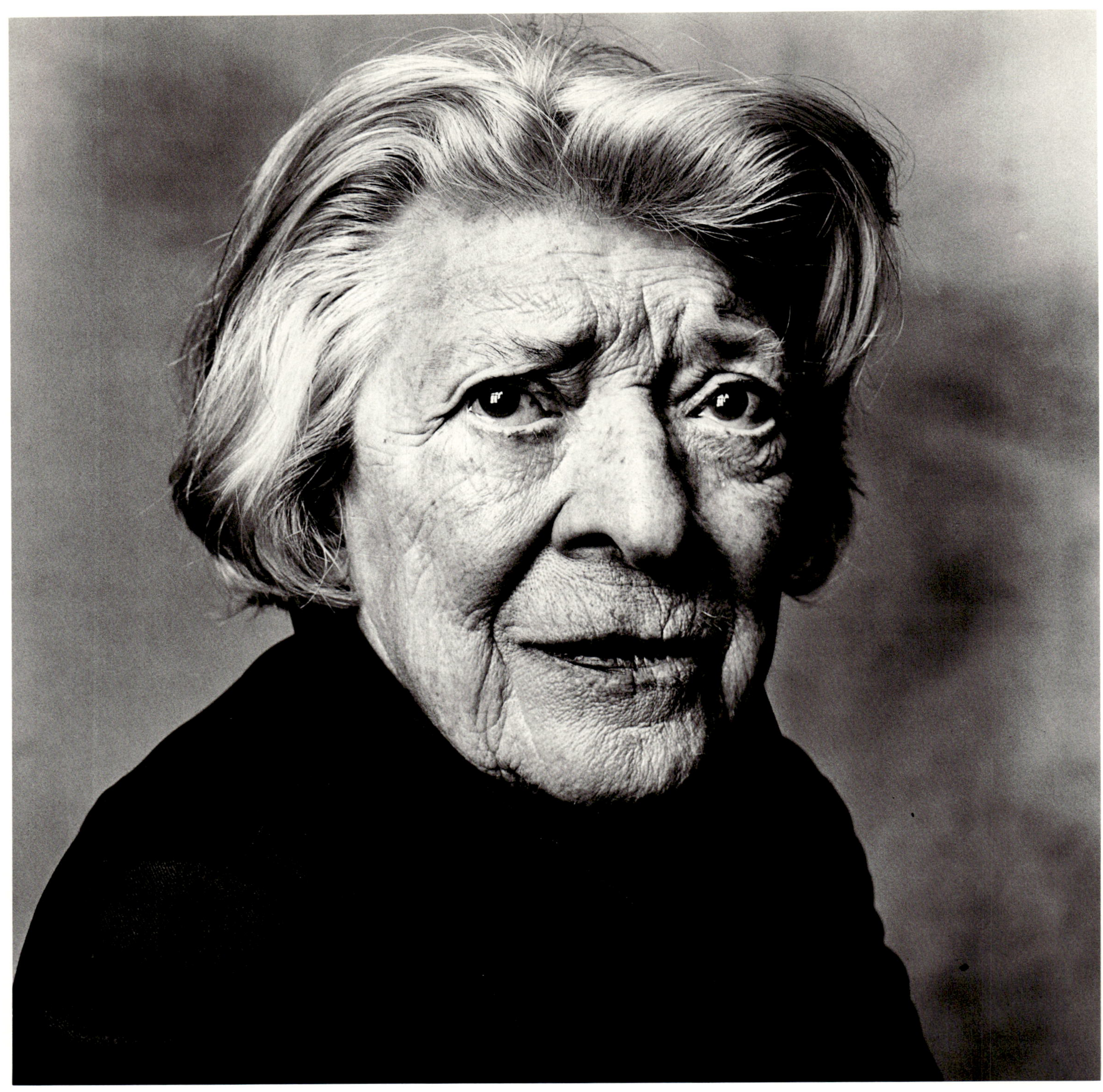

144. Janet Flanner. New York, 1971

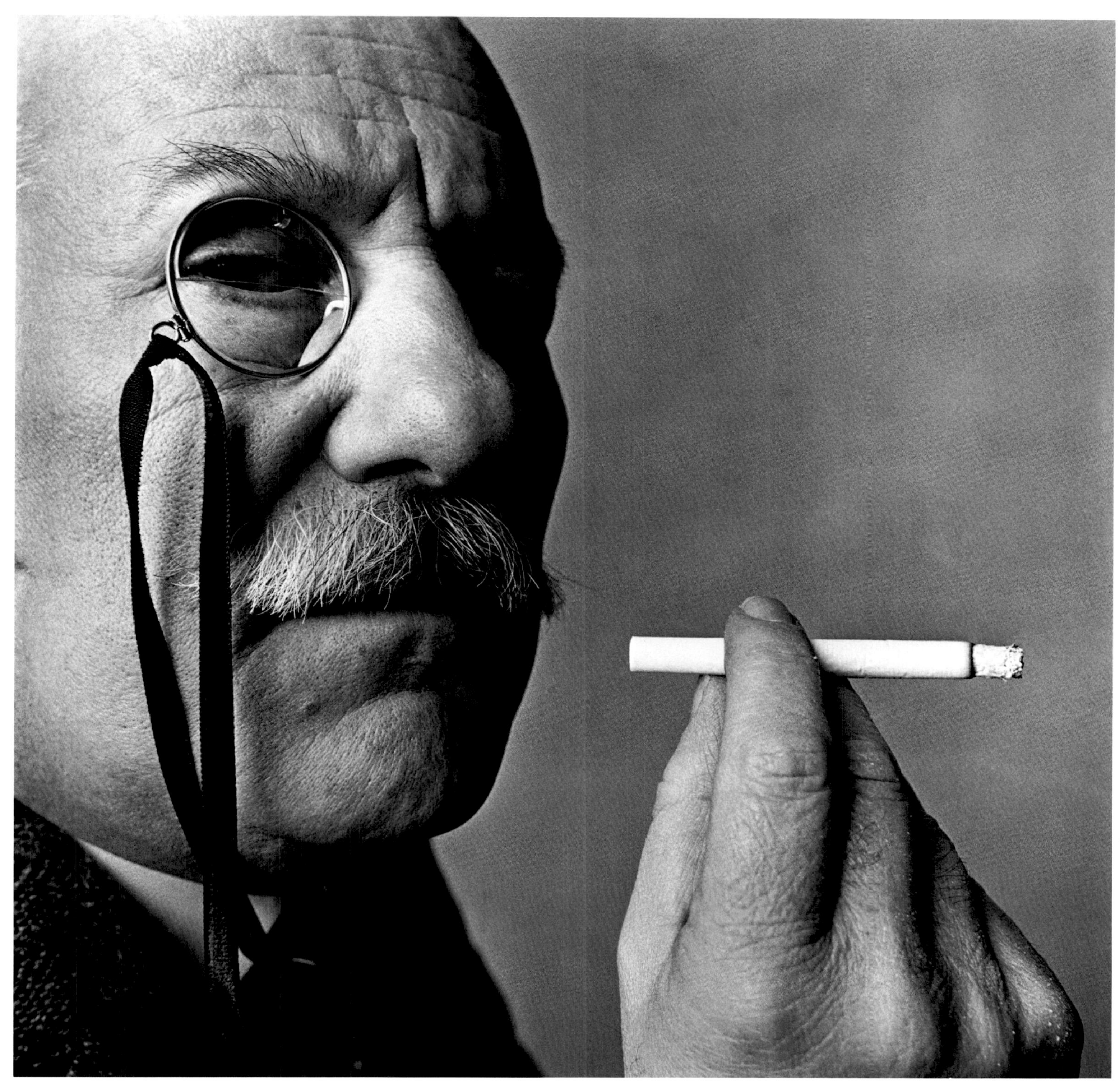

145. Barnett Newman. New York, 196€. Platinum-palladium print, 1980

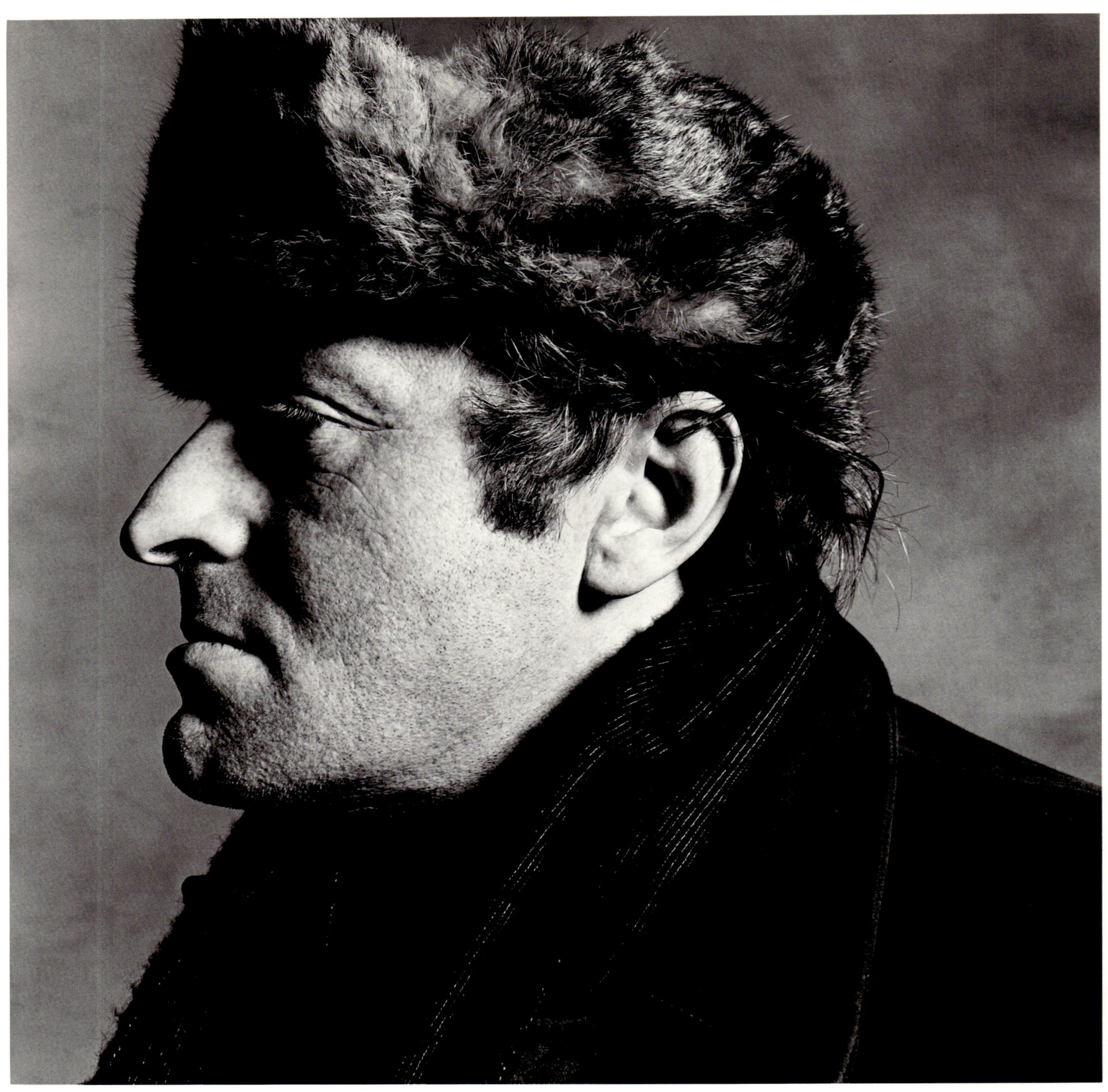

146. **Joseph Brodsky**. New York, 1980

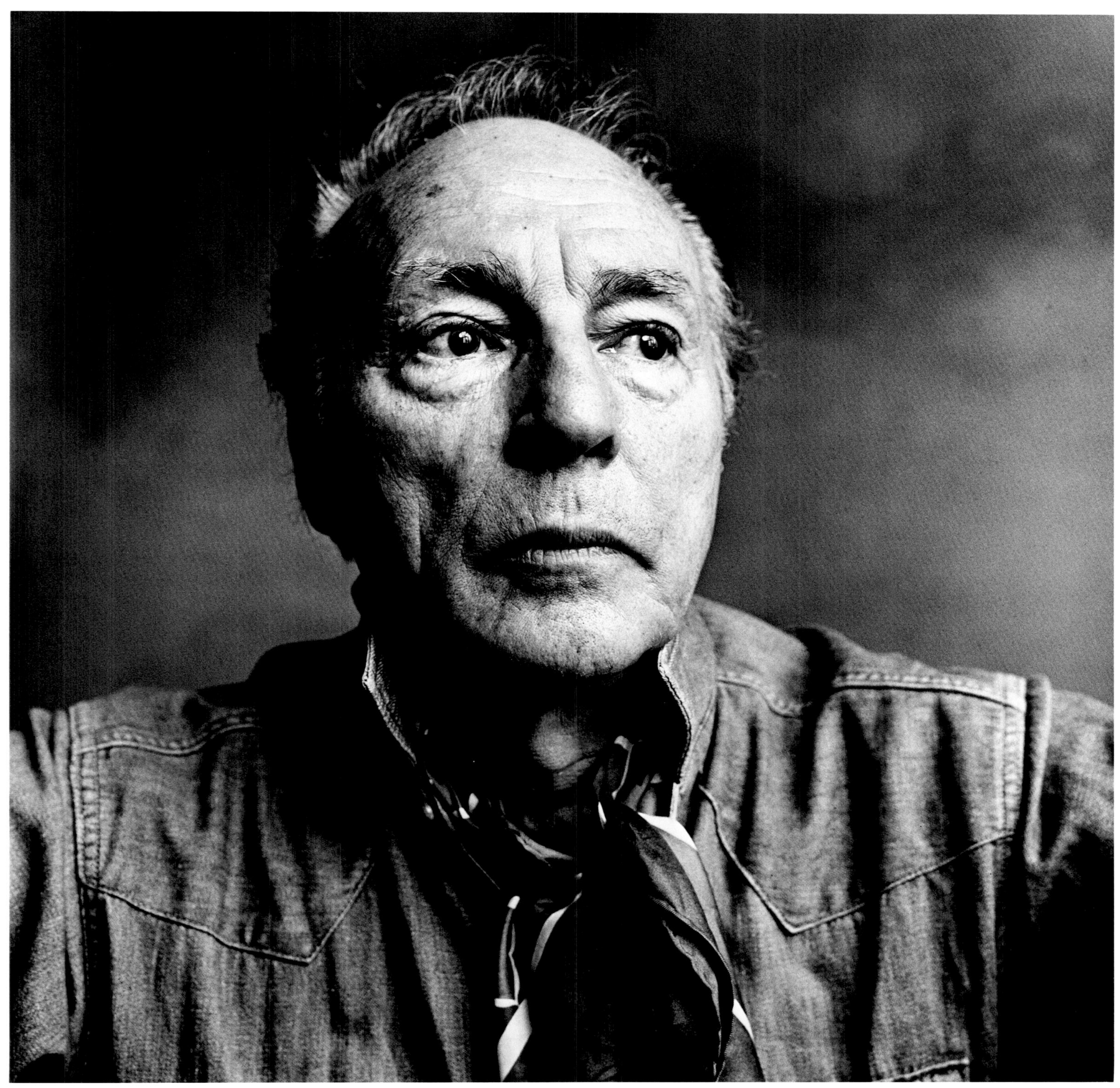

147. George Balanchine. New York, 1971

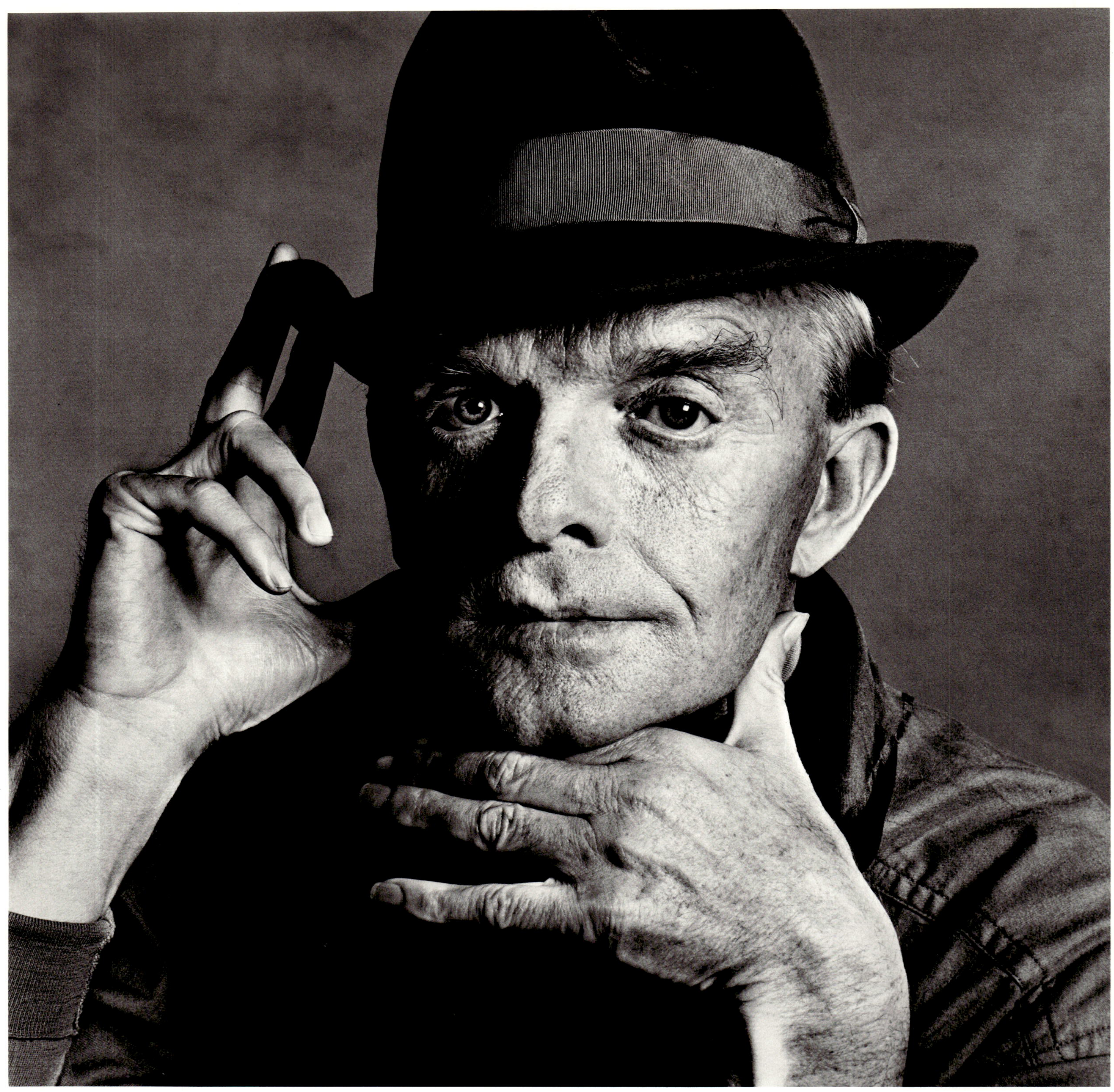

148. Truman Capote. New York, 1979

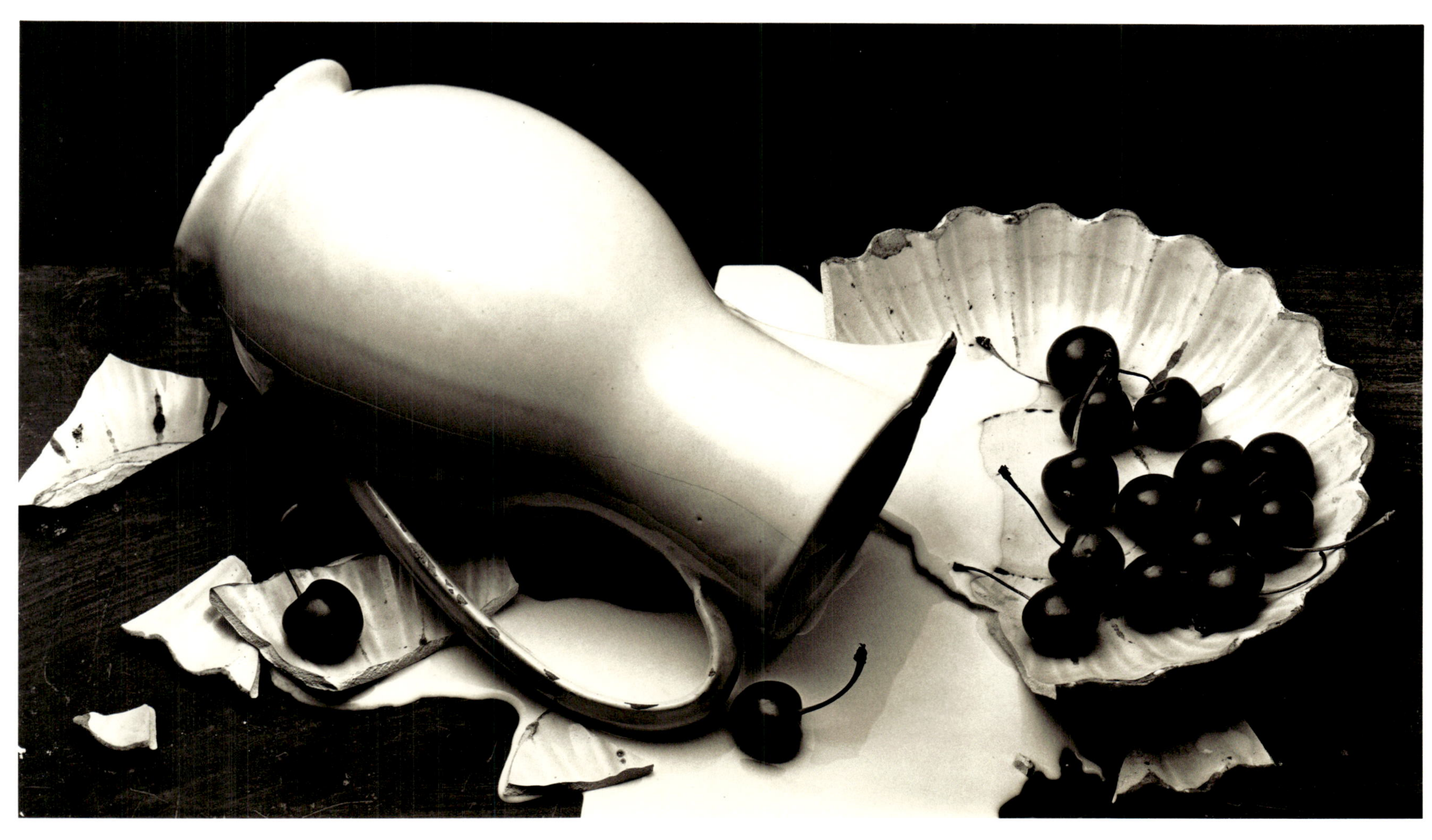

149. **The Spilled Cream**. New York, 1980. Platinum-palladium print

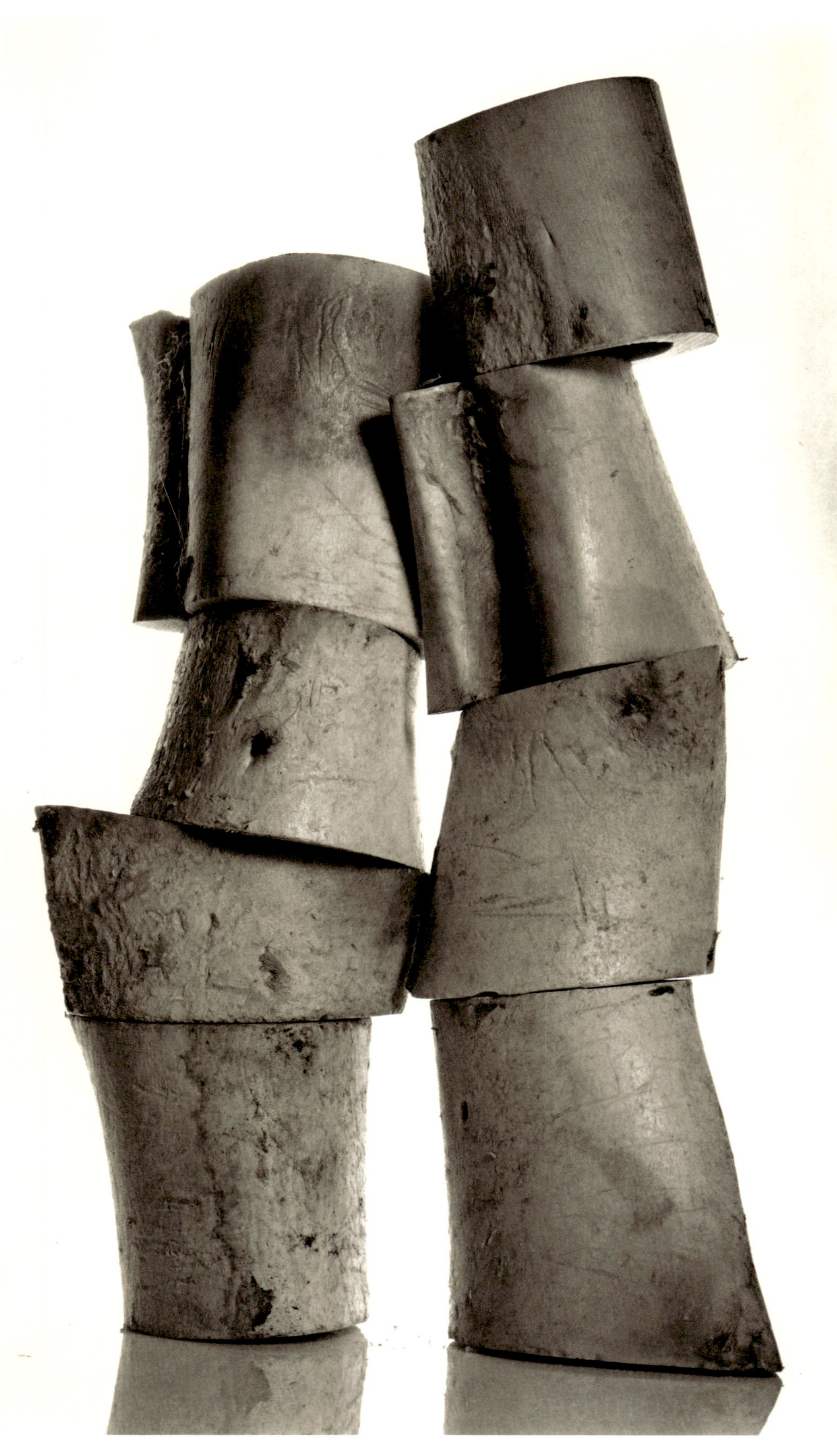

150. **Edifice**. New York, 1979. Platinum-palladium print

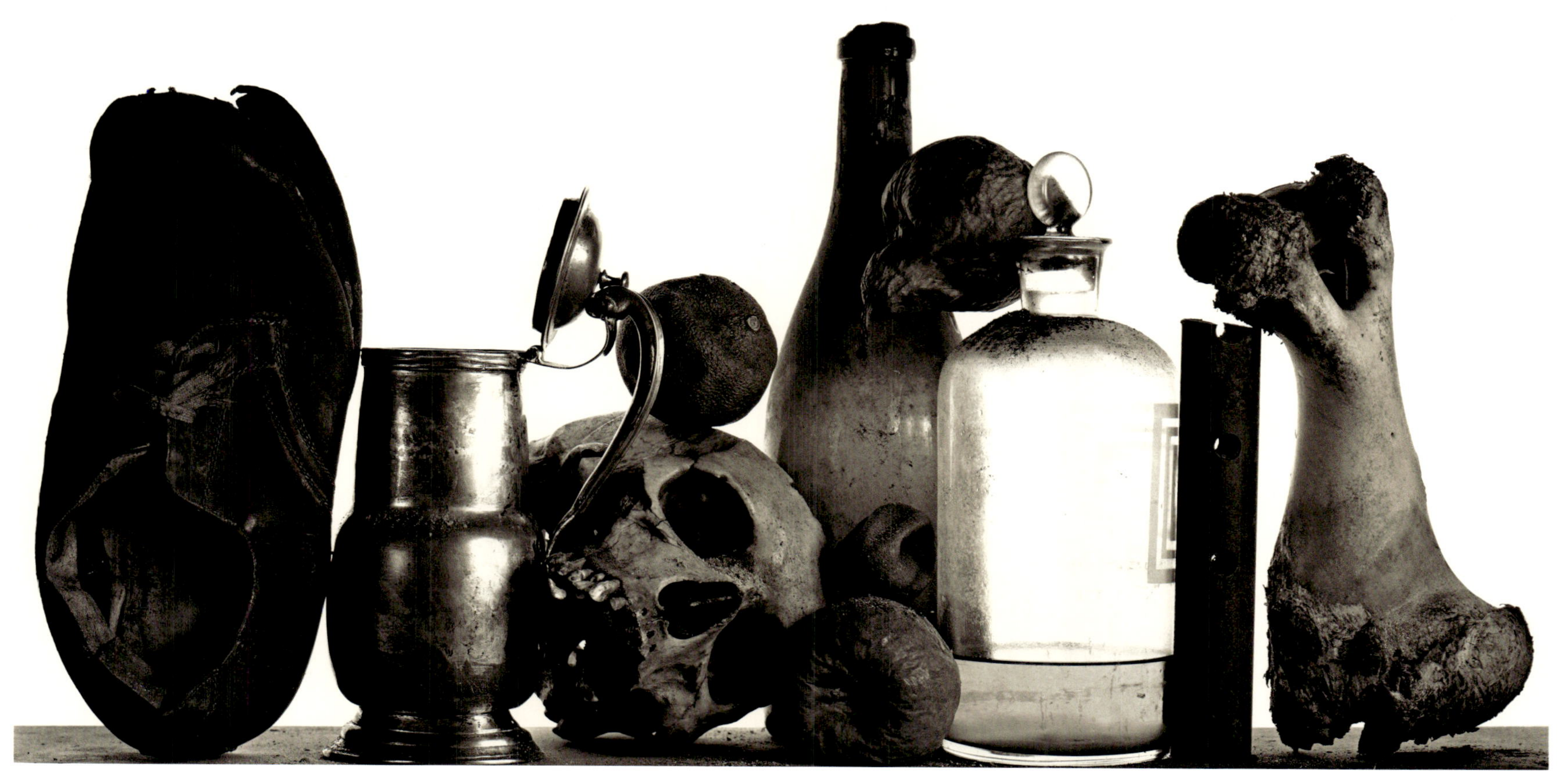

151. **Still Life with Shoe.** New York, 1980. Platinum-palladium print

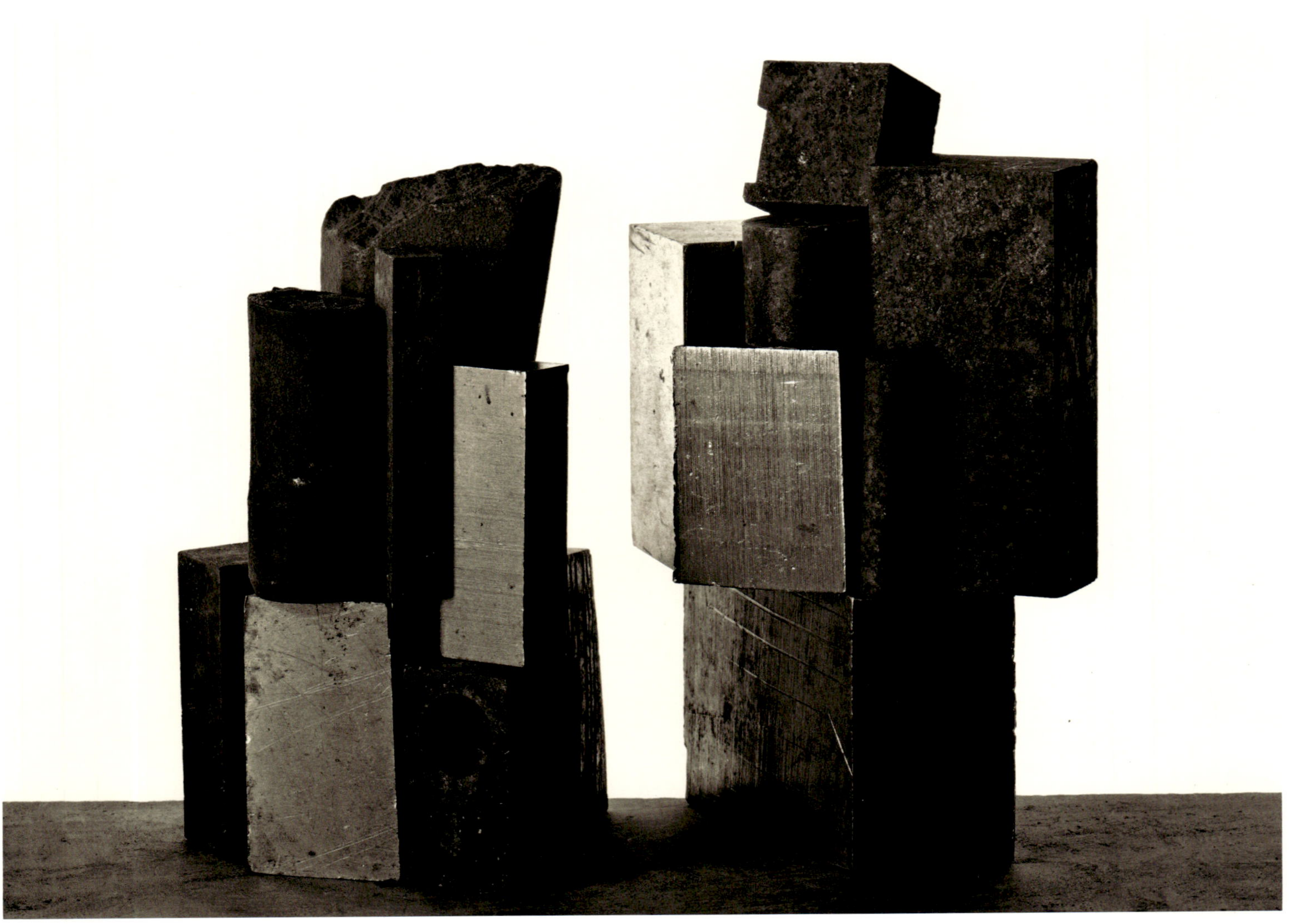

152. **Iron Couple**. New York, 1980. Platinum-palladium print

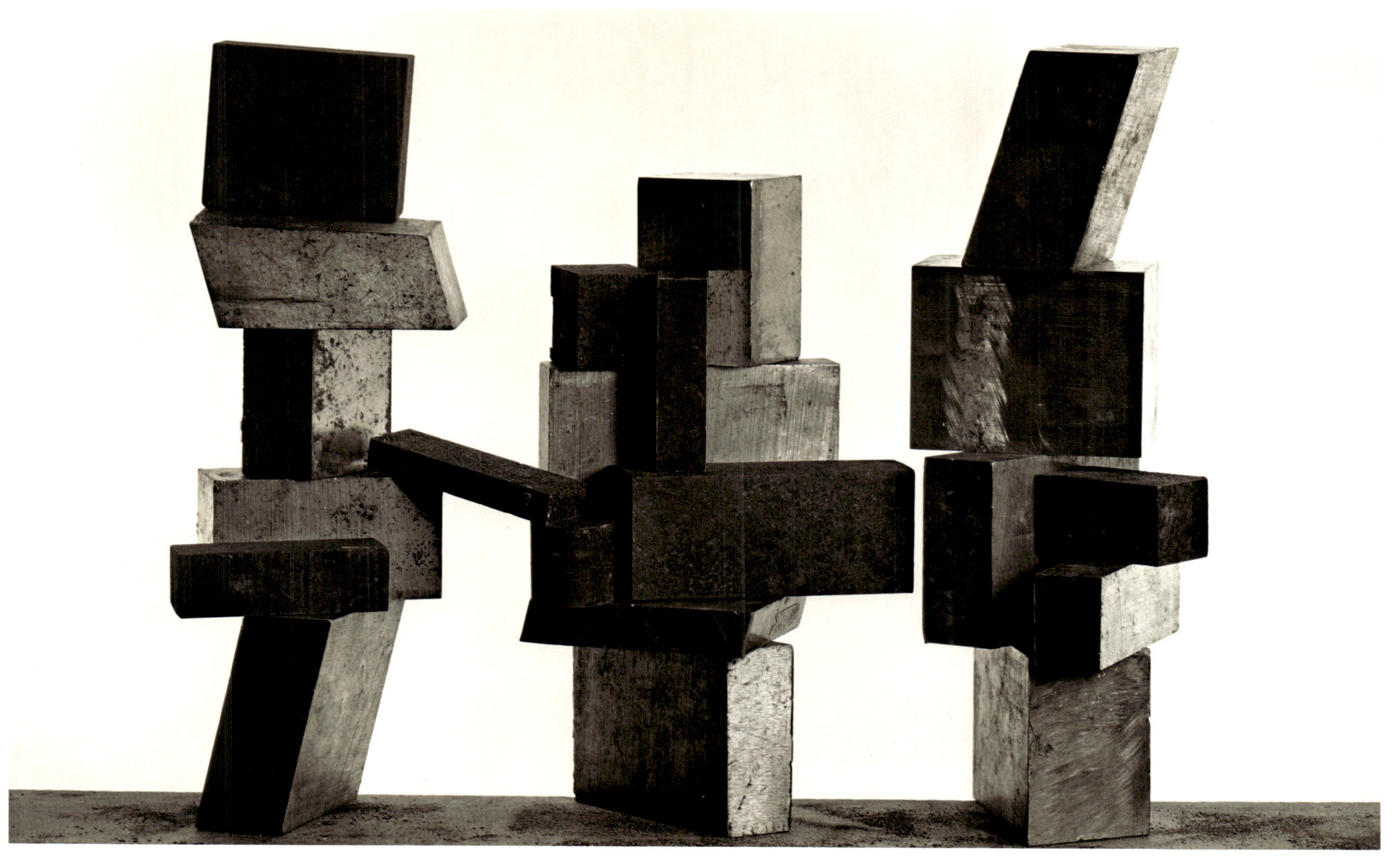

153. **Parade.** New York, 1980. Platinum-palladium print

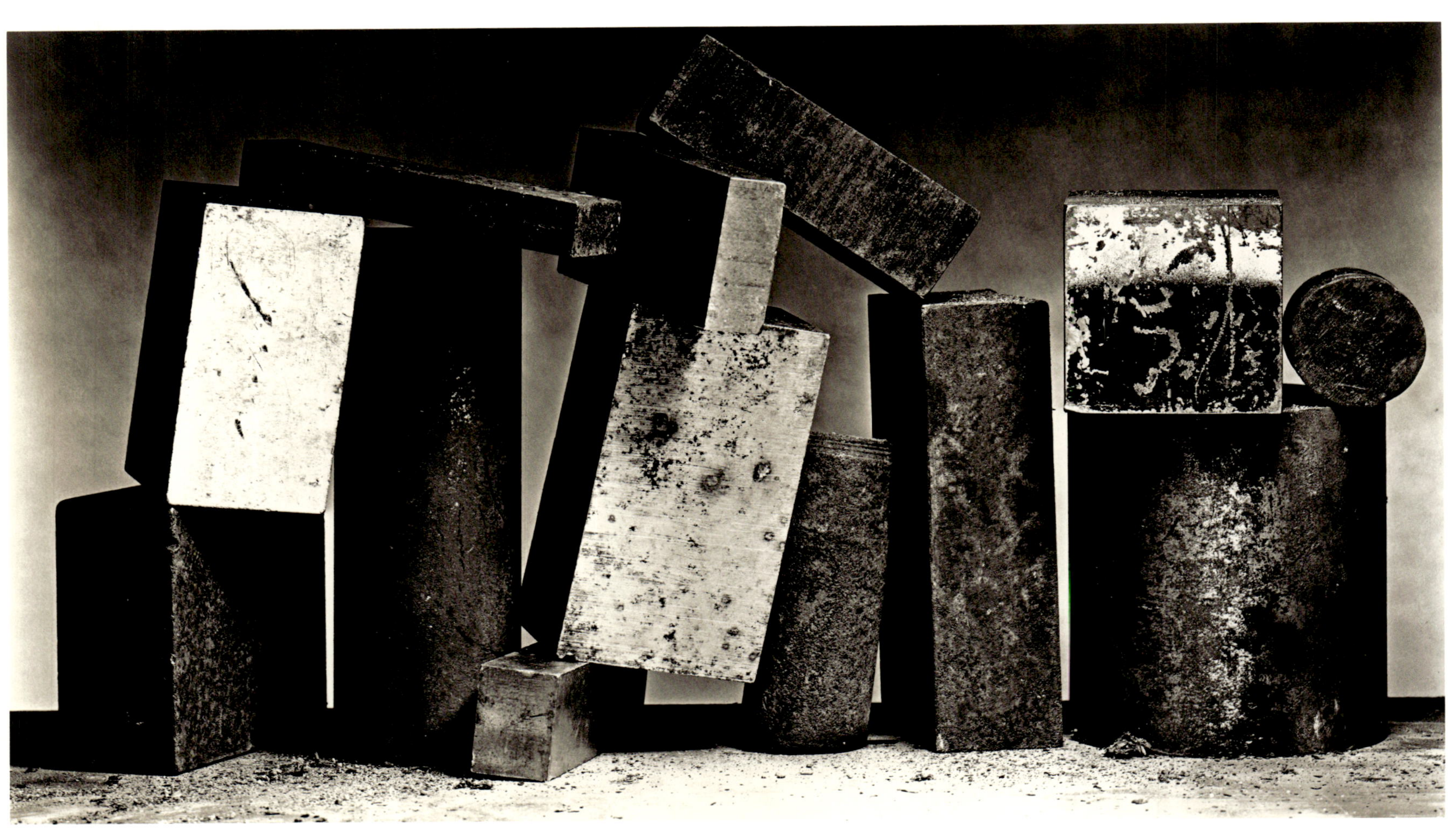

154. **Blast.** New York, 1980. Platinum-palladium print

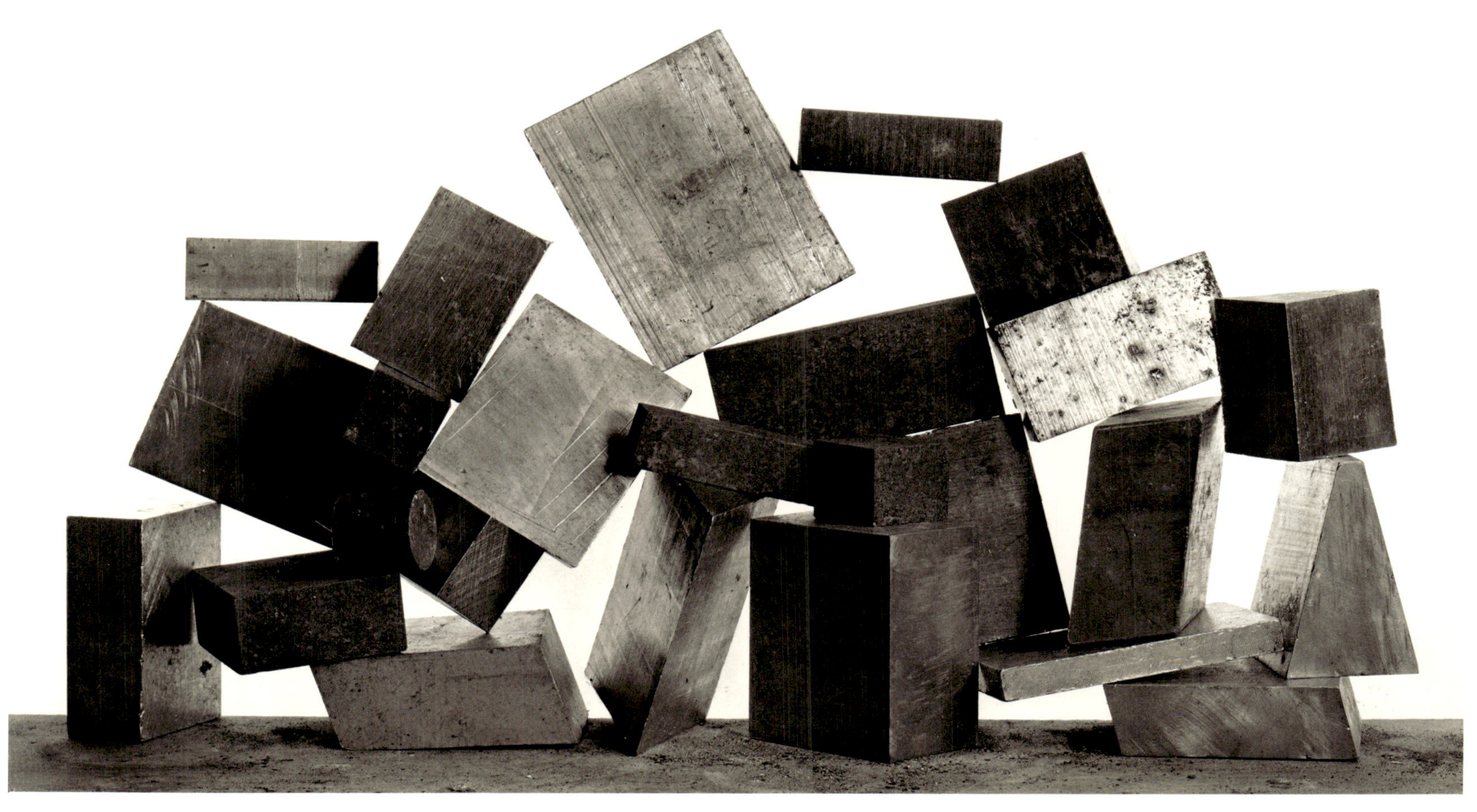

155. Collapse. New York, 1980. Platinum-palladium print

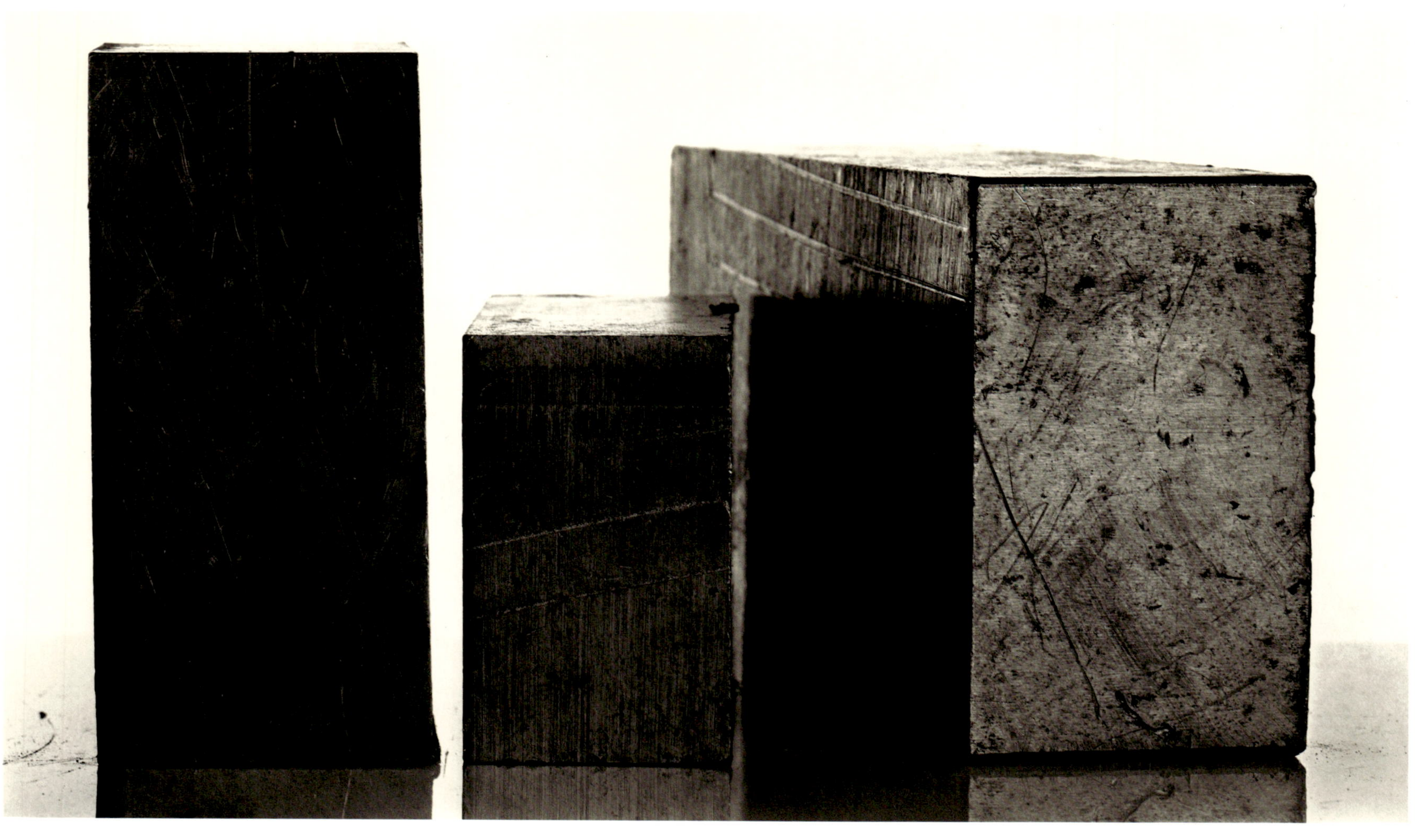

156. **Three Steel Blocks.** New York, 1980. Platinum-palladium print

The text for Irving Penn is set in Bodoni Book

Design by Christopher Holme

Type composition by M. J. Baumwell, New York, N.Y.

Halftone negatives and printing by The Meriden Gravure Company,
Meriden, Conn.

Color separation and printing by L.S. Graphic Inc., New York, N.Y.

Binding by Sendor Bindery, New York, N.Y.

CREDITS

Figure 9, copyright 1943 (renewed 1971); plate 66, copyright 1944 (renewed
1972); figure 10, copyright 1946 (renewed 1974); figures 30, 34-35, plates
28, 39, 67-68, 73, copyright 1947 (renewed 1975); figure 32, plates 1, 7,
14-15, 19-20, 63, copyright 1948 (renewed 1976); plates 12, 40-41, 43, 69,
99, copyright 1949 (renewed 1977); plates 32, 42, 44-49, 58, copyright
1950 (renewed 1978); plates 23, 25, 30-31, 33, 51, 55, 57, 85-86, 91,
copyright 1951 (renewed 1979); plate 53, copyright 1952 (renewed 1980);
figure 27, plate 64, copyright 1953 (renewed 1981); plate 72, copyright 1954
(renewed 1982); figure 24, copyright 1957; plates 29, 100, 102, 104, copyright 1959; plates 35, 59, copyright 1960; plates 65, 139, copyright 1963;
figure 26, plate 138, copyright 1964; plates 37, 133, 137, copyright 1965;
figure 25, plates 105, 135, 141, 143, 145, copyright 1966; plate 132, copyright 1967; plate 112, copyright 1970; plates 75, 136, copyright 1971; plate
147, copyright 1972; plate 70, copyright 1977; plate 148, copyright 1979;
plate 146, copyright 1980; plates 71, 101, copyright 1981; plate 103, copyright
1982, The Condé Nast Publications Inc.

Plates 26, 84, 87, copyright 1951; plate 22, copyright 1952; plate 34,
copyright 1953, The Condé Nast Publications Ltd.

Plate 54, copyright 1950; plates 88-90, copyright 1951; plate 21, copyright
1958, Les Editions Condé Nast.

Plate 5, copyright 1945 (renewed 1973); figure 17, plates 8, 11, 13, 36,
60-61, copyright 1960; plate 96, copyright 1967; plate 98, copyright 1969;
plate 106, copyright 1970; plates 92-95, 107-108, 110-111, copyright 1974;
plates 76-83, 129-131, copyright 1980; plates 9-10, 16-18, 24, 27, 50, 52, 56,
62, 74, 97, 109, copyright 1983; plate 144, copyright 1984, Irving Penn,
Courtesy *Vogue*.

Figure 8, copyright 1948 (renewed 1976); plate 38, copyright 1960; plate
140, copyright 1962; plates 134, 142, copyright 1967; figure 18, plates
113-118, copyright 1974; plates 125-128, copyright 1975; plates 119-124,
copyright 1977; plates 151, 154, copyright 1980; plates 149-150, 152-153,
155-156, copyright 1981; plates 2-4, 6, copyright 1983; figures 5-7, 11-13,
15, 31, 33, copyright 1984, Irving Penn.

Figure 22: JELL-O is a registered trademark of General Foods Corporation.

216